MAGICAL RITUAL METHODS

by

WILLIAM G. GRAY

SAMUEL WEISER

NEW YORK

First published by
Helios Book Service (Publications) Ltd
England

First American paperback edition 1980 by
Samuel Weiser, inc.
740 Broadway
New York, N.Y. 10003

ISBN 0-87728-498-9

Cover by Alden Cole

Printed in the U.S.A.by
Noble Offset Printers, Inc.
New York, N.Y. 10003

MAGICAL RITUAL METHODS

Learning about the "whats" of Ritual Magic is not very difficult—they are scattered far and wide throughout a number of books and other sources. But as such they are of no more value than a heap of electrical components would be to anyone without the skill or the knowledge to assemble them. The vital "hows" and "whys" are missing. The scope and intention of this book is to supply them.

Before starting any operation, it is advisable to consider the end-product intended. Ritual Magic is in itself purely a means of producing one end—a trained and disciplined consciousness capable of working on Inner causatory levels, together with a soul raised to full spiritual status in its own right. While none of us may ever reach the full degree of human perfection, at least we can make as much progress as possible along the Path leading to that point. Magical Riguals are capable of directing us in this way.

CONTENTS

RITE AND REASON

There is probably more rubbish believed and written about Magical Rituals than any other subject. From the wildest guesswork and the most fertile imaginations, magical rituals and their practitioners are invested with every conceivable impossibility or absurdity. Nonsense runs riot. As usual, the sensationalist writer catering for the willingly credulous reader is largely to blame. Most people want to believe in whatever stirs their sense beyond the average rate, thus providing them with lifts, kicks, thrills, or variations from their living-line. It is of course quite necessary to human progress and evolution that we should rise above our own levels all the time, but there are right and wrong ways of doing this. Magical workings can supply both.

We come from the Eternal and return to this same Source through an unimaginable circle of Cosmic Creative Evolution. In our attempts to relate ourselves consciously with our hidden origins and background of pure BEING, we have made a great number of mento-emotional structures which serve our purpose to their limited degree, according to our ability to use them. Religions, philosophies, and sciences have grown up with us, together with the arts and whatever else extends our awareness toward the Unknown—which is our Great Necessity. Yet the basis of *all* our beliefs is neither more nor less that what may fairly be termed "Magic"!

Definition of Magic is largely a matter of individual opinion, since it means so many things to so many people, and there are so many claims made in its name. Fundamentally it remains what it always was: Man's most determined effort to establish an actual working relationship through himself between his Inner and Outer states of being. By magic, Man shows that he is not content to be simply a pawn in the Great Game, but wants to play on his own account. Man the meddler insists on becoming Man the Magician, and so learns the rules the hard way, for magic is concerned with Doing, while mysticism is concerned with Being.

Magic seeks to translate energies from one state of existence to another in accordance with an intention of the operative intelligence. So does science. The difference between magician and scientist lies in method and materials, which sometimes are not so dissimilar as might appear. A circle-dance and a cyclotron have much in common. The symbolic tools of magi and mathematician both operate through Inner dimensions to cause Outer effects. Modern science has evolved far more ritual procedures in its techniques than ancient magicians ever dreamed of, and they all come from the same source—Man's curiosity concerning the Cosmos and what he has to do with it; human attempts at growing into Godhood.

Ritual is a major tool of magic and science alike for patterning the consciousness of its operatives so that calculable results may be obtained. Unhappily it is a sadly neglected tool, ill cared for and misunderstood. The scientist is showing more respect for it than the magician, so he is getting better results with it today. This is a pity, because ritual has incalculable value for those able to handle it effectively, and as a way of life it has everything to offer those who can follow the pattern of its paths. To some extent we are all ritualists of one kind or another, but we shall concern ourselves in this work entirely with ritual classifiable under the broad heading of "Magical". We will attempt to understand its basic fundamentals and set it in order as a practical art in its own right, having at least as great a value to human users as literature, drama, music, or science. None of our civilisation would be possible without those amenities, and none of them would have developed without magic, so we are assured of a worth-while study.

If we, commence our task by considering actual human practitioners of magical rituals both past and present, it will prove most discouraging, even though it provides much material and great hope for the future. The single indisputable fact is that magical rites and their workers have continued throughout the ages into the present time, and are unlikely to cease abruptly unless humanity ceases at the same instant. The actual happenings of magical rites vary enormously according to century and culture, but basics are the same, and those must be our main concern.

To obtain a reasonable picture of ritual magic in the world of today is a virtual impossibility. The image presents as nasty a mess as much modern artistic excretion. What with self-acclaimed "Witches" inventing ritualistic covers for sex-naughtiness, and pompous amateur Ipsissimi proclaiming themselves minor or major Deities, magical ritualism is touching an all-time "low" at this period of its tide. Its public image is decidedly poor to say the least of it. As against this, there do exist genuine and dedicated souls who keep ancient traditions going the best way they can, whether individually or in minority groupings. Magical rites have never been for the multitude any more than other highly specialised activities.

The peculiar secrecy surrounding magical practices is not altogether a matter of deliberate policy, but stems from inadequacy of verbal or other symbology to express their meaning. Bare descriptions of the purely physical aspects of ritualism cannot possibly convey the significance of their inner contents. Knowing this either consciously or instinctively, practitioners of magical rites have maintained silence or given out such garbled versions of their activities, that very little practical use can be made of these. We may know what was done on material levels, and even all the words that were said. This still does not tell us the hows and whys or wherefores to be properly placed and activated Inwardly before any rite will work to the slightest degree.

General ritual practice throughout individual and collective Occultism in the Western world of modern times is little to admire or consider praiseworthy. It lacks synthesis, cohesion, and even practicability. Few individuals have any qualifications as exponents of the art, and not many have the qualities necessary to acquire it. There are no authentic text-books to help basic approaches, and sham secrecy is too often used as a cover for sheer ignorance.

Despite all this, many souls are drawn toward ritual practice because of their need of it on deep spiritual levels which nothing else will fulfil. Unless they are provided with reliable data and basic information concerning ritualism, they will not only lose opportunities for gaining the art, but worse still, the art itself will lose highly valuable practitioners, which it can ill afford to do at present.

In the hope of offering practical and necessary means for the study and operation of ritual practice, especially as applied to Western methods, this present work is attempted. It is realised there will necessarily be many shortcomings, inadequacies, insufficiencies, and probably inaccuracies. Such is inevitable when human intelligence tries to enter the unexplored and bring back evidence of its journey. Nevertheless if sufficient interest is aroused in other minds and souls to make their own explorations and to synthesise their findings into better and fuller shapes, for the benefit of themselves and their posterity, the mission behind this effort will have been fully accomplished. The main purpose is to deal with basics and not launch into involved discussions or commentaries. It must therefore be assumed that readers are capable of supplying their own comments or philosophising. Whether there is agreement or disagreement with what follows is immaterial. If genuine thought

9

and action is evoked, the rite behind these writings will have proved effective.

Since a start must be made somewhere, let us begin by examining the nature of ritual itself. This is neither more nor less than dedicated human behaviour extended through varying dimensions of existence. Life and ritual are inseparable. Our morning tea is a ritual, so is evening T.V. Ritual is habitual, intentional, conventional, marking the numbers by which we live and die. There are religious rituals, military rituals, social rituals, and rituals associated with every possible type of human expression. We are concerning ourselves in this enquiry with magical ritual however, so we must decide what sets this apart from other species of ritualistic activity.

The distinguishing feature of magical ritualism is what modern slang would term its "Way-outness", or degree of extension from what might be termed average human ritualistic behaviour. It is not so much the methods of magical rites which make them unique, but the direction and intent of the operative consciousness behind them. They are only magical because they depart so far from the circles of consciousness controlling other human rites that have become commonplace activities.

It is Man the Magician who leads humanity toward the Unknown. The magician of yesterday becomes the scientist of today. Where are today's magicians? Those who will push so far ahead into fresh fields of consciousness that it will take the rest of humanity many incarnations to make use of what is brought through. Where a single human soul has been, others may follow—eventually. There is strong similarity between a magician and an astronaut, save the latter is exploring Outer Space, and the former deals with dimensions reached Inwardly. The two states are metaphysically identical. The training and launching procedures of both magician and astronaut are not at all unlike, and their objective is the same— extension of human consciousness toward Truth. Both must be in full disciplined control of their faculties throughout their respective operations, and should their sanity slip it means equal disaster in different ways.

It was once thought that magical ritual dealt entirely with what were then called Angels and Demons. It is still perfectly true to say that magical work is indeed connected with linking human intelligence to very different sources of consciousness than mortal ones. Otherwise it would have small value apart from entertainment. Whether or not we term such extra-mortal intelligences Angels, Demons, or anything else, makes no difference to their essential natures. They exist, we exist, and interdimensional contact can be made between our different spheres of consciousness. The nature and results of such contacts may be as variable as there are instances of occurrence. Terms of reference on the differing levels of being are so divergent from each other that only symbolic communication is normally possible. Hence the symbolic nature of magical rituals.

At first casual impression, it might be considered that such contacts would be useless to the human race as a whole, and of doubtful value to the rare individuals who could not even express them in writing or other normal human communicatory methods. In fact however, individual linkages with extra-mortal Intelligences have a greater effect than might be supposed on all humans.

However individual we may be as human units, and no matter how isolated we are from others physically, we are connected together on deep common levels of mind and soul. Energies operating at such depths affect us all or in part, depending on their nature and placement. Whatsoever a single soul feels, or one mind thinks, can be shared by the rest of humanity providing an energy-impact is made correctly.

In commonplace circles of circumstance, a single human consciousness affects little beyond its immediate contacts to any degree worth considering. Should it extend or intensify past these limits, the family or group with which it is associated will be involved. Further extensions and intensifications will touch ethnic or national and racial levels. Continue the process, and basic humanity will be reached. Nor need we stop there, for who knows the ultimate extension of consciousness?

It should be appreciated that an exact energy-occurrence at precisely the right point of existence could alter an entire sequence of eventualities. One thought might change a whole life, one individual deflect the destiny of a nation. A single microbe can mean the difference between physical life or death. The slightest variation at the absolute inception of any course means enormous subsequent differences. This is how magic works, by dealing with energies on far more subtle levels than physical ones, which nevertheless have appreciable and calculable effects throughout all or specific points of our existence.

We are learning even from modern science how to "track back" along lines of power until we discover the apparent source of the most enormous energies to be what seems to us—Nothing. We have been looking at Existence through the wrong end of our telescope, and found that what used to be considered insignificant, nebulous, unreal, and even unthinkable, is in fact the most solid reality in being. The further away we go from physical matter and materialism the more real does Existence become. Our once good sound sensible world of unquestionable solidity has treacherously turned vague, insubstantial, undependable, and positively doubtful of its right to exist at all. One nice atomic blast reduces it to fundamental cosmic dust, or beyond that, to resonant energy.

The art of magic may be defined as being like that of using Archimedes' hypothetical lever to move an entire world if properly arranged. The magical lever however, is extended through one dimension into others before pressure is applied, and fortunately this is an impracticability for the vast majority of human beings. Otherwise we should have destroyed ourselves long ago. We have already shifted ourselves into the greatest degree of danger we can possibly reach short of disaster. A few determined efforts by master magicians during the next several decades will move the lever beyond the safety or destruction mark.

The bulk of humanity is quite incapable of effective magical action except as mass-movement. Few minds or souls can extend sufficiently from their average level of existence to exert much influence at other points. Magic is not for the many except concertedly. This is not because most people have not enough power, they have infinitely more than they will ever suspect, and waste more energy in one life than is needed to complete a whole evolution. Most mortals make ineffective magicians because they cannot bring their energies to bear upon the right points with adequate skill. Magic is not unlike judo or karate which needs quality rather than quantity of energy, applied with exact precision of impact and intent.

Magical ritual practices are those which have been found by experience and experiment to be suitable for development and application of the specialised spiritual skills necessary to work with high-potency energies on Inner levels. Most of them are human responses to pressures applied in the first instance by Intelligences of a much more developed order of Being than mankind. This does not necessarily mean that such Beings are either pro or anti human. It means simply they are utterly different in construction and consciousness to a human being. We may call them divine or whatever we please, but we have no means whatever of contacting them with any ordinary sense linking a human body with its external environment. Since we are provided with such senses, it follows that we must find extraordinary ways of employing them if we are to go beyond their merely mortal limits. These unusual ways of using a human sensorium may be classified as ritual methods.

Some Schools of Inner Existence prefer not to use ritual sense-methods at all, but confine themselves to meditational or contemplative means of approaching the Unknown. In fact both Meditation and Magic are entirely necessary to each other for the full development of the human soul. Each fulfils the other's shortcomings.

In all ritual training work therefore, there should be periods of meditation carefully balanced with ritual activity. The one and only way any training can be effective is to outline a definite programme and adhere to it as closely as possible. This is valid in the case of magic just as much as mechanics and probably with more reason. Although it is totally against the best traditions of magic to provide correspondence or other courses in the art, some system and order is absolutely necessary if any proficiency in magic is ever to be attained. The ideal method of training is for the student to obtain it directly from Inner sources in accordance with his individual requirements. Since this is more than exceptionally rare, the next line of contact is a qualified Master on earth, who is a most unusual being to meet with. Even sham Masters are getting scarce today! This leaves only text books or working Lodges to learn from. How many of either are available on demand?

The situation prevailing in the Western world of modern times in relation to ceremonial magical ritual is that no authentic text-books exist, and apart from a very few working groups of doubtful competence, there are no practical means of learning or operating it. If ritual magic is to be kept in Tradition through the present transitions of the modern world, student-practitioners must take upon themselves the responsibility of their own training and development. There is no reason why this should not be a highly successful magical operation in its own right, for there are quite enough Innerworld teachers waiting to guide and direct the work once earthly practitioners have built their side of the bridge between the two different dimensions.

Learning about the "whats" of ritual magic is not very difficult. They are scattered far and wide through a vast number of books and other sources of information. As such, they are of no more value than a heap of components to someone with no idea of how to assemble and use them. The vital hows and whys are missing. In addition, there are no feasible rituals published for use by sincere students, who are faced with either medieval rubbish or totally unsuitable material intended for Group-working by genuine or pseudo-Masonic bodies. Ideally, they should learn how to construct and operate their own rituals, but how many are capable of this?

The scope and intention of this particular book will therefore be to direct attention toward the elements of learning and practising magical ritual methods. Although it will keep more or less within the framework of customary Temple procedure, the same basics apply throughout every differing variation of magical practice. Students will be shown how to arrange and direct their own studies, although nothing in the nature of a "course" is intended, but only the importance and use of methodical application indicated and advised.

Before commencing any operation, it is always sensible to consider the end-product intended. In the case of ritual magic we must never lose sight of the fact that it is in itself purely a means of producing one end. A trained and disciplined consciousness, capable of working on causatory and other Inner levels, together with a soul raised to full spiritual status in its own right. None of us may ever reach the full degree of human perfection, but at least we may make as much progress as possible along the path leading to that point. Magical rituals are capable of directing us this Way.

Ritual is not entirely a single type of activity, but comprises quite a number of separate abilities and factors conjoined for an overall reason. A ritualist must be a creative artist in a number of fields each needing its own skill and practice. Anyone adhering to the old tradition of making their own magical workings would need some abilities in the following; literature, languages, poetry, drama (mime and elocution), metalwork, woodwork, needlework, painting, designing, music, dancing, elementary chemistry, floristry, plus any other skill that might have a bearing on the rituals worked. Additionally, of course, many personal qualities would be essential, such as: creative imagination, patience, good humour, insight, determination, physical stamina, sound health, and indeed the entire gamut of worthwhile human potentials. Nothing less will achieve any magical success worth having. If for no other reason, magic is well worth practising for the sake of its valuable effects on the practitioner.

The problems of ritual magic are those attending any kind of energy patterning and directing. What is the nature of the energy involved, how is it to be generated and controlled, what are the technicalities concerning its use, and so forth. It is no more possible to answer the question concerning the exact nature of the energy used in magic than we can say for certainty what electricity is. As in electrical engineering, much is known about the generation, manipulation, and application of the energy in question, but its actuality remains concealed in the NIL of its origin. The more we discover about it, the greater its Zero-point becomes.

It has been known since time immemorial that the operative energy of magical effects is connected in the closest way with living consciousness and is directable therewith. Mankind is only capable of dealing with these energies according to his particular degree of awareness-ability in relation to them. The actually of such a degree is the real degree of Initiation.

Going back to primitive times, we find that animal and human life was ritually sacrificed or dedicated to the fulfilment of magical intentions. This crude supply of attuned energy was often effective among communities of conscious individuals with few inhibitions or complexities of consciousness. It worked because they could see no reason why it shouldn't. Nevertheless such methods of life-sacrifice are like burning a whole forest down to heat one cauldron of water. They would not work today because we can think of so many reasons against them, and have learned far more efficient means of obtaining much greater results.

The sex act and all its variations were (and still are), used as a power-provider in magical ritual workings. Among those with no other means of initiating energies, or ability to exercise control over the same energy on more effectual levels, little else becomes available, but the disadvantages of indiscriminate sexuality are so numerous and obvious they scarcely need repeating at length. Blood and sex may still make best-sellers, because they mean Life and Death, Mankind's two main Gates to the Mysteries of his being, but there are better ways of contacting and applying the energies behind them than with stone knife or fertility flagellum.

We must remember that copulating and killing were early Man's only ways of asserting his influence with Life and Death. Modern Man as a whole does not seem to have grown very far from the primitive practice of these fundamental magical Principles. In the case of the blood-sacrifice, life energy was directed from the Outer to the Inner worlds, and with the sex act the same type of energy was evoked from the Inner to the Outer. In both instances a force-flow occurred, and the human operators hoped to "cash in on the act" by superimposing their personal or collective intentions upon the process. Sound magic, but sad misuse of elementary energy. Sex and slaughter methods are like using dynamite to break an eggshell, or a pickaxe for precision work. Yet we should not forget that both seed and blood are life-essences linked directly with the energies we are approaching in practical magic.

What the early magicians (and many moderns), had not taken into account was that overt acts of sex and slaughter were but external-isations of natural processes occuring in and around us anyway. We are dying and being reborn all the time. The ritual acts of Birth and Death are going on inside us constantly. It is on these Inner levels that instructed modern Initiates seek to tap the power-points of Infinitesimal Infinity from whence all energy is directly derived. There is no especial need to take seed or blood out of a body already connected with Inner Life.

It may be germane to enquire here why any ritual procedure such as chanting, costumes, or other theatricalities should be necessary at all if seed and blood sacrifices may be dispensed with. Part of the answer is that such a sacrifice has not been eliminated, but simply altered in method. The rest of the answer is that only Adepts of a very high order are able to by-pass conventional ways of bringing a normal human consciousness into operative linkage with Otherworld energies. The principles of ritual have stood the stringent tests of many centuries, and although they may and should alter outwardly, they are fundamentally as valid as they always were. We disregard them to our disadvantage. Besides this, many ritual procedures are quite unconnected with sacrificial motivations, being concerned with arrangements of consciousness for quite different reasons.

In understanding and dealing with ritual usage, it is always helpful to contrast the most primitive practices with their present forms among us, and extrapolate their future developments as far as we can. A very great deal of valuable information can be obtained this way. If we look back carefully enough, the magic mirror of the past may reveal the future behind our reflected images.

For example, the rituals of early man were not planned and elaborate affairs at all, but purely spontaneous reactions to environmental stimuli from Outer and Inner levels. Man acted impulsively and irresponsibly in his attempts to adjust himself to the Worlds of his existence. He is still doing so, but experience has brought degrees of control resulting in the questionable structure of our civilisation. If we continue to develop control over our elements of existence, we shall ultimately become full Adepts in the Mystery of Life.

Early rituals of tribal man had little grace or glory to commend them. They were often spur of the moment affairs linked with human frustrations and attempts to be other than existing circumstances allowed. Man trying to break his material bounds through mental dimensions, or increase himself inwardly because no outward opening for action presented itself. Perhaps he might stalk some animal for hours, make his spring—and miss. His disappearing dinner sparked off a whole chain of reactions. Some root, stone, or other natural formation nearby had a vague or fancied resemblance to the escaped beast. The infuriated and disgruntled hunter attacked it instead, muttering the grunts and noises of the chase. Nowadays we should say he "got it out of his system". In those days it was a full scale ritual.

The apparently futile action of our unlucky ancestor had quite a number of results. Apart from relieving his tensions (and how much do we need that very relief today?), it helped to restore his self-confidence, gave him some useful exercise in spear-work, and on Inner levels sent a great many messages into what we now call the Universal Mind which were subsequently answered to some human advantage. The ritual may not have produced its worker an immediate meal, but it helped to bring about future skills and circumstances resulting in further feeding.

Our ritual reaction-patterns nowadays should have reached far higher levels than those of pre-historic times both as regards motive and methods. Nevertheless ritual is still a matter of reflex activity, however much it is brought within the control of the operatives. The conditioned reflex is a basic of modern ritualism, which seeks to apply calculated stimuli in order to obtain intended reactions. With any kind of Group-working, this means that those involved must accept some common mythos or base-plan in, on, and around which to work. Otherwise they will get no results worth having.

This is how the various Mysteries and magical Schools came into being. In order to fulfil the essential condition of operating with one mind in one place at one time, occult practitioners agreed to construct an Inner Cosmos of their own in which their Inner lives could be lived and related to the rest of Existence. Intelligences from Inner levels co-operated, and the resulting structure became established as an authentic state of being, capable of supporting the conscious activities of its particular Initiates for perhaps many human generations. Some made Temples, some Groves, some Landscapes, some Castles, and in fact people of different types made whatever appealed to them most in the Innerworld. Their rituals were directed toward the maintenance and improvement of these realities, for reality is neither more nor less than anyone makes it. Let us see what methods are used in the making of any particular Mystery, so that if none of the existing ones suit us, we shall be able to make our own.

MAKING A MAGICAL MYSTERY

An Occult or Magical Mystery is a psycho-physical inter-arrangement between intelligent entities existing in differing dimensions of being, for some mutual purpose. The world "occult" means that the matter has unrealised extensions beyond the normal limits of its operative consciousness, and also that it is concealed from those excluded from its workings. The word "Mystery" signifies the whole affair to be intentionally confined within an agreed framework in order to preserve its essential purity of nature. "Purity" to be understood as an unmixed condition of being.

The construction material of the Mysteries is derived from consciousness processed into suitable symbolic units for inter-dimensional exchanges of energy. The Master-Concept is that the whole of Existence or Being is made from differentiations of a Single Universal Element. This U.E. is conformable to applied consciousness according to nature of application. Conscious beings are thus theoretically able to construct and live within whatsoever type of Cosmos they please, taking consumption of the Time-Space constant into account.

Each "Mystery" is in effect its own particular type of Cosmos, functioning as a sort of spiritual state for souls coming within its circle of extended existence. It is almost as if souls got together in families, designed their own world, lived in it together, and dealt with other types of soul from that particular standpoint. This is more or less what happens. In physical terms, units would unite as families, families as tribes, tribes into nations. They would build civilisations according to their state of evolution. The "Mysteries" are the equivalent on Inner levels of being, and are therefore available for every soul-category.

This is why there are so many varieties of "Mystery", such as the Mithraic, Eleusinian, Qabalistic, Christian, Masonic, etc. At one time the word "Mystery" was synonymous with a drama or a craft, and the designers and participators in any Mystery do indeed use every rule of dramatic art and every craft known to human skill. The direction of production however, is reversed. Normally our staged dramas are set pieces arranged from material provided from our lives. The Mystery-dramas on the other hand, allow us to live Inwardly from the set pieces provided from the materials of the Mystery. They are really affording us an opportunity of living in quite a different dimension from our mortal limits, and further-more they give access to a realm wherein our conscious identities can exist apart from our physical bodies.

Once the general setting of a Mystery has been decided on by the type of people meaning to use it, the Dramatis Personae, are nominated. They will be the God and/or Goddess, the Pantheon, saints, heroes, demons, minor spirits, or other Life-characterisations. Their natures and spheres of action will be defined, and their scripts outlined. They are all the vehicles as it were, for the extra-human Intelligences participating in the Mystery from inside it. The characters are created partly by human and partly by non-human consciousness, but they have every reality in their own rights.

In order to make action and energy exchanges between human and other participators in the Mystery possible, a whole Symbol-code of consciousness must be devised. We are using these in normal life all the time. Our alphabets are such, so are traffic signs, numerals, or any other symbol holding a consciousness-content. They are valid currency for exchanges of consciousness, just as money makes acceptable symbols for exchanges of goods and services on material levels. The Symbols used in the Mysteries are not at all unlike money. They are particular to their own Mystery, and not usable in any other unless exchanged for that type of currency, yet all are valuable under the right circumstances. Some are universally acceptable like travellers cheques. Where they are totally different from earthly cash is that they can be spent to any extent and still remain in the possession of the spender. The more they are spent the more valuable they become. This is the meaning of Fortunatus' purse. His inexhaustible currency was not in mortal money.

Symbols are in fact the practical means of maintaining the Mysteries, and without them no Mystery would be possible. Skill and practice in the making and use of symbols is absolutely essential to all Initiates. Such is a normal occupation in Mystery-living and magical working. The entire structure of rituals depends on symbolism. It is an art demanding the highest degree of ability and intelligence. We could not even live ordinary earth-lives without the constant use of symbols, and life in the Mysteries is but an extension of our lives into other dimensions of existence. In those dimensions we are entirely dependent on our skills with symbolism for earning a living. First and foremost in Mystery-training therefore, the Initiate should be taught some means of symbol working. The skilled craftsman in the Mysteries is like the craftsman in earthly life, assured of good living and a valued member of the community.

Once the framework and permanent staff of any Mystery have been established, and its symbols of currency accepted, active life among all its members can commence and continue for as long as they intend to be together. It may be that their Mystery was created for some particular purpose which is always with us, such as Universal Brotherhood, or perhaps its scope is limited to achievement of specialised ends for national or sectional interests. There may be a mixture of motives, which is usually the case, but there is always a principal raison d'etre which supplies the keynote of any Mystery. This is generally indicated by the overall symbol for the Mystery itself, rather like a national flag or a trademark, though a family crest makes a better comparison. Just as the soul of any people is held on earth by their physical bodies, so it is held on Inner dimensions by their symbolic forms. The better these are, the happier the soul, and the fuller their lives Inwardly.

With the passage of time, distinct traditions and customs form the patterns of the Mysteries. They evolve their own terminologies, slang, costume, and other symbolic conveniences of consciousness. These may ultimately fade out through disuse or re-incorporate into different Mysteries. The Christian Mysteries are well known as the modern repository of many ancient ones. What may loosely be termed the Magical Mystery has survived rather tenuously in physical membership, though it is well represented by Intelligences operating through Inner dimensions. Those following Western Traditions as distinct from Oriental ones have produced a working system drawn from many sources which is designed to fit in with our external lives and customary living-habits. The present period of transition is not an easy one, but it is very necessary to bring the Magical Tradition intact through the various adaptations that must be made on account of the changes in living-patterns that that very Tradition has helped bring about.

Following these broad principles, anyone or any group of people can create and construct their own Mystery. Children do this in minor ways as they play, and could not successfully reach adulthood otherwise. If our childhood ability to make magic were continued through into adult levels of Inner existence, we should be different beings than we are at present. Prevailing forces of objective materialism, social customs, economic pressures, and many other factors tend to deprive us of incentives and opportunities for Inner living. Only those who realise the true value of Inner Life are likely to spend sufficient time and effort in maintaining conscious contact with it. The remainder will close their spiritual eyes and ignore their rights of that "second birth" to be undergone if we are to enter the Kingdom of Heaven which is literally within us.

The crucial point of the Mysteries to us is this. What is the extent of their reality, their influence upon us, and their outcome in terms of human living? Are they beneficial or detrimental to us? The materialistic schools of thinking are unanimous in declaring all Mysteries to be nothing but undesirable fantasies arising in immature unstable minds, to be strongly discouraged and eliminated from all civilised human workings of consciousness. Consciousness itself is regarded as nothing more than electro-chemical activity associated with specialised cellular tissues. Only unbalanced or diseased life-cells concern themselves with "Mysteries", and any such concern is an automatic symptom of degeneration or incipient insanity.

This is no place to argue the pros and cons of materialism and esotericism. Both are necessary in the broad scheme of human evolution through all levels of existence, and we are only concerned here with the training and control of consciousness and action through Inner dimensions. One vitally overriding factor does however emerge at this point which must govern the whole of our future conduct concerning the Mysteries. Each soul entering them must be its own complete master therein. Otherwise insanity and other sufferings will occur and probably involve those connected with the unbalanced individual. This is why the old Mystery Schools were so careful in their choice of candidate. Only those likely to succeed in keeping full control of themselves in the Innerworld were admitted. Even so there were many failures. Mastery over "magic" has not only to be gained but also maintained. The first and foremost essential was, and still is, sound human qualities that used to be called "virtues". Without these, no Mystery practice is likely to be much good to anyone, least of all the practitioner.

We are all familiar with the "awful warnings" given out darkly against occultism and magic of any kind. Such vague threatenings do rather more harm than anything else, merely arousing apprehensions without supplying any means of avoiding hidden pitfalls. The facts are that magical practices bring out fairly rapidly the normally hidden side of any person. Their latent characteristics will objectify. If these are good, then results are said to be beneficial, but if bad, then the opposite. All that happens, is that once a channel of communication has been established by magical means between Outer and Inner Self, a kind of short-circuit occurs, and surges of energy take place from one state to another. Objective and subjective energies coming directly together without adequate control cause tensions liable to result in serious explosions or erosions. Spiritual, mental, and even physical diseases are quite likely to be an outcome. So are opposite conditions of improved health, strengthened mind, and the greatest benefits of soul. It all depends on whether our circuit was properly arranged before the power was switched on.

For these reasons, the reputable Mysteries, whose operatives were deeply concerned with human welfare, instituted a large number of controls between Inner and Outer life. They established Deity-figures of benignant aspects and attributes. They personified the worst and most undesirable qualities of humanity as demons to be controlled and directed into useful service. They tied up magical practices with disciplines and training programmes calculated to bring out the best in the practitioners. One way or another, they did everything possible to ensure that their Initiates came to no lasting harm nor were able to inflict serious damage on others. At the same time it was necessary to provide means of development so that Initiates became capable of handling powers which might be used with considerable good or evil effects. The position was rather like that of the modern problems concerning the selection of suitable people for controlling atomic energy.

Those individuals likely to benefit through magical Mystery practices will be well-balanced, healthy, sound-principled, intelligent, patient, hard-working, and creatively imaginative people. This may sound like an old fashioned character reference, but moral qualities are of greater importance to humanity than magical abilities. Unstable, easily excitable people, with unsound principles, erratic impulses, nervous dispositions, or inadequate health and stamina, can injure themselves still further by magical means unless they seek to use these for making good the deficiencies of their own natures. In no sense is this intended to imply any type of Divine retribution, but simply the natural outcome of using an inadequate individual for functions beyond their ability to deal with.

During earth-life it takes us a number of years to grow into operative adulthood through a series of reactive processes supplied by life-circumstances. All that any school does for its scholars is to bring them in contact with a chosen variety of information and events so that they can form their own reactive pattern to these, and change their consciousness accordingly. We change ourselves in different ways and to different degrees depending on our reactive abilities. This is exactly what happens in the Mysteries. Initiates are presented with sets of symbols and circumstances (rituals) among which they are expected to react in such ways that calculated changes of consciousness take place. The result of this releases energies in the Inner dimensions wherein the Initiate is becoming an adult soul, and eventually the structure of the soul alters correspondingly.

The Mysteries are well called "Schools". Their function is to provide practical means for their Initiates to form reaction-patterns which will result in their own spiritual development and whatever other effects may be intended on Inner levels. This they do by applying suitable stimuli to selected souls in the correct order to the right degree. That is very important. It is useless presenting anyone with Calculus when they are still at infant school, and equally stupid to employ an honours scholar in repeating multiplication tables unless such were done as a nerve-calming exercise. The greatest weakness of modern Western occultism in general is an utter lack of order, system, training schemes, and a workable curriculum for an average student to follow for himself.

This does not mean a lack of occult information. On the contrary there is too much of it available in the greatest quantities of confusion. The necessity is for information on the practical use of this accumulated information. We might as well be in a technical library without being able to read and having no access to any tools or equipment. Our first need is to learn how and what to learn. Once this is grasped, the rest will follow naturally.

Experience has shown the best learning technique to be based on the Nil-principle, or the exclusion from focal consciousness of all but the essence of the subject under study. This ensures a direct connection between the subject and the student's deep Inner consciousness. Magically it is known as "banishing" or "dismissing" and has less to do with getting rid of demons than isolating a stream of pure consciousness by excluding all contaminating influences. The production of such true illumination is of major importance and maximum priority in any training programme, therefore we are justified in outlining its procedure here.

The first essential is acquiring the ability of "making the mind blank" while yet retaining the faculty of consciousness in full control. This is like being in absolute darkness with opened eyes and in total silence with alert ears. Outer negation, Inner positivity, a reversal of ordinary polarity. Until some degree of this art is obtained, nothing else should be attempted, for out of NOTHING comes ALL.

Different Systems have evolved various methods of achieving the same ability, but in the end everyone has to find the way best suited for themselves by trial and error. The Qabalistic approach commonly used in the West is to meditate on the Tree of Life as a whole, and then banish or dismiss one Sephirah after another up the Tree until the Nil of AIN is reached. This is a reliable method, but needs a great deal of previous work on the formation of the

Tree. Another system is to imagine oneself in the centre of a diminishing circle until the Nil-point is reached. Another is to simply let the mind or senses register whatever they will and refuse them all as they arise. A well-tried one is the "Not-I" method which starts by asking the question "What am I", and then rejecting all else specifically as; "I am not my body—let it cease to affect me. I am not my thinking—let it cease to affect me. I am not what I see, hear, touch, taste, smell—let my senses cease to affect me," and so forth in a sort of Litany. Eventually it is hoped to arrive at the Nil-point which is identical with the All-point, for a magical secret is that the more we are NOT, the more we ARE.

It is of course impossible to arrive at an absolute NIL while still attached to a physical body, but a magically workable approximation in principle is definitely attainable, and this should be aimed for before anything else is attempted. The reason for this is simply because once the ability is attained to some practical degree, everything else becomes possible. It is the one Key unlocking the door to all the magical Mysteries. The Cypher giving access to every value. The importance of the Nil-Concept cannot be over-estimated in magical work.

All Mystery Schools stress the necessity for "detachment" or "uninvolvement" as a state of being which must be achieved by any occult operator seeking spiritual success. Few are very helpful with suggestions about how to achieve this, which is probably because words are inadequate for that kind of instruction. Once the attention of students has been directed to the nature of the task, and they have been made to realise its importance to themselves, they are expected to carry out their own investigations and conclusions.

Whether it is called "detachment", or "uninvolvement," or any other term, this truly magical art amounts to a control of consciousness from a very high level. We live from one level higher than our activities all the time, because we work *on* something *from* somewhere. To fully control happenings on any particular level of existence we must operate on it from another. If we want to become anything, we must also "not-become" everything else. Before any vessel may be filled with any specific content, it must be empty. Before a single number is countable, Zero must be assumed. No Creation is possible without the Void. Writing can only be recorded on blank paper, or sound on a clean tape.

Whatever we choose to call this ability of "switching off" or zeroing ourselves, it is undoubtedly the pre-requisite for all other magical abilities, and unless we can develop some degree of skill with our consciousness in this direction, there is little use hoping for much success elsewhere.

In times gone by, people valued the power of Zero so much they devoted whole lives to its achievement, going into solitude and silence in search of it. This gave them an easy start toward finding the Nil-Concept, but no opportunity to control it. One adverse sound or disturbing influence broke their tenuous hold on what they had gained. They have achieved realisation of the incredible Energy and Omnipotence behind Zero, but themselves could accomplish little with it. The true Adept of Nil is one who can attain it at will amongst every possible distraction, and then direct a stream of pure consciousness in any direction required.

Though the Nil-Concept may be beyond verbal description, it is no condition of indifference, apathy, indolence, neglect, or other human inadequacy. Nor is it mere unconsciousness or any kind of sleep-state, hypnosis included. It is impossible to be consciousness *of* Nothing, but consciousness proceeds *out of* the Nil-state. Therefore such exercises as imagining black curtains or other neutral backgrounds are quite unhelpful. Zero is a state to be achieved by becoming it and unbecoming all else. Its apparent Negation is positive, definite, absolute. Once attain it, and everything would be possible. It is the complete opposite to ineffectuality or impotence, being concentration of energy to an ultimate extent, and an entire breakthrough beyond every barrier of being anything. It is utter and absolute Freedom in the true sense of its meaning. A transcendence of every possible limitation. Nil and All are identical.

The Nil-Concept can be a dangerous one if misunderstood, and is no toy for weak minds to play with. Though it is Absolute in its own state, ordinary human individuals can only attain it within their particular capacity while they remain incarnate. If they use its power for the wanton destruction of things held dear by other mortals, they must expect those mortals to react accordingly and retributively. Should laws be broken, their penalties will certainly be invoked, and the nearer to Nil the greater the effect.

In attaining control of All by Nil, the ability of unreaction must be cultivated. This means that no matter how intense the stimulus, there should be a nil-response. The maxim to remember here is NIL by WILL. A difficult art indeed to acquire, needing considerable practice for even the slightest degree of success. Every Mystery School has different teaching methods. One drastic example was to place the candidate in the middle of a circle of Initiates who then did their best to upset the candidate's balance. They hurled insults, offered inducements, and generally devised every kind of distraction they could think of, even to physical blows and noises of all descriptions. Throughout all this, the candidate had to remain imperturbable and maintain Nil-control, not by any tortured effort, but freely and easily as a natural ability. A Christian Initiate was supposed to demonstrate this reaction-control not only by withholding response to hostile action but by actually inviting more injuries.

There is scarcely much need for a Circle of Trial in these days when we live in such conditions anyway. Any Initiate seriously intending to test the condition of their reactions is advised to attend a screaming-session of teenage activity and remain utterly unaffected. Failing this, there are many alternatives such as a traffic roundabout at holiday time, or a public Baths on a hot weekend. The radio will provide all noise effects for a trifling cost. Such testing-fields are for advanced workers however, and others would do better to seek more favourable training grounds in the privacy of Lodges, Temples, or personal sanctuaries.

The conventional method of establishing relationships with the Nil out of which ALL must come, and especially whatever objective is being worked for, is by means of the Zero-Circles. These are the circles traced around the operator at the commencement of any rite. They should be no superstitious gestures made with a vague hope of expelling demons, but a highly efficient psychological structure forming the scaffold so to speak of the whole construction to follow. They are erected thus.

Standing erect at the point of operations, the magician pivots himself between Heaven and Earth by a brief direction of consciousness above to Divinity and below to all other life than Humanity. Attention is then focussed in his own centre and polarised outwardly like a rod, or a beam of light. Most workers face East and work Westwards like Light, but some prefer facing North and working Southward like Magnetism. With this focussed stream of consciousness, which may be directed with an actual physical rod, a circle is traced horizontally around the operator. This is the Zero of Time. Next a lateral circle is made from zenith to right-nadir-left, and zenith again. This is the Zero of Space. Lastly a vertical circle is made from nadir to front-zenith-back, and to nadir. This is the Zero of Events. With these three simple circles, the magician has outlined an entire Cosmos, and established himself its conscious creator. It will be noted they are made deosil. In theory they ought to be made instantaneously, but that would only be possible after very long practice.

Since this apparently easy exercise is the basis of all ritual magical practices, we had better continue with it for a while until its principles are thoroughly grasped, and at least elementary skill developed in its use. Its object is to make the magician "come alive" in Inner Dimensions, establish his identity therein, and set up an operative consciousness on those levels. To do this, all else must be excluded or "banished" from the Cosmos created by the magician. The Nil-concept must be established before any creation is possible. Therefore a Zero-state in relation to all other existence is essential.

The principle involved is outlined by the ritual questioning;

"What is most important of all?"

"God."

"What is more important than God?"

"Nothing is more important than God."

"Therefore let Nothing come before God."

We can see now the esoteric significance of the injunction to: "have no other Gods before Me". That is not a command to abolish idols or other God-concepts than IHWH, but a positive instruction to start from the Nil or Zero point before any concept of Deity whatever. Our most direct way to the One God is via the Nil from whence Deity first emanated. Anyone reading a hint of atheism into this has utterly failed to grasp the slightest inkling of what is indicated, and had best re-zero themselves.

Most Mystery faiths or schools have their own zeroing procedure. In Masonry the Lodge is squared and tiled, in the Church there is a procession and exorcism with holy water, and in ritual Magic the Circle is cast and consecrated. Each practice has the same objective, to exclude the outer and open the Inner Dimensions for the participants, which means swinging the direction of consciousness through the Nil-point toward its changed focus of attention. This is only possible to a very limited degree with most human beings, because it means they must exclude every kind of thought directly connected with the outside world, and work with a completely changed consciousness in very different conditions than those of their mundane awareness. Few people can achieve this necessary detachment by their own efforts alone, and a major magical secret is that of complete detachment or absorption at will.

Let us return to our zeroing. At first this is best practiced in a quiet room free of disturbance if such a commodity is available. Otherwise open country is good, providing it is possible to find this away from roars of road and air traffic. An ordinary rod about as thick as a little finger and the length of the spine is needed. It should be pointed at one end. Those are the essentials for practice. Other trimmings or decorations are optional—at this stage.

Now stand upright facing East with rod held against centreline of body by both hands so that its top lightly touches tip of nose. Eyes partly closed, breathing slow and natural, the whole attitude being easy and relaxed. Next let there be some transference of identity to the rod. Some thought like: "This rod represents me standing between Heaven and Earth. Where it points so will I, and we shall do things together. "Let us make a Cosmos to live in." The rod is then pointed down to waist level, held there, and the operator rotates on his axis for a complete circle, restoring the rod to upright again. Then the rod is circled to the right (south) down to the ground up by the left (north) and to zenith again, the operator turning all the while. Finally the rod is circled backwards to the west, down to nadir and up through the east to first position once more. The operator now takes stock of his situation.

This should have created a magical zone around the practitioner something like a complete globe. It is visualised as extensions of force rather in the nature of a magnetic field centred on the operator himself. The extent may be indefinite or only a few feet from the body. For experimental purposes it can be kept to the actual distance of the extended rod. It must not be thought of as any type of goldfish bowl or plastic bubble, but always as an energy-field. This must now be set to Nil-potential.

In the old days, such was called "exorcising" and consisted of adjurations to various demons who were commanded by different Divine Names to depart instantly on pain of frightful punishments if they continued to pollute the place. This would work, providing the Demonic Names were fully identified with the undesired qualities in ourselves to be neutralised and excluded from our workings, but it is a cumbersome way of carrying out a straightforward task.

The most practical exorcism, banishment, or zeroing, is to centralise energies around the Nil-point of the operator and allow this to open out to the extent of the surrounding force-field. Easy to write and say, more than difficult to do in practice. Endless attempts will be necessary before even a modicum of success follows, and yet it is absolutely essential to continue practising until some kind of results show up.

A good way to begin is to take some problem or other which is a matter of personal worry, annoyance, or to which there is a definite and constant reaction. Evoke and conjure it up in the consciousness until reaction sets in, then deliberately banish and neutralise it into Nil, the principle being that what is called up on purpose can also be dismissed on purpose. The diminishing effort is but a continued and inversed energy-flow of the original invocation. The purpose of all this is to bring the power of consciousness under control of the will and intention.

To ritualise all this is quite simple. It needs associating with appropriate circuits of consciousness through components of adaptation such as gestures, words of command, visual vehicles, and so forth. Suppose we try putting this in practice.

First the Time-Space-Event field is rapidly built up. Then a simple invocatory gesture and command is made while the subject of invocation is brought to mind as strongly as possible. Elaborate pentagrams and wordy pieces of prose are a complete waste of time and effort. A neat and effective gesture is opening a double door, which is that of bringing both hands forward together, then back

28

toward the body and out to both sides. At the same time the plain command; "Come in" is given either aloud or mentally, while the concept invoked is considered as advancing through the open portals upon the invocant. A positive reaction must be made appropriately. If the concept is enjoyable, then pleasure must be felt, or if otherwise, then whatever is called for in the way of aversion. We have now "called up" or "raised" a definite formation of consciousness and recognised it reactively, which gives it reality in mental dimensions.

Now we must expel the concept from our world. This is done by mentally pushing it through the open portal, making the closing gesture of bringing the hands together and forward again as if pressing the door shut, and saying clearly; "Go out". So far so good, a concept has been raised and laid, but not yet neutralised. This can only be done by deliberately bringing ourselves to zero reactivity with it. It must not affect us to the slightest degree in any way. We must make ourselves completely immune to it at will. One way of doing this is to mentalise the concept as reducing away from us in time and space until it means less to us than a speck of dust a millennium removed. The moment we are able to start reducing the influence of the concept on us, it is only a matter of pushing on and continuing the process as far as we can. Our aim should be to neutralise to the furthest extent of our ability and hold this zero as long as possible.

There are many ritualised methods of this. We can visualise our concept surrounded by the Cipher-circle which then contracts to infinity while we say firmly; "Nil—Nil—Nil" making diminishing circular guestures as if rubbing out a diagram on a blackboard. We can call up our concept, react with rapid and irregular breathing and jerky gestures, then banish it and reduce gestures to stillness and breathing to mimium slow regular while we do the equivalent on mental and spiritual levels. The best way seems undoubtedly to go right inside oneself as centrally as can be, and there make contact with the Great Neutral Origin of all, and release Its energy by simply relaxing all opposition and resistance to It and making oneself into Its symbol—a Cypher.

Even the faintest semblance of this is only possible with consider-able meditation and a very great deal of practice, but the time and effort must certainly be expended if worthwhile results are to be hoped for with ritual magic. We must discover how to be "All Nothing" about anything and everything. This is the Zero from which all magic starts. Such a Nil-state will be an individually relative one of course, but it will link into the Nil-Infinite which is the sole source of every energy.

Two good opportunities for practising neutralisation are first thing in the morning and last thing at night. The aim should be to zero ourselves as far as possible in relation to the days events and personalities both prospectively and retrospectively. Absolute detachment and unreaction should be sought, but under no circumstances should these be confused with indifference or callousness which are both involved reactions and completely wrong in principle. We must rise above and outside of the time-space-events contained within the daily cycle. In effect, we are banishing the worst that may be in us and making room for the best that can manifest itself through us. A religious person would say it consisted of pushing out man and asking in God. Whatever the terminology, the exercise itself is essential.

It can be ritualised to a formula easily enough. First adopt meditational attitude, then make the sign of the Triple Cipher which is not unlike that of the Christian Cross. With fingers of right hand as if holding rod or pointer, imagine such an extension, then move the hand to heart level and commence. While sitting quite still, draw an imaginary circle horizontally round the whole body from left to right. The actual physical movement of the hand will only be a slight one, but the end of the imaginary rod will cut through the body backwards and complete its circle. This is Zero-time. The next circle is Zero-space, and is made from left to right laterally inclusive of head and feet. Finally the Zero-event circle is made vertically from front to back over head and under feet. Hands are now returned to the rest position.

All this should bring us into a condition of theoretical timeless-ness, spacelessness, and uneventfulness. It is not that we have made everything else than ourselves cease to exist, but that we have made ourselves neutral thereto. We have not stopped anything happening, but we have stopped being affected by happenings by putting ourselves into a state where they all have equal significance. Once time-space-events of any world cease to have power over us, we start having power over them.

When, and only when, we are able to reach and maintain this condition of undifferentiated neutrality at will, even if briefly, we shall be ready to start building up our Inner Magical Cosmos. It will all come from the zeroed material we have made ourselves. That is the secret of Creation. Whatever we reduce to zero becomes available as raw material so to speak, for everything must be made into Nothing in order to become anything. To gain control of Universal Nothing, is to be a God.

Back to Nothing then. It will help if the Zero-circles have names or identities of their own. We could of course call them 1, 2, 3, A B C, or anything else, but those are not very enthralling names. A good equation is the Gnostic I. A. O. Let the horizontal Time-circle be identified with Iota the ninth (triply triple) letter, the Space-circle the Alpha the first of everything, and the Event-circle be Omega the last, connecting all else together. A Qabalist might perhaps name the circles I.H.V. or a Tantricist call them A.U.M. The nomenclature is purely a matter of System. The important thing is to have means of relating ourselves with all Existence through its Zero. It may help still further if we actually coin a word for Magical Zero. Let us combine the Latin for All and Nothing, and refer to our neutral potency as OMNIL. That will be a very useful word. Paracelcus tried much the same idea with his AZOTH, using the first and last letters of the Latin, Greek, and Hebrew alphabets to indicate a Universal Cycle.

All we need now is practice in establishing a neutral force-field until it can be effectively done in a moment. A whole long complicated rite must be compressed into as near an OMNIL state as possible. This is how we live anyway, because a printed page that once took us several years to read and understand is now taken in with the flash of an eye. We reduce things to OMNIL constantly if we but realised the fact. Magic only takes advantage of little understood natural laws.

We can now improve our zeroing technique. Using a plain rod about 32 inches long, we face East (Magical East is always front, whichever way we stand) and hold the rod something like a rifle at the "present arms". Its lower end is kept close to the solar plexus with the left hand, the right hand gripping it so that the extended forefinger is about level with tip of nose. Quieten breathing and take a slow inhalation. Direct attention to point of rod. Now begin to turn deosil while pushing rod down to horizontal position with right hand (near end held to solar plexus with left hand throughout exercise), at the same time expelling breath carefully to the resonation of "I" as a long EEEEEEEE. Mentally create a condition of timelessness. When the circle is completed, continue the move-ment by bringing the rod back to first position with right hand while taking a fresh breath, then start circling the rod on the South-North axis while still turning and expelling breath in a resonation of "A" as Ahhhhhhhhhhhh, and mentalising spacelessness. When the rod is reaching apex position, take fresh breath, change direction of circle to right angles through West-East axis, resonate the "O" as Ohhhhhhhhhhhh, and mentalise uneventfulness. Come to rest at original position, and either resonate the word OMNIL, or any such single name of similar import. AMEN is an old dependable. A Qabalist might resonate AIN, since it has the double meaning of Nothing and I. This completes the external part of the exercise.

It should be realised of course that all three circles are really different axes of the same force-field around the individual. The whole condition should be one of omnivalency and absolute equation as a universal state of Un-Existence. This can no more be explained verbally than we can be told how to see, hear, or smell anything. Everyone has to find their own method of attaining OMNIL. One practical way is the following.

Having established the I.A.O. axes, imagine oneself as a globe of pure force within it. Light is a useful medium, but it could be radiant energy of any kind proceeding from the exact centre. Unlike light however, it does not get weaker as it gets further from its source, but exerts precisely the same potency at all points of its three fields which are really one field. This energy does nothing, it simply IS. Now we start mentally contracting the whole energy field toward its centre where we are seeking direct contact with the Supreme Cipher or the Ultimate God. As we contract inwards, calling on the Ultimate by whatever Name we are in the habit of using, we are reducing our everyday selves to Nothing as we feel the circles of the Cipher closing in around us.

Simultaneously we should experience the compensatory "take-over" of the Supreme Cipher opening out from the same centre toward which we are closing. The more we negate our ordinary selves, the more positively does the Great Negation fill the vacancy we have made. Its Zero-circles should be felt opening out to occupy the openings we have left for them. When we have reached the absolute extent of our ability to follow this process, and our inwardising contraction has been equalled by the outwardising expansion of the Ultimate Zero, then we have established as near a neutral force-field of OMNIL as we can. Constant practice is needed to improve its quality and degree of depth.

It should be obvious that if we had to do the whole elaborate procedure of rod-swinging and resonating Names every time we needed to establish a neutral force-field of OMNIL, the exercise would have very little practical use. Therefore the practice must be carried out to a point when it can be done effectively, rapidly, and with a minimum of physical movement or none at all. A few seconds should suffice, and the OMNIL state need only be held momentarily. A good plan is to do it at random intervals during the day apart from morning and evening. Such intervals can be decided in advance to co-incide with any convenient random happening such as some distant noise likely on occasions only. An aircraft perhaps (unless one is close to an airfield). Again it might be decided to practise zeroing regularly. Possibly once an hour. Whatever plan is made must certainly be followed until some good reason occurs for its alteration.

The practice of zeroing is of major magical importance for quite a number of reasons. Firstly because it brings us into controlled relationships with our Inner and Outer worlds simultaneously, establishing a direct route between our human and divine principles. It is an exercise in all the rules of ritual, operates conditioned reflexes through every level of our being, and commences or completes any conscious continuum. Its side effects are quite surprising. Nerves are calmed, health improved, thinking made clearer, living ability increased, and a number of other beneficial results.

Once it becomes possible to induce an OMNIL condition by a single act of intent, the pre-creation of a whole Inner Cosmos has been accomplished, and it can be filled with whatever is needed. Wisdom, however, should caution us not to get into anything we cannot get out of, and therefore we must practise a quick-release back to ordinary mundane existence. This is done by deliberately "collapsing" or "exploding" our magical Time-Space-Event circles so that they re-align with those of our commonplace material world. It is most important to associate this action with a Key-concept which will provide a push-button for the whole operation. That is what "Magic Words" or "Names of Power" really are. Keys to entire states of being.

The quickest way out of the OMNIL Cosmos is that of the "hatching" method, so called because it resembles a bird emerging from an egg. Hands are brought to "prayer position" over heart, palms together, fingers pointing up. Live a diver re-surfacing, they are pushed up over head, parted, and swept down sideways, forefingers pointing to ground. Simultaneously we imagine the Space-Event circles above us breaking at intersection and unfolding outwards while the Time circle expands outwardly like an opening flower. This leaves us standing in the centre of a circled cross again, but now its axes are identified with those of our customary external world. The "Magic Word" we resonate for this performance should be quite different from the I.A.O. A good one for the purpose is H.U.A. It is resonated as HOOOOOOOAAHHHHH.

We now have two invaluable magical procedures, geared for entry and exit between our Inner and Outer Cosmoi. They should be practised and practised until we can switch ourselves on and off in either direction with at least some ability. First we should carry out the practice physically, and then purely mentally. On each occasion we should make a definite association of the Key-resonance, so that ultimately it alone will suffice to induce the required state. When we have conditioned our reactions to a degree that I.A.O. puts us into Inner OMNIL, and H.U.A. gets us back to mundane living, it will be worth while progressing to the next stage.

A tape recorder is very useful in helping this conditioning process along. If a tape is set up reiterating the two resonances with their associations for a set period of say ten to fifteen minutes, and this is listened to periodically during zeroing training, it will prove most valuable. It should be arranged in hypno-style such as: "HOOOOO-AHHHH. This is the ordinary Outer World. HOOOOOAHHHH. Consciousness is outward through the body. HOOOOOAHHHHH. Life is objective. HOOOOOAHHHH (etc, etc, until the changeover comes), Stand by to change direction of attention. The Outer World is closing and the Inner World is opening to Zero. Time-Space-Events are turning Inwards. The Inner Cosmos opens. EEEEEEE-AHHHHHOOOOO. Life is subjective. EEEEEAHHHHOOOO. All is Nothing. EEEEEEAHHHHHHOOOOO. Time-Space-Events are Zero. Nil. OMNIL. EEEEEEEAHHHHOOOOO. This is the Inner World. EEEEAHHOOOO. Consciousness commences Inwardly from Zero. EEEEEEEAHHHHOOOOO." and so forth until we switch back again via appropriate phrases to the Outer World on the HOOOOOOOOAHHHHHH resonance. A loop-tape of all this makes a convenient teaching accessory.

The outcome of all this hard work should be well worth the effort. With a single "Word" we can bring the whole focus and force of our consciousness to bear on whatever we want to be and do either Inwardly or Outwardly. We have found the control contact and developed ability in its use. In old Magical parlance we have become Doorkeepers like Peter holding the Keys of the Inner Kingdom, and we can let ourselves in or out at will. This is true Magic of a very high order. Now we must learn how to live and behave in the Magical Dimensions to which we have earned access.

SPEAKING WITH SYMBOLS

It is all very well discovering how to start with a clean magical slate, but it is next necessary to find out what must emerge from such a beautiful blank. This means learning a completely new language and system of exchanging conscious energies between different levels of being. Another way of describing this is ritual symbolism.

Symbols may or may not be ornamental, but their fundamental purpose is for practical use by intelligent energies. Just as arrangements and combinations of physical matter are needed for applying material causes to obtain specific effects, so is equivalent symbology necessary in other fields of existence. Each symbol has its meaning and content like the letters of an alphabet or the elements of molecular construction. When correct combinations are made, results happen.

The practising magician must therefore learn how to think, work, and live with the symbols of the art, using them for any and every purpose. Once the principles of symbol working are grasped, entirely new Inner worlds will open up for exploration and life. It is a fascinating ability with unlimited possibilities.

What is a symbol anyway? In effect it is the good old "outward sign of inward grace", or a practical link between objective and subjective existence. It is a body containing a soul, matter holding a meaning, a focus of force, a condenser of consciousness, or a "thought-tank". Anything and everything can be a symbol. Whatsoever connects consciousness and life together from one level to another, or even to different points on the same level is a symbol. Figures, letters, words and ideographs are very good examples of symbols, since these join thinking with living.

Magical symbols are fundamental concepts for energy-exchanges between very different levels (or "worlds") of living, and the intelligent beings operating through them. They exist in the greatest profusion and confusion possible. There is no difficulty whatever in discovering them, but they are valueless without an ability to synthesise and apply them. To learn their alphabet is easy, but to make words and meanings out of them is real magic.

Not many serious attempts have been made in constructing or learning a practically synthesised magical symbolic alphabet. The most noteworthy is that of the Qabalistic Tree of Life and its infinity of attributions, based on number-letter relationships, with the Tarot ideographs and astrological concepts attached. Once the Latin alphabet is satisfactorily substituted for the Hebrew one, the Tree will be of inestimable value to modern Western occultists. Whether or not we use this System, it is certain that we must adopt some method of symbolic constructional combination, supposing we want to pass the nursery grades of letter-learning and slate-wiping.

Our best way of relating One and All together in Nil is the Circle-Cross symbol, as we have seen. After all, it is the natural method by which we co-relate ourselves with our external and internal worlds. Hence the magical attributions of the Quarters and Pivots. The symbols of God-Names, elements, instruments, angels, and so forth attached to the four quarters of a magical cosmos are the basics from which it is built, and they must be properly realised before they can be used. The only way to accomplish this, is by thinking and living them until they become integral to existence.

We can start work on any symbol we choose, but it will be as well to begin the construction of a magical circle or cosmos with the four principal Instrument-symbols, the Rod, Sword, Cup, and Shield. These are the major formators and arrangers of the One Energy from which All is produced. Whatever exists, is what it is by application of the principles symbolised by these four concepts. Singly or in combination with each other they define all differentiation. It is therefore essential to gain some experience in their use.

The only way to realise a symbol is by a process of mutual absorption. We must enter it, and it must enter us. We must participate in its essence to an extent of identifying with it at will so that we can project ourselves into it, or externalise it in any manner necessary. This means a good deal of hard meditational and ritual work, but it will put us in possession of a fourfold Master-Key to consciousness, and train us to deal with any other symbols we shall encounter. A very well worth while end product.

There is no real difference in grasping magical symbols than with any other type. We must approach them from the outside consciously, and then simply keep following them inwards toward their primal principles. Then we continue the circle so to speak, and come out of them again with an ability to push them around in our own way. It is just like learning the letters of a strange alphabet, and amounts to much the same thing.

It is this principle and ability of "going inside" a symbol that constitutes whatever "magic power" we may personally acquire with it. If we remember that symbols are the tools of consciousness, the same rules in learning skills with ordinary hand-tools apply to symbols whether magical or otherwise. There is an initial drawback in connection with magical instruments. In the case of physical tools and symbols, our best way of learning their use is to watch experts demonstrating them and then copy those methods until we have enough skill to evolve our own styles. With magical symbols this is almost unheard of. We shall not even know they are in use at all, until we have developed enough practice with them ourselves to recognise the fact that others are using them. So we must rely on ourselves and our inner guidance to provide us with grounding in the art of symbol-working.

To make a start of some kind let us take an ordinary rod and proceed inside it. First, however, it must be obtained. Magical rods are traditionally procured in some special way, and it is precisely the unusual methods followed that make any rod magical. Suppose we adopt the procedure of cutting a particular type of wood at a chosen time and place, perhaps from an especial tree, and then preparing it in some selected way. It is the procedure which constitutes the magic. The rod will still be a wooden stick whatever we do. Yet magic has surely been made and changes of consciousness have accordingly occurred.

There are so many ways of making a magical rod that we need not recapitulate them here. The same principles of selection apply to all, the whole idea being to create a unique rod, different from all others in existence and identified with the individuality of its owner. This is the essence of the operation. There must be only one such exact rod in being. However many similar ones there might be in respect of general design or species of wood, every magical rod must stand as a unit in its own right as an adequate representative of its constructor. The rod is a magical simulacrum of its maker and/or owner, who should traditionally be the same person.

To obtain a rod in even the simplest way calls for quite a lot of thought and planning. It must be associated with whatever our requirements may be. Let us construct such a chain of associations. We will choose ash for strength and utility. It will come from an ashplant at or near some place for which we have respect or regard. It must be cut with a minimum number of strokes, preferably a single one, at an important time on an important day. The time may be decided astrologically, or by some other means, such as an anniversary or for any special significance. The rod should not be thicker than the thumb or thinner than the little finger. It should be capable of measuring some definite length-standard such as a yard or a metre. So far we have enjoined six separate specifications and we can add to them as much or little as we want. The rod can be trimmed, cut to length, and peeled with or without any ceremony. It should be pointed at one end (male end), notched at the other (female end), then the owner's initials or some personal cypher burned or cut in the middle. Finally some dedication should be made even as simply as: "This is my Rod, I hope it works."

All this may seem a lot of trouble and rigmarole to obtain a common piece of hedge-stick, but in reality it has become far more than that. It has become a Symbol containing a great deal of consciousness, and providing access to an unspecified amount more. The physical rod is an actual materialisation of a whole series of controls on consciousness. This is what makes it magically valuable and provides its linkage with the Innerworld for its possessor, which would not be the case at all if it were merely purchased in a shop. The "hand tailored" Rod becomes a practical symbol with which Innerworld contacts can be invoked all along its constructional lines. Materialising it is only half the task though, and its main function should be evoking energies on non-material levels and directing them where they are needed.

To do this, we must follow through the symbol of the Rod inwardly until we can deal with its pure principles on their own planes. The most practical method of doing this is by meditation on the Rod and materialising our ideas and information about it in words on paper or recording tape. Paper is best because it gives rapid sight-access to ideas. Taking for granted that all physical symbols have some kind of mental and spiritual equivalents, we start from the material end of the stick (or Rod), and keep pushing our consciousness along until it spiritualises. A good method is to rule off our paper into five columns with a heading for each and fill them in as we go. Like this;

SUBJECT	BODY	MIND	SOUL	SPIRIT.
Rod	pen	word	meaning	intention
	match	lighting	illumination	fire
	stick	support	help	aid
	bar	separate	forbid	prevent

The secret is that we must find Rods (or whatever the Symbol is) everywhere, and translate them into Innerworld language, so that all matter leads us to spirit, and all spirit is capable of materialising as appreciable symbols. This is the real "language of the angels" or "Enochian". We do not have to use words for filling in the columns of our categorical stages between the Inner and Outer worlds. Symbols or ideographs, or anything will do so long as it evokes a reaction from us. The guiding rule is this;

1st. Our Symbol itself.
2nd. Its material manifestation. Body. Presentation.
3rd   As we think it Mind. Formation.
4th. As we feel it   Soul. Creation.
5th. Its Principle. Spirit. Origination.

Using such lines, we can keep our consciousness pushing happily backwards and forwards between the Worlds bearing valuable freight on each journey. It may even carry passengers too.

A good plan is to use the "Symbol a day" scheme. We dedicate each day to one particular symbol, seeking and applying it in every possible way. At first a notebook will be needed until we can do it in our heads, hearts, and spirits. The symbol we chose will turn up in the most surprising places once we start looking for it, and success will come when it begins to call our attention to itself of its own accord. This is the Innerworld "talking back", and means we are making good contacts with it. We can make a kind of game out of the whole process, and enjoy it quite pleasurably. Something like this.

We shall devote our day to the Rod. On waking up we feel our own bodies and realise they are full of Rods as bones. Move our bones in getting up, and Rods have been applied. The room is full of Rods too, bars to windows, legs to furniture, curtain rails, all over the place. They are to be found and turned into thinkings, feelings, and realisations of principle. We look at anything and realise a Rod is a straight contact between two points, so we have just looked a Rod. We strike a match, and there are 40 Rods to a box. Before we have finished the day we shall be in a jungle of Rods (shall we need a Sword to clear it???), with a notebook full of jottings and a real Magical Rod coming to life for us rapidly.

The object of this exercise should not be merely to find as many resemblances to a physical rod as possible among household and other objects. It should be to recognise and realise the primal Rod-Principle to a degree where recognition can be translated into resultant energy-effects. By taking up the Rod in Spirit, we should be able to so use it on mind and soul that even physical effects will result. This is, after all, only the other half of the cycle begun by tracking the Rod back from its physical end. It is practical magic by symbology.

The Rod-Principle extends everywhere in very unexpected ways. It would not help to start listing them here, because it is essential that everyone should find these ways for themselves. An effective help is to keep a cheap notebook devoted to the Four Instruments of Magic alone under separate headings for each, and simply jot down odd words or ideas about them as they occur. In a mere few weeks there will be enough material to write a book with. A typical sample might be:

"Rods are long and thin—think long thin thoughts. Forked rods used for serpent catching—Rod and Serpent Symbol, R catches Wisdom. Rs probe and prod—use likewise. Rs are indicators—clock hands, compass needles, pointers. Rs are connectors—conductors—channels—pipes—cables—radio aerials. Rs are spears—darts—rod and hook catch fish—fish for inspiration with R in Infinite Ocean." Just heaps of odd ideas linking and connecting with each other via one Symbol—the Rod. Eventually we should only have to evoke the Rod-Symbol to obtain access to all other streams of consciousness it directs. Such is Magic, the art of concept-control over living and other energies.

As with the Rod, so with the Sword, Cup and Shield. So indeed with all Symbols that convert thoughts into things and things into thoughts, for such is their function. We must not only learn them but live them so that what we symbolise "comes true". This will only happen if we are able to convert ourselves into symbolic power-patterns. Hence the importance of systematised and patterned progress along symbolic lines. Once we evolve a magical life-pattern, we must keep it going somehow or other if useful results are ever to be obtained from it.

This is the value of the Magical Diary and Workplan. They keep us up to the mark all the time, and produce much more than any haphazard leaps in the dark could possibly lead us to. At first they may seem dull, slow, and quite unromantic, but if they are persevered with, they are certain to bring us nearer success with magic than if we took chances in other directions. They need not be onerous or boring at all. Everything depends on how they are constructed, and we can consider this topic by itself later on. Now we must continue concentrating on work with symbols until the technique is sufficiently mastered to develop itself.

The secret is to go beyond thinking *of* Symbols, and learn to think WITH them. It is very important to understand the distinction implied here. Using our Rod-Symbol, this means thinking not *of* or *at* a Rod, but *as* and *by* one. We must not only think into a Rod, but out of it too. This principle applies to all Symbols of course, but if we cannot succeed with one simple Symbol at first, we shall never be able to handle any others subsequently, so we may as well keep plodding along until some measure of success comes.

We learn the Rod or any other Symbol by identifying with it. This means using ritual exercises which are simple to devise, but must be regularly carried out in order to be effective. They will

40

obviously be all directed in this instance toward the assumption of Rod characteristics and abilities. For example we might set the Rod up and meditate something like this;

"I am a Rod. I can extend between any two points of Infinity. I can impell or repell. I can point myself anywhere, take the measure of anything. As a pendulum I can control time. As a Rod I rule myself. I chastise my faults. Support myself or anyone else. Probe mysteries to their depths. Push power wherever I want to. By conserving energy in breadth, I can concentrate it in extension. I am a Rod of Light, illuminating or seeing whatever I will. I am upright and straightforward. Firm but not inflexible. My behaviour must be in accordance with these factors, and others of a Rodlike quality. Being a Rod I must act like one. Etc etc." Making out meditations along these lines and taping them against appropriate background music is very helpful.

Having collected all this mass of information and impressions concerning a Rod, it remains to translate it actively (which is the magic), and so we begin Inwardising and Outwardising with it. Here are some useful exercises, and plenty more remain to be found from their practice.

ATTRACTION AND REPULSION. Take the physical Rod and hold it lightly in contact with centre of body at one end with left hand, forefinger and thumb pointing forward, the Rod to be horizontal with trunk. Right hand grips Rod lightly with pointing forefinger and thumb, ahead of left hand about half way along shaft of Rod. Stand upright and steady so that point of Rod is about two or three inches from a wall or heavy fixture that one need not worry about making marks or scratches on. Close eyes and vividly imagine being drawn forward to the wall along the line of the Rod. In a few moments this will actually happen, and the tip of the Rod will bump the wall, only the grip on the Rod itself preventing a further fall forward. Keep eyes closed and reverse procedure, imagining a powerful repulsion along line of Rod. Be ready to check a backward fall. A comfortable sofa or such may be handy to fall back (literally) on. Repeat this exercise until it comes fairly easily, then try it without physical Rod, but standing correspondingly closer to wall. Keep the idea of the Rod going without its actual physical shape. Continue until success comes. Next make an objective target on the wall or some person, place or thing to be attracted or repelled. Practice Rod-attraction or repulsion to or from the objective. First with, then without physical Rod. Maintain Rod-principle throughout. Keep practising until the mere concept of a Rod in or out of contact with the objective will push or pull one's body about while sitting quietly in meditational posture. After that, the body should be held still and the mind or soul moved accordingly.

CIRCLING. There are many ways of describing or working circles with a Rod. The simplest is to draw a circle around an objective with its point, and focus the whole attention in that area. The opposite to this is drawing the circle and excluding consciousness from its content. This is good training for handling the mind. In some familiar room choose a smallish suitable object such as an ornament or fitting which is normally in its place all the time and generally unnoticed. Trace a circle round it with the Rod, at the same time investing it mentally with any remarkable or interesting quality it may suggest. Build this up as strongly as possible until emotional or other reaction is noted, and the ordinary thing has taken on extraordinary meaning. For the next few days, whenever the room is entered let the attention automatically fly to that one hitherto ignored thing and rebuild its new significance. Much can be done by developing this practice.

To reverse the procedure, bring into a room some totally incongruous object and place it absurdly or awkwardly where it would normally attract maximum attention without actually impeding movements around room. Trace a circle around it and banish it to a degree where it fails to evoke the least notice or interest. (If desired, deosil circles may be used for invoking, and widdershins circles for banishing.) After that, simply ignore the object whenever the room is entered until such time as it is possible to stay in the room without even being aware of its peculiar intruder. The circles of invocation and banishment can be very much reinforced with mental commands such as "Come in" and "Go out". (Simple commands are best.) At the same time feelings of invitation or rejection should be experienced.

Another good circling exercise is to stand a tall Rod or staff upright and imagine it is the central post of a spiral stairway. Grasping the Rod like a post, commence circling round it deosil, imagining that one is actually climbing real stairs to something very wonderful at the top. Doing this with closed eyes to music helps, and it is necessary to make a definite number for this practice, 32 is a customary set. The ascent can be done to a number-count, and when the final step is reached, a sensation of emerging into conditions of beauty and light with perhaps splendid scenery may be felt. Descent is by changing direction and coming down with left hand on the post until ground level and ordinary conditions are reached.

It is important with all these exercises that they be worked out in equals and opposites as complementary pairs. No exercise should ever leave its practitioner struck out on a limb with no means of return. Nothing should be gone into with no means of return provided, or safe transit to another level worked out in advance. All work should be cyclic, and a banishing method must counterbalance invocations.

By means of these apparently childish exercises, ideas and actualities are interchanged by controlled consciousness, which is indeed Magic. Ultimately the "wielding" of a Rod Inwardly will produce Outward effects, since it is working through a chain of consciousness operating between both. To calculate such causes and effects and make them according to will is the work of a highly skilled magician.

As each exercise is discovered and practised, so it should be carefully noted in the Magical Diary and classified as to nature, results, expectations, and other comments. In this way a whole curriculum of magical exercises and rituals can be built up fairly rapidly. It must never be forgotten that the exercises are means and not ends. The end-product aimed at should be the ability to handle Symbol-concepts. Once the primary stages are passed, we should progress to combinations of Symbols and complexities of action with diverse types of energy, but there will be no running without crawling first, so let us continue crawling at a brisker pace. The present task is still conditioning ourselves to reacting with symbols through varying conscious levels.

There is so much to be done with a Rod alone that we might go on indefinitely with it, but that would unbalance development considerably, so only two more specimen exercises will be given here. The first is:

PREVENTING OR PASSING. Hold the Rod horizontally, thumbs to centre and touching tips, male end right, female end left.

Slowly approach open doorway or some entrance arrangement which is too narrow to allow the Rod through it sideways. Close eyes and move quietly forward until ends of Rod touch on sides of opening and prevent further passage. Feel the check and register it consciously, there being no need to use any great physical force at all. Build up a feeling of protection as if the Rod were a bar preventing a bad fall through an open window, or the bar across a closed door keeping out undesired intruders. Make this as strong as possible. Repeat a few times until the idea is grasped. Link the operation with some simple command such as; "Stop! Proceed no further" or any other "Magic Word" producing the same effect in the consciousness.

The complementary exercise to this is actually passing through the opening, or inviting some being into the room. For this, the Rod is positioned against the doorposts (or Pillars) and one hand turned at wrist so that grasp on Rod is now with both thumbs pointing to the same end, depending on which end is to be opened. Giving some Inner command like: "Proceed in peace," swing the Rod like the opening bar of a door to centre line of body, and either pass through opening, or step back to invite some intended being inside room with appropriate greetings. Repeat until the exercise feels right. Try opening to left or right for differing reasons.

The use of this exercise is that we can now associate an upright Rod with freedom of passage, and a horizontal one with security and stability. Upright means "Go", and crosswise means "Stop". We can even use the familiar red and green to implement our meaning, so long as the symbology remains sound. Once skill is developed in this direction, we need only be conscious of a horizontal Rod to prevent, or an upright one to permit whatever we will between Inner and Outer worlds. A pleasant way of doing the exercise is while circumambulating. The rod is held upright with both hands thumbs upwards in front of the body while moving round the circle. It is swung to horizontal as stops are made. The action can be worked to music or taped instructions. An important point here is concept lag or lead relative to action. If action is to be controlled by concept, then the concept must infallibly precede and govern the act. We must not alter position of the Rod because we have ceased or started to move, but we must stop or start moving because the Rod indicates one or the other. This means we respond or react to the will behind the Rod, and our actions become subservient to intentions.

THE LEVER. We should all be familiar with the mechanical principles of leverage, and of course they have Innerworld equivalents. The Rod is the lever, and our exercise is aimed at applying energy with it from one dimension into another. The major part of the problem is undoubtedly the fulcrum. Physically it is the fixed supporting point against which the lever moves, thus transmitting energy from one end of the lever to the other. Metaphysically, a fulcrum is a firmly fixed concept in which we have absolute faith, and in relation to which we can move in other directions. Without such a fulcrum, nothing at all can be effected from one state of existence to another. The question must be asked and answered: "What do we genuinely believe in with sufficient undoubting faith to make it a valid fulcrum from which to extend our conscious energies?" Perhaps an awkward question, but a definite answer of some kind must be found. Even if the true response is: "I believe in nothing." then Nothing Itself must become an Absolute in which faith is fixed. Whether any concept is accurate or not makes no difference. It is the belief and faith in a concept that must be held firmly at all costs, whatever the nature of the concept may or may not be. Belief and faith itself is the working power. The object or concept in which we believe is simply the focus for the faith-force.

To construct a magical fulcrum on which to work our Rod as a lever, we must use a Symbol. A very practical one is a Pyramid. An ideal one would be made of a single piece of stone only a few inches high, but any convenient substitute will serve. On the base of the pyramid let a plain circle represent OMNIL. The apex of the pyramid will be the dot in the middle of the circle, and the fulcrum point, while the four sides will be the arms of the cross to the four quarters. On each side must be the symbol or actual name of some absolute principle we infallibly believe in. There is no use putting vague names of unknown deities or incomprehensible sigils. Far better use ordinary words that have positive meaning. Occult sigils conveying in their shorthand outlines a whole series of beliefs are valuable providing they are comprehensible to the user. The attributions to the Quarters will preferably line up with our notions of the Magical Compass, so let us take four general principles as follows.

E. LIFE (in all senses)
S. LIGHT (in all senses)
W. LOVE (in all senses)
N. LAW (in all senses)

These or their Symbols should be on the sides of the pyramid, and it should then be aligned properly. Lastly the Rod should be balanced on the apex of the pyramid, or at least rested on it while one end is being held.

We now have a well-constructed magical instrument. Using basic beliefs as a fulcrum, we are theoretically able to exert energy anywhere around the circle of Existence by applying pressure to its equal and opposite point via the Rod of Will. It remains to get the Rod in exactly the right position, then apply sufficient pressure for the proper period, in the required direction.

So far, we are only scratching the surface of possibilities in using a magic Rod, but until it is "brought alive" inside ourselves, we shall not be able to use it at all. The same applies to any Symbol, and the art of bringing Symbols to life and making them real for ourselves is basic magic, to be practised and practised until we develop as much skill as we may. Our lives with Symbols in any state of being must build our lives in equivalent ways through other states until single Symbols will act throughout the whole.

To work with any Symbol, we must come to terms with its soul. The outside physical appearance of a Symbol is the body, but its inner meaning, principles, and application, is its soul, and this is what we must deal with magically. If we tackle the problem with systematic and purposeful effort, we shall succeed far better than by making wild dashes at it. Therefore it is advisable to work out and adopt a standard technique for dealing with all magical Symbols. This will produce the best results in the shortest time feasible.

First we must approach the Symbol from its exterior as an objective phenomenon in its own right. We should make a species of it physically, even if this is a sketch on paper. At all events we must materialise it in some way or other. It must be given a name and classification so that it takes on identity and individuality.

Next we must react to it, which means doing a lot of thinking and feeling, all of which should be noted, summated, and arranged in some patterned order so that it all makes sense and will be available on demand. Qabalists will use the Tree of Life for this task, and others may prefer a straightforward tabulation of some kind. Whatever method is used, the Symbol must be entered into to a degree where there is definite empathy between it and its percipient, and awareness of its Inner significances arises in the consciousness.

So much is pure Pavlov reaction-reflex, but we must now carry things far beyond the range of a dog, or even very many mortals. We have reacted *to* a Symbol, and must extend our abilities into reacting *with* it. This is the magic part. Boiled down to essentials, we should deal with Symbols in three stages. First MEET them, second MEDITATE them, and thirdly MEDIATE them. Another way of puting this would be; IMPACT, INTAKE, OUTPUT.

To meet a Symbol is easy, to meditate it is difficult, and to mediate it needs real effort during initial attempts. Mediating a Symbol means applying it, which in turn means directing its use purposefully. For example we have met the Rod-Symbol as a prepared artifact and its representations on paper. We have meditated it by thinking about it, following up its lines of communication with the worlds of intellect and emotion, and exploring its Inner possibilities. Finally we have mediated the Rod by making it physically, moving it mentally, and moving with it spiritually. We have worked it from one world to another in various ways, and realised to some extent the amazing possibilities of linking Symbols with life. We have learned that Symbols are indeed Keys that will open any closed door in Existence. They are called Keys because they give access from one compartment of consciousness to another.

What we have done with the Rod we can do with all Symbols, using the same procedures in suitably modified ways. Once we have developed even moderate skill with a few basic Symbols, we can start combining them with each other, and then they will begin "talking back" to us in very surprising "words". There are no ordinary human words in any language to express the kind of consciousness dealt with on Inner levels of life by Symbols. They deal with "Magic words" that are far beyond the abilities of human speech, yet not unreachable by a human soul in search of its origins. By means of symbolic "Innerwords" we can communicate with higher intelligences than our own, and alter the entire course of our lives for better—or worse. This was once called magically, "working the Will within the Word".

To make the most effective use of Symbols for magical purposes, it is necessary to learn and practice them as a kind of disciplined drill. With training, it is possible to gain sufficient proficiency to ensure that a minimum effort will produce its maximum result. By simply channelling energies that would otherwise be wasted, magic is worked. This means making out a training programme and sticking to it. Such a programme would also have to fit in with the sort of life normally lived by the trainee in mundane terms. The difficulties of this are obvious, but not insurmountable. If a genuine Will exists, a Way will certainly follow sooner or later.

To construct a practical magical training programme is not very different from arranging any other type. Available time must be divided among calculated events. If the time is only five minutes a day it must be entirely devoted to its best magical use as a time-unit forming part of a series with an overall purpose. Suppose we try to put such a scheme together and see how it works.

Using the base-plan of the Circled Cross, we make time cycles round the centre as in Fig. 1.

The Time-divisions are arbitrary. We might as well have put; Dawn, Noon, Dusk, Night, and called it a day, New, Full, Wane, Dark, and called it a month, Spring, Summer, Autumn, Winter, and called it a year, or Birth, Adulthood, Maturity, and Age, for a whole lifetime. The actual length of time is not so important as the principle involved. We take a whole Time-unit, circle it and cross it. Once this is done, we can Space it, and arrange Events through it.

The Event-cycle will also be quartered, preferably in relation to the consciousness undergoing its experience, such as: Approach, Impact, React, Result, or Listen, Consider, Reply, Reflect. The nomenclature can be varied to suit the event, providing it implies the four points of a Circle of Consciousness concerning the event under consideration. We could, of course, equally well say A, B, C, D, or I.H.V.H. Any suitable symbology to express firstly the essential nature of an event in itself, secondly our contact with it, thirdly our reacting with it, and fourthly the outcome in terms of end effects. Once we have a properly quartered Time-wheel, and an

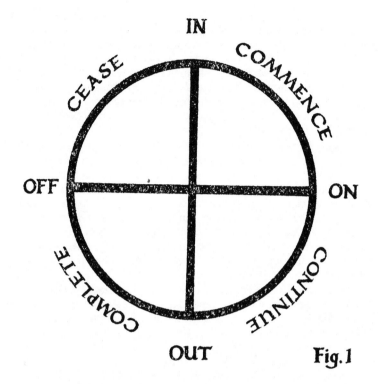

IN

COMMENCE

CEASE

OFF

ON

CONTINUE

COMPLETE

OUT

Fig. 1

Event-wheel, we can mesh them together just like any mechanical connection and drive them accordingly.

Now we must give the Time-wheel a value and the Event-wheel a name. Suppose we say five minutes for the Time, and the Rod-Symbol for the Event. This means living exclusively with the Rod for five minutes, during which we will first meet it objectively, then identify with it, next express it in some way, and finally reflect about it. This exact order of procedure is of the greatest importance, and must be kept to, whatever forms are used. We might for example spend the time in first visualising the Symbol, then reading about it, next writing of it, and finally thinking about it. So long as the sequence of the event is in harmony with its fourfold cycle of being, we can please ourselves as regards formalities. Magically our Event-experience is the "Utterance of the Name" or living through the Four Worlds of Origination, Creation, Formation, and Expression. There is no need to spend precisely the same amount of time on each stage, providing the whole Time-wheel is used for the specified Event.

48

In practice our magical Time-Event might work this way. First the objective Rod (or whatever Symbol) is set up in some way (perhaps purely mentally) and recognised as itself. A brief reinforcing phrase such as; "You are my Rod of Power" helps, though one can take any preferred invocation so long as it is short and incisive. The second phase of the operation is purely an Inner one, and consists of absorption and identification with the Rod-concept. We might say: "This is the Rod of my uprightness, my backbone, my sense of direction. It is my link with Life in all directions, the Divine Finger pointing my way ahead, etc." When we have put something into this phase, we can change over to the next, which is an output of what has already happened, and means doing something with the Rod in actuality. Perhaps we shall use some previously thought of exercise, or else invent a new one. It may be as simple as just pressing the point of our Rod against a hard surface, and then trying to sharpen the focus of our conscious attention likewise so that we can bring our forces of concentration to equal effect anywhere whenever we think of a Rod exerting pressure at one point. Lastly we embark on the fourth and final phase, which is one of summation. Here we should consolidate the effects of the previous happenings by making a few rapid notes on paper or tape. Conscious impressions at this point form the seeds from whence new experiences will eventually grow, so it is advisable to formulate them with some care.

With such a Time-Event combination we have compressed a whole lifetime into a few moments, which is a magical operation by itself. It must be but a single link in a whole chain however, and so this will now have to be thought out. Taking a Day-cycle, we take four points in it and place an event at each. For example, we might have a brief meditation-exercise in the early morning, a momentary invocation at mid-day, a few minutes meditation-exercise in early evening, and a final review of the day's events while going to sleep. Once such a cycle is commenced, it is most important to keep going, for it can lead anywhere intended after it gathers enough momentum.

A Day-cycle is only part of a weekly one, so we must work this out, for it presents much wider opportunities. We could devote each day to something aligned with its planetary attribution, or choose a "Symbol a day" system of some kind. Qabalists might adopt a "Sephirah a day" plan, thus getting through about three complete Trees in a calendar month. A reading programme is easy to arrange over a week, or a course of some special study-working such as "Words of Power", or "Tarot patterns". Little daily rituals are very simple to devise.

The Month-cycle comes naturally as Lunar tides. Sow at New

Moon, fertilise at Full, gather at Wane, consume during Dark. Whether plants or ideas are indicated, the principles apply just the same. Major magical rites should be towards the Full of moon, and others graded accordingly. By and large, the waxing moon is the time for activity, and the waning moon a period for reflection and recreation, but this is a very flexible interpretation. We might align the Lunar tides with the four Tarot Symbols, or any quadruple magical design. Once the principles are applied, there is great freedom of choice with actualities.

The Solar-cycle has the Four Great Feasts as its points, and they should be too well known to need detailed comment here. It may be as well to remember that a whole year as its Solar-cycle, is only an enlargement of a Moment-cycle at its centre. The life-cycle of a single instant is of level importance with that of a year—or any other time circle. Energy directed deeply and accurately enough for a brief moment can affect the remainder of a lifetime. Such is the practical use of magic. One good way to make a yearly programme is to choose some fitting topic for the Zodiacal sign of current solar progress, and an overall project for a whole season.

An ideal programme-pattern will thus consist of well-chosen events harmonising with Time-tides and projected through entire periods. The basic unit will be the Moment-Event cycle, the duration or nature of this to be variable, but its principle to remain unaltered. A good way of arranging a programme in advance, is to make out a sheet of paper for each Time-cycle with a large quartered circle representing the period in question. The chosen Event or Events can then be filled in as required, and changed at need.

The Magical Record or Diary can be followed with the same system, but using straightforward columns for convenience of writing. A Specimen page might read thus;

Date. 27, 3. — REMARKS. Disturbed night, See note.

DAWN	NOON	DUSK	NIGHT
1 Inv. Rght Ruler.		Come Cup	
2 As R upright. Tree. Strong. Support. Uphold.	X	Fluid in C calm while fluid outside agitated.	O
3 2 mins No 3.		No 16. (must vary)	
4 Felt braced. Ps 23. Fallen Tree like R making path through forest.		Drained. Warm feeling. Thought of L.C.	

NOTES Bad cough—abating—clear thought diff.

A few well chosen abbreviations in the right place are far more effective in linking Inner with Outer consciousness than screeds of pointless meandering and introspection. A Record or Diary is not for writing at length in, but for noting contacts which may be expanded elsewhere if needed. The Diary itself is a magical Symbol or Instrument constructed by a combination of Rod (Penholder), Sword (Nib or ball-point), Cup (Ink reservoir), and Shield (Paper). A good plan is to have separate Records for Days, Weeks, Months, and Season. They are much easier to keep that way. Days will carry only the briefest notes. Weeks will have somewhat more expanded ideas or comments, Months will perhaps carry accounts of ritual workings and magical happenings, while Seasons will deal with major matters at length.

As will be seen from the Specimen of the Diary, it is helpful to make out lists of specific magical exercises and codify them with numbers. They can then be selected or referred to with great simplicity. There is, however, no point whatsoever in trying to write masses of useless material and getting bogged down by unnecessary and irksome paperwork. Nothing at all need be written except to make magical life easier, neater, or more satisfactory. That should always be the aim.

A practical way of accomplishing this is by compressing and expanding consciousness. Let a chapter be taken from any book, or some suitable material chosen, read through carefully, and then summarised into a single paragraph. This again must be condensed into a few lines, then into a single sentence. So much is ordinary journalistic training, but we must take it further still and keep hammering away until we have translated the lump of consciousness into a magical Symbol of some kind. This may not be easy, but has to be done. The end-product is a Seed-Symbol from which all the material can re-grow. That is the value of magical Symbols. They are compressions or seeds of consciousness which will expand into all their original mass of detailed information or experience when they are allowed to do this under the right conditions.

Such is the significance of the Geni(us) in the bottle, symbolised by the open ended hexagram or Soloman's seal. Consciousness from one dimension was (and can be still), compressed into a container (Symbol) made from material belonging to another dimension. This can be released to work wonders, or can re-enter the bottle again. Details of the discoverer being a Fisherman, the hiding place an Ocean, and the finding place the Seashore (where the Four Elements meet), should all be of considerable significance to the occult student.

To make a Geni (Intelligence) enter a bottle, we must be as wise as Soloman and compress consciousness into symbolic containers. To release the Geni, we must remove the seal from the bottle by opening our own awareness of and to the Symbol and allowing its contents to expand into our Inner atmosphere.

Our magical records and Diaries should be a collection of such compressions and expansions of consciousness, for Symbols are a kind of spiritual shorthand, not invented to baffle ignorant minds, but to assist intelligent ones. They are made to help, not hinder spiritual progress. The better use we can make of them, the more practical our progress will be. Therefore we must not grudge some time and effort in learning the fundamental usage of symbology.

Expanding and contracting consciousness is equivalent to muscular exercises in bodily terms, though when we use Symbols we are contracting consciousness in one World by expanding it into another, the Symbol being a common link between both. Our exercises therefore, must consist of reducing the Time-event extent of a mass of consciousness into a single Symbol which may be of any nature suitable, whether sonic, written, painted, or perhaps not of a physical character at all. Once this is possible, we can reverse the procedure and extract masses of consciousness from the Symbol. It all depends on whether we push or pull the Symbol-door between the Worlds.

This "condensation of consciousness' is a most necessary part of magical art. All the Great Masters used it constantly. They never gave out their teachings in long windy sermons, but by points of power which have lasted for centuries. Their summations still guide us. Hillel said; "Do not to others what you would not have yourself from them". Jesus put it: "Love God and Man wholeheartedly together in you." Gautama said: "Truth is with the Not-Self". All genuine teachings are full of such condensations, and we must learn to follow the practice ourselves. Good examples are to be found among the Zen "haikus", a few words containing volumes of information in pleasing poetic forms. The conventional format of a haiku is in itself the Symbol. Suppose we take an already condensed formulary, and attempt to push it still nearer a pure Symbol. The Lords Prayer is a good exercise;

PHRASE	IDEA	SYMBOL
Our Father which art in Heaven.		Circled
Hallowed be Thy Name,	God	Point, or
Thy Kingdom come.		Hexagram.
Thy will be done on earth	Direct	Rod
As it is in Heaven.		
Give us this day	Sustain	Cup
Our daily bread.		

And forgive our debts	Liberate	Sword
As we forgive our debtors.		
Lead us not into temptation	Defend	Shield.
But liberate us from evil		
AMEN.	Us.	Pentagram.

So in two stages we have turned the Paternoster into six primal Symbols. God, Man, and the Quarternity. The One dealing with All equitably in every way. It now remains to combine the separate Symbols (or "letters") so as to make one magic Glyph expressing the sense intended. If we start by combining the signs of the Macrocosm and Microcosm (God and Man), we shall find that they will give an internal outline of the Cup as well, which signifies a state of love between the two. See Fig. 2. It will be seen that the Pentagram is not exactly an equilateral one, but it conveys the idea of Man being contained (Cupped) in God.

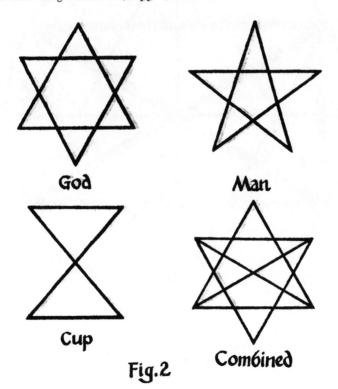

God

Man

Cup

Combined

Fig.2

If we now superimpose the Rod pointing upright to direct us from Earth to Heaven, and the Sword crosswise as an edge to cut free from tanglements, and then finally enclose the whole Glyph by a circle-cord to show all of us and Zero, we shall have Fig. 3. or the Lord's Prayer as a Glyph. This is not the only way it can be done, of course, but is a magically practical one. A much simpler Symbol would be to catalogue various prayers and merely use the reference number, but this would do no more than indicate a collection of words. A properly made Glyph or Mandala is magically alive with all the consciousness it contains, and can be used for meditation or mediation as needed.

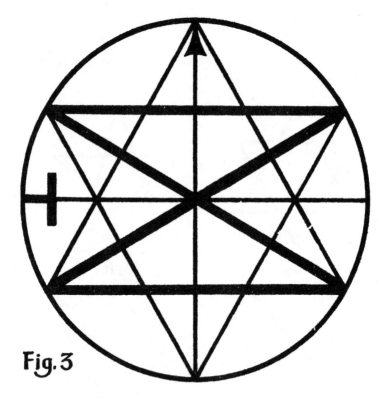

Fig. 3

To reverse the process by continuing its cycle, the Glyph is meditated on or ritualised until a stream of consciousness comes through it, to be interpreted as words or meanings of any kind which can be expressed in some form or another. It may come out in very different ways to the Lord's Prayer, but the fundamental energies of consciousness will be the same.

By using Symbols, we can translate or exchange experiences of consciousness or life-values in any way we like, from one dimension to another. The same unit of energy can be a stone, a plant, a colour, a shape, a sound, a sensation, or anything at all through the line (or cycle) it follows through the various worlds. It can only work along its own Path, but events on that Path may vary considerably according to which world and time the Path traverses. It is a branch of Magic to study and follow such Paths by means of Symbol-steps. They lead through all Time-Space-Event circles to and from the OMNIL Cipher. Qabalists have arranged them neatly enough on the Tree of Life Plan, and those unable to make their own paths might be well advised to look there.

The whole of Occultism and Magic is full of Symbols which are absolutely crammed with compressed energies and connected straight to direct supply-lines leading to undreamed of reservoirs of consciousness. Once we discover how to turn the Keys, an Infinity of Intelligence awaits us. This is why the art of Ceremonial Symbolism is so valuable. It teaches us how to manipulate Meanings in relation to Manifestations, and to work Will with Word.

The whole basis of Magic, is building up a foundation of Symbolic Energy-units out of which our Inner Cosmoi may be constructed. It is like establishing the material Elements from which physical matter is combined. Once we have established our working store of Symbols, we can go ahead and combine them in every way we are able. Nothing else will do this but patience, practice, and perception combined for the Purpose.

Now that we have some ideas about the nature and usage of Symbols, we must start arranging and working with them so that they will be available to us as and when we need them. This is the next part of the programme, and will involve a good deal of practical and repetitive effort.

CONSTRUCTING THE COSMOS

A Magical Cosmos is built up like any other type, relative to its centre. This centre is the Divine Spark within us, both individually and collectively. Nothing less is of any real value. The Cosmos is oriented to the Four Quarters around its Centre, and pivoted above by a God-concept, and below by a Life-concept. In such a way must we create our magic world about us.

It is of the utmost importance that we get this central nucleus-arrangement right at its very commencement. This is because the rest of our created Cosmos will be built up around it, and even the slightest initial error will mean a repetition of itself through the whole system in varying degrees. For instance, if we took an imperfect sphere and dipped it repeatedly in molten wax or any other congelant, the original faults would be reproduced each time in ever broadened forms. So called "Original Sin" is really an initial imperfection in humanity which succeeding generations have not yet managed to "true out" by compensatory action. It is the responsibility of every single soul to bring their own cosmos to perfection as nearly as they possibly can.

It may take a whole lifetime or more to get the nucleus of a Magical Cosmos together and working in harmony with itself inwardly and outwardly, but it may also be the work of a single instant. Both Time-units can be identical. In either case the same task has to be accomplished whether it takes a millennium or a moment. To make the vital nucleus out of which all magical power will come, we have been provided with a Plan or pattern for its arrangement. This is the simple Circle-Cross and the Concepts we build into it, relatively to the Time-Space-Event Spheres. Let us examine the overall picture.

Firstly we exist ourselves as an upright being with Divinity above and humanity below us, the Light of Life in our hearts. As such we are the Middle Pillar or trunk of the Tree of Life, the Direct Way between Heaven and Earth. Ahead of us all that aligns with our concepts of "Going forth", behind us our concepts of "Return", to our right our concepts of Positivity, and on the left those of Negativity (not Negation or Nil). Such are the dimensions of our magical world which we must build for ourselves with the instruments and instructions provided for us, out of the elements at our disposal.

Every Cosmos is built out of the remnants of a previous one lying in the state of Chaos. Order from Disorder. Reconstruction from Destruction. We must make what we want out of all that we do not want. The words of Khayaam-Fitzgerald should be remembered;

"Would we not shatter it to bits—and then,

Rebuild it closer to our hearts desire."

for this is just how a Magical Cosmos is made. Now we must have a look at our Do-it-Yourself kit and see what constructional materials are available. The nomenclature we shall use is arbitrary, but in accordance with Western Traditions of occultism.

Starting from the very centre of ourselves at the Monadic Principle emerging from OMNIL, we must begin creating ourselves by "uttering the Name above the water" and extending ourselves into the dimensions of our Magic World. The traditional Name is AHIH meaning "I breathe—I am". These Letters are extended quarterwise, and the Pivots become A above and Th below, the first and last letters of the Hebrew alphabet. At the centre of all these letters stands M, the Ocean of Infinity itself, as in Fig. 4. It will be noted that the letters are not produced successively around the circle, but crosswise as a single "exclamation". Read as sequences, they give some interesting results.

AMH signifies a common mother.

IMH means to be bright and warm.

AMTh means Truth.

Thus we have the idea of Light and Truth arising together from a common Mother-Deep. What finer focal-point could any Cosmos have? In the very centre we may read the sacred "OM" or "UM" sonic, which is neither more or less than the resonant frequency or "HUM" of Life itself.

This, or its equivalent in any acceptable form, must be the commencement of our Magical Cosmos. We "bring it to life" by "uttering" or living it ritually and practically. Having zeroed ourselves in a meditational position, we can literally hum a steady "MMMMMMMMMMM" while mentally extending the letters of the Names around us and keeping up the creative ideas of Parenthood, Light, and Truth along their axii. It should be realised of

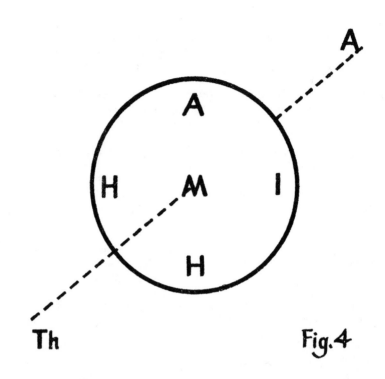

Fig. 4

course, that this takes place around the Divine Spark or Seed-atom in us which is NOT ourselves, but THAT which we become into. THAT is the Absolute around which our nucleus forms. It provides the BEING, while we have to provide the DOING of Cosmos-construction.

Once we have the nucleus of the nucleus in being, our task is to build up concepts around it not unlike the layers of an onion in theory. Each "layer" will be fourfold of course, uniting at the top pole or pivot in a "God-concept", and at the bottom or root in a "Life-concept" of human, animal, or other life-form. The nature of these "Heavenly" and "Earthly" concepts will vary according to the individual outlook of the soul concerned, but the upper extremity will always be the highest aspect of Divine Life imaginable at any particular level of being, and the lower extremity will be its complementary opposite as far down the scale of Life as may be reached. Metaphysically of course, these share an identity.

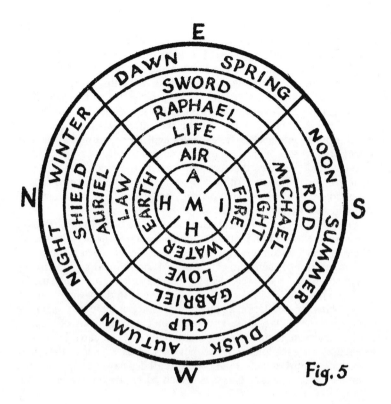

Fig. 5

The various major concepts of the Cosmo-circumference will be disposed around the central point on something along the lines of Fig. 5.

We now have a workable nucleus for a Magical Cosmos which is capable of indefinite extension by making further concepts at any suitable point of its structure. Given a well-designed nucleus, there is absolutely nothing in the entire field of Consciousness which cannot be co-related harmoniously with it at some angle or another. It is impossible to over-estimate the importance of this. The creator of such a Cosmos becomes a God in his own right, however minor this may be relative to other units of Deity. To such a one, everything makes sense, becomes true, fits in perfectly somewhere, and works at its best. They become healthy ("Whole-thy") happy, and harmonious beings, balanced at all points, and rotating (living) truly to their principles of construction. Whether or not the specific concepts of Archangels, Elements, Instruments, and other Magical formulae are used, or others substituted, makes little difference to the actual principle involved. It can be done with any formulation suitable to the constructor, provided the overall plan is followed. We shall remain with the magical system in this work however, because it has been proved practical by usage over many centuries.

The upright Magician drawing circles around himself is the Symbol of Mankind coming to terms with all the worlds of his living, and growing into a God. It "excludes evil" by organising all chaotic disruptive forces into regularised energies attuned to the creative cycles and serving the central God-Purpose of the Cosmo-constructor. Whether all this is done by one little human being, or the Logos of a whole Macrocosm, the principle is the same, and should be recognised as such.

The Cosmo-concepts of Magical Worlds are brought into effective being by reflection and ritualisation as we have already discovered. One of their advantages is that they have already been made use of by many skilled members of various Mysteries, and so are already "cut to length" as it were, leaving them available for ready use by those who recognise their value. All we have to do is work out our own plans for meditation and mediation and put these into operation on every level. We must remember that we shall not be dealing with inanimate lumps of matter, but *living energies* capable of auto-reaction on each other. If we put two ideas together, they may produce a third or cancel out others. It all depends what we use, and how we associate our concepts which form the molecules of our "immortal matter".

The ultimate idea behind all this working with, and arranging of conscious energies, is that the Cosmos of conscious individuals, singly or as a Group, should be held together at one point of control, or Nucleus, from which its entirety is directed. By identifying the structure of the Nucleus with Divine Names and principles, we try to ensure the best possible type of Cosmos. We also provide ourselves with practical means of directing our attention to or from any point of our Creation. By thinking about, or invoking, any particular concept, we automatically link ourselves all along its lines of communication. If we call upon or invoke the God-Name at the centre of the Cosmos, we invoke both its Supreme Spirit and every available energy throughout the whole of our existence. The "Magic Name" is in itself the Control of its Cosmos. This is why we should never "take it in vain". To do so is to break our own power in our own Cosmos.

In the Magical Cosmos we are dealing with, the Control-Name is: "The Living Truth", codified as AMTH AHIH. We can scarcely have a sounder nucleus around which to build everything from our

Universal Element, which now conforms to the pattern of the Cosmos by becoming the quarternity of Fire Water Air and Earth. These ancient elements of creation are magically called "The Elements of the Wise", to distinguish them from the physical phenomena of their namesakes. In their own right, they are standard frequencies of consciousness which if materialised to physical levels would manifest in a fiery, watery, airy, or earthy manner. We use combinations of them constantly in order to remain alive and sentient. To bring them under our control in our Magical Cosmos, we must accustom ourselves to deal with them by magical methods.

We begin this task by apportioning a sector of the Cosmos to each "Element", linking in with Time-Space-Event concepts, and personifying the Powers with an appropriate Intelligence or "Archangel". They will form the constants from which all the variables will eventually come and go. The Magical Instruments are the means and methods of operating and controlling the Elements, while the Intelligences determine the ways in which they should be employed. Therefore we had better start thinking about the natures of these and how to deal with them.

The actual Elements themselves should be sufficiently well known to need little comment. Nevertheless we approach them as basics of consciousness, and investigate their possibilities on occult or Inner levels. Using our notebooks and insight, while devoting both time and energy to meditation and mediation, we shall find a great deal to learn and practice. Let us commence with Magical East ahead of us, where we encounter:

AIR. Or the atmosphere of Life. The "ocean" (of gas) in which we swim around. We should study its physical nature and properties, translating these into Innerworld terms on their various levels. Just as we have a physical atmosphere, so we have mental and spiritual equivalents with their corresponding effects on us for good or ill. The rhythm of our breathing is more than physical, for we "breathe in and out" these mental or spiritual atmospheres with their contents of conscious instead of chemical constituents. If they are unhealthy, then we shall be affected accordingly.

Air carries sound, which makes meaning, and we can "hear" through the equivalent of air in other dimensions, once we have learned how to listen and interpret what comes to us by such channels. What air will do for us in a material way, it will do in other extensions of existence, and more besides. Therefore we begin at the physical end and "track back" until we find ourselves dealing with non-physical varieties of the same element.

Yoga "pranayama" exercises are invaluable in learning to live with "spiritual" air. The essence of these is that while going through controlled breathings of ordinary physical air, we synchronise those cycles with "breathings" of other atmospheres in different dimensions. Any reliable book on Yoga will explain the procedure.

Besides sound, physical air also carries scent, and so is the medium for two of our senses, hearing and smell. "Inner Air" or the "Air of the Wise" also acts as a medium for our extra-physical equivalents of those senses, and various meditational exercises can be devised for invoking sounds and scents on subjective levels. As our Inner senses "come to life" in their own dimensions, so shall we ourselves come to consciousness in the Cosmos they comprise.

In the Temple or Lodge, "Inner Air" is simulated by incense which modulates the physical atmosphere and superimposes a frequency in keeping with the nature of the Rite being worked. A correct atmosphere is of vital importance to any kind of action, and in setting up proper atmospheric conditions in a Temple, we are being just as scientific as a laboratory worker who sets up an artificial chamber to provide a simulated atmosphere of Mars or any other sphere for some experimental purpose.

The "Intelligence" of Air is personified in this case by Raphael, an Archangel of the Great Four. Archangels are indeed real Beings insofar as they are constants of consciousness constructed by the Overmind of the Superior Spirit Who is God so far as we are concerned with existence. Archangels operate within specified limits, each being a specialist for some particular purpose. Their fundamentals do not alter with any amount of centuries in our time, though of course they will use any available means for fulfilling their function at any point of time or place.

Raphael's work is instructing humanity and also healing injuries and wounds (not diseases) of any type. In another form he would be seen as the Great Hermes, Thoth, etc. Angels are actually sexless Beings constructed from pure Consciousness, so we may think of them as we like. Details of Raphael's appearance can be filled in from imagination and tradition. He is often depicted with a flask of healing ointment and the staff and hat of a traveller, since he is the patron of travel in any form. We can think of him as the Spirit of adventure into the unknown where we shall encounter and learn our destiny, together with sure healing for the injuries we are bound to meet with en route.

Raphael typifies the dawning of our Inner Light, without which we could not take a single step ahead upon our Path. We should continue to personify and objectify Raphael and the other Archangels until we can feel a very positive sense of "presence" when we invoke them. Techniques of this will be discussed later, for it is a specific magical practice needing special attention by itself.

The Sword-Symbol as a means of controlling the Element of Air may seem puzzling at first, but when we recall that it was originally an Arrow (which is a Flying Sword), the sense of the Symbol appears. An arrow depended on its feathered flights for accuracy, and the feathers of course had to come from some bird whose element the Air was. Today, a rocket or missile might be substituted for the Arrow, but the Symbol is adequate as it stands.

Just as we dealt with the Rod, so must the Sword or Arrow be dealt with, and its whole chain of connections with Inner meanings be followed up. Sword-exercises must be done in theory and practice, though we need not actually take up fencing or sabre fighting in order to gain skill. Normal sword-drill of drawing, saluting, and returning the weapon is an advantage to practice. So is thrusting and parrying, providing such manoeuvres are geared to magical exercises.

We must start filling pages about the natures and peculiarities of Swords and Arrows. Finding them everywhere from the razor blade in the morning to the last winged thought at night. Swords can be seen in keen observations, and pointed remarks. They can penetrate, decide issues, cut through Gordian knots, compel obedience, challenge stupidities and defeat them, uphold honour, and accomplish a great many actions along these lines. Swords are also surgical scalpels cutting away disease. They are the scythes and pruning shears of the husbandman, the scissors and needle of the good housewife, the lambfoot knife and shears of the shepherd. We can send thoughts directly to their mark like arrows, and we should remember that the bow is a type of Rod. A Sword is two edged, it saves or slays like most human inventions. In the body our tongues are swords, they can defend or wound. We are surrounded with Swords and Arrows to find and make use of as a single Symbol.

If we remember that striking steel on stone brings forth fire, a nice little ritual of the elements may be worked whenever we make a cup of tea, providing a genuine living flame is used and not an electric kettle. The striking match equates with fire from steel in the eastern dawn supervised by Raphael. Boiling the kettle on the stove is done with the element of Fire in the south presided over by Michael. Pouring the water in the teapot is like preparing a sacred drink in a communal Cup from which all will partake in the evening under the western care of Gabriel. Finally, setting out the tea things on a tray or table is comparable to arranging a Cosmic Plan or ordered magical Mandala on the Shield of Night with its pattern of Stars oriented by the North Pole Star shining from Auriel's forehead. Tea is more of a sacred ritual than we think even in fun.

The Magical Sword can be made in many ways and designs to suit its owner. From the humble kitchen knife with some sigil burned on the handle, to a beautiful and elaborate Lodge sword complete with scabbard and baldric, the physical aspect of the

Symbol may vary enormously. The real and true Sword however, like the other Symbols, exists Inwardly, created in our consciousness. No amount of money can possibly purchase it, for its price is effort, expanded for the necessary time to bring it into Inner reality. All the rituals and physical sword-drills imaginable, are for no other purpose than helping to make an Inner Reality of the Sword-Symbol, and developing our abilities for using it. We must never forget that external rites of any kind are only to aid the inducement of Inner effects, which might not otherwise occur.

So far, along this Quarter of our Cosmos, we have contacted its primary reference-letter of a Divine Name, (A), an Element of Existence from which we can make all sorts of things either singly or in combination with the others, (Air), a Symbol-tool to work the Element with, (Sword), and an Intelligence which combines both human and Divine consciousness who will tell us how best to proceed in this particular way. We have even dedicated times of the day and year as specially significant. Dawn, because we should awake to breathe in a new day with all the keenness of a freshly sharpened blade to learn what it offers us with the help of Inner tuition. Springtime, because life renews itself naturally as nature awakes from winter sleeping, and all must be cultivated with the cutting tools of earthworkers. Ritualists would be well advised to work out suitable Sword-ceremonies to fit in with Dawn and Spring. In primitive times a chosen victim was sacrificed with a knife or Sword to ensure fertility, but such is not advisable any longer. A brief mental working is adequate for an evolved consciousness.

Factual Sword-rites are simple to devise. A good one is simply to cut the Sword through the air in the design of a Pentagram while invoking some particular thought for each side of the figure. Perhaps a letter of some Name might be taken, or the vowel sounds made, or even 1, 2, 3, 4, 5, repeated. The idea is to start slowly enough and gradually pick up speed until the sword movement is much faster than the tongue can follow, and the syllables must be given mentally. Then speed must be still increased and concentration intensified to the point where it is even difficult to think faster than the flashing blade travels. Each Pentagram should be completed with a sharp little stabbing motion to the centre and a finalising "HMMM" resonated. This exercise and extensions of it, really sharpen up the brain first thing in the morning.

Another interesting Sword exercise is something along the lines of Zen archery principles of the "effortless effort". This needs a standard type of Sword with a blade of about thirty inches. At approximately eye level there must be a target with a central hole of about an inch and a half diameter. This target can be wood, cardboard, metal, or anything, and need only be a few inches larger than the hole. In fact a plain ring of wire will serve. This may be suspended from a ceiling by a cord, or set up on the end of a staff, but must have enough working space around it. Ideally there should be a light such as a candle flame at a distance away so that the light lines up with the hole and the observer's eye. The swordsman takes up a stance about six feet from the target, draws sword and salutes the Infinite Intelligence represented by the light shining through the Zero of the target. The sword is now raised to shoulder level with forefinger pointing along the blade which is considered as an extension of the finger, and the right foot advanced slightly. The tip of the blade, which may be only a foot or so from the target, is lined up with the centre of the hole and sighted along the whole of the right arm.

The exercise consists in lunging forward in fairly slow time so that the sword passes through the small aperture of its target. This is not so easy as might be thought, but the whole point of the exercise is that mere dexterity is not the object of its practice. The magical objective is that the blade should not be directed by our ordinary intent and skill at all, but by the "right intention" of the Superior Intelligence Whose plan is perfection in everything. It is an exercise in the surrender of the merely personal will to that of the Real Self which works with the True Will behind all manifestation, and to Whom the invitation is extended: "Do what Thou wilt".

Once the Sword is aimed at the target, the Zero of its circle should be concentrated on like a hole in Existence itself, which opens up into a totally different dimension. We should feel as if we were being sucked through this hole like a straw through a vacuum pipe, yet not be afraid of this happening because the cross-hilt of the Sword would prevent our being drawn further. Our whole attention should be focussed on the light through the target-hole, and yet we should feel indifferent or neutral as to whether our Sword hits it or not. Self-will in the action must be reduced to minimum, and the inevitability of the Divine Light drawing us straight to Itself through the hole felt to a maximum. Once everything "feels right", we will make our lunge with genuine "humility" or complete acceptance of the "Superior Will".

If the lunge was a "right" one, we simply withdraw the Sword and salute the Infinite with recognition. If the Sword missed the target, we bring it back so that the point rests on the ground before us while both hands clasp its hilt and our heads are bowed in the attitude of regret. This time we recognise that the fault for not striking true exists entirely in our ordinary selves. The True Self *must* necessarily be accurate, and *cannot* fail to direct the Sword (or anything else) truly. Therefore the fault has to be in the imperfect vehicle we offer this True Being. We put up a brief prayer or instruction for our fault to be rectified, bring the Sword to the salute, and try again. And again. And again as often as may be necessary.

Merely scoring direct hits through the target is of no use at all magically. It is the way such hits were made that is of importance. The feeling must be: "I cannot accomplish this by my own ability at all. It is not the personal "I", but THAT working through me which hits the mark." The Greater Being must operate the lesser one. Such is what matters before all else. We must not feel, "I hit it", but "That hit it". There is a Cosmos of difference between the two attitudes. Actually the whole of this exercise is very difficult to explain, and there is only one way to really understand it, which is to try it out practically. It may sound a trifle childish, but is of very genuine spiritual value, for it aligns consciousness and action between Divinity and humanity.

In all these single-element magical activities, we should build up the concept of acting *upon* the Element *with* the Instrument, guided *by* the Archangelic Intelligence, *presided over* by our God, and *based upon* our human status. That is the order of working, and we should equalise our energies through this system, no matter what names we may use to describe its component parts. The fixed relative point is always our Divine Spark at Absolute Centre. To continue our Cosmic circle, we must deal with the next Element.

FIRE. Fire of course means Light and illumination in all possible senses, and it has only been our control over fire that raised us from primitive animal level to our present dubious civilisation. Our further control of this Element on Inner levels is the only factor likely to raise us further toward Divine status, and it is controlled both Inwardly and outwardly by corresponding methods. As with other Elements, Fire must not be used, excepting under suitable conditions. No Element can ever be applied in its pure unmodified state without the near-certainty of causing destruction to materials unable to bear such energy. This is certainly true Inwardly, and is the cause of much spiritual damage to souls unprepared for Elemental energies.

A perfect person (if such a thing were possible) would be a being in which the pure energies of the Elements balanced each other perfectly and were expressed as a single Entity. Our imperfections arise at source from elemental unbalance, and if correctable at these primal points, all else would work harmoniously. Hence the vital importance of establishing a sound central nucleus to our Magical Cosmos. This is especially obvious in the case of Fire, which causes spectacular and obvious damage when incorrectly used. That is why it is so essential to construct sound control-concepts of Archangel and Instrument which exercise an automatic influence over the elemental energies of our essential natures. In doing so, we are fixing a built-in stabiliser and auto-pilot system for our Cosmos which will keep it going in as near perfect order as possible.

The Instrument of Fire being the Rod, it is scarcely necessary to add a great deal more at this point that has previously been said about it. Originally the Rod controlled Fire because it was a means of carrying it safely from one point to another, or keeping a blaze in check without being burned. Today, we may think of an electric conducting lead as being a Rod bringing a modern version of fire to our homes, and also the control rods of an atomic pile. Alternately we might think of a Rod as a fire-hose controlling fire with water. The principle of a Rod directing and controlling the Fire-Element can be applied in very many ways.

As the Archangelic Intelligence and Overlord of Fire, Michael is an admirable figure, with his Solar assocations. He personifies Right and Reason triumphing over Wrong and Ignorance. The best in us overcoming our worst. When we consider the damage possible by physical fire, the necessity for seeking safeguards from Inner levels against their Fire equivalents will be obvious. Michael supplies the Intelligence for taking such measures, also directing us how to use Inner Fire properly. He is too well known a Being to need much pictorial description, though a little known attribute of his is the scales (balance) in which he weighs souls after death to sort the worthy from the unworthy.

It is Michael that is said to heal diseases of organic nature by restoring the unbalanced condition to normal. His Spear is also the Balance-Staff. We should always visualise Michael as surrounded by brilliant Light which he modifies in any necessary way. The old legend of an emerald being struck from Michael's crown by Lucifer, which subsequently became the Holy Graal, is a most beautiful one. The Graal was not originally a Cup, but a Platter, which Symbol of course belongs to Earth. The significance of this Myth, is that Solar energy is brought by Light to Earth, where it is converted to sustenance for Life in the emerald green of fertile fields, and the herbs of healing.

Fire is the one Element we cannot touch directly in physical or any other form without being severely injured, yet unless we receive its modified energies we shall certainly suffer and die. Angels were said to be made of Fire or pure radiant energy. So we should see Michael, whose Spear is his Magic Rod transforming Elemental Fire into forms that are safe for us to handle or deal with. We should aim to study his methods and apply them to ourselves. Every time we light a candle with an ordinary match, we are deputising as Michael and his Rod bearing Fire safely. The same applies to switching on any electric appliance, and such is a very good moment to make a

Michael-thought. Opportunities for Element-control exercises exist everywhere if we care to look for them. It is all a question of entering extraordinary dimensions through ordinary keys.

That is how magical efforts are built up by the cumulative energy of thoughts. A number of little thoughts over prolonged periods will accomplish what might have been done by one intense thought for a moment. It should be part of ritual practice to provide opportunities for both methods. To think of Michael briefly for a week every time we switch on or off, will accomplish more than an invocation made only once a month. In fact, unless we are able to work these miniature rituals with very ordinary materials, we shall not be able to make much headway with elaborate Rites on full-dress scale. Principles come before practice, and are to be universally applied.

So we should be able to think of Michael if we strike a match, Gabriel if we turn on a tap, Auriel if we butter a piece of bread, and Raphael when we feel a draught. It is conditioning ourselves to find the supernormal through the normal that makes the best ritual training. Those unable to find Divinity in a Cup of water (or tea) are unlikely to meet It in a consecrated Chalice. Magic is to be found on the Inside of Outside—as every child knows, and most adults have forgotten. The most beautiful and remarkable rituals worked on earth are but sophisticated extensions of simple child-games founded on identical principles. Just as the play of infancy leads us to physical adulthood, so does its equivalent on Inner levels lead us to spiritual adulthood—and beyond.

Fire-exercises using a Michael-figure with a Rod-concept are very easy to devise. A valuable commencing one is:

Igniting. Or kindling a ritual fire and light. Since this is a commencement to the majority of formal rituals, it will be as well to master the technique at an early stage of working. Lighting candles should never be done indifferently or with lack of attention, since this would mean a considerable loss of valuable ritual experience.

The simplest requirements are a nightlight on a flat stone (preferably from some revered site), at floor level in the centre of the room or working place, a taper, a candle or nightlight at each Quarter, and a single match. (The match is a concession to replace traditional flint and steel). The room should be in total darkness, and the operator crouched down by the fire-stone, match in hand. Now the imagination should be brought into play, and dread of the dark evoked in some way. Perhaps the picture may be called up of being alone and lost in a cold desolate wilderness with no means of guidance or sense of direction. There may be unknown horrors lurking in the impenetrable blackness. At all events the darkness must be banished. A powerful invocation to Michael should now be made, and the sense of an answering presence felt. Michael should be visualised as appearing on a higher level in another dimension. He smiles reassuringly and reaches out his Rod or Spear to us butt first till it touches our hand and turns into the match. Michael has lent us his power from another world to use in ours.

We must attempt to realise with awe the power entrusted to us. With it, we can make Suns on earth, and it endows us with minor Godship. We can bless or blast with Fire, now that we have been appointed Guardians of the Flame. The tremendous responsibility of being able to produce Fire at will, and do what we want with it, should fill us with ambition to be worthy of our office. Invoking the Power of Inward Light, we strike the match on the stone, and light the nightlight, then squat back to contemplate the miracle which has appeared before us.

When we have reflected sufficiently on the wonders of what has happened, and meditated on the Flame that has appeared from Nil and will return there, we must realise that having obtained Fire from Heaven, we may pass it on through our own Cosmos. So we light the taper, which becomes a Rod, and slowly stand upright. Here we may picture ourselves like primitive man rising above all other life forms on earth because of his ability to handle Fire. With Fire-freedom, man began his ascent from earth to heaven. Heat rises over cold. When we were entirely in the dark, we were afraid to move away from the safety of our stone shelter, but now as Light-Bearers we can move anywhere we will, bearing the precious gift wheresoever it may be needed.

Full of such thoughts we advance the Way of Light toward the East, and light the candle there while we think of the dawn and possibly Archangel Raphael thrusting the Sword of Light into the sky. Or we may picture the candle as some particular person or group to whom we would wish Illumination. There are many possibilities. Then we repeat the process of illumination in the South and West with appropriate symbolism. When we come to the North however, we do not think of the Sun, for this is the point of night, but of the North Pole Star, our point of guidance in Heaven. Finally we come back to the centre of our Light-circle.

Now comes the extinguishing. The taper is put out first, but a realisation must be made that the Light has not been made to cease, but simply transferred back to where it came from. Perhaps we may imagine Michael "taking over" our tiny flame as it disappears on earth, and replacing it among his inexhaustible store of Celestial Fire. At all events we must appreciate its continuance in other dimensions of being. We repeat around the Quarters, and as the lights go out of earthly manifestation, we must "see" them still shining brightly Inwardly. In the end, although we are again standing in physical darkness, we realise that true Inner Light is inextinguishable, and can be evoked to dispel any amount of darkness. All we have to do is reach into ourselves and "light up".

With all this in mind, we can practice calling light back and forth from one dimension to another. We need only light and extinguish a candle to do this, while we consider the flame to be there all the time anyway in its true essence of Inner Fire. We simply act as agents moving it from one state to another. Naturally we cannot go through long or complicated rituals every time we need to light an altar candle, but the necessary Inner realisations must accompany the act which otherwise is meaningless. It can be done as swiftly as the time it takes to kindle a taper and light the candles. The order of lighting candles is always from the centre outward, and they are extinguished in reverse. The Circle of Light however is extinguished deosil as it is lit, for the simple reason that the Eastern sky darkens first, and the other Quarters follow on.

For normal ritual lighting of candles or lamps, something like the following procedure should be adopted. The taper should be borne as a Rod to the Perpetual Flame, and a momentary reverence made to the Light of Lights, an identification being acknowledged between It and the Divine Spark within the taper-bearer. The taper is then lit from the Flame with a sense of the Inner Spark shining forth with all its radiance. The Light at the end of the taper-Rod is now seen as Light exteriorised from the bearer's Divine Spark, and ready to be passed on anywhere. There must be a sense of responsibility and reverence toward the Reality symbolised by the Light. The candles or lamps are then lit in their correct order, identified mentally with whatever they stand for, and their Inner Flames seen to materialise as the taper touches their wicks. There should not be a feeling of "I am lighting a lamp" but of "Light is working through me". When extinguishing the lights, they should be sensed as only vanishing from physical sight into their Inner realities.

This, or some equivalent exercise should be persisted with until it becomes automatic, and its Inner responses are evoked every time it is carried out physically. It is of great importance, for it sets the tone of the ritual that follows, and opens up the way for more complex reactions leading to realisations of Divine Imminence. It is a good plan at first to perform this Lighting alternately with all its ritual meaning, and then as an ordinary action with no special thoughts at all. This will give us a sense of the difference between a similar action done ritually and non-ritually, and make a good proof of how valuable ritual can be to those able to use it.

From an ordinary standpoint, the foregoing will seem an absurd length to pursue in order to light a common candle, and a complete waste of time. Such, of course, is not so at all. An uncommon experience has been undergone by means of a common circumstance, and this is the modus operandi of ritual. The whole of our being has been enriched to the full extent of our ability to live Inwardly from outer stimuli, and such an enrichment is a positive reality demonstrable by alterations in our own person and consequently in all our contacts.

We are all familiar with the childhood game of "making pictures in the fire", and there are endless devices and gadgets depending on alternating light-effects to induce an hypnotic state. They all work on the principle of visual confusions causing a shut-off of conscious attention to normal objectivity, yet permitting the mind to superimpose its own subjective imagery on to the chaotic focal field. Otherwise sheer optical exhaustion is aimed at by prolonged staring at candle reflections in mirrors until the mind refuses to accept the picture presented by physical sight any more, and prefers to substitute its own from its secret storehouse. Such methods of using Fire may be diverting, but are not of much real value in serious ritual training.

Since any images observed by such means are actually formed on subjective levels and projected into conscious awareness as objective impressions, the best way of contacting them is to shut the physical eyes and look for them inwardly. No pictures are ever seen in a crystal or other means itself, but they are seen in the mental image of a clear crystal that exists in the observer's consciousness. A crystal is merely a symbolic means of suggesting a clear sphere where any picture can be made. We might as well think of a blank sheet of paper or canvas awaiting the attention of an artist. In making Inner occult contacts, we depend on our own intelligence constructing the clear field, and other sources of intelligence drawing the picture thereon.

In using the Inner Fire to illuminate our clairvoyance therefore, the best plan after zeroing down is to create a blank "stage area" in ourselves where images can arise illuminated by this Inward Light and be observed by our linked-in consciousness. Just as our physical senses only work by reacting to elemental energies of a material kind, so do our Inner senses operate by similar processes with the same elements on non-physical levels of being. Unless we develop some ability to work by Inner Light, we shall be spiritually blind, and unable to react with Inner Fire except by being burned by it. Hence it is as well to make first contacts with the Inner Elements through safely ritualised means. We now consider:

WATER. This comprises the bulk of our physical bodies and at the same time permits their mobility. As we emerged from the ocean primaevally by the action of Light upon Water, so must we be reborn on Inner levels through ocean equivalents thereon. This is ritually symbolised by baptism. Water will do everything Inside that it does Outside—and more.

Water is essentially the Element which is the medium of fertility and germination. It dissolves and disseminates the solid chemical elements of earth into a liquid state from which living organisms absorb and synthesize them. If we follow this through, we shall see that from the liquid state, these elements are transformed into gases (Air) and then into pure radiant energy (Fire). Thus one cycle of Creative Elemental Energy solidifies itself into "matter", and the inverse cycle subtilises itself into "spirit". So in "order of materialisation", the Elements are successively Fire, Air, Water, Earth. Water was anciently regarded as the seed of Sky-Father falling on Earth-Mother, and this beautiful symbology is valid still.

All this was expressed in the famous "Emerald Table" of Hermes, where it is said; "The Sun is its Father, the Moon its Mother, the wind (Air) hath carried it in the womb thereof. It descendeth from Heaven to Earth, and again it ascendeth from Earth to Heaven etc." The answer to this riddle of course is "Life". The radiance of the Sun draws up water into the air with its charge of living energy, then the coolness of Night (the Moon) condenses the vapour which descends to earth re-energised by the Sun, so that the Life cycle may continue. Water becomes the medium between solidity and radiance, and indeed mediumship (in the true sense) is the essential work of Water.

On Inner levels, Water is a container or carrier of consciousness, linking up conscious energies between all life-forms. Hence the Cup as a Communion-Symbol. By itself Water is pure and inert, no more than a combination of two gases, one inflammable and the other supporting fire. If the secret of "exploding" water were ever discovered, the whole earth would become the biggest atom bomb in the Cosmos. So Water is taken as the Symbol of purity, capable of dissolving impurities and superfluities, returning these back to earth for transmutation.

The Archangel of Water is Gabriel. He has several interlinked functions. As the "Messenger" he is a consciousness-carrier between Divine and human intelligence, which is symbolised by his speaking and listening trumpet. He is also a principle Fertility-figure as his name "The Potent of God" signifies, when his trumpet becomes a phallic Horn, the inside of which is the Cup, or female symbol. He "Bears news" on one level that fertilises minds, and he "bears seed" on another level to fertilise bodies. Gabriel is the Life-bearer, powered by Love, and he helps Force turn into Form. He resurrects life from death all the time, and Water provides him with a life-medium for its continuation.

Meditations on Gabriel are quite rewarding. As Ruler of the Western Gate, the Keyholder of the floodgates of Heaven, he links with Lunar tides and all the ancient fertility attributes of the Moon. There is no need even to regard Gabriel as exclusively male, for fertility is a bi-sexual matter, and Gabriel fulfils either function. On physical levels, we cannot see sex as anything else than the reproduction of our species from our bodies, but its equivalents on Inner Dimensions are very different, being related to force-fields and charges of energy. Pure Intelligence may manifest as it pleases in either direction. Humanity has not yet reached the stage of evolution where inter-sexual relationships are fully possible Inwardly. Gabriel is the Archangel for information on these interesting matters.

We can discover much about Gabriel from the legend of the Annunciation. Gabriel (the Potent One) brings intelligence (consciousness) to Mary (the Bitter Ocean) that it is possible to conceive spiritually, and that he is indeed charged Inwardly with Divine energy seeking expression through her. So much might be told any expectant mother, but Mary is given the realisation that in her case this Power will concentrate and focus to an unheard of degree through a child she will bear physically. Her realisation will act as a channel for such externalising energy. Gabriel personifies the mediation of Divine Power from its Source right down to material levels, and we know such meditation as—LOVE.

As the control-instrument of Water, the Cup has meanings as deep as the oceans themselves. Once more we must start finding Cups everywhere from the hollow of our hands to the Space that holds the stars of Heaven. A Cup is to liquid what a Platter (Shield) is to solid, and they are really extensions of each other as female Symbols, while the Sword and Rod are male. The Sword and Cup are partners, like the Rod and Shield (or Platter). This is shown by their arrangement round the circle as Cross-Points. In dealing with the Cup therefore, we must see its connection with the Sword so that we may keep it in correct balance.

We ourselves are Cups containing consciousness and Life. Our blood vessels and body-cells are Cups or Shields, just as our bones and nerves are Rods and Swords. The Cup is symbolised as a heart containing the Divine Spark, for a Lamp is a Cup holding Light. The Cup is linked with our sense of hearing on all levels, and we receive communications through it from other dimensions. The Cup is also a Form-giver, for without it Water could not remain as an effective Element. Uncontained Water would disintegrate. Even in its gaseous state of finest particles, water is "held" by the Cup of the atmosphere.

All hollows are linkable with the Cup. The Cave, the Womb, the Well, etc., etc. So far as spatial formation is concerned, we may say the Rods are Edges, Swords Points, the Cup Cavities, and the Shield Surfaces. In one sense we might say the Cup was a hollow Shield (which is a flat Cup). The Cup-Symbol is Female-fulfilling, and the Shield is Female-fulfilled. To imagine the picture in motion, we may think of a Cup being charged with fluid Life-essence which solidifies into its own identity, pushing the walls of the Cup flat in the process, so that we have a fully materialised Being standing freely on the Shield (or Field) of its world. If we carry the visualisation a stage further, and imagine the ex-Cup Shield curving in the opposite way, we shall see Man errect on the curved surface of the Earth. Spirit to Substance. Sacramentally we may imagine such a change from Wine to Bread, via Cup and Platter. Then of course, we can continue the cycle back from Bread (Substance) to Wine (Soul) back to pure Spirit. Cup and Shield are interchangeable like Rod and Sword.

The Cup and Love go together. Love holds, pours out, comforts, cheers. It may also intoxicate, poison, embitter, and even slay. The contents of a Cup may be anything at all in liquid (Soulful) form. Life, death, and resurrection come from and through the Cup. It is the Tomb as well as the Womb, and its circle represents Nil containing All. The upturned Cup is the Ocean, and the downturned Cup the Mountain. There is both an Inside and an Outside to the Mystery of the Cup. Onlookers may only observe it, but Initiates partake its contents, to signify they have been let into the Inside of the Mystery. The ideal Cup of the Mysteries is a hemisphere on top of a pyramid with no base, so that the design is a circled square. To use and understand these Archetypal Symbols, we must combine them with others and move them around in relationship to each other. Then they begin to "spell words" on Inner levels, and tell their amazing story.

So we start filling up notebooks or tapes with Cup-linkages, and follow these along their lines systematically until we have a working knowledge of the Cup, and can make good contact with it on different levels. As with the other Instruments, we shall meet it in very unlikely ways, but we must be ready to recognise it anywhere and anyhow. It is the *principle* of an Instrument or Symbol that must be sought rather than its form, which is apt to be misleading in any case.

As the Rod is a standard and a measurer of Space by length, and Time by movement (oscillation), so does the Cup deal with Space by amount, and Time by rate of flow. It is impossible to empty a Cup in actuality, for even if it held a vacuum, that would still be a content. Its essential nature makes a content inevitable, all we can do with a Cup is exchange one type of content for another. This is why it is such an appropriate Symbol for the Eucharistic

Transubstantiation (or exchange) of a God-Presence for a wine-presence. The God was there all the time, it is the "*emptying*" of the Cup that constitutes the Rite. If this seems unlikely, we might remember that our mundane Space (including the Empty Cup) is full of electromagnetic energy which we cannot detect except with special apparatus. As yet no mechanism exists to detect Divine Energy on higher and finer levels, so we must rely on our own inbuilt perceptors for that purpose.

There are so many Magical exercises possible with a Cup that it is difficult to single out particular ones as examples. Nevertheless if we select a few most likely to help with general Cup-principles, they will soon lead to any other that may be necessary. The most obvious to commence with is:

Filling and Emptying. As we have noted already, we can only *change* the contents of a Cup, and to fill it with anything is to empty it of something else. Furthermore we must "fill" a Cup by "emptying" another one, and "empty" it by "filling" yet another. To illustrate this, we need only take a Cup and plunge it under the surface of water. The Cup is now full of water. We empty this water by turning the Cup upside down, shaking it around and moving it away from that particular spot. Technically we have emptied the Cup, even though it is still full of water. Therefore we have emptied and filled it by one action. Let this be repeated in the Air, but this time try blowing the air out of the Cup by breathing into it. Do this to the Four Quarters with suitable actions for each. Fill the Cup to the brim with liquid, then realise that the jug or reservoir is empty by that amount, so that in reality the situation remains unchanged, only the identity of the Cup being altered. Drink the liquid and realise it has only altered its location from one sort of Cup to another, and in fact it can never be out of a Cup of some kind, whether such is made from metal, flesh, or anything else.

Discover various unusual contents for a Cup. Fill it with Light from the rays of Sun or Moon or artificial source. Try and "drink" the Light from the Cup. If a Cup can be full of Light, why not with thought-energy? God-energy? Fill the Cup with water, and then water potted plants with it as a ritual act full of meaning. The plants depend on their human friends for their life-giving water, and will otherwise die. In supplying them with their vital needs, we are performing a Divine act, and deputising for the Lord of Nature, the Great Mother, or whatever we call Divinity.

Take an air-filled Cup, and pour in water to the brim. Realise that the displaced air pours out back into the atmosphere to make room for the water. Providing this exercise is done over a sink, bowl (both are Cups) or somewhere suitable, pour sand into the water-filled Cup until it has displaced the water. Now we have seen a change of content from gas to liquid and then to solid. We could restore the status quo ante by washing out the sand and blowing out the water. It all depends on which element is active and which passive. The Cup is both a holder for the passive and an arena for the active elements either successively or simultaneously.

From all this, it would seem that the best way to describe the contents of a Cup would be as its "charge", and this is the usual magical term. The Magical Cup is said to be in a state of "Charge" with whatever is willed into it. That is to say the Cup-Symbol in the consciousness of the operator holds some specific and definite concept in its depths. Whatever we want to make contact with through the Cup, we place in it or invite into it on Inner levels. Let us try this ritually, remembering that our own skulls are Cups, and the thoughts impressed on our brains are held therein.

Drinking. The ancient custom of "toasting" anyone or anything is of much more magical significance than might be supposed. Genuinely magical exercises have a strange habit of persisting through the centuries, though probably as a formality lacking its proper soul. We must all have seen the ill-remembered practice of "drinking" someone. A raised glass (or Cup), a rapid inclination toward the person being "toasted", the saying of their name, or some good wish made, and then the Cup partaken of. Crude as this may be, the basics of very sound magic are all there. We will try and rearrange them properly.

Charge the Cup with some suitable drink. Think of some loved person with whom contact is sought, and if they themselves are not available or willing to take part in the exercise, obtain their photograph or some convenient likeness. Arrange this so that its image is reflected by the fluid in the Cup when it is held correctly before the eyes. Concentrate on the reflected image, and see it as its actuality or the person themselves in the Cup. Utter their name vibrantly across the surface of the fluid so that it ripples to the sound. The contents of the Cup have now received the charge of the name and likeness of someone. Magically, they are "in the Cup". It only remains to transfer them to our own Cups by the simple process of drinking them. This we do carefully, while making some good wish or kindly thought about who or whatever we are taking in. From thenceforth, the Cup-entity will become integrally part of ourselves in the spirit with which they were consumed. We may do this with anyone we love, whether human or Divine.

A Cup can contain any amount of beings. We may try the fore-going exercise with a photograph of a whole family group. Prefer-ably do not use photographs or physical reflections at all, but visualise the beings "live" in the Cup-content. Make them move, smile, respond, and even speak. Take a drink-charged Cup and hold it up with both hands (which are themselves a Cup), arms against the body, the liquid level adjusted so that suitable light-reflections are perceived rippling on the surface. Think of some loved person making a familiar gesture or expression, and "call them to life" in the Cup so that they are no static image, but a mobile presentation of themselves, very welcome to us indeed. See them held in the Cup, smiling, laughing, dancing, or in some way *living*, and being themselves. Look at them, *love* them, and drink them. Realise they exist thenceforth in the Inner Cup as part of the Inner Cosmos. Using the Magic Cup, we have transferred them from one Cosmos to another—our own.

By means of the Cup, we can put anything "into" our Magical Cosmos we want, just as by the Shield we can exclude anything. So far as the Innerworld is concerned, the Cup means IN and the Shield means OUT. The Inner Cosmos must have internalities and externalities like any other Cosmos. So with the Cup, we take into ourselves all that we truly love and hold dearest to us, which we want nearest to our essential being. All else we arrange as externalities around the demarcation circle of "Me and We" by means of the Shield. This makes the Cup the most "sacred" of the Instruments, since we should only use it for taking in and pouring forth the very best and finest energies we are capable of containing.

When the Cup is said to be an IN Symbol, this does not mean it has no OUT, or cannot be used for externalising. It means that the Cup provides a method of communication with our Inmost Inner being, from which of course we can pour out energies as well as receiving them. This is ritually carried out by means of:

Libation, or lustration, by which the dedicated Cup-contents are offered to human or Divine Entities by outpouring from the Offering-Cup in a suitably symbolic manner. For instance, an offering (or Link) through Air would be flung to the winds, through Water would be poured into a pool, stream or sea, Fire into flames, and Earth simply poured on the ground. At the same time some formula is pronounced to direct the purpose of the act. Libation is generally a good-will offering, and lustration more specifically intended as a purificatory rite. Sometimes the fluid was simply poured from one Cup to another, the act itself being the essence of the rite.

To libate, we must charge a Cup with our own energies and out-pour them in whatever Name we have chosen to be their recipient. If this is a God-Concept, we decide which Concept we need to contact; then what sort of energies we are offering, and to what extent; then how we propose to offer them. Should our offer be unconditional, the formula will be: "DO WHAT THOU WILT".

In which case we project our own image into the Cup and then outpour it appropriately.

The simplest libation, of course, is the rapid spilling of a little ale on the ground, and a brief wish for "good luck", still occasionally done by country folk. If it is to be properly done however, we must follow the principles of charging the Cup with whatever we have to give out, and then pouring it toward this dedicated purpose. Suppose we wished to make a libation toward some loved person no longer incarnate. We might have their photograph (or better, our own memory living picture of them), before which is placed a Cup in the shape of a vase. We charge a Cup of our own with water and loving thoughts as we hold it close to our hearts, gazing into its depths and evoking fond thoughts of its intended recipient. When this seems satisfactory, we pour the charged Water carefully into the vase while we say or think some sincere message, or merely: "From me to thee." To continue the rite artistically, we may repeat its principles while bearing some flowers on a small tray (Earth and Shield), which we then put in the water. The energies we have consciously directed in this fashion will certainly seek their intended mark. A great deal can be done magically with libations.

To lustrate, means that we are using Water for purification. The most natural way of doing this is by having a bath, or swimming. How many people try and get rid of their mental and spiritual dirt while they bathe or shower? Not to do this seems like a lost opportunity. To be physically clean while remaining mentally and spiritually filthy is a doubtful purity. Most of us are sadly encumbered with Inner dirt which only the Inner equivalent of Water can remove. Dirt, after all, is only misplaced matter capable of being re-used elsewhere. Even the worst filth can be reduced to the best fertiliser as our sewage farms show. In getting rid of our spiritual contamination, we are only sending it along its catalytic cycle for ultimate regeneration. It is stagnation or unsterile stasis that causes dirty corruption, so we must use mobile or running water to remove it.

This means that while lustrating in a bath, or by any other ritual method, we must make mental and spiritual cleansing movements as well as physical ones. Even though we may be sitting still enough in a bath physically, our minds and souls must be vigorously engaged in "willing away" our accumulations of Inner dirt. We do this by consciously loosening our attachment to the dirt, saying in effect; "I don't want this any more. It spoils me and endangers my health on all levels. I want to be free from it, and besides it is needed as fertiliser elsewhere. Waters of purification, take all this unnecessary Inner dirt away from me and put it where it ought to go. I shall not withhold it from its proper placement any more." If we can manage to "let go" of our Inner dirt, the Water will do the rest, but if we tenaciously insist on retaining it, then nothing but Fire will burn it away.

That was the real meaning behind the belief that the souls of the unbaptised were lost, or that sinners went to Hell-fire. For those refusing to get rid of their impurities the easy way of Water, there was no alternative except the Fire way. It had nothing to do with any non-existent Divine vengeance, but simply that what cannot or will not respond to Water, has only Fire left as a way of making spiritual progress. We shall be well advised to work the way of Water before we are finally forced through the way of Fire. In that way the Water will first purify us to the point where we may pass through Fire unscathed.

In ancient times, those about to act on behalf of many others shared any possible guilt the act might incur by washing their hands in water poured over them into a basin (Cup), which water was then sprinkled over the assembled people. The idea was that everyone involved accepted their minor share of responsibility, instead of the whole karmic burden landing on a single person. We see a relic of this today in the Asperges of the Mass, where the people thereby accept their share of the priestly responsibility for the Sacrifice about to be made.

The most practical lustration these days is to put the hands under a running tap while working Inwardly to rid ourselves of whatever undesirable influence we expect the Water to free us from. Even if it cannot do this completely, it will always help. We should never neglect to wash mentally and spiritually at the same time we use Water for physical cleansing. For ceremonial purposes we may only dip a finger in holy water and make a sacred sign with it, but the conditions of moving Water and a purificatory intention have been fulfilled.

The Cup can also be used as an aid to Contemplation. For this purpose, we charge it with some suitable fluid coloured according to the nature of our working, and sit in meditational posture holding the Cup close to our bodies, yet reflecting a beam of light on the surface of its content, at which we gaze steadily either in silence or sonically. The light-image will dance about as the fluid ripples slightly from our body tremors, and this acts as a mild hypnotic and tranquilizer. We should not forget that milk makes a good reflecting surface, and coloured lights are easily arranged. When the Moon supplies the light for this practice, it is known as "Singing down the Moon", and was a very old custom. Sometimes the Moon was also reflected from a mirror held by another person, and this image directed toward its twin, dancing on the cupped fluid. The degree of concentration and absorption necessary for this operation helped to work the magic.

Inspired by Gabriel, and with the aid of the Cup, we must therefore work out exercises for changing, discharging, libating and lustrating with the Element of Water in all its fluid forms. There are many other possibilities and potentials. Now we must deal with the last Magical Element—Earth.

EARTH. We usually take Earth to signify our state of "real stable solidity", which is an understandable mistake, for it is no more stable or solid than its associated elements. Magically however, it may be classed as a "heavy" Element, because it formates at a lower Time-Space constant than the others, and we have accustomed ourselves to living more on its rate than theirs.

Earth has many forces that make our lives on this planet tenable. Gravity is the most noticeable, and we need its magical equivalent very much indeed. Magnetism is an Earth-force without which no magic could be worked, for it is a different aspect of Light, and "illuminates" other dimensions of existence in which we are not normally conscious. When a planet "solidifies" from its original state of incandescent gas, its "Light" turns into "magnetism", and its "radiance" into "gravity". In "Inner Dimensions" however, this is not exactly synchronous, and so our apparently "solid" Earth is very much of a "surface" or "shell" on which we live in unawareness of what lies almost immediately behind it, which is just as well for our peace of mind.

Magical Earth is really the "skin and bones" of matter. Without bones we could not stand upright, and without skin we could not maintain ourselves physically "in one piece". Our personal identities as human individuals depend on our keeping a whole skin. Otherwise we should flow fluidly into each other and end up as a very odd mess. If, on the other hand, we were entirely "Earthy creatures", then we should simply be stones incapable of auto-mobility. Every thing depends on proportional balance of one Element with another so that they form a perfect Circled Cross relative to our Divine Central Spark. As the Cup "holds" Water, so does the Shield "hold" Earth, by acting as a surface, which is what Earth amounts to, and why the Shield is its Symbol. There has to be an Outside and an Inside to everything, and the Shield is the Outside as the Cup is the Inside of any Mystery.

Earth makes presentation possible between individual units of existence by allowing them to differ from each other dimensionally. This is necessary Magically as well as materially. To try working Magic without Earth is to make it utterly impractical. We must keep Earth-contacts while we are dealing with Inner as well as Outer forces and energies. They have Earth-equivalents in their own states which must be taken into account. There is a mistaken impression among many occult students that we should eliminate Earth in order to become truly "spiritual". Those who attempt this do so at their own peril. There are much higher types of Earth than the crumbly surface of our planet, but they are still "Earth" whether we recognise them as such or not. Truly spiritual Earth may be of greater value to us than physical, but both are entirely essential to our existence in either state of being.

Anyone holding notions that Earth might be a "lesser" or in any way an undesirable Element, will be well advised to eliminate such ideas as soon as possible. Earth is to Fire what Water is to Air—a counterpoise, and a control. Take Fire out of Earth and Water out of Air, and no life could inhabit this planet. With no Earth to retain Fire (heat) and no Water to vaporise into Air, life would still be impossible here. Hence Earth is placed at North of the Magic Circle opposite Fire to which it is Magically "married". By itself Earth is cold and sterile, only acting as a kind of reservoir (like the Cup) for the forces of fertility which condense into it.

We cannot keep Fire, Air, or Water apart from themselves without the means of Earth. Imagine a condition of Water by itself in its pure state. It would be a single mass, unable to form into anything. It is Earth which provides the material controls on Water and the other Elements, by affording ocean beds, channels, syphons, and other means of natural or artificial limitations. Earth has the property of conformability and resistance, offering the necessary inertia to other energies for their inter-relational manifestation. It is a bad mistake to think of inertia as a state of "deadness' or powerlessness. To the contrary, inertia is very much a power which keeps everything in proportion with everything else. It holds the planets in orbit round the Sun, keeps our feet to the ground on this earth, and must do the equivalent in the Magical Cosmos of our own creation. Such is the Magical value of Earth.

To realise this, it is only necessary to pick anything up, look at it, then put it down again with the question;—"Why should this thing stay where I put it? What power keeps it together by itself as it is?" We take a miracle for granted every time we move anything. On Inner levels, as we construct our Cosmoi, it is essential to master the Earth-Principle if we expect any of our consciousness to remain in a state of constancy with itself in an ordered variety of ways. It is Earth which allows us to make any number of different things, and yet relate them to one another proportionally to a common centre, so that they stay together as an expression of wholeness. We can make what we will out of and upon Earth. It is our Magical plastic, and our aim should be to utilise it Inwardly to construct whatever we need.

The Archangel of Earth is Auriel—the Light of God. He is said to preside over the luminaries, and he personifies the "other side" of Michael the Fire Archangel. Hence Auriel faces Michael across the Magic Circle. He was said to be the Lord of Awe, inspiring a sense of deepest respect for the wonders of Creation, and he could "put the fear of God" into human hearts. Those who have experienced natural cataclysms and disasters such as avalanches, earthquakes, floods, or the like, will know just how terrifying Auriel can be. On the other hand, Earth may be peaceful and wonderful. We have lost a great deal of contact with its natural power and beauty since we have been living so exclusively among the artifacts we have made from it. There is a lot to re-learn about absorbing energies from Earth at source, rather than from the mechanisms by which we adapt these at present. Perhaps Auriel has the means of teaching us.

Auriel is traditionally shown holding a Book of Wisdom. He is to be regarded as "Light" in the sense of Knowledge and Experience —our main reasons for being humans on this Earth. In the end it is Earth that provides us with all the bits and pieces whereby our knowledge has been put into practice to make this planet habitable. All physical things are made from Earth of one kind or another, and every World has its own particular sort of Earth which can be adapted in equivalent ways once we learn the secrets of handling it. This is why we must seek the acquaintance of Auriel, the Earth-Intelligence. Auriel it is, who links our consciousness with Earth so that we may penetrate its secrets and enter its amazing treasure-house. The Keys are in Auriel's hands.

From the "Book of Enoch", we read that Auriel controls the forces of the Earth's behaviour in its Cosmos. In those days of course, it was believed the Earth stood still, and all the heavenly phenomena took place around it. Nevertheless Auriel gave Enoch some sound advice when he said; "Look on the Book which Heaven has gradually distilled and reading what is written in it, understand every word of it." The comparison of Knowledge with a distilled essence is rather interesting, since it shows a practical technique for learning. From a whole mass of information (Mass = Earth) we must extract its spirit by a process analogous to distillation. Immediately we are reminded of Alchemy, the Emerald Table of Hermes in which: "it ascendeth from Earth to Heaven" etc, and the significance of the Ros-Cross, or *Dew*-Cross, where the Key was not the Rose in the centre of the Cross, but the apparently insignificant drops of *dew* (Ros) or quintessence of Wisdom lying on its petals. That was the real significance of the Symbol. By using the Four Elements (Cross) properly (proportionately), we arrive at the essence of them all expressed as Golden Dew. The dew was golden because it reflected the Light of the True Sun, and this is the Light personified by Auriel, when he reflects true Knowledge.

This idea of condensing all Wisdom to a single Golden Drop is an ancient Magical one, known as the Operation of the Elements. It was told of the Magic Cauldron, in which Fire was applied to Water through Earth (the Cauldron) and the resultant Air (steam) eventually condensed to the sacred Drop. This took a year and a day, or a complete Cosmic cycle, during which every possible natural influence should have been experienced, synthesised, and summed up into a single potency.

According to Occult Cosmogony, the whole of Creation arose from a Single Word "uttered" above the "Face of the Water", out of which developed every type and instance of subsequent consciousness. This was the Divine Way—OUT. Our task is to collect and re-form or distil all this variety of awareness and energies into single drops until we have arrived at the Ultimate. This is the Human Way—IN. If we ever become able to "utter" such a Word ourselves, we too shall be "as Gods", and the whole process will continue anew. Epitomisation to an Ultimate degree is a Divine Science. The Earth-Symbol is a Seed, holding in itself all the life preceding it, and all the life that will come forth from it. Auriel will teach us how to produce these Seeds of Consciousnes from whence we can populate our Inner Cosmoi.

There is often confusions in the minds of occult students concerning the Instrument of Earth, the Shield, sometimes called the Pentacle or more correctly Pantacle. Few agree on what it is, and fewer still on what it does, yet in reality it is a simple affair. Essentially it is a Surface. Precisely that. It can be any type or shape of surface, but for convenience and artistry is frequently circular, bearing whatever Symbolic patterns are needed for specific Magical operations. It may be made in any size from any material, and it represents the Earth. An altar-top is such an Instrument. So is a tea-tray, a cricket-pitch, a desk-top, or the lid of anything. Once more we must get out our little books and start writing about Shields. They may be called Pantacles if preferred, which means "All-keys" rather than "Pentacles", meaning "Five-keys". Earth certainly provides keys to problems arising on it.

All tools for controlling or moving Earth about are Surfaces. Spades, hoes, bulldozers, or machine-presses, one surface is applied to another in order to obtain some calculated change in Earth or one of its products. Even a bomb presents a surface of pressure, moving Earth in a destructive manner. The principle still applies. Furthermore, surfaces can be moving to some purpose. What nicer example of a Magical Shield than a potter's wheel, whereon Earth is shaped at will into useful or lovely artifacts? Another example might be a mason's trowel, with which Earth in the form of mortar or cement is applied to other surfaces, bonding them together for some united purpose. A wheel is a Shield as a mobile Earth-contact, enabling Earth (vehicle and passengers) to move in relation to itself. The platform of the vehicle itself is another Shield. In fact we are surrounded by Shields everywhere. Our own skins are such.

Walls are Shields, and so are mirrors. Coins are good examples, and garments can be so classified. By and large the material presentation of anything on Earth can be considered a Shield, even though its design and purpose may be of a Sword, Rod, or Cup nature. The aggregation of Mass into Matter is the Shield-Principle, and also the Field-Principle. Our Magic Shield is the "field" of any force, or is the field cultivated to supply us with food. It is a Field of Action or a static condition. Magically it represents the field of whatever operation is taking place.

For Magical purposes, a practical Shield may consist of a circular piece of material, some two feet or so in diameter, matt black on one side and shiny white on the other. This can serve as an altar-top or a scrying-mirror. It can be used as a background against which to set some object for meditation. Much may be learned by meditating on the same thing against a white and then a black background.

The beauty of a Magical Shield is its versatility. We can make it in any colour to suit any operation, or any shape for the same purpose. A red pentagonal Shield for instance suggests Mars-Geburah at once. There is scarcely any need to inscribe anything on it at all, if it is to be used for one single intention. Usually however, matters are not quite so straightforward as that, and the Shield will necessarily bear some symbolic design concerning both the operation and those engaged in it. The guiding rule is that the Glyph or other embellishments on the Shield should express as perfectly as possible everything to do with the energies and individuals, human or otherwise, which must be related together for the purpose of the Rite in question. The Shield is like the blackboard of a classroom, the circuit-diagram of an electrician, the chart of a navigator, drawing board of a draughtsman, or any other means of calling pure consciousness into humanly understandable terms of reference.

Our Shield thus becomes our means of communicating with the Innerworld, by placing some pattern on it which is understandable to both human and higher types of intelligence. We arrange its Surface according to the nature of our needs or wills, and it becomes a medium for translating thoughts into things or the reverse. Since it has to be readable on both sides of the Veil, we shall have to use some common Symbology. Mathematical values would be a sound method for those able to interpret or appreciate them. Hence the old idea of "Magic Squares" on Lamens. Otherwise pictorial or visual Symbology is a dependable method of working. We might, for instance, arrange the Sword, Rod, and Cup on the Shield to suggest our general intentions. We might weave patterns with a Cord upon the Shield. Black cord on the white side, or white on the black. There are endless ways and means of drawing up our Symbolic Schema. We can even draw it on paper with coloured pencils.

Before any Magical Operation therefore, its Shield must be prepared. We can either have a standard set of Shields for various operations, or arrange it especially for some particular purpose. It may be a wonderful piece of artwork, a simple tracing on paper, or scratched in the earth with the point of a dagger or rod. What really matters is its Innerworld construction and our ability to work with this. We may hang the Shield on the wall, lay it on the floor, suspend it overhead, put it on the altar, or do anything at all with it that seems appropriate to the circumstances, but in all cases it must present as complete a Seed-Symbol of the Operation as possible on its field. The neater and more effective this can be made the better. There is little to be gained by elaborating pictographs into intricate drawings or montages. Short and clear is best. Not a meaningless or unnecessary line should mar the Shield. It must be concise, incisive, and completely to the point.

The Shield in itself is like the cleared and receptive Field, waiting to be planted with productive seeds, or the prepared mind in a state of readiness for ideas and conformations of consciousness. The virgin soil in fact, and therefore a perfect Symbol of Earth. We shall build no Magical or material Cosmos without it. Therefore we had better start learning how to use it. The principles are simple enough, being those involved in constructive imagination and planned patterning.

We write Symbols on a Shield in the same way we write words on paper, the mind and consciousness working fractionally ahead of the hand, and putting the words down on the image of the sheet held in the mind, just before they are actually written or typed on the physical paper. The difference is that our Magical Symbols are written on the Inner Shield by themselves, and must appear on the Outer one by the means of imaginative projection. If we like to condense them to more material levels by drawing them on the physical Outer Shield, or placing solid symbology on it, well and good. Our first Shield exercises therefore, will be like those of a small child scribbling its ideas on convenient surfaces. Those help the child build its Cosmos, and ours will help us build a Magical one.

What sort of things should we draw or imagine? At first, whatever comes into the mind, and later we establish control over these until they respond to our Will. The most Magical Symbols of all are those which link directly with the deepest part of ourselves, and therefore bring the God-in-us into contact with our usual selves as humans on Earth. These are the Symbols we must seek in our first Shield exercise of:

Forming. Using a reasonably sized Shield of circular shape some two feet or so across, we set it up in subdued light (candle light or lamp light for preference), at convenient eye level when we are comfortably seated some four or five feet away. Some experiment may be necessary to find really ideal individual setting, since eyesight and temperament are such human variables. At first, the black side of the Shield will most likely be easiest to use. Incense or background music is sometimes helpful if it does not distract the mind from its main purpose. Once we are settled down in such conditions, we can make an enjoyable start.

First we need writing materials. These we obtain by imagining the Cup to be our "inkwell", and the Sword or Rod our "pen" or "brush", depending on the type of work we want to do. We could use both perfectly well, but to start with let us think of the Rod as being a beautifully soft brush, capable of applying our medium to the Shield. The "medium" in this case is to be "Liquid Light". We imagine the Cup to contain pure Light in a liquid state, and all we have to do is dip the brush end of the Rod in, and apply it to the Shield, when it will trace Symbols or patterns in glowing Light. We could actually use a physical Rod and Cup to begin with, but it is better to use their Magical counterparts on Inner levels, and just make the necessary movements with a pointing finger or hand gestures. Later on these will prove unnecessary.

We begin by dipping our Rod in the Cup and simply making a few squiggles in the direction of the Shield, trying to watch such patterns actually forming up over the Shield's physical counterpart. A plain Circle-Cross makes a good start. When we can trace this with the end of our Magical Rod-brush and visualise it shining away against its background, we are off to a good start. No use going any further until this is mastered. It is the base of the whole art, and may even take weeks to do. How often should we dip our brush? As often as the tracing gets faint, or we cannot see what we are writing. At first we shall be constantly dipping, but presently longer and longer amounts can be done without recourse to the Cup unless we want to change colour or Instrument.

Once we can see the Circle-Cross with any sort of clarity, we should proceed to writing letters of the Alphabet and basic Symbols, numerals, or anything else we fancy. The early goal to aim for is persistence. If we can trace a Magical Symbol on the Shield, and then some little time afterwards look back and still see it clearly, we have made good progress. From that point on, everything is only a matter of development and progress.

The next stage is to try using the white side of the Shield and do our Magical designs in black, still using the Cup and Rod as inkwell and brush or pen. From there, we visualise various colours, first of all simply colouring the whole Shield, and then making coloured patterns to suit our needs. These Magical colours should always be seen as "alive", glowing with their own illumination, and never as dead flat applications of paint. They must be felt as *living* in their strange Magical way, full of their own power and energy. The Cup of course supplied them. There is no real reason at this stage why we should not visualise the Rod as a beam of light from a projector (the Cup) and project full-scale moving pictures in colour on to the Shield. It is a degree of ability which may be worked for.

Once some degree of proficiency has been attained with pictorial formations on the Shield, we might try a hand on solid work. This is done by visualising the Shield as a potter's wheel with convenient lumps of wet clay, or any such device, and moulding the medium into whatever we like. Or we can imagine the Shield as any kind of a productive machine, and the Sword as a machine-tool. There are endless possibilities, all having the fundamental principle of the Shield being the holder and supplier of the Magical Earth-Element which is moulded by our wills into what we want.

One great beauty of the Shield is that it may be used anywhere at any time. If the worst comes to the worst, we can close our eyes and the back of our eyelids may be used as a Shield. We can think of it as a Universal background against which Magic of all sorts and descriptions may be made. There is one good warning against its use however, which is that it should never be indulged in while driving a vehicle or engaged in anything of a like nature. This should be obvious. The difference between Shield-using and "day dreaming" is that the former is a skilled exercise under full control of Will, and the latter a somewhat indolent amusement for no better purpose than drifting through existence on the easiest currents. Magic does not meander. It means what it moves.

The main purpose of the Magical Shield therefore, is for materialising consciousness from abstract to concrete types of energy so that we may deal with them objectively. With the Shield we can invoke or "call up" the telesmatic images of the Archangels or other Intelligences, and eventually even make intelligible communication with them. The Shield will become the "message pad", or recording tape by which we make contact with such Beings. It will also work in reverse so to speak, and dematerialise unwanted matter on Inner levels, or shield us from unhelpful energies likely to damage our Cosmos. To do this, we must proceed something along these lines.

Defending and Banishing. If we simply want to defend ourselves from disturbing or unbalancing influences or persons, we emblazon our Shield with a deterrent Symbol and interpose it between ourselves and the image of that person or power in our own minds. Should this not work at first, we must use it on deeper and deeper levels until it becomes effective. If it seems that no results are obtained superficially, then we must check very deeply down in ourselves and find out whether we genuinely want to be free from whatever it is. The chances are that we shall find some desire-attachment still forming a link whereby access is gained to our closest Innerworld. Only the Sword can sever that.

Against irritations and distractions on ordinary levels, the Shield is invaluable. With sufficient practice it is most effective, once developed to a reliable degree. We will suppose that some particular stimulus such as a person's voice annoys us, and we are seeking protection from it, yet cannot very well avoid its presence. First we must discover just what constitutes the annoyance, the sonics of the voice, what is said, or because it belongs to a person we dislike. Then we must find just what in ourselves reacts to such a stimulus. Does it offend our sense of harmony, jar the ear, arouse hostility for some reason, or precisely why have we something in us which reacts badly to another human vocality. Once we have cause and effect located as nearly as possible, we may apply the Shield.

If, for example, we discover the original stimulus to be a continually whining tone of voice accompanied by unimportant complaints, and our reaction to this as resentful dislike because we consider it unfair that we should be the recipient of this, then we proceed as follows. We make up in our minds a Magical Shield with a suitable Symbol on each side, and interpose it directly between our Inner Selves and the source of stimulus. We might put on the black side "SHUT UP!", and on the white side, "DON'T BE CONCERNED", then firmly fix the Shield imaginatively between ourselves and the other person, black side toward them. This would be crude and basic, but workable. It might be nobler to fix a Symbol typifying Divine Love on the external surface of the Shield, and human tolerance on the other. Whatever Symbology is used, the principles of Shield defence are the same. Identify external cause and internal effect, make a counter-Symbol to each on both sides of the Shield, then interpose Shield between the two.

Generally speaking, the black side of the Shield should bear some negative command or Symbol such as "Cease so and so" and the white side a positive instruction like "Be calm", and the polarities aligned as may be necessary. This need not be invariable however, and must be altered to suit circumstances. It is practical, of course, to have a sort of general purpose Shield with a Symbol of Faith permanently emblazoned on each surface, such as a Circle Cross or Hexagram. In fact an all-purpose Shield is a most useful Magical adjunct, and should be designed as early as possible in individual and Group practice.

Using the Shield in this manner will give us protection from influences affecting us temporarily. We must not forget the principle of Athena's Shield which she lent to Perseus for his Gorgon-slaying. This being a mirror, not only enabled him to see magically what he must do, but also came in useful for leting Medusa of the snaky locks (evil thoughts) paralyse herself by her own reflection from it. A Mirror-Shield is indeed a practical Magical one against envenomed energies of consciousness. By simply reflecting harmful thoughts directly back to their senders, there is seldom any need for further action.

To banish unwanted material from our Inner Cosmos we use the Shield as a centripetal disintegrator. This involves its visualisation as a spinning Disc in an anti-clockwise or laevo-rotary direction. On this Wheel, the Symbol may well be a Swastika made from Rods with Swords for angles at the perimeter. Coming into contact with this device, we think of whatever it is we need to be rid of. Our Shield-Wheel must be seen as whirling it into Nothingness so that it becomes less and less at every revolution until it fades into final insignificance. It may be necessary to persist with this practice for a considerable period before complete dismissal of the unwanted energies takes place. Before working this exercise at all however, it is wise to discover whether or not we may be throwing out valuable material which we should do better to use up otherwise. Complete banishment should only be a last resort when all else fails.

A great deal can be done with the Shield once we turn it into a Wheel and rotate it. Deosil rotation may be thought of as centrifugal, invoking, and calling into our Inner Cosmos whatever we need, while the opposite direction is centripetal, banishing, or throwing out of our Cosmos what we would be rid of. The Spinning Wheel was an old Magical concept, and its basic principles are fundamental to the Art today. We may think of it in terms of dynamos or cyclotrons, but the basics are the same as they always were and will be. The Rota-Cross of the Swastika or Periphery of Power explains how it works.

The Magical Shield thus becomes in Innerworld terms just what the Earth means for our Outerworld. It affords stability, protection, a mass-medium, a currency for exchanges of consciousness, and a focus for all forces into Inner objectivity. It is the Shield-working that makes the Inner World "come real" to the Magician, and lets the Inner Life become as practical as the Outer one. Its limits, however, are those of the users themselves, for it is as much a tool or

Instrument as its physical counterparts, depending on skill and ability for the quality and extent of its productions. In material terms we speak of *manu*facture, signifying "made by hand", and implying the work of competent craftsmen. With the Shield we may coin the word *mento*facture, to signify making with the mind, and calling for Craft on Inner levels. The greater skill we develop, the more and better Inner productions we shall construct. Therefore we must continue devising suitable Shield exercises for all occasions, combining these with the other Instruments. Though it is impossible to cover a complete range of uses in this short work, another important exercise is that of:

Spinning, or the Shield in motion as a Wheel. As already mentioned, this is a vital fundamental practice, since the Matter and Mass of our Cosmos comes out of Motion. All action being cyclic, everything has to start with the Primum Mobile, which we equate Magically with the Creative Word or Tetragram. Once this starts spinning around its Point, Creation commences.

All Motion, which is to say all Matter, has its Rate or Frequency which makes it precisely what it is. Alter that, and the whole structure of the material would change accordingly. Transmutation would become an almost instantaneous phenomenon under the control of the practitioner, and we could destroy our planet much faster than we are doing at present. It is a question of applying the correct frequency with sufficient energy to the specific item in the right manner. Fortunately these factors very rarely coincide to the destructive degree except over Time-periods which allow us opportunities for adjustment. Nevertheless the ancient belief in "Words of Power", or cyclic energies in sonic or other forms was well founded. It was discovered that specific sonics did in fact cause changes in consciousness and therefore affected body, mind and soul to the extent of producing appreciable changes through external circumstances. Small wonder such sonics were considered "Magic".

We should, therefore, study the possibilities of spinning the Shield or Wheel at various rates linked with sonics and colours of varying pitch or frequency. The rhythms will be based on the Tetragram for experimental work, and practical Qabalists will doubtless equate these with the Sephirotic values. Kether for instance would have a rate of one, Chockmah of two, Binah of three, and so on until ten. Non-Qabalists will equate the numeral values with whatever System they follow.

The "Rate" of anything is its fundamental pattern of potential between maximum and minimum energy compatible with its existence. This is to say that if more energy were applied beyond its positive limits, or more energy subtracted from its negative ones, it could no longer exist as itself, but would disintegrate one way or the other. A "cycle" of existence is related to Time insofar as this is the extent of anything from first to last point of its being. Its rhythm or frequency is its reiterative pattern relative to a fixed Time-unit. Once more we meet our Three Rings. Rates link with Space, Cycles with Time, and Rhythms with Events. The Rate of anything determines What it is, its Cycles determine When it is, and it Rhythms determine How it is.

Manifested matter is normally made from combinations of varying Rates, Cycles, and Rhythms. Suppose we have a blue wooden Shield which is a circular disc four feet in diameter. We can alter its Space-rate by making it square, triangular, or any other shape. Its Colour-rate can be changed with paint. Its cycles will alter in physical dimensions according to its speed, and its rhythms according to its fluctuations. We cannot, however, alter its natural Rate, which is that of its own particular wood. If we could, we should be able to turn it into steel, mud, water, or anything at all. To change its Nature-Rate, the wood must first be burned to ashes and these distributed by Water and Earth. Eventually every single atom of the original wood will find its way back into Formation again. Nothing can be lost, only changed.

So we must practise altering our Shields systematically. This we do by visualising and sounding specific Rate-Cycle-Rhythms according to whatever method we may be working. A practising Qabalist for instance, would operate something in this manner.

	SEPHIRAH	COLOUR	RATE	CYCLE	RHYTHM
1	Crown	White	Circular	Single	1
2	Wisdom	Grey	Oval	Double	1-1
3	Understanding	Black	Triangular	Triple	2-1
4	Mercy	Blue	Square	Quadruple	3-1
5	Severity	Red	Pentagonal	Quintuple	3-2
6	Beauty	Yellow	Hexagonal	Sextuple	3-3
7	Victory	Green	Septagonal	Septuple	3-3-1
8	Glory	Orange	Octagonal	Octuple	3-3-2
9	Foundation	Violet	Nonagonal	Nonahedral	3-3-3
10	Kingdom	Russet	Decagonal	Decahedral	3-3-3-1

For ritual and Magical purposes the Rhythms can be given as taps, knocks, knells, or any other convenient sonic methods. Any major Concept can thus be invoked by its own particular Rhythm, or combinations of Rhythmic arrangements may be made. Once we have associated numerical values with Concepts and Rate-Cycle-Rhythms, we shall provide ourselves with first-class Magical material.

Suppose for example, we wanted to make contact with the

Concept of Mercy by means of the System outlined. We should visualise or construct a square blue Shield rotating with a quadruple power-peak cycle to an incidental rhythm of 3-1 beats. Why the single and triple combination? First because the Qabalistic pattern on the Tree is composed of triads and units, and second because a four-pointed solid has the shape of a three-sided pyramid or 3-1. A square is only truly four-pointed in two dimensions. Furthermore, if we trace round the cycle of the Circle-Cross we shall find that from Zero the first three quarters are clear, but the fourth and last quarter ends at the Zero-beginning and is therefore the Quarter-plus. Lastly the triple beat aligns with the three Letters of the Sacred Name I.H.V., the final H being a balancing repetition of the first. A.H.I. and I.A.O. or A.U.M. are other examples of Triplicities.

We can spin our Shield very happily to these rhythmic sonics such as: "EEE (1) AYY (2) OOO (3) — MMMMM (I)" for the quarternal Mercy-Shield, shining beautifully with a blue Inner Light. Repeated often enough, we can invoke Mercy by humming the rhythm or tapping it out with the fingers or feet. It can be danced or mimed, once the fundamental frequency is practised sufficiently. Hence the need for practice and perseverance.

If we get our "background resonances" right by a proper use of the Shield-field, it will go a long way toward setting the correct tone for the whole of a ritual. Moreover these "Field-frequencies" can be used at any given moment for whatever purpose we have on hand. This was the principle on which old "Spells" were worked. Their efficacy did not lie in the actual words alone, but the rhythmics of the chant. These were found from experience and by copying sonics from nature itself. We might do worse than seek in that direction when setting up a "frequency-field" for our modern Magical operations. Any background music or effects may be classed under that heading and symbolised by the Shield, which may be seen as both a record or a reel of tape.

Such then, are the bare bones of a Magical Cosmos. With them we can go ahead and build endless operations of Magic until our Innerworld becomes a fit place for a God to dwell in. They are the Keys to our expanding Inner Consciousness which shape it however we will. Nevertheless they are not automatic in action, and have to be used consistently and persistently in order to get any practical results. Once we become even a little skilled with them, energies will flow between Outer and Inner levels of being, and Magic will start to become a practical proposition for us. Now we must turn our attention towards the different ritual techniques by which we can put these elements of the art into operation.

CONDITIONING CONSCIOUSNESS

The natural query arising at this point is why on earth spend so much time and trouble considering four Symbols arranged in a pattern. What use can it possibly be and to what practical purposes could it be put? Is it all worth while anyway? If we accept a plain answer, it should give us every encouragement in the world to go on with our workings. By setting up the constants of our Inner Cosmos in their most primal relationship to each other, we have gained the firmest possible foothold on the Innerworld. For those who do not feel at home with concepts of Archangels, other "Rulers of the Quarters" may be substituted, but the fundamental principles are structurally sound. Our task is to establish our own existence and life through Inner Dimensions, emerging therein as conscious entities capable of exchanging energies with others in similar or varying states of being. Once this is done by "uttering the Creative Word", or starting our "Inner Wheel of Life" rotating by means of our magical pattern-practice, everything else becomes simply a question of development and extension.

The Concepts we have accepted and built around ourselves become selective channels for conscious energy-exchanges between our various life-levels. They are reliable, effective, and practical, for they will deal with specific energies in calculable ways. Just as we must adapt the "wild" elemental forces of the physical world into patterns of civilisation and culture, so must we "tame" the same energies Inwardly, which is done along analogous lines by building up the equivalents of mental and spiritual "machinery" for channeling and using these "raw" powers. Such are our "magical Symbols" and "Words" put together in "ritual" patterns. They are items of Inner Existence co-related intentionally to produce specific effects.

A workable "Inner Universe", complete with all its trimmings gives every advantage to the soul dwelling therein. Provided it is constructed in such a way as to allow for indefinite expansion and progressive alterations, there are no known limits to its possibilities. We shall become what we make of ourselves inside ourselves, and the better we do the job, the better for all that live with us. That is the importance to us of a Magical Cosmos. It is very much worth while making.

Suppose for instance, we consider a God-Image, the Great Mother for example. If we are able to "invoke" such a Concept successfully by making mental and spiritual contacts with it, all the specific "mother energies" available will come through it and make their impact on us. The extent of such impact will be limited by circumstances of course, but the principles should be clear enough. Make the correct means of dealing with Inner energies, and they will act accordingly. This is the use of God, Angel, or any other type of Concept. Each is an Inner Means of contacting and applying pure Power specifically with purpose. Such is the Magical method, which uses selective channels of working, rather than a generalised appeal to Universal Energy.

This is why so many attempts have been made to link up Magical Symbols with alphabets and natural phenomena, associating these with God-Concepts or Power Principles. To extend our existence into Interior Dimensions, we need to be consciously operative in terms of thinking and feeling that are quite different from, yet still analogous with, those of the mundane world. It is like learning a totally foreign language which does not even work in any formulations we should recognise as "words" by standards of human speech, yet which exchanges energies of consciousness through formulated "word units" activating a type of awareness we do not possess as ordinary mortals except in a very rudimentary way. We use sonics for communication on earth because it has an atmosphere which conducts these resonances. In other states of being, we shall have to use different methods, but the principles still apply of formulating and channelling consciousness between individual and group Intelligences.

A sonic alphabet consists of consonants and vowels. The consonants are distinctive types of energy, but the vowels alone make them pronounceable and allow them to form into words meaning any sense. Without vowels, there could be no continuity of consciousness or development of intelligence through language. Hence the ancients made their most secret Names of God from pure vowels. The Semitics regarded vowels as so sacred they made no proper symbols for them, and used allusions or substitutes instead. The Tetragram I.H.V.H. simply indicated the vowels to be "uttered" in the spaces between the written letters as we might indicate G-D, or - - S-S The God-Names of I.A.O. I.E.U. etc are all based on vowel combinations. Take the "God-Name" out of any alphabet, and it made no sense at all and was unpronounceable. It was and is, "God" alone that makes any sense out of a whole Universe.

The Four Major Concepts are so to speak the vowels of the "Magical Symbol Alphabet" which make it pronounceable and sensible. All other symbols relate to and with each other by means of these "Magical Vowels" or Primal God-Names that bring continuity and construction into the Inner Cosmos. The fifth vowel—U —is really a double O which is symbolised by the circumference of the Circle as a Cord or Serpent, both of which imply a principle of outlining or forming into whatever is willed.

Matching up "Magical Alphabets" is always an arbitrary procedure open to endless differences of opinion, but a fair attribution of vowels to the Quarters would be A, AH, and derivatives, to Earth; E to the Air, with its whistling Sword; I to Fire and its Light-shaft; O to Water and the Cup; while U or OO is the spiral from centre to circumference and the "wave-forms" therein. If we can accept this, it is possible to figure out the "consonants" of Magical Consciousness from other Symbols, and then the whole of life through Inner and Outer Worlds will start speaking intelligently to us and we shall be able to "talk back" in its own tongue, because we shall "live the letters".

This is the true "Magical Language", that we actually live and exist as a series of "words" made up out of the "letters" or fundamental type-units of Life itself. We are all "utterances" of the Divine Breath, and each of us is a "Word" which is our real Name. If we can "speak the language" or make our own "utterances", then we shall indeed "be as gods", living the whole of ourselves in intelligent and intelligible patterns which will constitute our Cosmic consciousness. As we relate ourselves to Outer Life by means of our words in human language, so we must relate ourselves to Inner Life by means of our "Magical Words" of Divine "speech".

The most notable attempt at linking concepts of Deity, mathematics, ideals, and other values together is the Tree of Life pattern (or Mandala) of the Qabalists. By means of it, "Magical Words" are made on all levels. Life-factors (which are the Letters) can be combined with each other in sequences which speak the sense of "Inner Wisdom". The magical value of the original Hebrew attributions was that by putting the consonants of their alphabet together, totally different senses could be obtained by altering the vowels or "God-Name", and completely new meanings made out of existing situations. In theory, to change an Inner Word alters its Outer expression or equivalent to a proportional extent. The converse is also true, and the intentional formation of Outer Words automatically "speaks" their Inner translations. A major aim in ritual magic is the formation and "utterance" of such "words".

The basic principles behind this are simple. If everything in existence is a matter of resonant frequencies, and all that distinguishes This from That are variations of frequency, then Existence is in fact the "Language of God", or the "Music of the Spheres". Modern physics shows the practicability of this on physical levels, but Magic is more concerned with the resonances and frequencies inherent in Concepts, Symbols, and the materials of mind and soul. If these can be discovered and put to use, many marvellous results can be obtained. Even the greatest marvel of all, the evolution of human souls towards their Divine Origin, may be at least attempted if not always achieved.

The workings of energy by Magical methods are likened to speech by words and reckoning by numbers because similar principles are involved. Values and Idea-units must be correctly related together in OMNIL in order to obtain specified effects. To understand this, we must ask ourselves whether, when we see an "A" on blank paper, we make sense from the black ideographic letter, or the white space surrounding it. We may think we read the lettering on a printed page, but it is equally true to say we read the blanks.

The sense of words is derived from separations of silence from sound and emptiness from form. To demonstrate this, we have only to try listening to speech against an overpowering roar of mechanical noise, or read a page of writing obliterated by an ink roller. In both instances the wording would be theoretically still existent in one state of being, but impossible to reach through physical means. There must be variations in energy-levels relatively to their "background" before our consciousness can deal with them. To transcend such laws, we would have to change our being very considerably.

Just as there is a limited number of sonics a human voice can utter, out of which all the words of every national language and the sum of human knowledge has proceeded, so there is a limited number of Ideas and Concepts from which all consciousness operates. These basics are the "Letters" of the real Magical Alphabet. The Tree of Life attempts to outline this by providing ten Absolutes which are linked with numerical values, and twenty-two Characteristics, each of which is the distinction between two Absolutes. It is possible to obtain more than twenty-two Characters by adding more "Paths" to the Tree. The object of all this, is to make a workable means of operating consciousness through Inner dimensions otherwise inaccessible to human participators in Life.

Whether or not we follow the Tree of Life method, its principles must be used in one formulary or another. We must find the Lowest Common Denominators or Alphabet of Consciousness and learn how to combine these units with each other just as we put letters together to make the very words on this page. Once we start expressing ourselves in this way, we shall begin making Cosmic sense.

As to precisely what these Units are, opinions are bound to differ quite considerably, but if we base our attributions on the Sephirotic Numerations of the Qabalistic Tree, they seem fairly satisfactory. The list will read:—

Number	Sephirah	Type of Consciousness	
0	NIL	The Unconscious	(I AM NOT)
1	SUMMIT	Being	(The I AM)
2	WISDOM	Knowing	(This from That)
3	UNDERSTANDING	Feeling	(I and They)
4	COMPASSION	Attraction	(loving, wanting)
5	SEVERITY	Repulsion	(hating, rejecting)
6	BEAUTY	Stabilising	(equanimity, normality)
7	VICTORY	Increasing	(gaining amount of awareness)
8	GLORY	Improving	(quality gain of awareness)
9	FOUNDATION	Constructing	(arrangement of awareness)
10	KINGDOM	Continuity	(memory)

This gives us ten practical divisions of human consciousness from one end to the other over the broadest possible spectrum, and these are bound to co-relate with their Inner equivalents, whether the Intelligent Entity be human or Divine. By selecting any of the numerals, we are now in a position to choose the type of consciousness we will work with.

If we combine the numerals or relate them with each other in any way, we shall obtain results in terms of consciousness, which, being energy, can be directed accordingly. It now remains to make "letters" from junctions of numbers, and "words" from junctions of the letters. In this task there will be probably more varieties of practice than there are different languages on earth. The only rule to adopt, is that those unable or unwilling to use existing systems, must make up their own and speak to themselves with it. Otherwise they are at liberty to remain uncritically silent.

Scholars of Hebrew have a perfectly good system of letter-attribution in the existent Tree of Life Plan, but such is not very helpful to those accustomed to thinking in English. On Inner levels of course, consciousness is not expressed by what we know as "language", but by direct exchanges of energy values having equal validity to all intelligent entities operating on a common level. In this Outerworld however, we need a linkage-system between pure consciousness and the conventional terminologies of our standardised speech and types of thinking. Hence the connection between Concepts, typified consciousness, and ordinary alphabetical letters. Since our particular language is English, the letter-attributions to the Tree-Plan will have to be an English instead of a Hebrew alphabet.

Attempts have been made to do this, but one important factor has been overlooked—the vowels. The Hebrew letters are all consonants, vowels being added by "pointing" the words to make them pronounceable. We may think of the letters as objective externals encountered or arranged by an Intelligence, and the vowels as subjective internals putting the real meaning into words. The letters are inanimate and the vowels animate. It was said: "The letter killeth, but the Spirit giveth life", and that is what it signified. The soul of an otherwise pointless (unpointed) word composed only of consonants. Thus letters form a body, and vowels the soul of any word. Meaning was made out of the Qabalistic Tree attributions by observing the letters and injecting the vowels as moved by the Spirit.

To approximate the Tree-attributes in English, we shall have to extract the vowels, and then attribute the remaining letters to the Path-plan. Since we have already attributed the vowels to the Elements and their Circle, this leaves twenty-one consonants, whereas twenty-two are needed. If we add the "Th" (thomb), this solves the problem very neatly indeed, and restores an old letter very much used in the English tongue. It also allows Tarot and other attributes to be made in accordance with existing Qabalistic technique.

The entire object of this exercise is to devise a practical means of inter-translation between ordinary objective life, and the highest types of consciousness we can contact. Using alphabetical letters as symbols for Inner realities, and linking these with allied magical meanings is a very good method of communication from one level of being to another.

The methods of learning and using this "Magical Alphabet" are similar to those employed in teaching infants their letters. A major difference of course lies in the terms of association. The "baby Alphabet" has all its letters linked with familiar objects in the understanding of a tiny child. "A is for Apple, B is for Bed, C is for Cat", and so on. In some ways this is a pity, because those associations remain underneath all the others for life, and colour consciousness accordingly. The Magical Alphabet being linked with Eternal Verities, causes consciousness to formate on those Inner terms, and thus becomes a means of opening up contacts with Intelligences whose lives and existences are on far higher and different levels than

The Alphabet Rhyme

A   is good Earth as a Heavenly sod,
B   is the Being and Wisdom of God.
C   is the One, Understanding all things,
D   is the Crown and the Beauty it brings.
E   is the Element thought of as Air,
F   is Wise Understanding—uncommonly rare.
G   is Wisdom and Mercy, most blessed are they,
H   is Wisdom and Beauty—a perfect display.
I   is the Energy burning as Fire,
J   Understands Justice, yet never knows Ire.
K   Understands Beauty that shines like the Sun,
L   brings Mercy and Justice together as one.
M   is Mercy and Beauty—surpassingly fine,
N   is Mercy and Victory—truly Divine.
O   is the Watery Element pure,
P   is strict Justice with Beauty secure.
Q   is a mixture of Glory and Fear,
R   is Victorious Beauty made clear.
S   is the sign of both Beauty and Glory,
T   tells a well-Founded and Beautiful story.
U   Undulates round Elemental Accord,
V   is Glorious Victory—not of the sword.
W   blazons where Triumph is Founded,
X   marks where Victorious Kingdoms are grounded.
Y   is Foundation and Glory made fast,
Z   shows a most Glorious Kingdom at last.
Th   makes Foundation and Kingdom both meet,
     and this Magical Alphabet now is complete.

those we know in the ordinary physical world. Without the co-operation of such Beings, we cannot work effective Magic.

Our first task along these lines therefore, is to make our Magical Alphabet come to life, and then make meanings from it. A simple Alphabet-rhyme is given which may be helpful for rote-learning at the beginning. After that we must learn to spell "words", and indeed that is what is meant by Magic "Spells"—words spelled out of Inner Letters which changed basic conscious attitudes and the energies comprising them. Refinements like the grammar, syntax, and styling of the Inner Language come with experience and development. It will be difficult enough at first to manage even "baby talk" with it. Probably the simplest and most useful commencement is with the vowels.

For this purpose, we must devise an associative ritual. It is always best to keep the basics of ritual as brief and concise as may be consistent with the purpose in mind, so we "put the vowels on the Wheel". Centralising ourselves with a rapid fix of the Pivots above and below us, we spin slowly around intoning the vowels as we pass their Quarters. The sound should be kept up all the time, and simply altered from one vowel sonic to another as we go round. It will sound something like this;

E. EEEEEEEEEEEEEEEEEE   (toning to EI)
S. IIIIIIIIIIIIIIIIII   (toning to IO)
W. OOOOOOOOOOOOOOOOOO   (toning to OA)
N. AAAAAAAAAAAAAAAAAA   (toning to AE)

The U is brought in by continuing to turn while ululating an Oo Oo Oo Oo Oo Oo Oo almost like a two-tone siren. Lastly movement is ceased, and a central HUM set up. During the exercise, the Archangels and other Attributes of the Quarters should be meditated on and invoked as powerfully as possible. A very few of these exercises should be sufficient to associate the vowels with the major Power-Concepts.

Pictorially, we may visualise the E as a Delphic one, its long central arm being the Sword, and the supporting sides a scabbard. Male and Female uniting. The of course is the Rod and Spear, the O becomes the rim and base of the Cup, while the A can either be a pair of legs in the act of walking, or a primitive plough furrowing the earth. Any such means of association will be helpful. The entire purpose and principle of the rite, as with most rites, is for associating specific ideas with energies from Inner sources. As the vowels are intoned, we can imagine the sound taking the actual shape of the letters, or think of them condensing from light of any suitable colour. Anything that conveys the association of power and energy connected with the specific Elements. A might be a brown or field-green letter, E a light blue one, I a brilliant yellow, and O bluish green or "wine-dark".

As the vowels are the Powers, the other letters are the Paths through and by which the Elemental Powers flow and are controlled. As we arrange them, so will the power-patterns formate. The consonants are like the circuit-wiring of electrical devices, which determine the action of applied electric energy. Although we can alter them around, they make the fixed points that direct the mobile energies of the Elements. Ritualising them calls for a somewhat more complex process than the vowels. Since each consonant is linked with a dual Concept, it might be a useful idea to arrive at a common Symbol expressive of the whole unit. Luckily such a set of Symbols exists as the Trumps Major of the Tarot, though they cannot be attributed according to any system in general publication.

THE ATTRIBUTION OF ENGLISH LETTERS
TO THE TREE OF LIFE

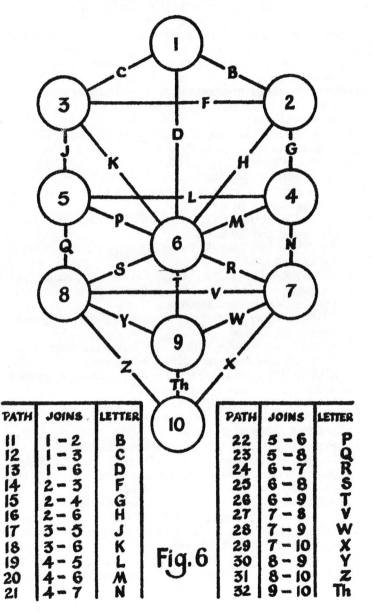

Fig. 6

PATH	JOINS	LETTER
11	1 – 2	B
12	1 – 3	C
13	1 – 6	D
14	2 – 3	F
15	2 – 4	G
16	2 – 6	H
17	3 – 5	J
18	3 – 6	K
19	4 – 5	L
20	4 – 6	M
21	4 – 7	N

PATH	JOINS	LETTER
22	5 – 6	P
23	5 – 8	Q
24	6 – 7	R
25	6 – 8	S
26	6 – 9	T
27	7 – 8	V
28	7 – 9	W
29	7 – 10	X
30	8 – 9	Y
31	8 – 10	Z
32	9 – 10	Th

We shall have to use a rather more arcane procedure, which follows fundamentals rather than misleading figures.

In the first place, we must totally ignore the present numbering of the Trumps, and concentrate entirely on the Idea and Inner Meaning that each card expresses. When this emerges, it must be linked with its letter associated with the closest Concepts of the Tree, so that each card typifies a particular Power-Path. In point of fact, they do this in a rather surprising way, very different from currently known systems. Our first break-down shows that the twenty-two Trumps fall into ten distinct categories of associated ideas. As follows.

1. The SUN, MOON, and STAR. These may be called Cosmic, and refer to the structure of our Universe away from our own Earth and into the depths of Space.
2. JUDGEMENT, JUSTICE, and the WHEEL OF FORTUNE. These may be called Fatal or Karmic on three distinct levels of compensatory energy.
3. HERMIT and HIEROPHANT. Inner and Outer consciousness, Esotericism and Exotericism.
4. DEATH and the DEVIL. Forces of change and disintegration on different levels.
5. TEMPERANCE and the HANGED MAN. Compensatory and stabilising energies which adapt and balance other factors by sacrifice or necessary adjustment.
6. EMPEROR and EMPRESS. Powers of integration and governing by rule and law.
7. TOWER and STRENGTH. Energy in kinetic manifestation, the first katabolically, and the second anabolically.
8. CHARIOT and the LOVERS. The dual Life-motive ennobled as the spirit of Enquiry and Affection.
9. MAGICIAN and PRIESTESS. These are the two types of devotion on the Path of Ascent. Rational and Emotional, Mind and Soul. Hermetic or Orphic.
10. FOOL and WORLD. The People and the Place. The Uninstructed and Innocent in general, coupled with the commonplace and casual. In a higher sense, the Spirit completely freed from atachment to material manifestation.

It will be seen from this, that the cards have become two triplicities and eight pairs. The pattern has begun, and we shall now be in a position to place the cards on the Tree. Its planetary attributions are a considerable help in this task, since they assist in typifying the specific energies of the Spheres. The associated colours are also of value in suggesting the lines of linkage. Looking back at our new associative-pattern, it assumes a sort of progressional chart from the "Man in the street" right up to the highest types of individualised

The Tree and the Tarot Trumps

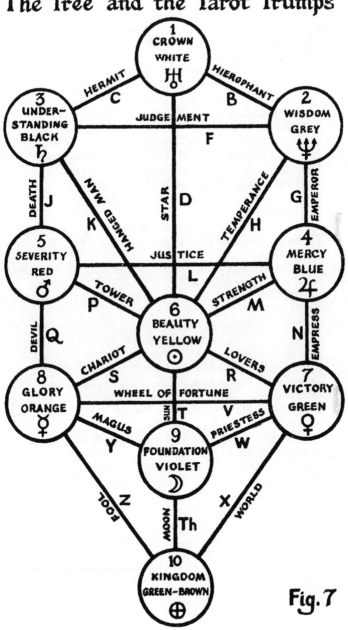

Fig. 7

souls, for we should remember that the HIEROPHANT may be "Pope Joan", an androgynous figure, and the HERMIT is also the "Old Lady". We therefore know roughly at least where to start working from, but let us erect the framework first.

1. MOON, between Earth and Moon, 10-9. SUN between Moon and Sun, 9-6, STAR between Sun and Summit 6-1. This gives us the Middle Pillar of Light on the Tree in the order away from our world toward Heaven. It links this Solar System with all others.

2. JUDGEMENT between Wisdom and Understanding 2-3, Saturn, Neptune. JUSTICE between Mercy and Severity, 4-5, Mars and Jupiter. WHEEL OF FORTUNE between Victory and Glory, 8-7, Venus, Hermes. This gives us the cross-bars of the Tree as three distinct levels of Karmic action.

3. HIEROPHANT between Crown and Wisdom, 1-2, the externalising consciousness.
   HERMIT between Crown and Understanding, the internalising awareness. We can see the soul on its outward and inward journey here.

4. DEATH between Severity and Understanding, Mars-Saturn, 3-5. This crosses the Abyss.
   DEVIL or Tempter, between Severity and Glory, Mars-Hermes, 5-8. This is the Misleader.

5. HANGED MAN. Karmic debts accepted. Between Understanding and Beauty. Saturn-Sun, 3-6. Peace though renunciation and sacrifice. Duty.
   TEMPERANCE. Intelligent dealing with all presented energies. Between Wisdom and Beauty, Neptune-Sun 2-6. Careful control of forces.

6. EMPEROR. Benevolent rule of awareness. Between Wisdom and Mercy, Neptune-Jupiter, 2-4.
   EMPRESS. Benevolent rule of feelings. Between Mercy and Victory, Jupiter-Venue, 4-7.

7. TOWER. Energetic break-down or katalysis. Severity and Beauty, Mars-Sun, 5-6.
   STRENGTH. Energetic build-up, or analysis. Mercy and Beauty, Sun-Jupiter, 4-6.

8. CHARIOT. Travel, the adventure of Life, Exploration, Discovery. Between Beauty and Glory, Sun-Hermes, 6-8.
   LOVERS. Attraction, finding truth in others, Life-urge. Between Beauty and Victory, Sun-Venus, 6-7.

9. MAGICIAN (Or Priest), The Hermetic type of Initiate. Rationalistic approach. Science. Between Glory and Foundation, Hermes-Luna, 8-9.
   PRIESTESS, The Orphic type of Initiate, Emotionalistic

approach. Artistic. Between Victory and Foundation, Venus-Moon, 7-9.

10. FOOL (or Innocent). At bottom the "common man" or Neophyte. At top the Emancipated Ego. This card can interchange places with—
WORLD. Living conditions in general amongst humanity and for any individual concerned. The "norm".
Positions are Glory-Kingdom. Hermes-Earth, 8-10, and Victory-Kingdom, Venus-Earth, 7-10.

Now if we stand back and look at the pattern produced by this arrangement of concepts on the Tree of Life Plan, it will make very considerable sense, and show a progression of consciousness from one end of existence to the other. Each stage is symbolised by a card, and these in turn can be linked to an alphabetical letter so that we can build up "Idea-Words" with them to operate our consciousness through Inner Dimensions. Used in this way, our Tarot Symbols will form the currency with which we shall be enabled to exchange ideas with other intelligent Beings in differing states than our own. This is their real purpose.

We shall not start getting results from these Symbolic associations until we have planted them very deeply into our consciousness, hence the necessity for ritualising or presenting them to ourselves in such a way that they will make a genuine impact on us, and reach the required levels. A practical way to begin this process is

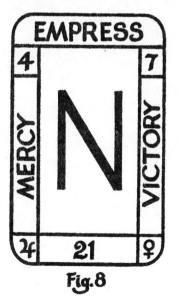

Fig. 8

Fig. 9

to make up a set of special cards of simple design with the appropriate Symbols on them. This is quite easy with thin cardboard cut to playing-card size, some Indian and coloured inks, and some round writing pens. Any suitable design may be used something after the fashion of Fig. 8.

To add emphasis, the side pillars with the Sphere-Concepts written on them may be coloured appropriately. The Vowel cards of course will have the Elements, Instruments, Quarters, and Rulers written around them. They form the aces for the Numeral pack or Minor Arcana.

This so called Minor pack, consists of forty cards, four to each Major Concept of the Tree, or each Concept seen from four angles or "Worlds" corresponding with the Elements. These are respectively:

1	The Originative world	Fire	Rods	Being
2	The Creative world	Water	Cups	Feeling
3	The Formative world	Air	Swords	Thinking
4	The Expressive world	Earth	Shields	Doing

Each card of course is capable of a wealth of interpretation, and in company with its fellows can hold an enormous variation of meaning. For purposes of rapid grasping however, they have been codified with a single concept for each card. So:

Sphere	RODS	CUPS	SWORDS	SHIELDS
1	Fire	Water	Air	Earth
2	Choice	Liberty	Uncertainty	Change
3	Intention	Affection	Suffering	Effort
4	Magnanimity	Hope	Truce	Reward
5	Retribution	Grief	Defeat	Adversity
6	Balance	Happiness	Safety	Benefit
7	Ability	Amusement	Deceit	Attention
8	Expediency	Enthusiasm	Danger	Skill
9	Endurance	Satisfaction	Misfortune	Means
10	Responsibility	Friendship	Disaster	Opportunity

Another set of cards can be made from these concepts, following the same simple scheme as before, but using a central number instead of a letter, something like Fig. 9.

We are now possessed of four Power-Concepts, ten Sphere-Concepts, twenty-two Major, and forty Minor Ideas. Seventy-six distinct pieces of consciousness all related with each other through a representative design or pattern of Existence. A valuable vocabulary indeed, yet now we need the people to utter it, and people come all sorts and shapes. They are represented by the "Court cards", which do not fit into any particular place on the Tree, because they are volitional, and may associate anywhere according to their circumstances. Being classifiable in alignment with the Quarternity, they can be grouped around the Circle. Strictly speaking, they show the human or Divine consciousness at differing stages of its development or evolution, rather than trivialities of personal sex or age groups, colour of complexion and so forth.

The King-state shows a being at the top of its category, evolved, effective, ruling in its own right, and capable of issuing its own orders for its own dominions. This is the ne plus ultra for any classified consciousness, and to "climb higher", it would have to change its fundamental nature altogether.

The Queen-state indicates a highly developed being who is yet bound up with the fates of associated beings by reason of emotional or other ties, and is *in*volved rather than *e*volved. Attachments are maintained with their Group-categories rather than individual advancement sought.

The Knight (or Prince) state refers to the average struggling souls seeking their best paths of development and attempting to advance themselves both individually and collectively. At least they are making efforts, even if they make frequent mistakes.

The Page (or Peasant) is the member of the masses who drifts along with the general currents, sometimes forward sometimes backwards, following whichever particular broad category is theirs basically. Insufficient initiative to be an Initiate, but with a natural potential for rising in whichever direction their natural inclinations allow.

It will be seen that people of any age or sex may come into one of these categories, but for purposes of codification, a word-formula is given for approximating the sort of people these cards would indicate if they were plain humans.

	Fire	Water	Air	Earth	
	RODS	CUPS	SWORDS	SHIELDS	
KING	Incisive	Magnanimous	Severe	Reliable	Fire
QUEEN	Capable	Affectionate	Serious	Practical	Water
KNIGHT	Astute	Idealistic	Aggresive	Ambitious	Air
PAGE	Diligent	Cheerful	Troublesome	Amenable	Earth

The above of course are necessarily generalisations, and would have to be considerably extended to cover more detailed particulars. If anything, they err on the optimistic appraisement of human nature.

The addition of these sixteen sorts of people (or one person in sixteen ways), gives us one hundred and two specific conscious units to play with and combine with each other in order to make Magic and Meaning associate together. We can make cards of the "Courtiers" also, and bring them into the growing family of transcendental thoughts. This will provide us with three distinct packs:

1   The 22 Letters or Principles
2   The 40 Numbers or Practices
3   The 16 Courtiers or People

Nor should we forget the 4 Powers. It remains to work out the Plans and Patterns into which all these items can be arranged.

It is not in the least intended that such home-made cards should supersede the orthodox Tarot Pack, but only act as a study-method and adjunct, in which capacity they will prove invaluable. Their main use is for opening up the lines of communication between objective and subjective consciousness, which give entry to the Inner Magical World. This of course is possible without cards or other accessories, but their advantage is that they provide controls and conditioning which give access to an Innerworld governed by factors coming within the will and ability of the entrant. Without safeguards of any kind, experience of "wild" Innerworld life can be so terrifying and damaging that it will throw a soul completely out of balance for a considerable period, if not inflict worse injury. This is the disadvantage of Innerworld entry via the hallucinogenic drugs. The entrant is helpless. Using trained Magical methods, an adventurer into other dimensions is not only equipped with "survival gear", but is permitted entry into the "right circles" among "civilised people". Anyone can "break into" the Innerworld, where they will receive the treatment due to intruders depending on the circumstances of their break-in. The Magical technician prefers to enter the 'Innerworld as a rightful inhabitant who is welcome to his own place among his own people.

What happens is very roughly this. When anyone sets up a "Magical" behaviour-pattern, its specific "wave-forms" release typified energies through what has been called the "collective consciousness". This naturally is the case with any behaviour-pattern, but its nature determines the response it receives from other intelligent pattern-makers on different levels. The "Pattern-makers" of Magical Systems and behaviours are Cosmogonists of a very definite Order, who readily recognise and respond to energies of their own frequencies. Once a positive pattern of cyclic magical action is set up and maintained, it will most certainly attract reciprocal energies from Inner sources of power and the Intelligences operating them. The effects or outcomes of these energy-exchanges may vary through an entire gamut of possibilities, and the time factors involved are so divergent that it is useless to speculate on hard and fast issues. All we can be certain of is that if our associations are made with discrimination, we shall put ourselves in the best possible position for making good progress. That is why it is so important to build up a sound associative chain, or in Magical parlance, our Links of Light.

Working regular and dependable Magical rites and practices will most definitely put the operators in touch with Inner Intelligences and conditions of life natural to other dimensions than ordinary physical ones. Types of contact vary from one individual to another, but it will always be made in accordance with prevailing personalities and circumstances. There are distinct species of Intelligence, just as there are distinct races and types of human beings. It is advisable to seek contact with those having closest harmony with the spiritual state of the human operatives involved. Each to their own circle is a good Magical maxim.

The consciousness-pattern of the Tree-Tarot-Alphabet, gives access to an ordered and disciplined Innerworld which has been under careful construction for a very long time by highly developed Intelligences. It is neither easy, nor yet impossible to enter. When signals are received from human beings using the consciousness-code already outlined, observers will note and check them from Inner Dimensions. If it seems worth while establishing closer or more intimate contact between the human and the discarnate Intelligences, the "Inners" know perfectly well what to do and how to "lock on" to the human end of the line. It is most unlikely that anything spectacular or "phenomenal" will be noticed by the human entities. The aim of the Inners operating this particular Mystery-System is a natural and sound expansion of awareness as rapidly as may be consistent with true spiritual growth at its best possible degree.

The System we work will therefore determine the type of Inner company we keep. Each System has its own "administration" and adherents which may or may not be compatible with differing Systems which cater for souls undergoing different sorts of development. There is no reason however, why all Systems should not operate perfectly well in their own ways for their own people. They are all serving a common cause in the end, which is the evolution of the soul, and the supremacy of Spirit. The System of consciousness outlined in this chapter happens to be the one generally acknowledged as suitable for the "Western" Traditions of what is loosely termed the "Occult".

To operate this systematic Inner Consciousness and Life, we have the dual method of Meditation and Magic. These are but opposite ends of the same Rod, depending on the direction of force-flow.

With Meditation, the physical body stays relatively still as a fulcrum while the Inner Being is roused into action in its own dimensions. With Magic, the physical body is moved into active patterns while the soul remains relatively still in its own state. In Meditation, we are pushing the power Inwards from the physical, and with Magic we are pushing power Outwards from the spiritual end of Life. The two cycles are complementary to each other and must be used together to obtain a total effect. To put is basically, what we push in one end will come out of the other. Meditation and Magic are the cyclic alternations of the same Circle of Consciousness expressed from one Dimension of Life to another.

Therefore we must now start making patterns of our own with the material provided. These will be our Rituals out of which Inner (and Outer) living will develop, and the "Words" of inter-Dimensional speech. Once the principles are grasped, they can be transferred to the levels of practice by the commonplace method of expending sufficient time and effort for that purpose.

The most practical way to set about this task, is to make up a sort of curriculum which first of all deals with things one at a time, and then begins putting them together with gradually increasing complexity. If we take the Powers, the Principles, the Practices, and the People in that order, dwell on each with both Meditation and Magic, then combine a few of them with each other, we shall be off to a good start. The main objective is to form the closest possible personal relationship with each unit of consciousness so that instead of being merely an observed item of awareness, it becomes an actuality of experience in existence. That is what makes the Magic. It is the old formula of "making a wish come true", or objectifying subjective energies.

Everyone will eventually find their own best methods for accomplishing such an achievement, so the exercises given here are only broad suggestions and outlines to follow. Using our old friends the pen and paper, we set up our subjects into Inner and Outer categories. The demarcation line between the two will be the limit of our personal extensions in any state of being. This is a theoretical variable of course, depending entirely on the individual, though in principle it is a constant. On the Inner side, we must put down the ways and degrees to which we are able to identify ourselves with, or include the study-subject *inside* our own being as it were, and on the Outer side, we must write the various means we have found of relating ourselves *externally* to the same subject in a ritual manner. It is quite amazing how one side of the line will help the other side extend, which is the principle on which Ritual Magic works. A rough-state specimen of this might appear something in this fashion.

The lists can be extended far beyond this point of course, but it

SUBJECT	INNER	OUTER
	(Realisation, Meditation, Subjective, etc)	*(Ritualisation, Magic, Mediation, Objective, etc)*
Water	Ocean of Life feeling. Fluidity. Flow of ideas. Adaptability to formation Tides and currents. Flotation. Suspension, etc.	The Cup and contents. Drinking. Libating. Purifying. Plunging. Pouring. Depth-gazing. Green-blue. Blood and body fluids. etc.

is of the greatest importance that everyone construct their own sets of relationship between Inner and Outer qualities connected with any subject. It is the effort of making such distinctions that really matters to anyone, for this constitutes a Rite by itself. Once we arrive at a point where the inside and outside of a subject are distinguishable from each other, we can start being a little more particular about the specific equivalents themselves. For instance, we might decide that the act of pouring water into the earth from the Cup could signify the nourishment of some seed-idea we had planted in the "ground" of our own minds. To make up a Rite from this connection, it only remains to do the one thing while thinking of or actually being the other. This makes Magic.

It was for the sake of establishing such relationships with Internal and External Life that the Invocations of the Ancient Mysteries were so frequently cast in the first person singular. The invocant positively identified himself with natural and Divine energies, which had the ultimate effect of actually "raising" those energies in himself. Nowadays we might call this "auto-suggestion", but it works under any name. One important task of any practical magician is to write or collect a series of these Invocations phrased suitably to whatever System is used, so that the various categories of consciousness can be conveniently contacted. There are large numbers of these Invocations to be found in various works, but unless they harmonise with each other they will only produce confusion when wrongly mixed. The skilled operator should be capable of producing his own, whether or not he is accustomed to using others for Group working. For instance, a Water Invocation might be made along these lines:

> I am the Waters of the Infinite
> That Ocean of Eternity
> Whence living creatures spring
> To individual life, evolving endlessly

According to the Word within.
I am the Cosmic tides
Of incident and time.
In me, the motionless is motion
And my restless waves
Lap every shore of Space.
My womb is full of worlds
Awaiting bodiment.
To me each life returns
For its rebirth.
I am the totally engulfing flood
Absorbing force,
Obliterating form,
Till all distinction drowns
Within my deathless depths
And mine are one with me
etc etc.

Whatever method of identification with specific energies is adopted, the invocant must feel happy and confident with it because it is his own natural way of uniting with what links his Inner and Outer life. It must be remembered always that WE BECOME WHAT WE IDENTIFY OURSELVES WITH, and if we can successfully identify ourselves with Divine principles having an immortal and eternal nature, then we shall indeed "become as Gods". Such should be the aims of ritual practice.

Continuing with our Water-example, we must think of as many ways as possible to unify with Water in principle and practice. While swimming for instance, we should try and experience the sense of *belonging* with the sea or river, entering its spirit so to speak, and acting as part and parcel of it. There should be an "I the drop, AM the Ocean" feeling. This is impossible to explain in written words, and can only be *lived* in Inner language. It is a sort of floating out of one small human body into the unknown vastness of all the Water in existence, and yet at the same time retaining a sense of identity, or rather of enhancing this to an nth degree. It is a becoming. An exchange of little for much. A growth toward God-hood. The external of the sea keeps us linked to Outer Life, and the internal of the Water-principle joins us with Inner Reality.

It is not necessary to actually plunge into an ocean and swim around to get this linkage. Skill in ritualising should make it possible to obtain a similar feeling if a finger-tip were moistened in holy water blessed for such a purpose. This is the very essence of ritual, that Internals and Externals are joined together like the back and front of a door, and it all depends whether we face Inwards or Outwards as to what happens when we place ourselves between the

Pillars that form the Pylons of the Gateway from one dimension to another. To go inwards, we must grasp the physical end of anything and follow it along like a cord or Rod until it leads us toward its spiritual nature, and to go outwards, we grasp a spiritual principle and feel our way along its line until we reach material manifestation. Nothing is purely physical or spiritual in itself, for whatever exists in any dimension must necessarily have extensions beyond those apparent limits, or it could not be there at all. All Consciousness is a whole Energy, and we only deal with its wave-variations which seem to us separate from each other, though they are really pattern-formations which allow auto-consciousness to remain in being. As Zen followers would say: "IT is aware of ITSELF", or put Qabalistically "I AM THAT I AM".

In ritualising anything, we simply do not stop when its physical limits are reached, but plod steadily past them bringing NOTHING and SOMETHING closer together with every step. It is a matter of application and training which can be done by anyone with the necessary dedication and ability to continue working past points where less devoted individuals lose interest and give up the effort. The only secret is "stickability" and refusal to be discouraged by seeming failures.

Having dealt with the Water Element systematically as far as possible for the time being (extensions are always possible to Infinity), the other Elements must be tackled likewise. Each must be given its own Invocation and associative train for helping the practitioner identify himself with that particular Power-Aspect. Colours, shapes, tones, scents, tastes, and every possible link should be brought together in connection with each Element. Each must be meditated and mediated to a degree that means automatic response in terms of energy. For instance, it should be possible to invoke Earth-energy by simply feeling greenish-brown, or specific Earth-energies by thudding tones or drum-beats. Sonically, Air is invoked by wind instruments, Fire by string, Water by resonant metal, and Earth by heavy percussion or drum. These are only general categories. Any instrument can link with any Element depending on its method of use.

Once the Elements have been successfully ritualised, the Sphere-Principles must be attempted. Again we Internalise and Externalise them. Since this has already been done for us over and over again by various authorities, the task should be reasonably easy. As always, the aim is to identify ourselves with each Principle both inwardly and outwardly. A valuable aid to to start asking ourselves questions and then seeking for the answers. This is why queries and replies form such an integral part of Western Rites. It was not for the sake of supplying clever answers, but to get the participants into a habit of seeking knowledge for themselves by asking intelligent questions and then following them up in search of a reply.

Suppose we are trying to identify with Glory, the eighth Sphere. We have already made associations with a Divine Aspect of the Gods of Everyone, an Archangel Intelligence of the Teacher-Healer Raphael, angel-agents of the Children of the Mighty Ones, and a planetary presentation of Hermes. All these go together to make up the nucleus we typify as "Glory". What are they in ourselves? How did they get there? What are we to do with them? What will they do with and for us? These are not questions for answering by any particular "authority", but for enquirers to *discover for themselves*. That is what really matters. First, sufficient interest and intelligence must be attained to ask the questions, and then enough initiative developed to go out into the Unknown to find the answers. All that any genuine Magical System can offer is a means of doing both those spiritual necessities for Inner Life.

So we literally or metaphorically place ourselves between the Pillars and continue the experience of remorselessly pushing ourselves along the eighth Path of Glory. Apparent failures in Magic are mostly due to the primary failure to push hard or far enough in order to "get off the ground". Tea-party "magicians" normally accomplish no more than what is due to them. Real Magic is only worked with the efforts of a whole heart, a whole mind and a whole soul. There is no point in trying to work with less. Attempts must be repeated for a lifetime if necessary, and no seeming failure allowed to hold back progress. Success is no more than the summit to a mountain of failures. No effort is ever a failure in itself, but only fails in sufficiency or efficiency, to accomplish what was over-demanded of it. The Magician who fails himself will fail everything. At all costs, we must keep going once we are committed to the Path. It is like riding a bicycle on a tightrope—cessation means disaster.

The practical worker on the Glory-Path therefore, will secure himself from interruption, trace his circle around himself and say one way or another; "I refuse to leave this circle until I have made some realisation of Glory, whether this be much or little." It is important that we do not specify at first exactly what is wanted except in the broadest terms. To do otherwise is to invite failure because of imposing impossible conditions. Commonsense is the best controller of consciousness. Once committed to a Circle however, it must not be quitted on any account until some achievement is attained. We can take the nonsense about evil spirits lurking around the perimeter to destroy those who pass it with a pinch of salt—which will work the exorcism! Worse than evil spirits will happen to those who quit their circle without attaining the end for which it was entered. Their faith will suffer a set back, and their links with their own Inner Light be weakened. Every Circle must succeed in order to pass its dynamic impulse along to the next one.

The success of any Circle, is that something has been accomplished within it towards the end for which it was formed. Such an accomplishment may be but a single thought, the flicker of an emotion, the briefest realisation, the least exchange of energies between Something and Nothing. Success is entirely a matter of degree. Little or much, both are successes of their own sorts. What matters in the Circle is that when we leave it we have changed our condition in which we entered it. Preferably changed it for the better, made more of ourselves, adjusted our living to our satisfaction or advantage, but in any case done something with ourselves that means a valuable change for the effort made. We should never cast a Magic Circle in the first place, unless we seriously intend to make good use of it, and once it is made, it must be used only for its constructional purpose.

In the circle dedicated to some discovery of the Eighth Path, the worker will make every conceivable effort to align himself with it. The order of working will be: Objectify — Subjectify — Identify Those are the three prongs of the Magic Trident. Objectifications might be orange lighting, the play of "Mercury" from the "Planets Suite", invocations to Hermes, Raphael, the All-Gods, the adoption of characteristic postures or movements, "mercurial" perfumes, display of the Caduceus, or any other ritual means that ingenuity can suggest. These objectifications may be either factual or simply present as mental conceptions. They may be as simple as a small orange button, or a whole Temple full of accessories. What matters is the work accomplished.

Subjectifications may be feelings of rapidity and lightness, quick-wittedness, "sharpshooting" intelligence, amusement, desires to heal, a sense that everybody's Gods must have something in them, and the like associations with the Sphere. If impressions arrive that are not "in keeping" with the Sphere-framework and Nucleus, they must be "banished" by firmly rejecting them and only opening up to those "on the Hermetic beam". Such a discriminative ability is chiefly developed by practice. It is very rarely inborn.

Identification is the actual experience of *being* the Glory itself approached from both Objective and Subjective angles. There must be an I AM realisation which comprises and transcends all that has led up to it. We must unify with and not only become, but pass far beyond the Externalities and Internalities we have been using to attain this very end-product. Such is the essence of the exercise and the whole purpose of its performance. This is what we are really working for and must definitely achieve to even the slightest degree, for it is the means of making magic.

The precise technique of identification is no more possible of instructional description than the ability to keep afloat in the water may be put into written or spoken words. How does one "become" anything? Obviously by effecting a change in an existing state so that it becomes another one. We "become" an adult by changing from childhood, or we "become" sad *because* some event has made us change our pre-sad state. We all "become" all sorts of things and conditions in very short spaces of time. Our whole life is a becoming. There is no difference between a Magical becoming and any other kind, except that instead of being dependent on outside circumstances, Magical becoming is done in accordance with will to a predetermined pattern. It is a controlled art, and this is what makes it unique. In Magic, we must never pass beyond the limits of our own recall. Otherwise we are no more than disposable life-units.

To identify with Glory, therefore, we must arouse and arrange our consciousness in that Sphere, and that Sphere only. We must be absolutely determined to stay in that Circle until some form of that realisation comes. We must go on until we sweat blood if necessary, or fall fainting on the floor, yet we must never lose control of our consciousness no matter how great the temptation to "let go" or "let it drift" may be. We must "enter the Sphere" as a responsible self-controlled being in our own right, and not allow ourselves to be "sucked into it" as a vacuum cleaner might pick up dirt. That is the important point. It is easy to "abandon ship" and sink ourselves into various psychical states of being, but this is quite the wrong thing to do. Our aim should be to direct the energies we are contacting, and not drift about as they impel us. From first to last in any Magical operation, we must remain the Masters in our own Circles, and not go drifting out of them pointlessly into the swirlings of Inner Space. That is what is meant by the injunction to "stay in the Circle" all the time. In other words, never lose control of our associated nucleus-framework. When we can stay still in the middle and revolve everything else at whatever rate we choose around that Absolute, we shall have attained some degree of mastery.

The Externalities therefore, are only to arouse the Internalities, and the Internalities balanced against Externalities should arouse Identification. It is an $\dfrac{\text{Ext}}{\text{Int}} = \text{Iden}$ formula. An "I AM" affirmation as distinct from the "I AM NOT". Together these make up the "WE ARE". The "I AM" This, That, and the Other of the Ancient Mystery Invocations is a sound method of achieving a sense of identity. When cast into poetic rhythm, and reiterated over and over again, a definite identification will be made according to the operator's degree of capability. A formula for Glory may be made in this or any suitable fashion;

"I am Glorious Honour. In my hand is held the Book of Hidden learning, and my words in every world speak wit and wisdom. I am Initiator to the Temple of Intelligence, and Instructor of all minds that seeks enlightenment therein. In me the Gods of everyone proclaim themselves and show the way of One in Many.

I am also Raphael, Archangel of the Teaching and the Healing arts. The whisper of my wings holds hope for every soul. Mine are the Orange rays of power and beauty, stimulating every mind to rise in search of truth.

In me the Children of the Gods reach out for reason. The scent of storax causes me to strive for commonsense.

Hermes am I to all mankind. Silver is my speech and quick my mind. The Caduceus is my Sign. Words are mine in rites and rituals. The ancient Craft adornment of the apron is mine own. Glorious indeed am I among the Great Ones!"

Such an Invocation is composed out of the various attributes of the Glorious Sphere, put together in such a way as to make a continuity of consciousness circling round the central point of Glory. The idea is to build up sufficient pressure on that point to make it penetrate into Inner Dimensions. This is bound to be the case once applied pressure reaches the required degree, but may take a great deal of effort and skill only acquired by constant practice. Invocation is an art in itself. The word means "in-speaking", and we have to learn how to speak into ourselves for what we want to bring out or *evoke*. If we invoke properly, there will be an answer evoked from the Power on which we have called. It is as elementary as an energy-reflex. What goes in must push something out. The question is: can we push it in the right place the right way? Knowledge of how to do this is Magical wisdom.

Since Invocation needs special consideration by itself, we will deal with it in more detail later on. It is a very individual matter, and styles vary enormously with workers. They must necessarily vary with types of Rite as well. Each different species of Rite has its own particular sort of Invocation which must be adhered to in order to make it work. Some depend on lyrical poetry, others on brief reiterated affirmations, others gain on descriptive prose. There are as many sorts of Invocation as there are methods of dramatisation, and probably every sort of worker thinks that theirs and theirs alone is the "right" one. The only rights and wrongs of the matter are whether or not the Invocations used prove suitable for the people and circumstances involved.

In using Invocations, we are really appealing to qualities and energies *within ourselves* to "come out" and objectify themselves. We ourselves are the "medium" through which those energies must manifest themselves. They have entire Reality of their own on Inner Dimensions, and we are simply calling on them to "come through" into our state via the vehicles of our consciousness and personality. This is the Identification. Everyone has their own most "invocable" Inner energies, and degrees of ability vary from one extreme to another, but the Principles of the Ten Spheres are spiritual necessities for all of us, and therefore are fundamentals we should infallibly identify with.

In the Glory-identification, we are trying to sell ourselves the idea that we really are creatures of such a Sphere, do in fact have some vestiges of the powers and potentials connected therewith, and are that very sort of person, standing for those principles as a God-image in our own right. The Invocations might be called "sales talk" of their kind, and if we keep on long enough and convincingly enough, an energy-transfer will take place between the two ends of ourselves, and the "sale" will be made. We are in fact "talking ourselves into it," and that is what Invocation signifies. It may be that we only had the merest traces of Glory-qualities to start with, but if we continue our ritualisations, they are bound to arise in answer to our calling, and we shall ultimately gain increased contact with them, and incorporate them more and more in our own natures.

The main danger to avoid in these Magical Invocations is loss of control over the situation, and a consequent unbalancing leading to delusions of all kinds and a lack of co-ordination between Inner and Outer life. It is easy to be swept into the power-vortex we create by Magical practices, and very difficult to gain equilibrium again. As a safeguard, it is advisable to keep an anchor attached to External life by holding fast to some commonplace fundamental as a kind of "grounding point". A relic of this old precaution was the skeleton at the feast, or the official detailed to ride behind the Hero during a Triumph, whispering "Remember Man, thou art but mortal" over and over again. This had the effect of "bringing things to earth" safely.

Each energy invoked by our Rituals must be safely "earthed" so that we do not remain in a state of unbalance or tension. If we neglect this elementary precaution, severe emotional or spiritual trouble will result. Having "raised" power and used it, the power must be carefully replaced in the neutral position until needed again. So much is commonsense. At the end of each Rite therefore, even of the simplest kind, we must put our Magical gear lever into neutral. This is done by making a realisation of Outer life Identity and unifying with it by a similar process used for Inwardisation. We may say in effect; "My name is so and so, I am a so forth, living at such an address. I have had an Inner experience that will help me express this Outer Being to better effect. Now I am coming back to be my ordinary self improved by what I have just been." All this can be done in one simple effort such as the Sign of the Cross, or stamping on the ground, or even snapping the fingers.

It is a bad thing to emerge from a "working" all starry-eyed and exuding psychic trails in all directions. The end of any working should bring the participants back to their point of beginning, leaving them externally in a calm rational state as firmly balanced as they were before the working began. Thus rituals should be designed with a suitable "tail-off" or descent, which allows the re-integration of the "normal self" and the re-assumption of a sound everyday personality. The Circle should not be quitted until this has taken place. It is a great help to "switch over" in a mundane direction by eating some food, or undertaking some normal domestic task. Eventually it becomes almost second nature to "switch" from Inner to Outer life without loss of balance either way.

One good way of "opening and shutting" is to visualise a Door between Inner and Outer life, and use it for opening and closing a rite. The Door can be typified in any suitable way, such as a Golden Gateway with some Symbol on it between a Black and a White Pillar. To "open", we visualise ourselves on the outside of this Door, at which we knock with the code-signal of the operation we are undertaking. We should try and feel the response from the Doorkeeper on the other side who slowly opens the Door inwards while we take the three ceremonial steps across its threshold. To return, we reverse the process, and experience the Door being shut behind us, securely sealing off the Innerworld. On entering, the Black Pillar will be on the left, and on leaving, we must turn round in our minds so that it is on our right. This Door method is a very useful one, and can be simplified or elaborated to any extent. Some such ritual device must invariably precede and conclude all contact between the Worlds. Our rule should always be to start and finish at "normal".

For each Sphere, we must devise a simple rite calculated to "work ourselves into a state" of that particular Sphere, and then get ourselves back to where we came in. This is the real Circle of any rite, the completion of a whole energy-cycle from zero to zero. Once we have covered the ten Spheres, we may turn our attention to the Paths shown by the Tarot trumps. Similar procedure to that of the Spheres may be used with this important difference. In the case of the Spheres, we were concerned with being united by all the various associations around a single point. In the case of the Paths, we are seeking unification with energies arising from two distinct points, which must contrast each other into equilibrium through us. In a Sphere, we are metaphorically surrounding ourselves with a whirlpool, and on a Path we are in a river flowing in both directions at once (which is the same as a whirlpool flattened out). With each situation, we must equilibrate the polarised power relatively to ourselves, and direct it in accordance with the effect required.

When "working the Paths", our previously described cards are extremely valuable, since they provide the necessary data. Let us try an experimental effort. Taking the "Path pack", we cut at random—obtaining the Sun, classified as T, or the 26th Path between Beauty and Foundation, conjoining both Solar and Lunar influences. We go through the stages of Objectivity, Subjectivity, and then Identity, and make a little rite of the process.

The Sun of course may be represented by a light of any kind suitable that has yellow rays, and the Moon by a mirror, silver plate, surface of water, or anything that reflects. We may place ourselves literally between the light and its reflection so that we are illuminated by both during the rite. We now subject ourselves to the dual energies inherent in the Concepts of Beauty and Foundation. The God-Aspects are respectively those of Knowledge and Life. Archangels Michael and Gabriel. We connect these two together, with ourselves in the position of the Sun uniting them. At first we may think of one and then the other, but in the end they must both be held in ourselves as a whole polarised power of which we are the product as a Solar being.

Nothing must enter our field of consciousness except awareness along this particular Path. All else to be dismissed and altered into Sun-Moon thoughts which make us into a Sun of Righteousness, shining and radiating a type of energy comprised of Beauty and Foundation. We can build up mental images of Archangels, or any suitable symbology that will help to expand our Inner awareness along these lines. Music and rhythms having Sol-Luna connections may be used, or appropriate incense if required. All these adjuncts are only to help us get Inner results. The less we depend on them, the more skilled we shall become. We must remember that a Path is an *harmonic* resultant of a dual Sphere-frequency which should be a perfect blend of both to make us what we are seeking to be. Our Identity-Affirmation might be something like this:

"I am between both Beauty and Foundation. My name is Lord of Fire above the World. My Intelligence is called the Active, or Exciting, since from hence all creatures of the supreme orb receive their spirits and the action of their nature. My sign is of the Sun, and I am Power personified in Light, commencing and completing every cycle throughout sentient Life. My watchword is ILLUMINATE, and I am radiant because of the Eternal One who shines through me."

It will be seen that the structure of this Identification comes from the titles of the Spheres, the Tarot trumps, the Paths of Intelligence, and a Watchword. Source material for most invocations is easily obtainable, and only needs an ability for construction to link them all up into a pattern.

In "Pathworking", we are trying to "get off the ground" and extend ourselves into Inner Dimensions by pushing ourselves up between a dual-concept. Metaphorically, each concept is like the side of a ladder, or perhaps the confining walls of a channel or conduit. We must bring them in as close as possible to ourselves on each side, and then make step-junctions between them so that we may progress or ascend. If we imagine this literally with a couple of poles or Pillars, each painted the colour of a Sphere, it will give us an idea to work with, and even make some of the Rite with. Our special cards are a help here if we have coloured the sides correctly.

It is essential during this exercise to learn the knack of "un-wavering", or keeping the concentration as fixed on the task as it would have to be if we were trying to cross a dangerous chasm by a desperately narrow yet possible bridge. This is what the Abyss-Symbol means, namely that we must bring the whole of our consciousness to bear in focus upon the single task in hand. We no more dare take our minds off it when once commenced, than we would let our attention wander while on a precarious rock-face, or hanging over an Abyss. In old Initiations such dangerous practices were actually carried out for no other purpose than to demonstrate and arouse the degree of concentration necessary for accomplishing the attainment of Enlightenment. We never live so intensely as when within a hair's breadth of death. To effect any radical change in our conscious condition, the intensity of its degree must be increased to a point where it can penetrate the normal veil separating the distinct conscious states from each other. For this to occur, some external stimulus must be applied to us, or else we must provide such a means of our own accord, as indeed we should in working rituals.

The principle of Pathworking is not unlike squeezing a tube of toothpaste. Apply pressure at its sides when its cap is removed, and the paste can only go one way—out. By imposing the limits of the Sphere-Principles upon ourselves, and squeezing them towards us, our consciousness can only be forced up between them so to speak, and emerge on a higher level. It is like decreasing the area of a light-beam in order to increase its penetration in length or height, as in the case of a searchlight. Our normal consciousness is scattered all over the place rather thinly. The "occult" exercises are aimed at getting it together in one polarised beam so that it becomes effective in whichever direction we aim it. Such is Magic.

If we are working the Sun Path therefore, we must set up the limit of Beauty on one hand and Foundation on the other and stay as firmly between them as we had to remain in our Circle to make a Sphere-Principle. The specifics of the sixth Sphere must become an absolute in one direction, and the ninth Sphere in the other, depending which way we want to face. Each Concept must be clearly constructed to a point where we can actually feel them beside us like two forces exerting pressures on us. We can identify the two Spheres with our two arms if we like, and press these to our sides physically. Any such device to make our Inner images "come true" is useful. We may even imagine the Archangels Michael and Gabriel pushing us together like a pair of book-ends. Then we "point ourselves" upwards, hold our Solar image, and keep up the pressure till we "rise in the planes". It is essential to keep "pointed" as we feel ourselves "going up", or the whole structure will collapse like a ladder falling apart, and we shall fall back with it and have to start all over again. To climb higher, we pull the Pillars in towards our mid-equilibrium line, and to descend safely, we gently let them go apart while coming quietly down again to ground level.

The result of this exercise is to produce a greatly intensified beam of conditioned consciousness, due to controlling its variable properties with fixed pressure-principles. This works almost the same way as producing an electric effect by physically pressing the sides of certain crystals. By limiting consciousness to fixed lines, we have made a sort of "railway effect" in which the limiting Pillars are the rails, the overall concept becomes the passenger or contents of the waggon, and the ultimate aim is the destination of the whole trainload. We have actually taken hold of our consciousness and made it operate among the lines we ourselves have constructed, and that is a most important step in Magic.

It is difficult at first to "think between limits along set lines", but it comes with practice of Pathworking. There are a number of "ritual devices" which encourage the art. One of course is the two Pillars, another is the cowl which limits a field of view, or a sighting-fork on top of a Staff. Two-tone chanting or a double beat may be used. Anything that compresses consciousness along one axis and extends it along another. This forms the corridor between the worlds. Again and again we must remind ourselves that no ritual adjunct will accomplish anything by itself, and everything depends on the extent we are able to make conscious use of it. Some can make a magic Rod from a matchstick, and others could not make one from the most expensive materials. There is no substitute for skill.

Each Path will produce its own particular type of conditioned consciousness, and they must all be worked until we are familiar with each and can induce it in ourselves fairly rapidly. Different practioners all have their fancy methods of doing this, but the principles are the same. The product of a polarised power must be projected in accordance with Will or Intent. Later on, experience will teach us what sort of powers should be used to effect specific intentions. By the time we have worked through all the Paths from top to bottom, or in whatever order they come from the pack, we should be in full possession of the necessary information for continuing and developing the process, which, after all, is simply a normal function of consciousness pushed to an abnormal extent.

Reduced to its simplest terms, Pathworking is taking two preconditioned factors of consciousness, associating them so as to produce a calculated result, and then continuing the line of pressure into a different dimension of awareness. It is as if we said, 2 and 2 make 4, and instead of taking that as a complete statement with a final result, only accepted it as part of a calculation, and went on pushing it into the Unknown in search of the rest of it. In other words, we are breaking past the artificially imposed barriers of awareness, and entering new states of consciousness, or rather extending ourselves into dimensions that have few purely human occupants. It is like a new birth, and indeed is the being "born again" to enter the "Kingdom of Heaven" or Inner Life.

The secret is really to "carry on thinking and being after the rest have stopped". Nevertheless this might lead to serious trouble if done the wrong way, and for this reason the Paths have been planned as they are, to give the very best and soundest basis from which to work our way toward Inner living. Having taken a pair of first-class Concepts to start with, we equate these with a Symbol we can work ourselves into, and when we can reach no further point of ordinary conscious progression, and Nothing stares us straight in the face, we must simply *go on* pushing ahead into that Nothing without deviating from our pressure-point. Providing we apply a strong and steady enough pressure behind a fine enough point, there will be a penetration to the Innerworld, and we can open up the field of our awareness to take in more of what we shall find there.

Mystics have described this actual penetration as being like an experience of becoming first "all Light" (Illumination) then of "Limitlessness" (Expansion) and finally "Nothing", or Nirvana, wherein consciousness has outstripped its own speed, and therefore has passed the limits of awareness until it catches up with itself. In effect this is what happens during the phenomenon known as death, except that in that case an actual severance takes place between the base and apex of our consciousness, and an Abyss or "Great Gulf" is formed. The state of being we shall extend ourselves to after death is but that of future conditions which will be common-place to humanity in times to come. We can only go ahead of ourselves to a limited degree without breaking the Silver Cord. If we really want to improve matters on Earth, we shall have to alter them in "Heaven" first. At every meditation therefore, we should take the opportunity to make even the smallest improvement to our Innerworld which we shall have to live in when the Outer Gates close behind us. This is the value of "laying up treasure in Heaven".

Once some skill has been gained in Pathworking, we can take up the "Court cards" and begin Personifying. These "people" are the presentations of individualised consciousness in human form. They are a cross-section of single or collective human states of being. We are provided with sixteen "characters" in search of an author, or a single being capable of playing sixteen or more character parts. To Personify, we must project ourselves into each card, and relate ourselves with others.

Suppose, for instance, we decide to be an energetic and aggressive type of person. The Knight of Swords is our man for this. If we want to be warm hearted and loving, the Queen of Cups offers herself. The actual physical sex of the personificator is not of importance when relating with the Court cards. They represent various qualities inherent in humanity regardless of sex, and must be so considered. By and large, the Courtiers cover the sixteen points of the Compass surrounding any human being, and we are bound to be in line with one of them at any given moment of our lives. By gaining an ability to alter our personality-pattern, we can change our living-course to suit ourselves. Hence the need for practice with the personifications.

It will be noted that the cards only represent acceptable human qualities. There are none to typify vicious, cruel, evil, or bad types of individuals. Such undesirable traits of human nature form no part of the Plan for the Innerworld outlined by the Tarots. We must leave malice behind us when we enter it, for no provision has been made for such nastiness. It is an Innerworld designed to exclude evil. The Tarot Devil is not the Spirit of Evil at all, but the Tempter who has a specific task to undertake in the testing of humanity both incarnate and discarnate. The Court cards therefore only offer us a choice of personalities suitable for souls aspiring toward betterment of their being. If we make a Compass out of them, they will look like Fig. 10. Since there are not only four cards to each Element, but each card carries the sub-significance of an element by itself, Kings being Rod-Fire, Queens Cup-Water, Knights Swords-Air, and Pages Shields-Earth, we can specify a personification to be one of "Earth-of Fire", or the Page of Rods for example.

All kinds of combinations and arrangements can be made with

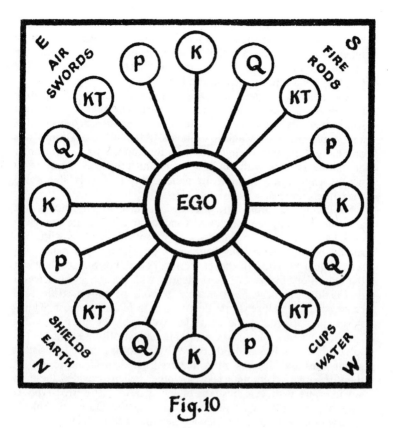

Fig.10

these Court People. We can see which are harmonious or inharmonious together, and calculate the likely effects of one with another. An Earth-Fire person (King of Shields), is opposed or compensated by a Fire-Fire one (King of Rods). There are many aspects and relationships possible between the cards as there are between flesh and blood people of corresponding categories. What is more, we can adjust the one state from the other.

A personality is an effect of power-projection from Inner sources and appears to be what it is because of the way its primal pattern of energy is arranged, and because of various filter-screens interposed between the personality and its source. It is a long way back to our original undifferentiated Energy appearing like pure Light, but we may make temporary alterations to our personalities by the voluntary assumption of pre-set characteristics. This is done in the same way that an actor "assumes" a role, except that our repertoire is taken from the Tarot and the Tree. The reason for doing this, is because eventually such characterisations do indeed lead us to Inner Realities. They are the "Unreal" leading to the REAL, the "False" leading to the TRUE, and the "Darkness' leading to the LIGHT. Such is their purpose and use.

Any reliable textbook on acting will give techniques for "getting into" and "assuming" any character part. The practical occultist will be well advised to make a study of these, extract their principles, and apply them in Magical exercises. After all, the Drama was originally a sacred art, intended to afford humans an opportunity of sharing identity with Divine powers and principles. There is no reason why we should limit dramatic ability to merely identifying with other humans.

So, taking the Court Cards, we assume the characteristics of one after another until we can actually induce an appropriate change in ourselves according to whatever Card we are dealing with. We should be able to cut the Court-pack at random, and make ourselves identify with whichever Person comes up. Suppose we cut the Queen of Shields. We must identify with her to feel ourselves a thoroughly practical hard headed person, perhaps a trifle self-centered, but intelligent and determined to make the most of ourselves, and expecting the same from others. Not given to being over-sentimental, and maybe a little impatient of those who are too soft with themselves and others, yet by no means unkind. Insistent about likes and dislikes, more materialistic than idealistic, but at the same time accepting a need for other beliefs provided these do not interfere with "the business of living". An extroverted type. It may be that different individuals will see the Queen of Shields otherwise and each must classify her and her associates as they think most suitable, provided this task is actually done. It is the effort made to do such work that is important.

It follows that just as we must "raise" each Tarot character in ourselves, so we must be able to "lay" it again. Failure to do this will result in hopeless confusion. There is no need to make a uselessly elaborate rite of this simple procedure. A brief Word-Act association is ample. The cards will help us here again. We place the People-pack upside down, and then cut, turning the card towards us, which of course "raises" the facing card to right angles with the rest. At the same time we say or think simply "IN". The card is then personified to the best of our ability in ourselves, just as if we were looking at our own reflection in a mirror, and realising "That is me!" When this realisation has been made, we "banish" by turning the card flat with the rest so that is lost in the anonymity of the pack and saying firmly "OUT". This dismissal must be accompanied by "letting go" of the image we have created. Any gestures that suggest effacement, such as a wave of the hand, may be used if wanted, but they are superfluous. It is however, most important that a deliberate "raising" and "laying" be done with each card, even for a fraction of a second. This, and this alone ensures that we keep control of the operation, and it does not begin to control us. With practice, we can raise and lay Personae with the speed of turning cards, and a face-image will invoke, and an edge-image banish. Associative practice is the key.

The next thing to attempt is encounter-reaction. As our normal selves in the everyday world, what happens when we encounter some other human and exchange energies with them? Anything from indifference to the most violent effect, but invariably *something* passes between us no matter how slightly. We try and approximate this Inwardly by use of the Tarot People. If, for instance, we are the Queen of Shields, what is likely to happen should we have an encounter with the Page of Rods? To discover this, we must try it and see. The Queen must be "assumed", and the Page encountered. This time we make the Page *other* than ourselves, and imagine ourselves encountering this different person who will act, speak, think, and be completely in character as a Rod-Page person. We must experience our reactions to this behaviour in the character of the Shield-Queen, and identify with her in thoughts and feelings. We must never let ourselves be so carried away by the situation that we lose over-all control of it. Should there be a likelihood of this, the banishing "OUT", must be firmly pronounced, and neutrality restored. We may always re-raise the situation again for better handling. Empathy may be established to any degree at all, *providing* that we still keep hold of the Master-switch. It must always be used when the danger-point of losing control is reached.

There are enormous possibilities connected with the use of the Tarot People. We can select a Person by decision or chance cutting, and then cut any Person at random to encounter. Ordinary conversations will arise in our minds quite naturally, but the surprising thing is that we shall learn a great deal of information from these "talks". At a casual thought, it might appear that we are only using one part of ourselves to talk to another one, but this is less than a half-truth. The Personifications link Inwardly with what might be called the Universal Mind, and most equally with those individualised minds that actually lie behind them. In using the Tarot People therefore, we are linking in with real minds other than our own who operate along those particular frequencies. We can actually use them to make contact with incarnate or discarnate individuals. It is all a question of practice and establishing connections. The cards will give access to a *type* of individual. To reach one single entity among that entire type is a far more difficult matter.

For this, we would have to be responsive with their particular base-pattern which distinguishes them from all others. That is their true "Magical Name" which cannot be "uttered" by anyone else, however closely it is approximated for communicative purposes. We can only communicate with others to a degree, whether or not they are incarnate. The extent of this degree depends on our ability to "empathise" with them, as we do with the cards.

When we have attained a little skill with the Card-People, we can try using the Practices. After all, we react with people in various ways in different circumstances and conditions. These are represented by the ordinary numbered cards. Looking at their list, we can pre-select or random cut any of them, and consider what happens if we find ourselves environed by such temporary affairs. Suppose we have identified with the Solar Principle, expressed through the Person of the Rod-Queen who is encountering the Shield-Page. The circumstances of this encounter to and with which we must react, will be determined by whichever figure-card comes up. If, say, it is the Four of Swords (Truce), we may assume that there has been a disagreement or quarrel between the Queen and Page, but this has now been suspended. To find out what led up to the trouble, and if it will ever recur, we should have to use a lot more cards.

By using the figure-cards, we can put ourselves in or out of any situation likely to arise in connection with human living. Each card is the basic of some circumstance which is capable of affecting human beings or has been caused by them. If we took the whole of every life to pieces and classified its events to their lowest common denominators, we should obtain—a Tarot pack. There are but a definite number of possibilities which apply to human living, and our events are combinations of those basics. There are but limited types of people we can be, however much we individualise these. Reduce those types to their minimum, and we have the Tarot-People. The same applies to the Principles and Powers. The whole Pack is an Alphabet of Life which will spell its words in any dimension of living. This is its essence and value.

Now we can see the real use of the Tarot pack. It is for living in and arranging our lives with. The cards are the exchange-symbols between Inner and Outer life. The way we arrange and link them Inwardly will reflect into our Outer living. Conversely, the way we identify them in Outer life gives us an opportunity to dispose their Inner relationships so as to deal favourably with their Outer dispositions. Altogether the Tarots are a most valuable collection of psycho-physical currency convertible into either dimension. The only reason why they have been successfully used for fortune telling, is because they form patterns of life likely to arise in the experience of most human beings. Basics of life are to be interpreted differently on different levels. A Tarot spread only links with past or future insofar as the same things happen over and over again to different people in various ways.

By using the Tarot as a Magical Alphabet, we should be able to extend and condition our consciousness so that it will operate intelligently through levels normally unreachable by an average human mind. In point of fact this would be possible with totally different symbols, but since the Tarot is a perfectly valid and serviceable system, there is no reason whatever why it should not be used. Unless of course some genius invents an improved method, which does not seem a near possibility. The "Live it Yourself" kit of the Tarot pack is likely to be the most efficient means of magically relating oneself with Existence for a long time to come. Its designs may alter to suit styles and centuries, but its principles are fundamentally too practical for unnecessary alteration.

The value of skill with the Tarots in this Magical way, is that we gain control of our Inner living so as to relate it most effectively to Outer conditions, and eventually we may alter the Outer conditions too. Once we get our deep causal energies properly linked with a set of Symbols reachable by the focal point of our consciousness, we affect the depths by manipulating the screen of Symbols at the height. A general moving toy-soldiers in a sand-tray can make their human equivalents do the same on the battlefield, *provided* the proper links are established between the actual field and G.H.Q., which is what Magic aims to do.

The working principles of this System are not limited to the Qabalah. By making a "breakdown" of life-factors, and linking each with some guardian Saint, the Christian Church attempted to formulate its own System, which seemed to work in its own way. Linking Symbols with life and cross-working was a well known art in the Ancient Mysteries. Their designers may not have known of (or approved of), modern "psychology", but they knew Inner Life intimately from their own practical experience of it, and they used this knowledge to formulate their Symbol-sets. By linking-in the Symbols with actual Intelligences and types of consciousness personifiable as Divine, Angelic, or otherwise, the Mysteries offered their human members an opportunity to participate consciously as active partners in the Life-Plan at director-level. Surely this is worth working for, and keeping before us as a major Magical aim.

Once we have done sufficient meditation and ritualising of the Symbols, we should be able to build up the sort of Innerworld around ourselves that we need. What really matters is that they provide us with the means of organising our Inner Life in a sound, sane, and sensible way, which is the Great Work lying before every magician. Every Magical exercise, practice, ritual, or process can be constructed from the basics already outlined, just as all the scientific books of the future can be written from the thinking-units known to our ancestors. Our task is simply to re-arrange what already exists.

How we use the Symbols is largely a matter for individual and group experience. Everyone must do their own work for themselves, and then hope to combine this with the efforts of others so that mutual modifications will produce more perfect patterns. Eventually each individual or Group will evolve their specialised styles to suit various needs, and providing tolerance-limits are agreed upon, the greatest benefits for the human soul may ensue. There should be no end to the possibilities of symbol-combinations, so there is no reason why there should not be room for everyone's particular ideas of procedure.

A good starting point exercise is the daily "brain-brightener". We set up a problem with the cards and let our Inner consciousness get on with its solution. For this purpose we sort the whole pack into four groups. The Powers, or the Elements represented by the four Aces, the Principles, or the 22 Trumps, the Practices, or the numbered cards, and the People, or the Court cards. By selecting a card from each group, our Problem will emerge. Suppose we draw the King of Swords, Temperance, the Ace of Shields, and the Eight of Rods. This makes a situation in which a somewhat austere or serious person finds himself involved in an Earthy way with principles of Temperance in circumstances of expediency. Using that framework we can identify ourselves into it in a great variety of ways, gaining valuable Inner experience which will reflect back toward Outer living. If we use our Tarots for practical purposes such as these instead of haphazard fortune telling, they will show their worth to no small extent.

The cards may be used for "Magical manoeuvres" following the same principles of military exercises with maps and models, and will produce excellent results. They can be used for training schemes and experiments with consciousness that will make really solid contributions to our advancement in mental and spiritual dimensions. Altogether the Tarots are far too valuable to be confined to mere sorcery, or treated as medieval curiosa. Once put to proper use they will more than justify the necessary time and effort spent in learning and practising their lore. They are indeed the "Hermetic Bible", out of which all the books of Magic may be written by everyone able to put one thought with another in the right patterns. What more can be done for any Initiate than providing them with the means for making their own magic?

However there is more to Magic and its rites than classifications of consciousness. To understand and appreciate the techniques of ritual, we shall have to study and practise them in detail with the heightened consciousness that should now be available for us. This should prove a most rewarding pursuit.

SENSORY RITUALISM

The entire technique of ritual depends on an ability to take one piece of consciousness and stretch it two ways at once, Inwardly and Outwardly. This sounds simple, but is far from being so with humans accustomed to a one-sided materialistic view of Nature. It would be equally difficult for those whose attention is fixed on nothing but the immaterial. Ritual is essentially an art of extensions between differing dimensions. It works on the principle of patterning in one scale so as to re-produce the equivalent in another. Ordinary human beings can only extend ritualised consciousness to a very limited degree. If it is to go further, it must be "picked up", channelled, amplified, and processed by Intelligences operating through Inner Dimensions. Without such co-operation, no purely human efforts are likely to do a great deal. It is the "Inner contacts" that continue the cycles of energy beyond their usual point of neutrality, and push them along the Inner Paths to accomplish their release-purpose.

Nevertheless, it is a skilled matter to generate and direct specialised energies toward the Innerworld sufficiently far for them to be "picked up" by the "Inners" and carried on from there. It is even more skilled to determine the course of such energies so that they will reach their intended Innerworld destination before they are neutralised and rendered ineffective. We also should be able to reciprocate with the "Inners", and "pick up" energies they are directing toward us for expression on our material levels. There are many such problems to be considered when studying ritualism.

As usual, the best place to start any studies is at base level, and if we consider the crude simplicities of primitive rituals, we shall find the elements we are looking for. Mankind's initial attempts to raise himself from earth-level toward the Stars of his immortal origin, resulted in rites having only two factors, sex and violence.

Those are the twin Pillars that primitive Man depends on in any age including our own. They are the only extensions into other dimensions reachable by undeveloped and unevolved humanity. By sex the world of the unborn was contacted, and by slaughter the sphere of the dead was approached. Man knew no other means of reaching beyond his earth-state, and yet the overpowering instinct that he must infallibly strive for existence in the Innerworld drove him along the path of sex and slaughter for centuries, and still continues to do so.

There are many sex and slaughter schools operating today in various ways under different names. Some might be very shocked to hear themselves so described, yet the basics are there. The Christian Mass depends on the Sex symbolism of the Incarnation, and the Slaughter symbolism of the Crucifixion. The so-called "Witch" rites linked with primitive paganism depend on ritualised sex practices and symbolic slaughter dramatised in the forms of sadism and masochism known as "bonding and beating". The Christian figure of the Scourging at the Pillar takes the place of this in Church practice. Man always oscillates wildly between the Pillars of Pleasure and Pain in order to prod himself even a little further along his Path.

It is probably only sex and violence that moves an average human powerfully enough to produce any very noticeable effect in Innerworld terms. When young thugs are questioned as to reasons why they have beaten some helpless fellow-creature to the point of serious injury or death, their common reply is: "We did it for kicks". Perfectly true. They are so low-graded in responsiveness to Inner energies, that nothing else except the most vicious and violent events will move them. Yet the necessity for reaching out of themselves proved stronger than their own natural inertia. This is an important realisation. Sex and violence are not motivational causes, but effects. The original motive behind both extreme human acts, is the compulsive necessity *stronger than life itself*, to extend existence beyond womb-tomb states. The incredible power, energy, and force behind such compulsion, drives Man past his average point of desperation in each direction. It all depends on evolutionary status as to what reactions follow this initiating Impulse.

Humans do not primarily kill each other for the sake of the act, but for the sake of the Inner effect such an act produces. They do not go in for sexual intercourse for the sake of re-populating the world, but because the act itself results in Inner reactions they enjoy. It is important we see which is horse and which is cart in this case, because motivations behind rituals come from the same source. Impelled by the same Force, an inarticulate savage might beat his mate's head in with the nearest stone, while a more advanced soul would use the energy for eliminating some fault in his or her own nature. There are only two currents to the same Power, Anabolic, or building up, which is sexual, and Katabolic, or breaking down, which is slaughter or violence. That is the Primal Power we are seeking to utilise in a modified manner by channelling it through ritualised Paths. The methods of use depend on ourselves.

The Holy Mysteries evolved away from the levels of blood and seed, titilation and torture. Those Intelligences behind the Mysteries knew well enough that better ways existed for Mankind to contact the Innerworld than being driven by greed or fear, yet these two sides of the human mainspring are still beneath the Pillars of the finest Temple. They are the extremes between which we have to steer a Middle Course up the Pillar of Mildness, and we shall not be able to eliminate them from our calculations. All that can be done is to alter their expressions to ever nobler forms, and reach higher and higher levels of usage until the two meet perfectly in the middle, and our evolutionary cycle completes itself.

Behind each ritual act therefore, exists a deep-level motive of increasing our reality through Inner dimensions, or "Godwardising". Even the vicious little thugs seek "Life-and-Death" powers when they murder or rape, and so usurp the Divine perogative. They too, are "greedy for God" and admit to "feeling good" after their brutalities. In their stage of evolution, they are incapable of expressing themselves otherwise, and are unreachable except retributively. "God-greed" and "Devil-fear" will be with us as long as the Ladder of Life extends itself on both sides of us. They have to evolve with us to the Gates of Heaven or Hell. Between the Pillars of Pain and Pleasure, there is only one Path of Initiation. It is named "Peace".

It is the intention and use of any act that ritualises it. Otherwise it is nothing but an action. Every type of act, practice or thought can be ritualised, but especially in Western Occult Tradition, ritualism has become considerably stylised over the centuries, and definite ritual patterns have emerged and continued because they have proved practical. Unfortunately we have lost touch with the Inner side of the rites to a considerable extent. It is high time we made serious efforts to re-establish contact with the Intelligences using such means of working with Mankind. This will only be possible if we are prepared to put as much study and effort into the task as we should with any other specialised activity.

The basic of ritual-study is to realise and experience the difference between a ritualised and non-ritualised energy. This is done very simply, by contrasting one event from the two directions. Suppose we just pick up an ordinary pen or pencil from our desk, press the end of it lightly against the centre of our forehead for a few moments, then replace it. No particular thoughts of any kind should be attached to this act, nor any feeling experienced except the physical pressure. It should be one of those vague things done automatically with no particular significance. At the conclusion of the action, its effect should be noted in relation to the person. This will probably be insignificant. Now the same action should be repeated in a ritualised manner.

First we must bring ourselves to order by making the Sign of the Circled Cross. With the thumb and first two fingers of the right hand touching each other, we raise the finger tips just above the forehead saying:

"In the Name of the Wisdom."

The hand is now brought down to heart level saying:

"The Love." Then to right shoulder saying:

"The Justice", Then to left shoulder,

"And the Infinite Mercy". Followed by making a complete circle deosil of the four points while saying;

"Of the One Eternal Spirit." Finishing by bringing the hand to the centre of the circle while intoning:

"AMEN."

Now let the entire attention be focussed on the pen or pencil. A sense of purpose and clear intention must be felt. Let us suppose we seek a Michael-contact. Since this Archangel's position is in the South, we slowly turn the pen clockwise around its middle till it faces either true or Magical South. Magical South is on the right hand whichever physical direction we may face. As we turn the pen, we change it in our imagination to become the Rod, the instrument of Fire—Michael. When we pick it up, it must feel mentally a lot longer and heavier than it is physically. Then we close the eyes, and press the end of the pen against the forehead, just as before. This time, however, the rod must be figured as a direction connection between the holder and the Archangel. Somewhere in another dimension, Michael, whatever this Intelligence may be, holds the other end. He or it must be reached out for along the rod until there is a sense of response. We may send a definite formulated thought such as: "I seek Light. Lead me thereto O Michael." A picture of the Being in traditional armour etc may be mentally built up. Then we make ourselves receptive and try to receive whatever impression will be reflected back to us along the channel of consciousness we have just made. There may be only a single word, a sense of light, a momentary flicker of awareness, or some far more illuminating experience, but there positively will be *something* worth making a note of. At the end of the exercise, some closing sign, or the Cross, must be made to restore "normality", and bring the circle of the operation to its completion.

We must now compare the ritualised and non-ritualised activities and see what may be learned. The main difference lies in the objective. There is a vast difference between idly scratching our foreheads with the end of a pen, and focussing up a beam of consciousness directed toward a specific type of extra-mundane Intelligence and Energy. If indeed we have been able to extend this beam efficiently enough, we shall also have received some kind of response from the Intelligence we were aiming at. To some extent we have made an alteration to our existence by an act of intention operative Inwardly and Outwardly. The entire fundamental principles of Ritual Magic have been demonstrated. All else is a matter of degree and application.

It must be understood that no ritual act of any kind at all will push us Inwards and Upwards, (or anywhere else), automatically, any more than a tree will lift us into its branches. The motive power must come from within us. Ritual appurtenances do no more than provide us with a build-it-yourself Ladder to get off the ground. Nevertheless we could not rise very far without it, so we may as well gain proficiency in the art of magical climbing. Once the realisation has been made that nothing except our own efforts will get us a step away from material levels, we shall rise much more rapidly toward the Inner destinations we are seeking.

The whole secret of Ritual Magic is nothing else than developing an ability to use quite ordinary physical means in an extraordinary way so as to obtain metaphysical results. Such an ability is as much an art as music, painting, writing, or any other expression of consciousness via material media. It is inherent in many humans, and may be trained, developed, and made to serve evolutionary ends like any other capability. Without sufficient practice and direction there will be little result worth considering. Hence the necessity for rational and regular use.

Unless we have either a natural or an acquired ability to "Inwardise away" from the material accessories of Ritualism, we shall never achieve very much by its means. It is true that certain ritual patterns over the centuries have built up their own Inner contacts which bring about specific results, but these depend very largely on "mass-production" methods needing sheer weight of numbers, and there is an enormous efficiency-loss between input and output energies. They can be classified as religious rites rather than Magical. The main difference between the two is that Magical rites fall more within the province of limited skilled and highly specialised workers, concentrating on pressurised points; while religious rites are the unskilled but devoted efforts of the masses in a general direction. The principles of ritualism are exactly the same in both cases of course, the only distinction being in usage-method. A Magician is a trained ritualist, whereas a worshipper is an untrained attender.

It is the difference between players and spectators. Each gains from the rest in their own way, but the specialist is always ahead of the others, though only along that particular line.

If we want to become an athlete, we shall have to perform training exercises, and we shall never be an artist without colour and brushwork, or a musician without finger and scale practice. It is equally impossible to become a ritualist without spending a good deal of time and effort over the basic exercises which alone will give proficiency at the art. Unless a worker is prepared to devote himself to these, there is little point in proceeding along the Ritual Path. No angels are going to do our work for us. The first steps on the Path must be made with our own energy. True we may receive unobtrusive guidance from Inner Beings during our magical infancy, but we are unlikely to be very aware of it. The main drive must come from inside us, and unless we release it ourselves with our whole wills, we shall make no progress.

To say: "I am so busy I have no time for magical exercises" is futile. Those who *need* time for anything *make* it. Either they cease devoting it to less worthy uses, or they discover how to "fit it in" with existing practices. If anyone really wants to practise magical rituals with sufficient strength of intention, they will find means for doing so somehow. If they have not sufficient interest in the matter to discover this for themselves, they would be useless ritualists anyway. Unless people care enough about magical rites to sacrifice their own comforts and convenience to gain time and experience, they have no hope of success anyway, and had better leave well alone. Such is probably the first test they will have to face. The Magical life presents one challenge after another at every step, and until the right answers are given, we can go no further. So far as time is concerned, how much of it does the average person devote to "pastimes" such as television, social occasions, etc? If the worst comes to the worst, it is always possible to rise a little earlier in the morning. Of course "time-gaining" goes against the grain. It has to. Yet we simply must find enough strength and ingenuity to achieve the precious moments necessary for Inner workings. The less time available, the more important it is to discover how to do a lot within a little of it.

As regards the place of working, few operators are fortunate enough to possess their own private Temples, or even to have access to a Magical Lodge, let alone own a whole set of Instruments. Such things take years to acquire, if ever indeed they do materialise. Nevertheless it is important that an effort be made to achieve some form of such necessities, because the magic lies more in the effort than the things themselves. A penknife for a Sword, a thimble for a Cup, a coin for a Shield, and a twig for a Rod, circled with plain

137

string for a Cord, will make a Magical pattern to an equal degree of any produceable by the finest artifacts. It is the work done with the Symbols that counts far more than their physical vehicles. If the working-place be no more, externally, than a small altar-shelf, or the corner of a room, it will be effective, provided it is used regularly and devotedly.

One important point is that magical accessories of places and instruments should be the best available to the practitioner. For a wealthy individual to use shabby or tenth rate material would be just as wrong as for a poor practitioner to bankrupt himself and his family by buying things far beyond his reasonable means. The Middle Way is the one to follow. All magical equipment should reflect creditably upon the user within his circumstances, leaning neither to extravagance nor ineptitude. Traditionally, it should be made by the practitioner himself as far as possible, and this is an ideal to strive for, because in perfecting the skills necessary for the work, the practitioner will also develop his own "Magical" ability. Craftsmanship and creative skills go together in any dimension of existence. Of the equipment, there will be more to say later, for it is entirely secondary to the ability of using it, which must be considered first, and may be trained with very ordinary materials available in most households. Unless a reasonable degree of ability can be gained with simple primitive means, it will be quite useless to obtain elaborate or expensive appurtenances. In Magic, the tools are made with the Craft, not the Craft with the tools.

The best basic of ritual training we can begin with is the disciplined use of the physical senses, or perhaps more correctly speaking, the physical ends of our senses, for our Inner awareness comes through extensions of these senses in other dimensions. Consciousness is consciousness in any state, and we simply shift its focus within the limitations of our vehicular faculties wherever this happens to be. During incarnation, the ends of our awareness extending into this world manifest via the four bodily senses. Taste and smell are really a single sense linked with oral and nasal receptors. The senses line with the Elements as follows;

FIRE	WATER	AIR	EARTH	
Sight	Taste-smell	Hearing	Touch	**PHYSICAL**
Perception	Savouring	**Learning**	Grasping	**MENTAL**
Vision	Absorbing	**Concording**	Empathing	**EMOTIONAL**
Illumination	Communion	**Harmony**	Incorporation	**SPIRITUAL**

This list has only been made in the broadest possible way in order to indicate the sensory extensions through the various types of channel. In reality we do not possess a number of different senses, but only one sense, Consciousness itself, operating in differing ways on diverse levels. It is important to approach our sense-study from this angle, otherwise we shall be lost in a maze of irrelevancies. There is an unfortunate heritage of belief that all matters of the senses were either wrong, immoral, or somehow undesirable. This is simply not true. Our sense-information on physical levels is very restricted, and bears only a distorted relationship to Inner realities, but the senses of our bodies are linked with those of our souls and united in the single Sense of Identity at our Origin. We must "track back" or transcend our senses until they lead us up the steps of their own ladder toward their Inner Source of Divine awareness. As always in ritual procedure, we start at the most available end and process along it as far as practicable.

A good commencement for sense-training is by re-constructing memories and then projecting them. Let us take a photograph of some familiar person and place from the past, look at it, and then "live ourselves into it". This must be done systematically and constructively as a controlled activity, rather than a haphazard jumble of impressions. We may use the traditional Question and Answer method, provided we let the Questions be asked as if the picture itself were posing them, and the Answers be given as a wholehearted reactional response from ourselves. Each sense must be taken in turn, and evoked as definitely as possible. Suppose we have a picture of a friend or relative taken in their garden. Our session with it might run like this.

The Person in the picture speaks to us, we must try and recall their tone of voice, way of speaking, and vocal mannerisms, reproducing these from our memory. We shall hear them in our minds via the Inner equivalent of Air. The words they speak will be made up out of our memory banks of course, but the control will be our own. Let the picture open.

Them: "Do you remember who I am?"

Us: "Yes. So and so."

Them: "What colour clothes do I wear?"

Us: "Such and such."

> *(Here we must try and see the right colours appearing. The picture should preferably be a black and white one for this reason.)*

Them: "What sort of aroma do you associate with me?"

> *(Here we recall any particular smell, such as scent, cooking, paint, or anything at all likely to connect with the place or person.)*

Us: "It was so forth, and we used to enjoy such which together, didn't we?"

Them: "Can you hear me speaking, or remember what we listened to?"

Us: "Yes, very well."

> *(Here any favourite tune, or other sonic association is evoked.)*

Them: "What did this feel like?"

> *(Here the "picture person" must indicate some physical object such as clothing, a utensil, tool, or whatever may be handy in the picture.)*

Us: "It felt like this".

> *(Here we must reproduce in ourselves the feeling of actually touching whatever it was, trying to experience the sensation it gave us.)*

This bare outline should provide us with the essentials of the exercise. It is important to work along these lines, so as to develop the reactive pattern between objective awareness, and subjective realisation. We are using a control to evoke a creative reply from our Inner being, and following the principles on which ritual is carried out. We may elaborate the picture exercise as much as we like, and we shall learn a great deal about processes of consciousness by devising variations of it. Its use is to help us "come alive" in our Innerworld, yet keep full control over our senses therein, because we ourselves direct what they do. We could have a lot of fun and entertainment playing with pretty pictures in this fashion, but such practices are minor games meant to lead towards major abilities, and we should treat them as such. What matters is that we have activated a Symbol (the picture person), in such a way (the Queries and Responses), as to cause a genuine Inner experience related to distinctions of consciousness (our sensory evocations). In other words we have successfully "worked a Rite." All we have to do now is apply the same principles according to the various Mystery customs.

If, in place of the picture-person, we substituted a "God-Form", or "Telesmatic Image", and replaced the homely sensory-suggestors of the picture with Magical Symbols, we would be working ritual magic. The difference is that we would be using an established method of "Bridge-building" between the physical world and Inner Dimensions which should make contact at the "Inner end" with definite Intelligences using the same patterns or Symbols to establish contact with *us*. Whether we call them "Gods", "Masters", "Brothers", or anything else, they really exist, and inter-relate with us in the same Great Plan in which we are all participants. Normally we are unaware of their existence because our senses are focussed into physical limits. It would be useless for us to be aware of such Beings unless our Inner senses were fully under our control. Hence the need for disciplined exercises.

So we must proceed methodically to take one Magical Symbol

after another and "rise from it" by transforming an Outer sense to an Inner one. It may help if we think of our circled cross with the senses lined up with the correct quarters, the circumference representing the Time-Space rate, and the centre being the Stillness-Silence cessation point, or interval-factor. This will give us the procedure. If we exercise the senses one after another, and then make combinations with them, we shall be able to build up whole impressions of our own, or receive them from other sources of consciousness.

Using our Sphere classification, we can sense-Symbolise our way up and down the whole Tree. Suppose we select a Venus-contact in the Sphere of Victory. We visualise a predominance of green, suggesting perhaps grass, or maybe the sea from which Aphrodite sprang. Beautiful forms also must arise in our minds. Then we try and call up the thrilling and lovely perfumes associated here, rose and sandalwood or such. Now we switch on the sound, and evoke inwardly the sort of music or sound effects we link with this Sphere. Lastly we evoke in ourselves the type of touch we would expect here. The touch of some loved person perhaps. An embrace. We should not forget that Venus links with pet animals so we might imagine the feel of some animal friend's coat, or the way they pushed themselves against our hands. What matters is that we should put ourselves through the whole series of classified sensory experiences associated with the seventh Sphere as a controlled evocation. We must really feel the whole exercise as something which has genuinely happened to us Inwardly because we have "put ourselves through it". Each Sphere should be sensorily dealt with in this fashion, building up events and experiences according to their nature. It is most important not to place the associations of one Sphere into another, though those of any can be mixed with others externally via the appropriate Paths.

This needs further comment. While "In" the Victory Venus-Sphere, we must be "In" that sensory-state and none other. The moment we quit that frequency-range, we quit that Sphere, and in Magic we must learn to "keep tuned" to any state of being with which we seek contact, just as a radio must stay tuned to one station even though it will receive all. In order to develop this ability, we therefore practice the sensing of the Spheres in such a way, till we can switch on and off at will, keeping station as long as necessary.

To make a nice little ritual practice of this, we might try the elementary procedure of using a green light, rose perfume, playing the "Venus" section of the "Planets" by Holst, and touching something pleasant, while we direct our whole consciousness towards the Idea of Love, which we may personify as a beautiful Being of either sex or neither. Every Sphere should be treated in this manner until the associations really begin to make their homes in our consciousness, and will arise when any of their links are contacted. Theoretically we ought to be able to look at any colour and call up its whole chain of associations, hear any type of sound and do the same, or link any sense with its correspondences in connection with any other sensory linkage. What matters is the fundamental process of associative classifications, and their control by use of the Magical Symbol pattern in which they unite.

If we take each sense in turn, and make an association train through the ten Spheres, it will help to show how ritual magic may be studied and practised. Individuals vary considerably about what they link with which, but there are broad overall lines on which most people agree, and everyone must fill in the gaps for themselves with their own particular bits and pieces. So long as we choose something to see, smell-taste, hear, and feel, in connection with each Sphere, we shall be provided with ritual material. There is no one particular thing alone for each category, but rather types of things from which we may select specimens as suitable Symbols linked with their associates. We should end up with a cross-reference sensory-linkage broadly covering the whole of represented Creation. Each sense will link with the ten Spheres, and each Symbol with the senses throughout a whole Sphere. A specimen list might read thus;

LIGHT TYPE	VISUAL SYMBOL	OLFACTORY SYMBOL	AURAL SYMBOL	TACTILE SYMBOL
1 Bright Spot	Focussed Light point	Ambergris	Highest audible note sustained	A fine point just felt
2 Alternating Flashes	Circle	Musk	Reiterated rhythm	Oscillatory vibration
3 Very dim	Triangle	Myrrh	"Saturn"	Heavy weight
4 Blue	Square	Cedar	"Jupiter"	Firm comfort
5 Red	Pentagram	Ammonia	"Mars"	Sharp painful
6 Yellow	Hexagram	Frankincense	"Hymn to Sun"	Warm and cheerful
7 Green	Heart	Rose	"Venus"	Soft and pleasing
8 Orange	Caduceus	Storax	"Mercury"	Light and springy
9 Violet	Crescent	Jasmine	"Moonlight Sonata"	Cool and smooth
10 Ordinary	Cube	Dittany	"Bolero"	Rough and knobbly

These Symbols though perfectly workable, are quite arbitrary. Many other associations are possible or necessary. It is unlikely that many workers would have a complete range of perfumes or sound effects. Where these cannot be used physically, they must be evoked mentally, and everyone should make up their own list of equivalents. Coloured lights are not very difficult these days, and we might draw Symbols on cards for visual purposes, or use actual pictures. Musical effects may be taped easily enough, and all the examples of music given are available on popular records. Still, some workers might prefer the rhythm-taps instead, or use natural sounds such as a burning fire for Solar contacts, hollow drumming for Earth, swift whistling for Mercury, and so forth. It sounds like a Zen koan to ask: "What is the smell of Wisdom?" but that is a necessary question. The traditional link given is Musk, but there may be associations with school smells, or perhaps a strong sea breeze. There is no reason why there should not be a great many sensory links with each Sphere, but the first task of an investigator is to accept or work out a practical set of such links and then commence utilising them experimentally.

Let us try a training session along the Justice-Mars lines. For this, we will select a red lamp, a Pentagram, sword, or some such visual Symbol, a smell of ammonia or any acrid scent, the "Mars" section of the "Planets" on a record or tape, and something to cause us a sense of discomfort if not pain. A good arrangement is to trace or imagine the Pentagram on the floor to a convenient size, and tightly grip the hilt of a drawn sword in the right hand, held at the "carry" position. The music is switched on, and carrying the sword firmly, we start patrolling the sides of the Pentagram with a military step like a sentry, turning the angles smartly as we come to them. So much for the purely physical side of the operation. The real Magical work is to translate all these sensory-impressions into Innerworld effects, and this is where effort and energy must be liberally expended to get results.

Every single sense-stimulus has to be firmly linked with an Inner equivalent in the most definite manner so that these combine into an overall pattern of operative consciousness. The whole action is not unlike focussing a microscope. First there is a general light impression, then a series of blurs which gradually take on formations, colours, becoming sharper and more distinct until the maximum point of definition is reached, and the picture impinges on the consciousness of the observer with sufficient clarity to cause an effect therein. This is what we must do with our ritual practice, except that we are focussing past the point of our merely human observer-awareness, and reaching the Inner Consciousness behind our ordinary minds. It all depends how strongly and clearly we make this degree of definition, as to the level of Inner consciousness it will reach. The Qabalah postulates the levels of this in four general stages behind humanity. The Intelligences, the Angels, the Archangels, and the God-Aspects. Names are arbitrary, but the idea of a Single Awareness extending gradually from Its Source through all Its channels including ourselves is common to all Systems of belief and practice.

Most operators will do well enough if they can "focus back" far enough to reach even a degree or so behind their normal consciousness. In a full-scale Rite, this should reach an immediately contacting Intelligence, who "relays" it to "Angelic" level, from whence it is re-routed via "Archangelic" to God-level. Response-effect should return via the same channels in the reverse order. It is important that we realise our purely human limits, and fully understand that once we have extended our energies as far as we can along our lines of Inner existence, these must be "picked up" and carried on by other types of conscious beings than our own. Most of our human energies expended in processes of consciousness are dissipated and absorbed normally through immediate living. Comparatively little is sufficiently channelled and beamed so that it will reach higher levels as an individualised distinctive effort. Unless we are able to do this, we shall receive no response in defined terms. It is like picking up a telephone instrument without dialling a number. We would be in potential contact with every subscriber in the world but none in particular until the coding numerals select our choice. The aim of ritual training is to learn how to dial specific codes and keep in contact with our Inner "subscribers" once this has been made.

So we will return to our tramping around the pentagram while we try and keep ourselves aligned with the Fifth Sphere of Justice to the exclusion of everything else. This is the whole object of the exercise during its first stages, and we must employ every sensory impression and reaction for such a purpose. To begin with, we shall be seeing everything in a red light at the lowest end of the physical spectrum. We are looking mostly at the Symbol of the Sword which our tight grip assures us we are holding. This tells us a great deal, for it links us with all the meditations we should have worked on the Sword. Mainly it suggests that we have to sharpen up our attention until it is literally as keen and pointed as the Sword itself, being like the edge or point which theoretically fines down to a NIL extension beyond physical matter. If we could sharpen our consciousness like a Sword until it entered NIL dimensions, our object would be achieved. As we concentrate on the Sword, we must try and make ourselves as like it as possible in principle.

Our sight and touch is also linked to the pentagram pattern and method of partolling it. This "pattern-treading" is a very old magical custom common to all Systems, and equates with "pacing up and down" to aid thought. It can be turned into any form of dance or rhythmic motion, and its principles will be considered more fully when "Magic Circles" are dealt with. The Pentagram may be simply patrolled like a sentry, or a sort of emphatic dance-step is easy to evolve by slapping the feet firmly down, pausing between each advancing step, and moving the Sword sharply up and down a few inches vertically as if its edge were severing whatever obstacles might prevent our progress. The more determined we make ourselves, the tighter we must grip the Sword hilt. It may help if we attach some particular meaning to each side of the pentagram which will connect with the main idea. Perhaps the concepts of Duty, Discipline, Requital, Respect, and Firmness may be suitable. As we make our way along the sides of the figure, we should think of each in turn.

The sense of smell is tuned in to the pungent aroma of ammonia or something similar which suggests severity. A practical method is to soak some into a wodge of cotton wool which is held in the left hand and wafted toward the nostrils occasionally. With a range of perfume bottles and an old fashioned vinaigrette or similar means of holding scented pads, the entire gamut of the Spheres may be very neatly scent-linked. A really modern method which is practical but unaesthetic is the wearing of a cheap "smog-mask" which has removable filters. The merest trace of the requisite perfume on such a filter ensures it beings literally "under one's nose" all the time. There is no real reason why the expensive and somewhat rare traditional perfumes should be the only ones used in magic. Nowadays there exists an enormous choice of reasonably priced synthetic scents which will adequately serve as associative links. It is a question of making suitable attributions to the various Spheres, and this is a task for individual workers themselves.

Conjoining smell, taste may be linked in by sucking something rather sharp such as peppermint, or for really tough palates a fragment of chili. We should not forget the sweetshop and the kitchen as providers of magical materials. By aligning specific flavours with the Spheres, we shall be able to establish that much closer contact with them. With the Sphere of Justice and Severity for example, we need smell-taste stimuli to evoke these Principles. Not exactly soft or pleasant perhaps, but something to arouse a sense of necessity, strictness, or other responses suitable to the Fifth Sphere. Smell-taste is a leading sensory director, meaning more to many animals than either sight or hearing. A single whiff of some associative scent, and we are reminded of persons, places and circumstances in the most vivid possible way. Distances in Time or Space are bridged more rapidly by smell than most other means, and perfumes have always played a major part in Magic.

One old "Magical secret" connected with the Rod, was that it had a built in perfume point which could be altered to suit the operation. This was usually a twist of coloured wool or material heavily impregnated with animal or vegetable odour. The officiant would either smell this themselves from time to time during a ceremony, or waft it toward others to call their attention towards its significance. Nowadays, this might be much more neatly done by making a cylindrical "scent cartridge" for insertion in a cavity near the tip of a Rod. This could be changed to suit every different operation, and the cartridges would be easily rechargable with a drop of the appropriate scent. As the Rod is moved around, any good modern perfume should be plainly perceptible around a small room with an average temperature. Such a "scent-Rod" is well worth making, even if it is a ball of cotton wool on the end of a stick, because it makes scent-stimulus control possible.

Although we have chosen the "Mars" section of the "Planets Suite", there are many others suitable, and it is possible that "Mars" may not be long enough for experimental exercises. Really consciencious workers should put about half an hour of "Fifth Sphere" music and sound effects on tape. The machine can always be switched off at will. Even without music at all, the stamping of feet on the ground in a determined manner suggests advancing armies, alert sentinels, the approach of Fate, or the "Left-Right" of the Scales of Justice. A very great deal is possible with suitable footwork, and types of mime-dance should be worked for each Sphere. They will suggest themselves easily enough with a little thought, because they fit in with the base-pattern marked out on the ground.

If all, or most of these conditions have been fulfilled, we should find ourselves in the middle of a magical exercise aimed at "keying-in" with the Fifth Sphere of Justice. The totality of our physical senses will be engaged in responding to stimuli specifically linked with this particular Sphere by itself. This is the simple part of the operation. Now we must begin "lifting off", or "rising away" from the purely physical level, and penetrating as deeply as we can toward the Innerworld on this controlled frequency alone. It is most important to keep "on the beam" and not deviate from the exact line of consciousness we have evoked. This is the difficult part of the exercise for a Western mind untrained in holding concentrated thought-projections for any length of mundane time. Such is the only type of consciousness that is able to "slip between the worlds" and establish intelligent contact from one world to another.

This can be illustrated easily by setting a radio set to Medium or Short wave, and rotating the tuning knob very rapidly from one end of the range to the other in quick succession. No programmes will be heard, but only a series of odd little noises as the sensitive focus of the radio whizzes back and forth across all the stations. The briefest sound or so from a large number of programmes makes no sense at all. This demonstrates the confusion resulting from an average human mind skating hurriedly across the surface of consciousness receiving only the merest fractions of the innumerable channels connecting at right angles as it were, and leading to the Innerworld. To receive or transmit consciousness along any of these channels, we have to do the equivalent of keeping our tuning dial still while we "home in" on our target. This is almost as difficult, and certainly comparable with, guiding a missile across Space. Yet Magicians must learn the art of "Micro-cosmonauting" and guide their "consciousness-capsules" through Inner Space until the intended target is reached.

The purpose of physical procedures is to provide the initial "thrust" to get off the ground with, but once away we must stay on course and maintain velocity or we shall return to base with a bump. To keep course, we shall have to "think very thin" which means that rigid control must be applied to both sides of our consciousness so that it stays on the mark we are aiming at and remains there. This calls for intense concentration which is very far from being a static procedure. To concentrate, means that though we must prevent our normal consciousness from wandering sideways away from where we have aimed it, we must push it as far and as hard as we can along the Inner course we have selected. We must make a right-angle turn away from our normal direction of awareness and follow the projection-path we have chosen into Inner Dimensions.

Since this is a major magical method, it needs a little explaining. Our normal life-consciousness as human individuals follows a progressive line through a state of existence to which we relate ourselves via sensory contacts. It seems to us that we are doing or being an enormous number of different things, but in reality we are only varying the ways and times we encounter the same fundamentals. All we meet with are re-combinations of the same basics, or constants, from which our conscious existence derives. These are what we should concern ourselves with in Magic, for once we master them, we master Life itself as we have to live it. The force-flow of these constants is cross-wise to that of our normal awareness, and there are whole states of existence intersecting our own of which we are usually quite unconscious, or only vaguely aware.

So far as we are concerned, the lines of consciousness leading from our normal state to what we know as Inner Life, are distinct from each other as specific categories (or frequencies) of energy.

Hence the Qabalistic classification of them as "Spheres". Other Systems refer vaguely to "Rays" or "Planes", but the principles are the same. Normally our depth of perception is only concerned with physical living, and we only have minimum conscious extensions Inwardly. Our Magical practices should enable us to turn our awareness through a ninety degree arc so that as our perception swings away from the material line, its depth extends more and more into Inner Existence. What matters above all, is that we must keep full control over this process so that we can use it at will. Otherwise we shall experience nothing but the wildest confusions.

The whole purpose of our physical ritual behaviour is to direct and focus our consciousness along the depth-axis of its fundamental frequencies. If all our material senses are actively engaged with stimuli that point in only one direction, we shall eventually be bound to turn ourselves that way Inwardly, and respond to whatever reaches us from thence. Practice and perseverance will positively produce results. It may be that at first we shall have to tramp around the pentagram for a solid hour before feeling that anything has been accomplished, but once the bridge has been built over the division between the Dimensions, contact becomes progressively easier

Therefore we continue our pentagram-patrol until it gets to an automatic level and we are consistently reproducing our sensory pattern as a mechanical activity. This may sound terribly monotonous, but it provides the working basis or foundation over which we shall attempt to build the turning-point of our Inner awareness. With practice this process may be reduced to moments, but the initial work of laborious sense-patterning is absolutely necessary. Primitives do this by drumming and repetitive chanting while making rhythmic movements. We can see this in operation on modern dance-floors, and it is quite effective. Indian yogis reduce the practice to such a fine art that they can accomplish it by mental "Mantras" alone. The exercise of the "Rosary" works along the same principles. In essence, we are converting purely mechanical physical efforts into specialised Inner energies directed toward categorical Intelligences operating through their own particular channels. It is this intentional selection of the whats, whoms, and wheres of consciousness that makes our activity into an act of Magic.

There are very many Paths which will lead us from Outer to Inner Life, but the Spheres and their Pathways are, so to speak, the safe highways that offer us the best possible protection and means of contact with other types of consciousness than ours. They have been designed for that very purpose, and if we keep within their framework we can at least rely on receiving responsible guidance from those who control their Inner workings. All concepts of malice or evil have been excluded from the Spheres, and in the Fifth Sphere of our present working for example, there is no room at all for vengeful or angry thoughts. There may be fearsome or painful matters to face there, but only on principles of the strictest Justice and correction of unbalanced conditions. Sheer necessity for taking drastic measures toward perfection would motivate Fifth Sphere activity, and any ideas of wrathful Gods are completely out of place and inaccurate. It would be quite useless to attempt directing the energies of this Sphere against other human beings out of personal spite. Being fundamentally based on the Principle of Justice, all released energies would first tend to correct any injustice motivating such release, and the ill-wisher would be duly dealt with. It is as well to bear these points in mind while we plod the pentagram.

Once our sensory-pattern has built up, we must translate it into terms on the next level of consciousness and repeat its process there. The Qabalah calls this level "Angelic" or "Formative", and here we are concerned with the forms of Justice and the specific ways it may be applied by "Angels" or agents appointed for this particular purpose. Therefore we must keep our consciousness entirely to this mark and none other, until this too becomes an automatic affair. There are many methods of this. We can visualise "Angels" with fiery swords engaged in purging away filth and corruption from anything. Whatever images we choose, we should respond in ourselves to them, and feel we are actively engaged in furthering their work. Perhaps we may take some particular circumstances about which we have strong feelings in connection with Justice—or the lack of it. As we plod round the pentagram we bring this to mind and imagine as powerfully as possible the Angels of Justice and ourselves engaged in doing all we can to put things right. When this becomes a repetitive process, we should start shifting our consciousness back another level to that of the "Archangel" or Creative Intelligence.

Here the actual forms that Justice takes on material levels ceases to interest us. We must concern ourselves with creating Justice wherever a need for it exists. We have already admitted such a need, and now we must assist the Great Archangel of Justice to create just the type of Justice to deal with the circumstances we have been considering. There are many varieties of Justice, each applicable to different necessities. It is the responsibility of the Archangel (working through us) to select precisely the right choice and create it to suit the occasion. When this has been done in our own minds, and is operating automatically, our "rising" consciousness must be directed to the highest or "God-state".

On this top level of working, we must deal with nothing except the pure Principle of Justice itself. The "God-Aspect" is the Origination of Justice, from which Point this Principle extends throughout the whole of Existence. Here, Justice emerges from NIL and exerts its influence throughout our entire state of being. This is where the Universal Consciousness we call "God" typifies Itself into a specific stream of energy resulting in what we recognise as "Justice". In our present magical practice, we are attempting the same thing on a very much lesser scale.

Assuming all these processes of consciousness have been followed, it will now be necessary to "return to earth" by descending the ladder in reverse order. From the realm of pure Principle, we come down through the Creative and Formative levels until finally we find ourselves back in our pentagram-patrol which may now be ceased while we think things over.

If this exercise has been worked with even the slightest degree of success, it will have accomplished several remarkable things. From simple physical sensations concerned with Justice, we shall have progressively lifted ourselves through three successive stages of consciousness until the Divine level is reached as nearly as we can, and then a return made to physical levels by the appropriate channels. A direct chain of linkage will have been established between our purely physical and most abstract spiritual states of being. Furthermore, these links will have been formed through a category of consciousness which connects directly with Inner realities. We shall have practised and learned a controlled method of relating ourselves with Inner Life throughout its different levels.

Training-patterns on similar lines to the foregoing one should be worked out for each of the other nine Spheres, and persisted with until they become familiar processes. The fundamental procedure must be along these principles:

1. Selection of Sphere.
2. Contact on Sensory levels.
3. Raising consciousness from Sensory to Formative.
4. Raising consciousness from Formative to Creative.
5. Raising consciousness from Creative to Originative.

Then of course the return journey will be made in reverse order.

All these alterations of consciousness which seem so cumbersome and elaborate when described in detail, are only momentary matters after a reasonable amount of basic practice. Eventually even a single sensory impression should provide a key for the rest. It is only necessary to think of any Sphere-colour in order to evoke the other associative sense-data. Since we are surrounded by such colours in normal life, we must establish some kind of control to prevent ourselves "drifting away" from ordinary living on such slight provocations.

This practical safeguard is called the "Entry-Symbol". We must make an arrangement with our own consciousness that unless we use it, we shall remain in our ordinary states of mind occupied with the affairs of this world. What is more, we must keep such an agreement scrupulously, and never under any circumstances attempt even minor magical operations without using the Entry (and Exit) Symbol appropriate for the task. It is most unwise to seek entry into exalted or mystical states of consciousness except through doors to which we firmly hold the keys. All that is needed is a suitable Symbol, and an association with "Inning" or "Outing". Often the Pylon or Gateway is used, a visual impression being built up in the mind before each operation of the Portal between its Black and White Pillar, and the definite thought of "I am coming In" or "I am going Out" evoked. Sometimes the .Knocks of the Sphere sought are mentally given. For most average work however, it is quite sufficient to make the Sign of the Cross saying at the Entry or commencement: "*In* the Name of the Wisdom etc." and in conclusion; "*Out* of the Wisdom, etc." What really matters is that we keep our various types and levels of consciousness to their proper channels and courses by means of simple Symbolic Keys.

Suppose, for instance, we have so conditioned ourselves that we could not possibly feel angry until brought into contact with the Symbol of a blood-red Sword in flames burning downward instead of upwards. Such an unlikely combination controlling an entire emotion, would mean that we should never be angry unless we wanted to be with sufficient force to evoke this triply complex Symbol. By using Symbols to control our various energies, we are making the most practical use of Magic, and it is with ritualised practices that we learn this art. Given the minimum necessary number and species of Key Symbols, we can control every energy we are likely to meet with in our Existence, provided sufficient time and effort is put into the task. More than one lifetime may be needed.

It is all a question of operating from a deep enough level of consciousness. The laws of consciousness are very similar to those of Light, for consciousness proceeds from a common Source we sometimes call the Divine Mind, and "illuminates" all matter from "Inside" much as the Sun "illuminates" the same matter in our Universe from "Outside". Once this principle is grasped, most occult affairs become much easier to understand. Each one of us consists of an atomic arrangement or "body" capable of being "illuminated" by Inner and/or Outer Light. The breakup of our bodies at "death" does not put out our Inner Light any more than a decaying leaf puts out the Sun. Our real Life *is* the Light. Once we identify with It, we attain immortality.

Just as we focus and deal with ordinary Outer Light in physical ways, so can we make use of Inner Light by equivalent methods. It can be concentrated, diffused, set to specific colour-frequencies, or otherwise produce calculated effects. Colour "therapy" works along these lines by inducing response from individual patients. It is not the physical light that does anything, but their own Inner Light responding along an equivalent frequency. Hence the importance of colours in ritual Magic. We should be able to "set ourselves" for any colour frequency we choose to suit the particular operation.

This is quite an important basic exercise of a very rewarding nature. Most Occult Systems teach methods of "Inner Lighting," though few are very specific as to details. Teaching a Light how to shine presents the same difficulties as teaching water how to be wet. Fundamentally, we must realise that as our very bodies consist of radiant energies locked into atomic structures, we really do emit Light from ourselves along frequencies beyond those normally visible to our purely physical eyesight. Just as we "see" the material world around us by means of light emanating from physical sources, so do we "see" the Innerworld by means of light radiating from our own Inner beings. We must become our own "Suns", capable of illuminating the Inner states around ourselves.

A good training exercise is to sit in a darkened room or Temple before some devotional Symbol and try to see it clearly with the Inner Light radiating from ourselves. We may start with an electric torch or spot-lamp held on the knees. This is switched on and off quite rapidly and the Symbol observed by its momentary light. Then we go to work on the after-image, building it up as strongly as possible in our minds, but making ourselves the source of light by which it is seen. We should think of all the little atomic "Suns" in ourselves shining together because they are powered by the spiritual. Sun releasing Light through us. We do not have to *make* this Light, but only *clear ourselves* sufficiently for it to shine through. It will come by itself once we open ourselves to it from inside.

Undoubtedly the most concise instructions for "putting on the Inner Light" are given at the beginning of Genesis, and we cannot do better than follow them. In meditation we must "brood over the darkness within us" until we get the feeling of floating like God upon the face of our own waters. Then we must "Utter the Word" by willing with all the force at our command: "LET THERE BE LIGHT". At this point we picture and experience the Divine Spark at our very centre opening up into a Light that radiates through every particle of us so that we become a Shining Being, pouring forth Light everywhere. We must not look into the Light, but out of it, so that whatever we see will reflect the Light coming through us. At first, it may be helpful to sit with an actual lamp which is switched on when the command of "LIGHT" is given. This is only to give us an idea of what to do in ourselves so that we can imitate the effect with our Inner faculties. No amount of purely physical light will induce Inner Light to shine, but it does encourage us to "switch on".

Once the "knack" of "lighting up" is developed to even a slight degree, we should try the experiment of looking at things Inwardly by our own light. Let any Symbol be taken at random, a Tarot card will do admirably, and concentrated upon with the realisation that we are illuminating its Inner content ourselves. We look at the thing physically, and proceed something after this fashion;

"I am seeing this Symbol with my physical eyes by the ordinary light in this room. That is not all I see. I myself am shining strongly at the Symbol, and my Light is becoming brighter all the time. By this Light I am seeing the Inner meaning of the Symbol. It is becoming more than signs on cardboard, and is presenting its actual Inner reality to me. Now I see clearly what it signifies. This is what is meant by revelation. This is Insight. I am seeing with the eyes of my soul."

At this point the physical light may be switched off or dimmed down, and the Inner Light intensified as much as possible, so that physical appearances mean little, and Inner appearances mean much. As the physical side of the Symbol fades out, so must the Inner side become plainer and plainer, because of the Light we are focussing upon it. Finer points of the Symbol should be singled out and illuminated with all the power we command. It is quite surprising what we shall learn by the use of this exercise.

Although we must feel ourselves to be, as it were, entirely incandescent with Light, the phenomenon should always remain in our control. The main point from which this Light is projected is not in the physical body at all, but from a position somewhat above the top of the head. We may think of ourselves as not unlike a lighthouse, having a beam of Light coming from just above us, which we direct to any degree of direction or intensity we like. The Light above us however, shines directly downwards into us, and our non-physical receptors situated approximately at forehead (Originative), heart (Creative), Solar plexus (Formative), and reproductive centre (Expressive) levels, act as prisms turning the rays at right angles to their primal course. This picture is far more metaphorical than literal, but it provides an idea of the general principles. What really matters is that we achieve the ability to turn this Inner Light on or off at will.

Another good exercise with Light is to remain a while in a very dimly lit place and try to brighten it up with "soulshine". This may also be done Inwardly during periods of despondency or depression which can be "shone away" by turning on the Inner Brilliance especially from the Heart centre and letting it radiate gloom away. Not easy perhaps, but positively possible. Difficult situations or problems can be considerably lightened by using the Light technique in even the most elementary way.

It is useful to link Inner Lighting with breathing exercises. Just as physical air brightens a flame with its oxygen, so does its Inner equivalent help the Inward Light shine more clearly. We should adopt our meditational attitude, accept the Light Above through its focal point at the top of the head, then breathe slowly in physically, at the same time indrawing the Air Element from the Inner atmosphere around us. We must imagine the Air and Light meeting each other particularly at whichever centre we wish to illuminate especially. As we exhale, the Light must be "blown up" much as a fire is blown up with bellows or a gas flame increased by air pressure. By this means Inner Light may be intensified and concentrated very considerably, until it becomes what used to be known as the "Holy Fire". A great deal of practical magic may be accomplished with its aid.

Once the ability of "Light-breathing" is developed to any degree, specific portions of the spectrum should be experimented with. We should be able to shine in any particular colour suitable to an operation, and change our colour at will to adapt ourselves with any given set of circumstances. The Sphere-colours are the keys which make this practical. Once the Sphere of an operation or circumstance is known, its necessary colour may be selected easily. If we consider the three primary colours, it will be found they correspond with the three Pillars. Red for works of stringency, Blue for works of mercy, and Yellow for the harmony between both in the middle of the spectrum. These three will be our standing colours for elementary practices.

A useful training-device is either a lamp with three primary colour filters, or three coloured lamps which may be selected at will. A working-Symbol must be set up, and then dealt with by different lights. Instead of the abstract Magical Symbols, a photograph of someone may be used instead if this makes reactions easier. The essence of the whole exercise in all reactions on physical, emotional, mental, and spiritual levels must accord with the nature of the light frequency being used.

Let us suppose we have switched on the red light. We follow this by "shining Red" out of ourselves, and directing this end of the Inner Spectrum toward the Symbol or picture. Our whole being must be "tuned red", and the Symbol approached in that particular light only. This does not mean we must hate the subject of the

Symbol, or the person represented, but that we deal with it or them as if we were the power of Justice and Severity. We must see our subject strictly and stringently, though without anger or irritation. All traces of sentiment or pity must be eliminated, and absolute firmness insisted upon to the utmost degree. Adjustments are made on all levels. Physically we should be taut, emotionally stern, intellectually critical, and spiritually just to a hairsbreadth. Our watchwords —Discipline and Duty. Every energy we are capable of calling up must be directed along these lines toward the subject at which the exercise is aimed.

After a period of "being Red", we swing ourselves to the opposite end of the spectrum and "go Blue". Here the blue light is switched on, and everything geared up to the keynote of compassion and mercy, in which light we must deal with the same subject. It is important that the identical subject should be approached by the various lights at this stage of working. By the blue light emanating from ourselves, we now approach our subject with all the compassion and mercy we can command. Beneficence should pour out of us toward our point of aim. Physically we must make ourselves relaxed, emotionally tender, intellectually tolerant, and spiritually as merciful as we ourselves hope to receive mercy. Our watchwords will be Kindness and Forbearance. All this while we pour wave after wave of blue light from ourselves toward our Symbol-subject.

Lastly, we must swing back to the centre of the spectrum and "shine Yellow". Again the lights are changed outwardly and Inwardly. This time the whole keynote must be one of balance and harmony between the two extremes. In the yellow rays, we should see our subject in the light of sound judgement and intelligent appraisal. Physically we should be poised, emotionally responsive, intellectually appreciative, and spiritually balanced. We must take the mid-line attitude toward our subject, and try to see it in its own light. Since we are shining yellow ourselves, there will be a green side-effect if the subject is shining blue, or an orange one if it shines red. Otherwise our own yellow light will intensify with that of the subject. So far as possible, we should try to keep the yellow illumination focussed on our subject while we realise this will reveal its broadest band of truth. On the other hand we must never forget that only the red and blue ends of the spectrum will disclose details peculiar to their respective frequencies. Everything must be seen from all points of its spiritual spectrum if we are to make the best possible analysis.

After some experimental work in viewing various Symbol-subjects by different sorts of Inner lighting, we should repeat the experiments without use of the physical colours, but creating colour-conditions purely by our own constructive imagination. Once a suitable subject is set up, it should be approached in one coloured light after another all the way up and down the Spheres. Notes should be made of anything learned during this process, and the experience evaluated as far as possible. This will prove a most valuable piece of research into ritual, and provide the soundest possible basis for future colour-working. Given sufficient practice, it will also provide means for dealing with most situations in ordinary living, and be helpful for maintaining sound health of body, mind and soul. If we once master the art of controlling our feelings and consciousness by the use of simple colour-keys, we can relate ourselves in any way we like with the rest of Existence.

The secret of this depends on being able to keep our Inner Light in the proper channels of its spiritual spectrum, and shine however may be necessary to obtain effects on various frequencies. It is most important to keep the colours separated from each other and only blend them for particular purposes. Otherwise the Inner Light will produce nothing but confusion. An illustration of this may be made by running three brushes of colour in the order red yellow blue down a sheet of paper side by side. They make three perfect lines of colour. If at any point we stop and run them horizontally across each other's tracks, the result is a muddy mess. This, in effect, is what most people do with their Inner Light all the time. Run the separate colours into each other till they muddle themselves into a murky morass of meaninglessness. We must learn by ritualising with Inner Light, how to maintain its colour spectrum brightly and clearly so that it will paint perfect interior pictures for us.

One of the principle reasons why many working ritualists wear white robes is because white combines all colours and reflects them equally. Black, on the other hand absorbs all colours and neutralises them. Thus the use of both black and white vestments signifies an absorption of the unwanted portions of the spectrum, and a radiation of the selected light-frequency. Ideally, a magical operator should wear the colour of whichever Sphere is being worked with, or whatever colours are appropriate for the reason or subject of working. No amount of external colour however, will compensate for lack of Internal Light which must provide the real colours of any ritual. External colours of lights, robes, or other accessories only serve as reminders and guides for Inward activity. There is no use putting on the most colourful or gorgeous robe if you do not put on Inner colours to match it.

Since robing-up for ritual is basic to the rite itself, some practice in the art is called for. Robing should never be done carelessly or casually as if putting on fancy dress for fun, or hurriedly cramming oneself into some dubious disguise. The whole purpose of robing-up should be to make the necessary Inner adjustments for tuning the operator to exactly the right pitch for the forthcoming rite. Properly done, robing will accomplish exactly this, though not unless it has been practised sufficiently to make it effective.

The types of robes worn vary enormously with the System worked and the resources of the wearer. Most magical workers favour a cassock-like garment with close sleeves that are unlikely to knock candlesticks over or catch in other equipment. There may or may not be a hood attached to this robe. Hoods are not primarily worn to make the wearer mysterious, but to assist concentration by excluding side-views, and also for the practical reason of keeping the head warm during open-air workings. Hoods are quite a useful aid during meditation, since they also muffle distracting noises and give the sense of being "wrapped up in the subject". If an outer cloak is worn, the hood is often attached to this instead of the inner robe.

Traditional ceremonial dress of a magician consists of an Inner and Outer Robe, sandals (usually slippers nowadays), girdle, pectoral or collar, and cap or headgear. Adjuncts such as rings, stoles, or other ornamentation will depend very much on the nature of the rite being worked. All these robes may be simplified down to an apron with symbolic embellishments worn over ordinary clothing, or more simply still an appropriately coloured cord worn round waist or neck. What matters is that something physical is assumed to represent an actual non-physical change of appearance and personality for some particular magical purpose. This Inner change must take place in fact, and constitutes the real "robing up". It is an exercise in its own right, and must be treated as such.

Let us suppose we have the robes ready to assume. They should be neatly laid out in their order so that they may be put on with a minimum of trouble. First and foremost, we contemplate the robes briefly and make a realisation that we propose to change ourselves Inwardly to suit the occasion. It is understood that our ordinary everyday selves are inadequate for the magical task before us, and therefore we must become different in some way that will make us fit for such work. Somewhere in our own depths we really are the sort of person who is able to perform our proposed magical operation, and it is this individual we must now become. If we reach inside ourselves deeply enough, we can bring that aspect of us to the surface and link it with the symbolic clothing of its proper appearance. These are the clothes of our souls which we wear quite apart from our bodies, and this is how we look when our bodies will no longer be wrapped round us. Strictly speaking, we propose to remove the garments of flesh, and assume the robes of spirit. We intend to shine forth in our own true colours, and let our Heavenly beings appear through our earthly counterparts. For this reason the Inner Robe of Glory is worn beneath the Outer Robe of Concealment.

These are the type of thoughts to prepare us for robing. They can be summated into a prayer or statement-formula if required, but it is quite necessary that some such approach be made to the robing procedure. The realisation must not be "I am going to change my garments," but "I am going to change *myself*, for the purpose of so and so". Then we set about actually making this change while we assume the physical robes. It will help to quite an extent if the robes are arranged so as to give a general impression of bodily outline, or suggest a human figure in some way. They may be hung on separate hangers on the wall, one over the other with the head-gear above, and the slippers at the bottom. Ornaments should be by themselves on a side shelf or table.

We must see the robes as a characterisation of the being we would really like to become in order to work magical rites. A better, nobler, and far more competent being than the human standing before them. Our own selves of the future perhaps, whose likeness we intend to borrow for the moment so that this advance contact will help raise us even a single degree toward the reality. Such a better self will naturally have far more powers and abilities than we possess at present, and with the robes we shall assume at least a vestige of those powers and be able to exercise maybe a minute proportion of them. We must build up the best picture possible of the ideal individual into which we would wish to evolve, and realise that the robes before us present the symbolic appearance of this being which is our not-yet, but hoped-for Self. We must have absolute faith that we can and will become such a one if we spend the necessary time and energy for the purpose. Perhaps this thought of the difference between what we are and what we might be makes us feel rather humble or dissatisfied with our present inadequacies, and so we kneel before the Highest Power and send up a brief petition that one day we may indeed reach the reality our robes signify.

The first thing to do is be upright and face our task fairly and squarely. We therefore rise to our feet and join our hands close to the body about heart high. This will be the neutral position for the hands which is to be held between every use of them, and they should automatically return there when they have finished whatever they have been engaged with. The robes before us now become a portrait or mirror-image of the self we are going to assume, and it is as if we shall step forward into that personality, turn round, and emerge from the picture-plane as a new being. In fact it may be helpful to hang the robes over a reasonably sized mirror so that in the end we shall get an impression of our transformed selves. A tall narrow mirror for a full-length view would be ideal.

There is a proper sequence for robing if we are to get the most from the exercise. First come the sandals or slippers. We take the initial step by putting the left foot into its slipper and realising we have started our progress on this particular path. Then comes the right foot, and we know we are irrevocably committed to our present course of action. A dedication or affirmation should be made at each stage of robing, and we might say for instance:

"Firmly have I set my feet upon this Path of righteousness, nor shall I falter from it till my present purpose is accomplished."

The phraseology of such affirmations will vary to suit the user. Some prefer petitional prayers, and others plain statements of intent. What really matters is the clarity and sincerity of the formula which is best expressed as succinctly as possible. It may be spoken aloud or in the mind, but at all costs it must be uttered in the heart and meant with the whole soul. Once the footwear is on, we should feel able to go anywhere, and willing to walk across the whole Universe in search of the Truth we are seeking. Every step we take in them will carry us nearer our aim, and every inch of the journey be crammed with meaningful events. These magic shoes will take us the whole of our Way.

Next comes the Inner Robe of Glory. This may be either white or golden-yellow. The left arm is inserted first, and with the robe, we must "turn on the Inner Light" as strongly as we can. The breathing exercises will help. Here we should try to feel as light as possible, shining and rising with the Light of Glory pouring out of us. This is our Garment of Light in which we live apart from our physical bodies, and we should pray that when we attain the reality behind this symbol, we shall indeed be amongst the Shining Ones.

Now follows the controlling symbol of the Girdle. It forms the immediate Circle into which we are bound by our own wills, and its free ends connect with all other Links which join us up with Divine and Human entities. The girdle must be tied tightly enough so that we can feel its grip, and the knot is usually a "reef-knot" which cannot slip. Right over left, then left over right. This knot is the Hexagram, and carries the symbolic meanings thereof. As the girdle is tied, we should feel ourselves being tied in with all others who follow our particular paths, so that everyone is bound by a common Cord of Control. It is the umbilical cord attaching us to the Great Mother, and its colour or design should accord with the general intent of the Rite. If we are working on the Left Pillar, then the ends will hang on our left sides, if the Right Pillar is being used, our cords will hang on the right, and for the Middle Pillar the girdle will be central, hanging down in front of us. It should be noted that if the Cord were tied round our necks it would choke us, if round our ankles trip us, but being round our waist will support us where-ever we may be led by the Intelligences who hold the end. We should visualise ourselves as being a climber on the Holy Mountain, securely roped by our girdles. Our nearest Guide will have one end of the girdle, and we must offer the other end to whoever seeks our guidance along the narrow Pathway. In fact we may put this in practice when we have knotted the Girdle, by offering up one end with a prayer for its acceptance by a Leader in the Light, and holding out the other end with the sincere intention of helping any-one needing our assistance. The girdle ought to make us feel linked in with the Great Chain of Life, and as we are pulled up by those above us, so should we pull our weight for those below. Such should be the experience of girding ourselves, and the girdle is the horizontal limitation of the Three Rings.

The stole follows the girdle, and is tucked behind it to keep the ends in place. As we assume the stole, we should realise it indicates our limits of action in breadth as the second of the Rings. In effect it is the Right and Left Pillars, between which we have to keep an exactly Middle course. It should give us the feeling of defining our Path precisely. We are, after all, committing ourselves to our present course with a sense of dedication. We must not stray too far from it in either direction, but remain as poised and purposeful upon it as if we were walking a plank bridge across a chasm and relying entirely on the handrails each side to stay balanced. The stole and symbology embroidered on it, provides us with the necessary ideas for keeping ourselves between the bounds of our present purpose, and defines the edges of the Portal we intend to enter. Once the stole hang over our shoulders, we should feel as if we were supported on our right and left by guiding angels whose responsibility is to keep us upon our appointed way. Invocations may be made to such angels if required. The left-hand angel is supposed to tell us what not to do, and the right-hand angel informs us of what we ought to do. Together they make up the Yea and Nay of any matter. We may imagine them holding the ends of our stole, and trying to lead us along the Middle Path. When we have related ourselves to Inner Life by all the means afforded by the stole, we pass on to the pectoral.

This Symbol may take a number of forms. It hangs upon the breast suspended from either an ornamental chain or a cord of whatever colour harmonises with the rite being worked. Sometimes elaborate embroidered collar-pieces proclaim the wearer's status or office. The pectoral itself may be an ornate piece of jewellery or some very simple glyph traced on a metal plate or medallion. If it is square and flat with engraved designs, it is usually called a Lamen.

If the wearer happens to be a Christian, it would probably be a cross or crucifix, if a Jew, the Star of David, or if a Qabalist the Tree of Life. Otherwise the pectoral Symbol must bear some design which indicates the nature of the operation being undertaken, and the confidence of its wearer in the whole affair. Appropriate Divine Names and symbology are easily contrived if required, though a plain succinct statement or forceful written expression of intentions and beliefs will serve equally well. The fundamental principle of the pectoral must be that it expresses as concisely as possible the faith-pattern of its wearer. It must represent whatever we believe in with our whole hearts, and will stand by with our very souls. The pectoral shows what we proclaim ourselves to be before everyone else, and what we will defend with all our might. Without this quality of belief no magic would be possible in any case. Therefore it is no use making up pectorals from merely fancy designs that mean little or nothing to the wearer. Whatever Symbol we hang upon our breasts, must really and truly stand for what we genuinely believe in with all the force of our Inner Being.

As the pectoral is assumed, we should realise we are bringing the entire structure of our faith to bear upon the purpose of the rite to be worked. We must think "This is what I am in myself, and this is what I intend to do." The pectoral symbol and its cord fulfils the third Ring of Being, and completes the Limiting Principles. Our robing pattern begins to reveal itself. We first manifested Motion with the slippers, then became Light with the Inner Robe of Glory. After that we applied the Three Rings of Limitation by means of the girdle, stole and pectoral. We are creating our new personality according to the esoteric laws behind Creation itself. Let us continue what we have begun.

The next process in robing is the cloak or mantle, otherwise called the Outer Robe of Concealment. It signifies all the externalities surrounding our purpose and ourselves, in the midst of which we have our Inner Being. The mantle is the body in which we live, the Matter which Spirit animates, and everything extraneous to the essence of the rite in which we are engaged, yet which will prove necessary for its fulfilment. It is the Outside of the Inside we have been creating, and as it settles on our shoulders, we should feel the full weight of our responsibilities and burdens in bearing the consequences of all our actions, magical or otherwise. For this reason, mantles ought to be made of reasonably heavy material, and capable of the edges either coming together at the front, or being secured by a chain so as to reveal the central portion of our other vestments. Putting on the mantle should give us the experience of aligning ourselves with the objective part of our subjective Inner-world. Just as we are ordinarily conscious of ourselves with a whole material world full of other humans around us, so we must now make ourselves aware of our existence spiritually with an entire Inner creation peopled with other souls than our own. This is the "mantle" that surrounds us Inwardly, and that is the way we must try and feel when we assume the Outer Robe. Ideally it should be the colour suited to the magical operation, but otherwise it can be a true purple which is an exact balance of Red (Justice) and Blue (Mercy). Between its opening in the front, we should try and radiate the colour needed for the rite.

Assuming our mantle, means that we have accepted our position in the spiritual world around us which we are entering. We can send out recognitions to the Beings we believe are its rightful denizens. After all, we are adopting the dress of their country, and claiming citizenship among them. Prayers or invocations to such effect are very helpful here. If we expect to be recognised by higher intelligences than our own, then we must show ourselves capable of behaving in a way that arouses their sympathy towards us. It is only when we are able to assume our robes in such a way that they become evident to Innerworld entities, that these Beings are likely to accept us on terms of fellowship rather than patronage. With the mantle on our shoulders, we must attempt to put ourselves in the presence of our Inner Spiritual Superiors and Companions. We have become more than a solitary soul, and one of a Company, dedicated like ourselves to works of Light within Omnipotent Love. The mantle is our uniform proclaiming us a member, however humble, of the Holy Mysteries. It must be unthinkable we should ever dishonour it. We cannot act entirely on our own any more, but whatever we do will automatically make a contribution (or a detriment) to the Great Work on which the Company of Light is engaged. This is a thought which should add much to the weight of our mantle.

Now comes the headdress. There is no need at all to invent some wild and wonderful affair reminiscent of Bali dancers. Qabalists will adopt a plain square cap not unlike a biretta without its top adornments. Others may use some metallic circlet or fillet. It should fit the head firmly so its pressure can be felt without any particular discomfort. The whole purpose of the headdress is not to decorate ourselves or look important, but to symbolise and signify the Higher Consciousness to our own under the direction of which we must place ourselves in order to evolve spiritually. As ordinary humans, we are the intellectual product of many other minds than ours. All the thoughts of others we have encountered had their effect in making us as we are. Spiritually we must open ourselves to the consciousness of those Superior Intelligences who seek to lead us along the Path of Light if we are able to accept what they offer. They do not command us, but expect us to command ourselves.

Our assumption of the headdress means that we are willing to open our Inner Minds to the Wisdom that comes from contact with such Beings.

The headdress is therefore held above the head with both hands, and slowly lowered into position. As we feel it grip our head, we should send out as strong a thought as we can toward our Spiritual Leaders under whatever names we call them. We must ask them to make contact with our Inner awareness even more firmly than the headdress presses our temples. This pressure we can consider the token of their linkage with us, and as we feel it, so should we feel them pressing against our minds. We may think of our headdress Inwardly as being like a receiving apparatus tuned into our spiritual directors who transmit truth towards us. Qabalists may choose the Four Great Archangel Intelligences to line up with the four sides of their cap, and thus keep themselves aligned within their Creative Circle. Whatever method or system is used, the fundamental of linking our own consciousness with that of our Spiritual Superiors and co-operating therewith, must be tied in with the headdress.

Finally comes the Ring. It should be worn on the right forefinger, and signifies our own "marriage" with the Eternal One. We must literally put our hand out towards God with perfect faith that it will be taken hold of and we shall be led in the best way for us. The action is not unlike that of a child holding up a finger trustingly for an adult to grip while the child tries to stand or walk. The ring is held above the head with the left hand, and with eyes closed, the right hand with extended forefinger is raised slowly towards it. It should be felt that we are reaching as far as we can out of ourselves toward the Highest Power while we ask to be "taken in hand" and guided aright in the Path we have chosen. As the ring slides down our finger, it should seem like the answering grip of the Divine Hand.

Providing the whole robing procedure has been properly done, it will prove a most uplifting experience to prepare the practitioner for whatever rite may follow. When fully robed, it makes a useful meditation to gaze at the reflected image in the mirror and see not the ordinary self dressed up, but a preview of the personality we hope to reach in the course of our evolution. It will help the imagination if we view our image in semi-silhouette by the light of a single candle some ten feet from the mirror directly behind our backs while we are about a yard from the mirror. There is no point in making ourselves appear improbably wonderful or decorating ourselves with too-distant Divinity. It is best to choose the sort of individual we might feel sure of becoming within at least an incarnation or so. Even a brief glimpse across such a gap of time will bring our hope and its attainment closer together. As we think today, we become tomorrow, therefore we should think ourselves into someone worth becoming.

Disrobing naturally takes place in the reverse order, and as the robes and ornaments are taken off, their Inner equivalents must be restored to their places with acknowledgments and thanks to the various Powers linked symbolically with them. Eventually we come to the end of the robing-cycle at the point we commenced it, enriched by the entire experience to whatever degree we have earned. With practice, a full robing-up need only take a few minutes, yet it is capable of offering a gamut of spiritual stimuli which would otherwise take far longer to meet with. Such should always be the purpose of robing, which is pointless apart from its Inner opportunities. To assume a set of robes without going through the spiritual exercises which justify them, is a sheer waste of time and a total loss of advantage.

Few practitioners living in modern conditions are likely to possess anything resembling a full set of magical robes. Apart from Lodge aprons and collars, the simplest substitute for robes is the Cord. Anyone can make one, though it takes training and effort to use it in a ritual manner. The cord comes traditionally in three colours, White for the Neophyte or First Degree, Red for the Initiate or Second Degree, and Black for the Adept of the Third Degree. It should best be of silken material (or Nylon), but may perfectly well be made of plain hemp. The overall length of the cord should be the height of its owner. At one end is a spliced loop (female) and at the other a knot and tassel (male). By putting the tassel through the loop we make a running noose and all the symbology that may be attached to this. There are various systems of placing knots in the cord so as to give these meaning. One way is to line up the knots with personal body measurements. A knot is made so that it engages with the loop when the cord is tautly placed round the waist. Another knot checks the loop from tightening fatally when the noose goes round the neck. A further knot brings the loop to heart level. Others may be made to suit requirements. The cord then becomes the measure of its owner and none other. As such, it may be considered as a piece of personal clothing or with a stretch of imagination, a universal vestment.

To robe-up with only a cord needs the same precision as if all the robes were actually worn, which they must be—Inwardly. The general procedure goes along these lines. After preparatory prayers, the ends of the cord are held in each hand according to the polarity being worked. If female, the loop will be in the right hand, but if male, then the tassel. First the feet are set in the Path by standing on the centre of the cord and pulling it against the insteps while we dedicate the steps we propose to take. Then the Inner Robe Is assumed by throwing the cord centre over the neck and looping its tassel at its extremity. This gives the symbol of ourselves in the middle of an oval, which we then project mentally to the dimensions of our Inner Light shining around us with all its auric energy.

The Limitations are then applied. For the Girdle, we put the cord around our waist, for the Stole we hang it on each side of our neck, and for the Pectoral, we fix it with the loop at the heart-knot so that the tassel hangs down the middle of our body. To assume the cloak, we cast the cord around our shoulders and pull the ends with our hands to give a sense of weight. For a headdress, the cord is wound deosil around the head with tassel fixed so that it is just visible exactly between the eyes. This gives the Serpent of Wisdom Symbol. The cord may well be left in this position or in any other considered suitable for the rite. As a Ring, of course, the finger is inserted in the loop, and the other end offered to whatever Intelligence or Divinity is sought as a Leader.

A very great many occult exercises are possible with the aid of a cord, which was why it became so popular with almost every System. Its cheapness and adaptability made it an ideal tool for even the poorest worker. By and large, the secret lay in making the mind perform in its own dimensions whatever the cord could do on physical levels. Mind patterns could be "woven" like cord patterns, and these mind patterns were what "move" Spells. Different coloured threads indicated different kinds of consciousness, and their physical arrangements had to be projected into equivalent Inner patterns of power.

To demonstrate the principles of cord-working, we need only utilise the time-honoured custom of tying a knot in it to remind us of anything. The best way of doing this is to follow the procedure now outlined. Write the problem to be dealt with or remembered as neatly and concisely as possible within the compass of a small circle. A few keywords will do. Take the cord, or an ordinary piece of string a foot or so long, and make the beginnings of a knot with it. Hold the string so that the wording is read through the circle of the commenced knot. Concentrate strongly on the essence of the words while pulling the ends of the string slowly and steadily apart, keeping the tightening circle of the knot lined up over that of the words all the time. Keep the attention absolutely fixed through the knot while this is going on, and visualise the meaning of the words as caught up into the knot. The idea must be as if the problem were actually surrounded by the tightening knot and lifted bodily off the paper by it. As the hole of the knot gets smaller, so must our concentration become sharper like a beam of light being focussed to a point. When the knot is closed up, the ends of the cord should be pulled really hard while the mind tries to follow suit. Finally one end of the cord is released, and the thought made: "The end I hold belongs to me. The other one I offer to ————" naming whichever God or Aspect of the Universal Consciousness is firmly believed in. Quite a nice little rite may be built up along these lines, and the principles are applicable to a large number of various practices.

The mental and spiritual mechanics of such an exercise should be obvious enough, and serve to illustrate the practicality and value of ritual. If a simple piece of string can be used as an aid for evoking enough powers of concentrated consciousness from an individual to stay focussed on a single point for more than a few moments, then the string has done a remarkable job of work. The magic of course, lies not in the string, but in what it led a human mind to do. In its way, a cord or a piece of string supplies the raw material for magical manipulations rather like a lump of wax or modelling clay. It was not the wax image that had any effect in witchcraft or magic, but the mental moulding of it into patterns linked with Inner realities. The wax image only served as a medium for concentrating the consciousness of the operator with sufficient sharpness and duration upon the person or thing it represented in order to release energy Inwardly aimed at causing an Outer effect. Nevertheless the practice as such could produce results if deep enough levels of release were reached. Seldom an easy condition to guarantee, especially in a complex modern society.

Since the principles of the wax image or cord are magically associated with the sense of touch, we may as well deal with this extension here. Like other sensory phenomena, touch may be Ingoing or Outcoming relative to ourselves. As we have already seen, all the various ritual symbols may stimulate our touch-sense in ways which are ultimately destined to form power-patterns at effectual depths of consciousness—if they reach their objective. If we continue this cycle, we shall find that Inner power-patterns should project themselves from our depths via the return half of the circle, until they materialise into Outer forms of expression. In other words, if we think deeply and strongly enough about anything, it will formate into material levels eventually. True enough, they do indeed in one way or another. Practice will improve our production, and is basic to ritual work anyway, being frequently used during most rites in the form of manual gestures forming definite patterns. Let us consider this.

Supposing we were able to think right back into ourselves until we reached Originative level, then started thinking forward until we became Creative and thought about the idea of a Cup. From there, we pushed on again into Formation, and thought out a beautiful silver chalice, ornamented with gems in the most wonderful way. We could almost feel it at our very fingertips. Now comes the miracle. Out of those fingertips pours an amazing type of plastic energy capable of becoming anything at all we can fashion by shaping it up with our hands. After a few moments of imaginative work, a real solid chalice develops between our fingers and becomes a physical object that we set down and consider what to do with. The fantasy of this conjecture lies in the instant materialisation of exactly what was demanded. The rest is theoretically factual and practically applicable.

A working magician thinks and projects Inner power as far as possible towards materialisation, and relies on other agents to continue the cycle commenced. Of all sensory paths, that of touch puts us most finally in contact with material manifestation. Therefore, touch-projection is essential with magical practices, and our hands are the most specialised means of touch-contact with other units of matter than our own. So our hands should become our symbols for Inner touch outwardly expressed. This is natural enough in sign-language which uses hand gestures to convey intelligence between differently embodied minds.

What happens in the case of a hand gesture? We are in fact sculpting with air as a medium. In effect we are moulding the Element of Air into symbolic shapes intended to contain our meaning. It is not actually our hands, but what they have done which must be considered. Air has been touched, moved around, given form, and made to mean something in connection with our Inner intention. If we can do this with Air, why not with the other Elements? So we can with Water and Earth, but we cannot directly handle Fire, which requires intermediary instruments before humans may touch it. Let us begin with Air-touch.

Standing or sitting in an easy position, we select any suitable subject, such as one of the Ten Spheres, and make as clear a concept of it as we can. Then we project this concept along our arms and into our fingers, asking them to respond by moving and moulding the air around them into representative formation. We realise that air is just as physical as earth in a different way. True, the images we make with it will have but momentary existence, but they will have been made in actuality. We cannot take an air-sculpture and put it on exhibition, for it unsculpts itself as fast as we form it, yet nevertheless it has a validity of its own which may be used in magic.

We shall not need artistic talent for forming our Air-images, helpful as this might be. The true necessity is that we respond to our Inner concept and attempt to impress it into the very air of our atmosphere by means of manual expressions. However clumsy these may seem to us, or however inadequate they may feel, what really matters is that they come naturally in answer to our Inner impulse. They should, as it were, "come by themselves", and so far as possible be the outcome of the originating concept directly, rather than second-hand ideas drawn from other sources. This means our movements ought to be quite spontaneous, arising straight from Originative levels, and not from anyone elses notions of what ought to be done. It does not mean we must not do what anyone else does, but our movements must come purely because we impell ourselves to make them on our own deepest authority. In accomplishing this, we control ourselves from our Inmost levels, which is very highly desirable.

To familiarise ourselves with air-touching, it is only necessary to close the eyes, reach out the hands, and attempt to handle air like any ordinary plastic material. It should be felt between the fingers, pulled about like elastic, and generally treated like any other amenable substance. We can poke our fingers into it, throw lumps of it about, press pieces of it together, tear bits of it apart, or do whatever else we please with it. We must try to feel the air as a barely palpable material, only just discernable by the touch but undoubtedly solid enough to deal with manually. To anyone unaware of the purpose of this exercise, there might seem something ridiculous in the thought of an individual, or group of people with closed eyes waving their hands about in an apparently aimless manner, yet this would not be so at all. The exercise has a very real purpose, which is to sharpen the conscious attention to its finest point so that it is conditioned to deal with what is normally intangible. By attempting literally to feel air, which is the finest physical matter around us, we are bringing our consciousness to the very threshold where matter and un-matter meet. We shall be trying to solidify thought.

Few people think of air as "real" because our concepts of reality are too earth-based, and there they will remain unless we are able to rise toward Inner Reality. Of course air is real, and so is electricity, magnetism, light, and the remainder of impalpable existence. By treating air as an objective reality and applying ourselves to it with purpose, we train ourselves to mould mind-matter along equivalent Inner lines. It is just as hard to grasp and manipulate the substance of thought as it is to handle free air on physical levels, and the practice of one provides training for the other, so we should continue the exercises.

Suppose we have chosen the Sphere of Mercy for experiment. We "enter the Sphere" by "going Blue", and locking our consciousness on to the frequency of Compassion. Nothing other than this should occupy our field of focus, and we must stay tuned in to Mercy while we are working with it. Once we are able to project the power from this Sphere, we push it out of our fingers into the surrounding air and simply let our hands make whatever reactive movements they are impelled to do by the Origin-impulse. It is most important not to interfere from lower levels by being critical or interposing suggestions. We should simply keep our whole attention fixed to the Mercy Sphere, and let its energy work directly through us so that it controls our hands manipulating the Air-Element. At first, the hands will move awkwardly and uncertainly, like those of an infant. Since our eyes are closed, we will not see this physically, but we should try and look Inwardly at what our hands are doing, though merely as an observer at this point. The "top" part of ourselves must stay contacted to, and projecting the power of the Fourth Sphere all the while, our "middle" section must simply take orders from the top and do no more than pass the original power along to our "bottom" part, which connects with our external world via our handling of air.

Little by little, we shall become aware our hand movements are taking on a pattern and purpose which is definitely an Outer expression of our Inner contact. The movements may not be what our "normal" mind might expect, but then, Inner Life is full of surprises, and we must learn as we go. One strange result of this exercise will be that when it "goes right", we shall experience a most peculiar sense of satisfaction and achievement, which is actually an effect of Inner energy "getting through" effectively into Outer existence. The exercise will not feel in any way pointless or inane, but we shall realise its potentials and possibilities of extension with perhaps quite a sense of amazement. Nevermore do we make ritual gestures carelessly or emptily. Every move will be as full of meaning and power as the turning of this planet. We shall touch the air with purpose, and it will respond to the Will within us.

Once we are able to "make Mercy", or anything else out of air, we should work our way through all the Spheres until we get results from each. There are numerous side avenues that may be explored along these lines of investigation, and entirely new fields of experience may be opened up. The main object however, should be that of developing magical touch, and so from Air, we may progress to Water, since we cannot handle Fire directly with our fingers.

Water-working is apt to be messy unless done under ideal conditions such as sub-aqua or while swimming. However, it is possible to obtain some practice by immersing the hands in a generous basin or bucket of water, which may be hot or cold to suit the method being used. The same principles apply to water-touching as with air or any other material. We are aiming to impress consciousness into it by hand-contact. In effect we are practising the "laying on of hands" as a calculable skill rather than a merely superstitious belief. Consciousness is indeed a transmissible energy like any other, and can be made to affect matter or anything else in existence. By linking consciousness with touch, we are bringing it down to the closest and most intimate points possible between individuals. Touch is usually reserved for friends, lovers, and revered beings. Rings and priests are consecrated by touch. Humanity and Divinity meet each other by a touch-sacrament. These magical touch-exercises are designed to join the extremities of both Divinity and Humanity from one end of the practitioner to the other.

So we should repeat all our previous experiments with air while using water as a medium. It will probably be noticed that movements will differ from those used with air for the same subjects. Once more we must try and squeeze the energy released by our concentration into the very substance of the water. If we are dealing with Wisdom, then we should attempt to impress this Principle into every molecule that slips between our fingers. We may push it in, stroke it in, or manipulate it in any way that comes to us, so long as we try to impart Wisdom to the water we are touching. It should be remembered that what goes in will also come out, and there is a reverse-technique for extracting these energies from the Elements via touch-contact. We instinctively dip our hands in water over the side of a boat, or absorb fire-force from the Sun. Once we train ourselves to select specific frequencies of energy, we can take in Wisdom, Mercy, or any Principle we please. They are communicable from the Highest Source when the channels are cleared. All these magical exercises we are engaged with, cut the necessary circuit-grooves into our consciousness.

When we have familiarised ourselves with water, it is time to try earth. There are many ways this might be done, but we may as well begin with modelling clay, of which our ancestor Adam was reputed to be made. When we have selected a suitable lump of the material and obtained the necessary working conditions, we contact our upper consciousness with the Sphere or subject we have selected, and then with closed eyes let it work through our fingers with the clay. It is important to work with closed eyes so that sight impressions do not interfere with touch-projection. We are not trying to make the clay *look* like our subject, but *feel* like it. This makes quite a difference at the outcoming end. If we keep concentrating on the Origin-impulse, and manipulating away at the clay, some energy at least from the first will find its way into the second.

Whatever our production in clay looks like, we are here concerned with its tactile qualities. The test is, can we reverse it and reproduce a proportion of its initial energy in ourselves? In effect we have made a recording just as much as if we had cut a disc. Therefore we should try reversing the polarity of our consciousness, and by feeling the outlines of the modelled clay with our fingers, "pick up" whatever impressions we receive from it and pass these along to the top of our consciousness. The shaped clay should "play back" tactile impressions that will eventually add up to some approximation of its Origination. Theoretically, other individuals should be able to receive these impressions from the same clay, but few people translate energies equally. Experimentation along these lines is interesting.

Throughout these exercises we have gradually solidified our thoughts right down to earth, and have realised that consciousness is a solid in its own state. Thoughts and things are interchangeable, and if we train ourselves to exchange them via their appropriate media, we shall become practical magicians. Just as we must practise materialisation of thought via the Elements, so should we continue the cycle and spiritualise matter by working from earth to water to air with physical contact, and then making the Fire-contact by Inner Light.

From the foregoing, it should be clear how talismans, images, and the like magical accessories are made. At their inception, they are linked in with specific types of consciousness which are carried right through to their physical finalisation. It is not the personal consciousness of the operator which provides the power behind them, this being only the linking channel, but the effective energy comes from other sources, depending on which category of the Greater Consciousness we are capable of making contact with. It matters only to ourselves how we name these Inner Realities. If it makes us happier to euphemise everything except our own awareness under the heading of "The Collective Unconscious" or any such terminology, there seems no reason except that of common-sense why we should not. Whatever makes our ability to REALISE spiritual Principles easier is worth considering, and *realisation* means making our most nebulous consciousness solid enough to touch. If ritual practices assist us in this work, then we are fully justified in their use.

There are endless opportunities for ritualising touch. We might simply close the eyes, pick up the nearest object or lay our hands on it, and then try to place it in whichever Sphere it suggests to us. A categorical list of touch-contacts with each Sphere is a necessity for every serious worker. Everyone would have to make their own list of dependable contacts, since the tactile sense varies so widely with individuals. It is only possible to outline broad principles. The Four Elements may be generally outlined as Fire being a warm touch, Air a dry one, Water wet, and Earth cold. These sensory stimuli are easy to include in any rite, but the Ten Spheres are rather more complex, and can only be particularised by workers for themselves. Their general natures have been given already.

Naturally the largest proportion of tactile sensation during a rite comes from the contact of clothing with body surface. One reason for the school of nude operators, mainly working primitive pagan systems, was to obviate clothing-contacts altogether, and plunge their persons directly into Air, Water, leap through Fire, or roll themselves into Earth as occasion demanded. They claimed these direct Elemental contacts provided them with considerable power, and so indeed it does on lower levels for very limited periods. If inadequate controls are imposed on the Elements, they will take more power from the operator than they donate, and manifestations of energy will be in the nature of the Element extracting this from the worker, rather than the other way round. Our aim should be to master Elements, not allow them to master us. Nude rites may be spectacular in one sense, but they are very liable to go wrong when participants abandon themselves to the aroused Elemental energies. It can be fatal to underestimate the power of the Elements, or over-estimate one's own ability to hold them in control. Group nude working is not recommended for those intending much beyond ground level in spiritual Inner dimensions.

The majority of Temple-method operators have found from experience that whatever materials their external ceremonial clothing is made from, contact-material with the body is best chosen from those with a good degree of insulation. At one time only silk fulfilled this condition, which made magical underclothing an expensive item. Nowadays there are so many excellent alternatives such as rayon, nylon, terylene, etc, all of which are highly electro-static, that ritual underwear presents few problems. Whether modern plastic materials like Polyvinylchloride have any value or advantage in ritual clothing remains to be seen. As yet there is insufficient evidence for judgement one way or another, but possibilities may exist. On the whole, no ritual clothing should produce sensations of discomfort unless these are intentionally aimed for. Shaman magic, for example, frequently calls for a considerable weight of metal plates, talismans etc, sewn over the leather coat, and these rattle and clank while the magician dances. It is unlikely this method would be of any help to advanced Western workers.

There is enormous scope for the study and patterning of touch-techniques in magical rituals, since it is a somewhat neglected aspect of the art. We must always remember that the sensory side of any rite is to provide the externalities of an actual Inner experience from which we may expect some degree of spiritual result. By the gamut of touch from its end of the sense-spectrum, we may be pushed to any extent between the Pillars of Pain and Pleasure, or subjected to the influence of both at once. To apply the right touches in their correct order is an essential part of ritual procedure. In ancient initiations the candidate was literally handled by the initiators, sometimes very roughly or violently. Shocks by striking or scourg-ing were delivered at the right moments for the proper reasons.

A fundamental maxim or percept uttered while the impact of a sharp blow accompanied it was seldom forgotten. The physical shock acted as a fixative for the spiritual truth. When such practices degenerated into sadism and horseplay, they were gradually dropped or relegated to very minor affairs such as a light prick with a sword point or a purely technical blow.

A good case exists for restoring the touch factor to ritual workings by modern methods. These days we need not rely on crude applications of a scourge or the like. Physical vibrations of any perceptible frequency can be selected and applied by electro-mechanical apparatus. Electricity itself may be harmlessly but effectively used for tactile purposes. There are many ways that electricity might be introduced into rituals apart from lighting them. Mild electric shocks are a fairly well known method of psychological conditioning, and if correctly blended into rituals could prove extremely valuable, provided a qualified electrician was responsible for the technical arrangements.

At the pleasure side of the touch-gamut, there are many possibilities for ritualisation. Individual tastes vary a lot of course, but the joy in handling fine craftsmanship or physical excellence of any kind is indescribable, giving rise as it does to most notable Inner experiences. Some shapes are far more satisfying to hold than others. The difference between holding a globe and an irregular lump of rock is remarkable. Experiments can be carried out with handling a selection of widely differing stones much about the same weight, and noting the varied Inner reactions to them all. A set of similar checks may be done with regular geometrical solids formed from light material. Any sensitive individual with closed eyes will get surprising differences and results with these. Nor should we forget the touch aspects of our Four Instruments. The flat Shield, hollow Cup, sharp Sword, and round Rod have a great deal of touch-data to offer. Each stimulates and responds to its own type of touch, thus causing its specific Inner effect.

We neglect the touch angle of ritual working to our own great loss. The best way of using it is to educate our tactile ability by exercising it through the magical channels linking our Inner and Outer extremities. Eventually we shall touch our Inner spiritual contacts with an equivalent certainty to that of touching our own finger-tips together. A touch is a contact on any level of being. If we accept our physical reality by pinching flesh between fingers, then we must accept our spiritual reality by pressing our own souls until their reaction assures us of their existence.

It would be possible to continue dealing with ritualised touch for a very long time because it is such a fascinating and fruitful topic. Probably few investigators would agree on more than very broad lines. All would admit the importance of the subject however. Our contacts with Divinity are closer to touch than our other sense extensions. We do not see, smell, hear, or taste Spiritual Life in any way resembling these physical abilities, but most of us *feel* the Power of Presence to a noticeable degree. We develop the sensation of touch even before physical birth, and its equivalent comes to us before our emergence into Spiritual Life as distinct entities therein. So many of our old prayers are that we may be *touched* in some way by Higher Beings than ourselves. Instinctively we seek contact with them by the most certain route. How many times have we attended ceremonies during which we have seen, heard, smelt and tasted nothing except the purely physical adjuncts, yet have felt touched Inwardly by an unmistakable Inner contact? Touch is surely the most reliable basis for extension into Inner Dimensions.

Now the time has come to consider the hearing aspect of sensation in ritual, and because this is so specialised and detailed, another study-section must be opened up. Once more it is the Western Tradition that will be principally dealt with, and methods described will be those most suitable for Occidentals.

RITUAL SONICS AND INVOCATIONS

Before applying ourselves to the study of sound effects in ritual, we should disregard all wild exaggerations still circulating in some occult literature about the Pyramids, Stonehenge, or Atlantis being "raised" by "Sound Magic". These, and similar distortions, bring nothing but discredit to a valid art, and are an insult to the hard-working teams of long dead labourers who piled one stone on top of another.

The origin of the Pyramid rumours can be traced to Herodotus. He quoted an amusing travellers' tale of his time to the effect that magical chanting raised the Pyramid stones. So it did in a way, for the chanting came from the workmen themselves as they hauled the enormous blocks up the long ramps, and heaved on the tackle manoeuvring them into place. Oriental and Mediterranean peoples have always believed in music while they worked, and it was only by rhythmical chanting that they were able to haul in unison and move the ponderous masses of stone by exerting their efforts together. That was the magic they used and none other. It is a mystery why misguided minds still insist in crediting this ancient canard.

There most certainly is real magic in sound, and it produces far more wonderful effects than heaping up stones, or knocking them down like the Walls of Jericho. Applied sonics alter life itself. They bless or blast, heal or hurt. The meanings we have imposed upon sound waves have built up whole civilisations—and destroyed them again. The Word has literally brought Cosmos out of Chaos, and the Anti-Word is capable of reducing us to Chaos once more. Words and magic are inseparable, but they work within a framework of laws which are calculable and controllable by a consciousness able to comprehend their structure. All sonics are "words" in their own way, even if we have attached no especial human phraseology to them, and many of these so-called "meaningless" sonics have their magical uses.

For practical ritual purposes, we shall deem "Sound" to mean whatever movement of matter on any level of existence comes within the "audio frequency" range of resonance. We know of course that indefinite extensions of frequency and resonant-energies occur above and below the "Sound-section" of an "Existence-Scale". Some of these are reachable by humans, and the rest lie far beyond our present grasp. Within the audio-range however, there is considerable scope for ritualised activity with vocal and instrumental sonics, so we shall confine ourselves to this particular field.

The majority of sound during most rituals consists of invocations addressed to various categories of Divine or supra-human consciousness. Then intelligence may be exchanged among participants with the intention of directing their consciousness into specific channels. Particular sounds may be introduced in order to cause reactive effects on the hearers. Such would include gongs, bells, raps, or meditational music. Orchestral and choral accompaniments provide a very great amount of sonic energy for ritual use. Literally anything that makes a noise at all may be ritualised to some purpose or other, yet the fundamental reason for every sort of sound is the same. To provide linkage between points of consciousness operating through different dimensions of being. This identical motivation is found behind all ritual practices.

Ancient man called upon his Gods with yells, shrieks, howls and cries of the loudest kind. There has always been an impression in the human mind that sheer noise makes the best substitute for sense. We still tend to raise our voices when speaking to foreigners. A baby screams for attention. A bully bawls down a victim. Sometimes a noise is made purely for the sake of self-assertion, and sometimes for obtaining a response. Early man heard the Gods answering through Nature around him. Everything spoke. Eventually man began to listen inside himself, and there, in the Silence, the Voice was heard. The story is beautifully told of Elijah who first listened in the old way to tempests and natural sonics, then finally went into his own silence and heard the Inner Voice utter the I AM. We can scarcely do better than follow his example.

When we call upon Deities and Intelligences during rituals, just how do we imagine such entities are able to hear us? They are not embodied individuals with ears like our own. No matter how loudly we call towards an altar or into the air, we shall do no more than make a noise if we cannot direct our intentions more accurately than that. Beings that live beyond the boundaries of physical matter will only "hear" us if we address them with Inner sonics uttered through our own Inwardising consciousness. In other words, the

176

Gods hear us in ourselves—if we are effectively connected to Them by Inner channels. During ritual working, sonics are usually divided between utterers and listeners, choir and congregation, or priest and people. The job of the utterer, is to aim sonically at whatever Inner contact is sought via the hearers, whose function it is to link themselves with that particular contact and no other.

This consideration is important, because it indicates precisely the modus operandi for intentional sonics during ritual. It means that while a skilled Invocant is emitting meaningful sonic energies directed to some category of the Universal Consciousness, those hearing them physically are acting as receptive relays sending the message backwards through themselves along their Inner linkage with the Contact they are all trying to reach. The priest speaks to the God in and through the people. Using this system of a single mind conducting the concerted energies of many, great amplification of consciousness is possible. It is seldom this happens in fact, for it would need a highly trained and co-operative congregation, which is more than rare in human associations.

Suppose under ideal conditions it was proposed to invoke the Merciful Mother Divine Aspect by sonic energy. A suitable formula has been worked out for intonation. The Invocant directs the focal point of his consciousness to this Aspect through the consciousness of all present, vocalising at them as if they were the Merciful Mother Herself. These hearers should call up the Mother Aspect in themselves as if She were indeed listening out of their ears. Some do this by thinking of the Divine Contact in miniature situated in their heads between the ears, others imagine the Contact as a Being overshadowing them and listening intently, others again try to identify with the Contact and realise that what the human ear hears and the mind translates, is transmitted as Inner Sound and meaning to the Contact with which they are attuned. Everyone finds their most effective method of relating themselves with Divine Aspects or Inner Intelligences. Provided they remain tuned to the Aspect being invoked, and all work together properly, the power-circuit will be completed by the Inner Contact, and the strangely interesting phenomena of reactive resonance should occur.

In principle, this is initiated by the Invocant who gives the Call, or whatever the sonic is. The energy emitted from this will vary according to ability, but is unlikely to be a great amount, being divided by the number of receptive hearers. Each of these individuals now reproduces the sonic (or their response to it), and directs their share of energy towards the Inner Contact. This means a very considerable gain of total energy on the original. If it reaches and invokes a response from the Contact, there will be a return-cycle of Inner energy from thence, which will impinge upon the receptive

177

faculties of the human invocants causing a proportional increase of the next energy-cycle. This continues to increase with every cycle according to the capacity of those in the circuit for absorbing and conducting the force-flow. It will manifest among them as an expansive sense of uplift along the lines of the Contact to a point where physical symptoms such as strong tremors or even violent spasms may occur. The onset of physical effects is a sign that the energy is approaching maximum load for the individuals concerned, and control should be applied to hold the power at that level. If it is increased beyond this safety limit, damage is likely to happen somewhere about the weakest link, whatever this happens to be.

The psycho-mechanics of this are observable at revivalist meetings, "beat" type dances, or other gatherings where sonic energy is directed at a crowd of people who respond rhythmically and intentionally. In common language, they get "worked up" to whatever pitch they are capable of reaching, and their Inner contacts respond through them. With the revivalists, contacts are likely to be no higher than sentimental and emotional ones. In the case of the screaming youngsters, their contacts will probably be limited to sexual levels. In both instances an objective has been aimed at and attained by the use of sonic energy directed betwen differing dimensions of being. Initiated members of the Holy Mysteries seek far better results when using the same fundamental principles.

In orthodox religious practice, reactive resonance may be studied in Litany-working, and the chanting of Divine Office, although these are unlikely to provide good examples. The theory behind Divine Office is that sonic energies should be equally divided between complementary choral teams, each of which "calls out" the Divine Aspect Contact from the other, thus holding a considerable amount of Inner energy in balance. This answers the problem of stability, which is always a crucial matter with sonic energy. Once it goes off key, or its rhythm breaks, or feed-back occurs beyond the limits of harmonious response, sonic energy "goes wild" or "explodes" into break-up dissonances which ruin the whole structure being put together. Sound is a very unstable constituent of Being, and its fluctuations are responsible for most rapid changes therein. When using sonics in ritual, this must always be remembered.

For ritual usage, sonics may be classified as Outsound and Insound. The former consists of audible frequencies discernable by our physical ears, and the latter of the Inner equivalents or harmonics they are related to. No amount of purely physical sound will penetrate to Inner Dimensions. We may shriek to our hearts content in a ritual room, but unless we are able to translate some of this noise to Inwardly directed energy, not a single squeak will be heard by Inner Listeners. It is quite possible to be loudly vocal in one Dimension and dumb in another. The much quoted "Words without thoughts, never to Heaven go" is perfectly true, though it should be counterbalanced with "Thoughts without words, cannot to Kingdom come." To each state of being its own laws of manifestation. We have attached formulated consciousness to sonic sequences on earth, but if we want to project those beyond the limits of physical matter, we shall have to do so along carrier-waves of Insound. Before we attempt serious ritual work, it would be just as well to make sure we can utter such Insonics. Otherwise we shall be acting in dumb-show Inwardly, no matter how hoarse we make ourselves materially.

To "invoke" means literally to "voice inside" or call *inwardly*, and that is precisely what we must do if we are aiming to make contact with higher Intelligences through the Great Consciousness. There is no use our shouting through Outer Space instead of Inner Space. External wordage and sounds are only useful as material to be converted to Inner Sonic Energy, which alone is capable of reaching the contacts we seek. Invocation does not mean bawling our heads off before some altar. It means using our Inner Voices to reach those able to hear them in ourselves and other human beings when we are speaking spiritually rather than physically.

"Evocation" means calling out of. It signifies that we are calling upon our Inner Contacts to approach more closely toward our Outer terms of consciousness. If we evoke, we ask the Inner Ones to come out of us so that we may meet them as nearly as possible at material level. For this to be effective in any way means we should have to provide our Inner guests with at least a mental semblance of humanity and all the limitations of intelligence and speech that this implies. We cannot expect to be met by Divine Ones in human guise, using human language, without allowing for the distortions and errors of which we are capable. If we insist They confine Their consciousness to human phraseology, then we must accept the shortcomings of our language and the degree to which we understand it. This is not likely to help communication. Provided we are prepared to make such allowances, evocation may be of some value when seen in its proper light.

Invocation or evocation only forms part of ritual sonic procedure. A great deal of it is concerned with effects in the minds and souls of the participants. They are being encouraged to think, feel, and undergo experiences aimed at processing their consciousness for various reasons. This needs skilled psycho-physiological techniques of sound. At one time these were kept secret, but most of them are now being used by commercial or political groupings for influencing whichever section of the Mass-mind they want to dominate. As reactional resistance to such methods increases, they will become

179

less and less useful for ritual working. Once Mystery-methods are prostituted, they lose their original virtue. When Church and Supermarket combine their tactics, the former loses customers to the latter. There is little use producing effects in Lodge or Temple if these only remind their hearers and viewers to buy Boggs Baked Beans on the way home. Nor are ritualists likely to accept colours or sounds associated with political parties they loathe. We have so many built in psychological antigens in our systems these days, that entire ritual structures used over the centuries need re-building in conditions clear of these disadvantages. It might be suggested that new methods of ritual be designed to arouse anti-commercial or political reactions from participants. They would thus be in no risk of usage by either faction, though in danger of suppression and persecution from both, which might not be a bad thing, since the Mysteries have always thrived most in secret.

There is no doubt whatever that close relations exist between sonic patterns and consciousness on all levels. The sole problem ritualists are concerned with, is the selection and use of specific sonic arrangements for operations of consciousness outside the range limited to material manifestations. We may use the word "psycho-sonics" if it helps. How do we translate human speech into energies that make meaning in other states of being? How reverse this force-flow so that we can make sense of what we receive from elsewhere? How shall we arrange sound-effects physically, so as to cause definite reactions from our minds, souls, and spirits? What is the famous noise of one hand clapping? These are the kind of question with which the practical ritualist is concerned. To extend the Koan, how shall we strike a physical hand against a spiritual one and hear the noise both ways?

None of this should seem very extraordinary. Musical composers and instrumentalists are constantly faced with it. If a musician wants to convey sadness, joy, or any other emotion, he is perfectly well able to do so in music. The spirit of natural grandeur such as thunderstorms, moonlight, scenery, etc, has been "painted in sound" countless times by different composers. From the extremes of exalted spiritual experience, to the depth of howling sexuality, a sonic medium exists to link the In and Out of these typified energies, and they are all applicable to widely varying sorts of ritual. Religious ritual has its own appropriate sonics, so does military ritual, social ritual, or any other formalised pattern of behaviour. Even local rituals classified as "Folk" practices have their own songs and dances, possibly limited to one place or time. The study-field of ritual sonics is so enormous, we can only hope to touch on basic principles and confine ourselves to those generally applicable to the Western Tradition of occult ritualism.

Possibly a noteworthy example of psycho-sonics in use among some circles is the so-called "Gift of Tongues" or "Enochian speech". In effect this is "automatic speaking", which like automatic writing produces endless amounts of "scribble" and occasionally connected sequences of intelligence. The fundamentals of this are simple enough. Anyone can make noises with their mouths without attaching meanings to these with their minds. If this is done, and the normal mind control withheld, such a control point may theoretically be handed back to a level of intelligence originating beyond physical limits. If in fact it were possible by such means to establish audible contact with Beings in other dimensions of existence whose spiritual development is in advance of our own, there is no doubt we might obtain great benefits. Like most forms of automatism however, the "Gift of Tongues" is extremely unreliable in practice and tedious to deal with. Very little sound sense comes out of mountains of nonsense. Yet in principle the subject is worth some investigation.

There is no necessity these days to use similar methods to those of Dee and Kelly who gave sonic automatism the title of Enochian or angelic language, yet they did attempt to attach grammar and syntax to what they received. This resulted in their famous "Calls", which were a recorded collection of "utterances" having no direct connection with any known human tongue, yet which were capable of being "understood" on deeper than normal levels of conscious perception. They were actually making "abstract" words like a painter makes abstract colour associations. The mind reads into it whatever interpretation the consciousness is capable of constructing on different levels. We may make what we will of abstracts whether they are visible or audible.

To practice sonic automatism it is necessary to have someone capable of making the sonics, and another person or persons able to direct the outcome along intelligent lines. It would be very difficult to combine both conditions in one individual. The "medium" may first be got into the right mood with music and perfume, or merely silent sitting, then they "drift away from themselves", letting their jaw muscles in particular slack off and relax. Breath is expelled steadily between parted lips, while the tongue moves about in the mouth with as little supervision from normal control as possible. It should be free to move in any way it is impelled by the subjective part of the mind taking it over. This will result in "whispering" or "muttering" sound, which if persisted with, settle into a kind of rythmic pattern resembling uncertain speech imperfectly heard. As the "medium" allows the control over these sonics via the musculature of the tongue and throat to become increasingly remote from their volitional centres, the others taking part in the exercise do their best to link in with whichever Inner contact is aimed for. The hope is that direct control over the "utterances" will pass from the "medium" to the Innerworld intelligence making contact.

Such are the elementary basics of spiritualist mediumship, the "Gift of Tongues", oracular utterances, or the "wizards that mutter" condemned in Hebrew scriptures. The practice may be disguised in a thousand ways yet remains fundamentally the same. Over the unknown centuries of its use among mankind it has produced remarkably little coherent intelligence, and yet has had considerable effect on the development of our perceptive faculties. Its value lay not so much in the passage of intelligible information couched in earthly languages, but in the more subtle exchanges of energy through the psycho-sonic channels of communication which only the Inner ear receives. It is not the externals, but the internals of these contacts that matter.

The difficulties and disadvantages of this inter-dimensional sonic system are many and great. A main problem is that of directing the control point deeply and selectively enough to establish communication along conscious lines between the human end and a reliable Inner source concerned with the welfare and benefit of those human beings. It is relatively easy to contact Innerworld entities on the lower grade levels of existence, with less intelligence to communicate than we may find in the ordinary course of life on this planet. In fact it is difficult to avoid them, though they have remarkably little to offer worth the acceptance. They benefit more from contact with us than we from them.

The whole question of so-called "spirit communication" is an exceptionally complex one. Without adequate safeguards and commonsense methods of working, more harm than good is possible to human operators. Indiscriminate contacts with irresponsible or otherwise undesirable Innerworld entities are always unwise and productive of trouble. Nor are "spirits" helpful whose hobby seems to be interminably sermonising and lecturing, or relaying inconsequential gossip from the world of wishes. These seem to be Legion. The conscientious ritualist does not welcome their attentions during operational exercises, for they are nothing but a hindrance to serious work. They have their proper place in the scheme of things, but this is emphatically not within the Circle of Art. Sonics likely to attract unwanted contacts should therefore not be used during rites from which these must be excluded. This should by no means imply any kind of hostility toward the unwelcome ones, but is simply a question of specialisation. A ritual is a dedicated, selective, sensitively attuned operation to its particular purpose. It can no more succeed as such if invaded by inharmonious entities, than a Chopin recital would be effective during an artillery bombardment.

Unless we have means of co-relating sonics with some scale or spectrum calculated in Inner terms of effect, we shall never be able to use them properly for rituals. Primitive people replied on screaming themselves silly during their rites until an exhaustion orgasm occurred, and they experienced a temporary catharsis. This works equally well today, but is rather like using a megaton bomb to kill a mouse. Sonics will produce far better effects with fractional energy if intelligently directed, providing we know which sounds to apply in what manner to obtain what outcome. Once more we are faced with making an associative classification of sensory phenomena (this time sounds), in relation to our standard scale of Inner values, such as the decimal system of the Spheres. Again we encounter the difficulty of attributions because of individual opinions and reactions.

Our friends the pencil and paper will stand by us faithfully. If we take ten separate sheets, number them, and then write on each a description of any sound we link with that particular Sphere, we shall obtain a good amount of working material. At first we may jot all this down just as it comes to us, and everything can be sorted out when we have enough to deal with. As a start, we might attribute the notes of an octave plus one at each end to the Spheres. These may be whistled, played, or simply thought up and down the scale until they are firmly fixed in the mind to a point where a single note will suggest its Sphere to us. A tape recording is a great help here, and the possessor of a voice true enough to sing the actual names of the Spheres on the correct note while also sounding it on the piano, is indeed fortunate. Enough meditation should be done to establish this simple sonic linkage with the Spheres. Even if we just Do Re Me Fa them, it will be helpful. They may even be spoken from deepest to highest tone of voice.

Once more it must be emphasised that everyone is responsible for making their own attributions to the Spheres if detailed results are to be obtained. A good system to follow is listing various sonic sources, and then attributing specific classifications of them to the ten Spheres. Here is an example:

It is very unlikely that all would agree with these attributions. That is immaterial. What matters is that none should disagree without being able to supply their own satisfactory alternatives. The important outcome is to link specific realities of Inner Life right down to the most ordinary sounds in our world, so that even the clatter of dishes being dried will put us in contact with something wonderful from the Innerworld. Providing we are able to do this one way or another, methods are matters of choice.

We must not forget classifications of sound to accord with the Elements. These should present little difficulty in general terms, for they will be mainly mimetic. We do it instinctively when we use

Sphere	Note	Type of Voice	Instrument	Natural sound	Artificial sound
1	D	faintest whisper	flute	breath	clicking
2	C	quietly authoritative	violin	wind in trees	ringing
3	B	deeply sympathetic	cello	rain	tapping
4	A	kindly genial	harp	gentle breakers	pulsating
5	G	justly severe	drum	thunder	exploding
6	F	richly melodious	organ	cheerful fire	humming
7	E	emotionally satisfying	guitar	swishing grass	rustling
8	D	intellectually stimulating	piano	rushing stream	rattling
9	C	strongly clear	horn	echo	whistling
10	B	ordinary accented	orchestra	footfalls	rumbling

words to describe elemental activities. We say something *whizzes* through the Air, *bubbles* in the Water, *crackles* in the Fire, and *thumps* on the Earth. Each word is an Elementally linked sonic of a descriptive type. In olden times the Elements were ritually invoked using the Flute for Air, Lyre for Fire, Sistrum for Water, and Drum for Earth. Anyone caring to take such trouble today would be well advised to try playing the flute or recorder in a hill-top wood on a windy day, strumming a guitar or zither beside a nicely crackling fire in an old stone circle, shaking a sistrum or striking tubulars beside a waterfall, and drumming away in an echoing cavern. The four experiences will amply repay the efforts necessary to undergo them. It is unnecessary to be able to play these instruments properly. Impromptu handling as the elemental influence inspires will give very satisfactory results—to the instrumentalist. Hearers are not likely to enjoy them, and the experiment is best done alone.

Sonic sources principally used in Western occult ritual practices are not as extensive as they might be. They are mainly:

The Voice. Used for embodiment of the rite's intellectual and rational content. Vocal instructions and directions to participants are given, consciousness directed verbally toward Inner Intelligences. Characterised vocalisations suggest or link with specific Entities and energies. Tonal qualities carry emotional charge, and evoke responses from recipients whether embodied or otherwise. All other sonic sources are mechanical, but the voice is directly connected with the consciousness concerned in the rite on both sides of the Veil. It is thus the most important of all instruments. One great disadvantage of the voice is its need for adequate training if finer types of Inner energy are to be worked with. Voices will only "bring through" whatever lies within the Inner range of their users, and if this does not extend beyond the lower reaches of the Inner Octaves, then results will be limited to these coarser effects. Unsuitable voices will wreck a whole rite, and it is most important to find competent vocalists for whatever working is proposed. Without efficient vocalisation, no rite using sonic effects can entirely succeed in its objective. Voice training is an essential prerequisite for magical practices involving ritual.

The Organ. For sheer sonic power on a grand scale the organ has never been superseded. Its physical vibrations literally enter hearers and shake responses out of them. When handled with skill, the organ is capable of affording unique Inner experiences. Its main advantage lies in the fact that it appeals principally to the best and highest in humanity. Disadvantages are its great cost and immobility. Organ recordings form a semi-substitute, but they do not provide the actual amount of sonic energy released by the instrument itself. As a vehicle for Inner Voices speaking directly to human hearers, the organ is invaluable.

The Click. Sometimes produced with a slight tap, and sometimes with a small clicking instrument. It can be made with fingernails in intimate workings. Its object is to focus attention from Silence to sonics, bringing all points of consciousness together in unison. It links the Unmanifest with the Manifest in a natural way without violence or shock, and allows its hearers to adjust themselves to conditions about to change considerably. The click should always be used in moving out of silent phases in any rite. In place of the click, some workers substitute a very soft handclap. The click is actually an important ritual sonic, and ritualists must be trained in its use. Responsibility for producing it lies with the principal Officer, or the Director of Ceremony. A brief interval should always follow a click to allow time for the hearers to make their reactions and preparations for the phase to follow. The click must be of minimal intensity which can still be definitely audible. This calls for some degree of ability in its production.

The Bell or Gong. In one sense, this is precisely opposite to the

Click. The Bell or gong produces a sonic which reverberates with diminishing resonance into silence. Trained hearers should be able to follow this sonic into the silence on its particular frequency. This they do by picking up its resonation in themselves, and as its physical amplitude decreases so must the attentive point of awareness be withdrawn from material and increased in spiritual depth. It is a matter of transference from audible to inaudible energies, or Outsound to Insound. The gong is mainly used for directing outward attention toward inner meaning at moments when this is of paramount importance. Consciousness should be allowed to flow inwards along the diminishing wave-crests of sound, which necessitates practice in the art of audio-response. It is possible to reverse the gong action if it is rapidly struck with ever increasing strength so that its sound grows louder and louder, but this must be taken up by the hearers and translated into Outsound activity in other forms. The Bell has an advantage over a gong in having a pure tuned note, but the gong covers a broader sonic band. It is important that either bell or gong has a good period of reverberation, for this is what gives it ritual value. Minor bells with varied characteristics are useful for directing attention toward activities which might otherwise fail to attract sufficient consciousness. Such bells are sometimes fitted to thuribles for that reason, or attached to the ceremonial clothing of officiants whose movements have especial meaning. Bells have quite a wide variety of ritual applications. They are used as an anti-sonic during exorcisms, or to produce temporary psycho-stasis by constant ringing at sufficient amplitude to hold the hearer within their sonic circle. Bells have been used to evoke conditioned reflexes for centuries before Pavlov, and crowns of bells were old devices to induce extensions of consciousness by their incessant jingling close to the ears. These survived as the jesters cap-bells, supposed to evoke wit.

The Knock. Rapping according to rhythmic patterns seems to have always been part of ritual procedure. Whole codes of knocking sprang up from identification signals to the elaborate modern Morse code. Each Sphere, as we have already learned, had its own basic raps. The different grades of Initiation became associated with appropriate knocks, and in fact a very complicated language of knocking exists in many forms. It is used to convey intelligence without formal words, and can be inter-lingual if a coding is agreed upon. Knocks are either based on numeral groupings of rhythmical formation. The first system depends on hearers counting the knocks and their intervals, then relating these to letters or other means of encoding consciousness, so that whole concepts are consecutively constructed unit by unit. The second method simply associates pure rhythms with definite ideas or experiences. For instance, we can easily rap out the rhythms of the human heart, a galloping horse, a railway train, etc. This principle is extensible into rap-patterns for specific emotions, Inner types of consciousness, and even the different Divine Aspects. Carried to such extensions, the raps would become prolonged drum-rhythms performed with hands and fingers or sticks which might even have small bells attached to them. The nature of raps may be varied according to the surface from which they are produced. Wood, metal, or a drum-skin are usual. Ritual raps are normally intended as a kind of shorthand instruction of some definite kind clearly understood by hearers. They are for clarification, not mystification. One rap may indicate "Stand up", while two signify "Sit down". Raps can mean anything at all provided the hearers know and accept their arrangements. They are most useful for controlling the concerted activities of group-working without intruding irritating or confusing vocal remarks. Just as soldiers become accustomed to behaving in unison on shouted orders, so ritualists must concert their energies by rapped signals. Knocks help to conserve vocal energies for better purposes than directing general behaviour during a rite. Ceremonial dancing or processional pacing can be controlled by knocking out the tempo, which may be speeded or slowed as necessary, and stopped at exactly the right instant. An otherwise completely inaudible rite may be perfectly co-ordinated by a system of knocks, which is indeed a most impressive and effective working if properly done. Altogether, knocks and raps are an indispensible ritual sonic to be carefully studied and applied.

The Horn. This is seldom used except for traditional summoning to the four Quarters, though at one time it not only acted as an instrument for producing sound, but as an amplifier for the voice or a hearing device. As a megaphone, the horn was capable of adding an almost supernatural quality to an ordinary voice. The "voices" attributed to the various Gods were simulated through horns and trumpets of different kinds. As a listening aid, the horn both increased the amount of sound in the ear, and gave it an "other-worldly" effect. Listening to natural sounds with a horn or a large sea shell produced a variable sonic background from which it was possible to imagine all sorts of Insounds or voices. (Compare this with the modern habit of creating a "noise curtain" with radio.) Mixed sonics of high intensity known as "White sound" act as an anaesthetic on the principles of a scream. By forcing sound into the ears by means of a horn, it was hoped to eliminate or considerably lessen awareness of other physical stimuli, and substitute Inner sonic experiences instead. This is quite practicable, but far from desirable as an indiscriminate method of inducing sonic shock-stasis on physical levels. Intensification of sound directly into the ear of a recipient by artificial means greatly increases its effect on the receptive consciousness. Of old, this was done either by whispering with the mouth against the ear, or speaking into a horn held to the ear. Whatever was uttered in such a way made a very deep impression on the hearer. Information given thus was remembered well, because it penetrated closely to basic levels of the mind. This is why the Qabalah is called the "mouth to ear" Tradition. Not to indicate its secrecy, but the method by which it was transmitted. The teacher either whispered it directly into the pupil's ear, or the student whispered it into his own by cupping hands so as to connect mouth and ear. A stethoscope or a deaf-aid are good modern accessories for close aural approach. It should be remembered that in Tibetan practice, prayers and instructions for and to the dead were whispered into the cadaver's ear, and it was an European peasant custom to whisper messages for dead friends into the ear of a corpse awaiting burial. As a concentrator and disseminator of sound, the horn could be applied to either mouth or ear, and was therefore valued as a ritual instrument. It can of course be used for such a purpose today, but has been largely superseded by electronic improvements. Nevertheless a horn is still a useful adjunct for basic ritual training, and forms of it are easily made from cardboard tubing or the like.

Miscellaneous. While it is true that any source of noise might find some ritual use, however obscure, the Western Tradition tends to be rather conservative in practice. Neither the flute nor the harp, both excellent instruments, are greatly employed. Nor is the drum heard to any extent on account of its military associations, its close contact with earth, and its stimulation of the sexual centres. It seems a pity to lose such an amount of sonic energy if it can be put to good use in well-designed rites. Whistles too, are capable of ritual work. Prolonged high pitched whistling has quite a penetrating effect on hearers, and whistles have always been connected with calling up winds or familiar spirits. Explosions are sometimes used to provide a shock-element in certain types of ritual. In some eighteenth century Masonic Lodges the "Grand Shock" was delivered by firing a pistol close to the unsuspecting candidate. Not a practice to be recommended very highly for general purposes, yet one to bear in mind should need arise. By and large, if any source of sound can be put to reasonable and legitimate ritual use, it ought to be permissible. Human beings vary a great deal in their reactions to sonics, and if an intended effect can only be produced in individual hearers by odd or unlikely sounds, then those must apply in such cases. It is necessary for each ritualist to discover precisely what sounds affect them in which way, and this information can only be obtained by themselves. When dealing with sonic sources for ritual purposes, we must infallibly include two major modern advancements:

The Record Player and the Tape Recorder. The finest musical effects in the world now become available to the humblest Temple. A record library should be built up containing associative themes with ritualised concepts. There should be music or effects for the Elements, the Planets, the Spheres, different emotions and states of mind, topics for meditation, the Seasons, and in fact sonic arrangements to fit in with any or every rite likely to be worked. It is best to plan these beforehand and tape them in their proper sequence for particular rites, since a tape is much easier to control than fiddling around changing records during the rite itself. There is no doubt that records and recorders have provided ritualists with a whole new and glorious extra dimension of sound to incorporate in their workings. It seems rather strange so relatively few workers are fully exploiting such a remarkable opportunity. For voice training, a tape recorder is a virtual necessity. Nothing else shows up errors and fallibilities so clearly or indicates improvements so soon. It takes care of routine exercises, records rites themselves for subsequent technical study, and the small models make excellent note-takers for on the spot comments or ideas which might otherwise be lost or forgotten. Natural sonics, such as waterfalls, cavern echos, wind, fires, etc, may be recorded at source and used as backgrounds. Yet in the end, recorders remain machines with no ability for extension into Inner Dimensions, and they cannot supersede human consciousness or replace human participants in ritual. Mind soul and spirit must always be given top priority and consideration over any mechanical equipment. Provided this point is never lost sight of, and all sonic accessories used in service to spiritual principles but never otherwise, we may be sure of our ground when arranging the sound effects of any rite. Each single sound should have its positive purpose and meaning. Literally every smallest sonic must only be used for the sake of its depth-effect on and in hearers. If rituals were put together with the same precision as a musical composition, their efficiency would be enormously increased.

Since the voice is of paramount importance in ritual sonics as being most closely related to consciousness and will, basic vocal exercises and ordinary elocution practices should form a fair proportion of a ritualist's elementary training. Faulty speech with only an irritating or laughable effect on hearers will produce little other result. The major quality to aim for, is a resonance that automatically evokes a maximum response from recipients on its particular frequency. This is no easy matter, especially for anyone without natural physical characteristics for producing such sounds. However, resonance comes as much from mind and soul as from body, and this is why it should be cultivated for ritual practice. To be truly resonant means uttering sounds with entire feeling, sincerity and conviction arising directly from Inner reality. The soul of a sound must be put into its body from Inside. Otherwise it is nothing but a noise.

Superficially, it might seem that the foregoing means nothing more than any trained actor accomplishes in portraying a part. It means a great deal more. Actors know the part to be foreign to themselves, but ritualists must make their sonic utterances integral with themselves. They must no longer be John Smith trying to utter a Divine Name, but the Divine Aspect Itself uttering the name John Smith associates with It. True this utterance is made with all John Smith's limitations and imperfections, yet even such a degree of distortion and fading should not entirely conceal the faint echo of the Inner Voice behind it. When genuine contact is made Inwardly, it will become apparent Outwardly by sonic alterations varying from the most subtle to almost incredible degrees.

As a start to uttering any ritual sonics at all, let us try a single one by itself, relating Outer and Inner components with each other. If this can be done successfully, the rest will be but a matter of practice once the principle is mastered. To begin with, it should be realised that the "Divine Names" IAO, HU, AUM, etc., are natural sonics of the vocal range which are ideal for "power-practice". If we simply produce a pure tone while steadily opening the mouth and drawing the tongue back and then shut the lips again, we shall have uttered EE A AU O MM in that order. IHVH is the sound of a laugh—YO HO WO HO, and AHIH can also be chuckled as He HE HE HE. The old saying: "The Gods created Man with a shout of laughter" is highly significant. Therefore let us commence practice with sonics which have stood the test of time down the centuries.

Suppose we take a nice middle "OOO' sound pitched about mid register. The exercise consists of adopting a suitable position, taking a full breath and intoning the "OOO" for at least 15 seconds. What matters is the quality of tone. It must not "wobble" or be uneven, but come out as a steady resonant vibration or "straight line" of sound. A tape recorder is useful here. Until some success is gained with this practice, it is useless going on to others, for it is the key to them all. It provides the ability to produce and control vocal sonics essential to ritual workings, and must be persisted with until at least a little mastery is gained. Any good book on voice production shows the technique. The secret is to set the mouth, throat and larynx for making the sound, take a full breath, then press the air steadily out of the body by means of controlled contraction of the great diaphragm muscle. In case of difficulty, the following is an exercise calculated to achieve good results.

Lie flat on the floor face up. Clasp hands over abdomen and breathe steadily in and out so that hands rise and fall with breathing. Apply pressure over diaphragm so that breathing is done against resistance. Persist with exercise a few minutes at a time for several days until the muscles are able to lift against strong pressure. (Non smokers will find this easier than smokers.) Next obtain a few large books such as encyclopedia volumes. Place these one after the other on the abdomen while breathing steadily until several can be raised and lowered with ease. When this is possible, start breathing in through the nose, fix the mouth and lips in the "OO" position, then at maximum breath, simply let go and allow the pure weight of the books to press the air out of the mouth. No sound apart from the breath should be attempted as yet. Continue until the outbreath becomes quite steady from the constant book pressure. There is no need to consciously contract the diaphragm for expulsion of breath. Let the books do the work as if artificial respiration were being applied. When this is possible, repeat the exercise up to this point, but this time activate the larynx gently so that it makes the "OO" sound. The weight of books alone must decide the outbreath, and since this is a constant, the result should be as near a pure outsound as possible at that time for the individual practitioner. The continuation of the exercise is to practice with less weight and more muscle control until a good quality sonic can be produced without the books. Then of course, the same results must be obtained in the standing or sitting position. No real attempt at volume ought to be made during the initial stages, and only quality should be dealt with. Apart from anything else, the whole exercise has most beneficial effects on general health and temper. If the breathing can be regulated by metronome or tape, so much the better. Otherwise mental counting must be used.

When (and not before), a reasonably pure note can be sustained for between fifteen to thirty seconds, we can start alternating Outsound with Insound. Insounds of course, are supra-audible sonics only received on mental and higher levels. We continue with the "OO" sound for the present because it is best to practise a principle around one point until perfection is reached before we start leaping from one point to another imperfectly. The next exercise consists in uttering the sonic audibly for its period, and then while inbreathing, continuing to make exactly the same sound inaudibly within us directed toward the Innerworld. No more than that at first. The "OO" is thus kept up continually, half its cycle being physical, and the other half psychosonically uttered. The aim is to produce a constant note varying from one dimension to another.

An artificial aid which facilitates this is to put several minutes of equally timed sonics and intervals on tape, say thirty second periods of sonics and silence. When this is listened to, exactly the same sonic should be uttered during the tape-silent periods, then when the tape sounds off, we must echo the sound inwardly as clearly as we can. Thus we fit Outsound and Insound together to make a whole. Eventually it has to be done without any tape until the Insound becomes as definite as the Outsound.

This little exercise has more in it than might appear at first, for it links speech and hearing together via Inner dimensions. What we hear Inside ourselves becomes converted to what we utter Outwardly, and vice versa. This is quite a normal process of consciousness, but the point of interest to a ritualist is the depth and location of origin for an inter-dimensional sonic signal. Everything we say comes out of our consciousness, and everything we hear goes into it, but how deeply? Where does it get to? What effect does it have upon whom other than ourselves? In ritual, we are concerned not only with keeping the sonic tuned to its correct frequency, but also with directing it accurately and deeply enough to make contact between ourselves and whatever Inner Intelligence we are aiming at.

It is no easy matter to either make or maintain such contacts for any appreciable period. Our normal amplitude of awareness is not very great, and to exalt it to sufficient peak-intensity for direct contact with Inner entities on even lower Divine levels is both rare and difficult. How many times in an average lifetime do we really experience any degree of positive relationship with extra-mundane Beings? Perhaps occasionally when we are young, in love, or under some severe pressure which forces us away from our normal focus. Certainly not very often, and possibly under unhappy conditions. We tend to insulate ourselves from such influences for the preservation of our ordinary personalities. Yet here we are attempting to harness ritual activities for relating ourselves directly with the Inner Ones. For such an event to be realised, we shall have to penetrate our own "Heaviside layer" which we have built around ourselves. Moreover there must be no general shattering of our natural defences, but neat and careful communication channels cut through them at strategic points where these will be open to trustworthy Inner Ones and none others. Controlled sonic energies will make these penetrations as scientifically as focussed sound can drill holes through physical matter. It is a matter of applying the same law in different dimensions.

"God Names" are really specific call-signals linked with typified Spheres of Divine Energy. Their use over the centuries by highly trained minds has established almost automatic connections between Divine and human Intelligences. They are certainly the best and safest to commence practice with. These "Names" have the advantage of extreme simplicity and universality, since they join up directly with absolutely basic Life-concepts. If we consider some of the better known ones, this will soon be apparent.

AMEN	(UM EN)	The Mother am I. Primal Parent.
HU	(HOO)	He. The Father-God. Primal Parent.
AHIH	(EE HEE)	The Life Breath. Life itself manifest as indrawn and expelled breathing.
IOA	(EE OH AH)	It was, it IS, and Will be. The whole of Existence as a complete Cycle. ALL.
AUM	(UM)	The Mother. Matrix. Producer of all.
AHVH	(EE VAH)	Love between sexes. Life from Love.
AL	(EL)	The. IT. IT IS. God is It and It is God.
IHVH	(EE AH)	I shall be what I will.
VHVH	(OH AH)	We will be as we will.
AVR	(AU ER)	Light. Illumination. All seeing.

A few elementary syllables to mean so much! Furthermore, they can be "overmeant". We can put any meaning we like into those sonics, provided it is compatible with the basis. They are indeed universal words, capable of containing all kinds of consciousness. The sonics of entire understanding. A good example is a single sympathetic murmur, perhaps no more than "Oh" or "MM" in response to some woeful tale. That one sonic conveys a depth and wealth of human feeling and kindly intent far beyond whole chapters of words to express. If we could only utter our invocations with the same degree of responsive sincerity, they would work every time, and this is precisely what we must learn to do.

Suppose we start with the three "Mother letters". **A. M. Sh.** They are called Mother letters because they are the three sonics which mothers of all nations and times use toward their babies. The first attempt at speech any human hears. We may as well begin at the beginning. Each letter, syllable, or sonic, conveys considerable meaning like the God Names.

A. (Ah Ah Ah Ah Ah etc) is an attention attracter, a warning, a signal to concentrate consciousness on some definite point. It is minatory in a friendly way, and intended to rouse awareness for some particular purpose.

M. (Mm Mm Mm Mm Mm etc) is a "middle sound" of sympathy, harmony, companionship, enquiry, acknowledgement of relationship, happiness, poise, satisfaction, and is intended to establish balanced communication between the utterer and the hearer.

Sh. (Sh Sh Sh Sh Sh etc) is an allayer of agitation, a pacifier, a restorer of lost harmony, an assurance of supporting help, an avowal of fellow-feeling, a healing of hurts, a silencer, and is intended to show that the utterer has the welfare of the hearer at heart during any adversity.

These three Matrix "Pillar Letters" demonstrate the principle on which God-Names and Words of Power are put together. They are Force-foci, or concentrators of consciousness. The more meaning that can be got into the smallest sonic space, the greater its pressure to a point provided it stands the strain without breakdown. It is the old $I = \dfrac{E}{R}$ formula, where I is Intensity, E is Energy, and R is Resistance. The greater amount of pressurised consciousness that can be compressed into a verbalised sonic, the more "Magic" does it become. By imaginative extension, we can follow the reasoning that attributed the Divine Consciousness with sufficient power to create all Existence with one Utterance. Even though we cannot possibly do this, we may yet work along the same principles so far as we are able.

The basic exercise needed is compression and expansion of consciousness through sonic symbols or vehicles. We have encountered this idea already. Take a page of material and condense to a paragraph, then condense the paragraph to a sentence, the sentence to a few words, and the few words to shorthand squiggles. The magician must simply go on compressing from the point where others are forced to stop for lack of ability to contain consciousness in greater concentration. It is perfectly possible, only requiring enough determination and practice. We may compare it with winding up awareness like a spiral clock-spring until it arrives at maximum tension. Possibly a clue of this was given by the Macbeth witch in her line: "Peace—the charm's wound up". Expansion, of course, is accomplished by releasing the compression through controlled channels.

If we make use of the three Mother-sonics for linking the principles and practice of this essential exercise, the rest will follow in its own time as a matter of natural development. Suppose we start with compression on the letter A, which may be sounded "EH" "AY" or "AH" from top to bottom register. We will also invent a couple of words (why not?), to describe the process. Let "Insonate" stand for internalising consciousness by means of sound, and "Exsonate" mean the opposite, or externalising consciousness via sonic vehicles. In the first place, how do we insonate, or attach meanings to sounds at all? What makes a word different from a noise? Only our own associative efforts. We could make any noise mean anything we wanted if we really tried or insisted hard enough. The different languages in the world show this. Very well, our present task is to take the single sonic "AY" and keep pouring meanings into it along its natural frequency until it will hold or convey enough consciousness to lead us "In" or "Out" as far as we are able to go. We shall have to revert to our babyhood method of link awareness with sounds in order to relate ourselves with other individuals. This time however, we shall be seeking contact with supra-human intelligence as we try to use sonics which will operate inter-dimensionally.

First of all we commence by simply resonating "AY" as an ordinary physical sonic for a few breaths while we "get a grip on it". Then it must be transferred Inwardly by ceasing it externally and continuing it as an Insound until even the material body tingles to it. Now we can start "packing" or "loading" it, which is the important part of the operation. While we carry on making the Insound, which must be kept going the whole while, we push into it every possible meaning we can find to associate specifically with it. For instance, in addition to those already noted, "AY" can be used in the sense of "Hey you!" as a call-signal; "EH?" as expressing a desire to be informed; "A" as singling anything apart from everything else; "AI" indicating "This is me"; "AY" signifying "Yes, it is so", and a number of other meanings along those lines. Every available meaning must be thought of and literally forced into the constantly resonating sonic by increasing the intensity of awareness to the sharpest focus possible. This is not unlike recording, where the resonating sonic equates with the turning disc, the focus of consciousness to the engraving needle, and the varied meanings impressed correspond to the indentations made in the sound-track.

Tradition always tells us to make the "Words of Power" long drawn out. The reason for this is now evident, which is to give us enough time for putting sufficient consciousness into them, or getting it out properly. True, some are "explosive", but if "Innerworld time" is to be geared down to our "Outerworld time", there has to be some relative factor compatible with both, and "Words of Power" are sonic attempts to fulfil this very function. It may take us hours to "load" a sonic which can be discharged in a millisecond, or conversely a charge of consciousness can be compressed instantaneously into a sound needing a lifetime to pass through an ordinary mind. What else is a "Magical Name?". Time is really measured by degrees of conscious compression. If we but realised this, we might do a lot more with our lives.

Once we start Insonating properly, we can keep any "Word of Power" going as long as we like, or to the limits of our patience. Insound does not depend on our physical breath or any material factor. Physically, we can move around, talk about anything, or think of all kind of things while we still keep resonating away inside ourselves on the same Insonic frequency. It is a useful practice to try this while doing some ordinary job not needing meticulous attention. It should be possible to make an Insonic background against which we occupy ourselves with other matters just as if it were a radio sound or any external noise. It is of paramount importance however that we should be able to switch this on or off at will. That ability must be developed, and control maintained over the sonic, at all other costs. Better not to acquire the faculty of insonation at all, than live against a chaotic background of Insound.

If the exercise has been progressing favourably, we shall be juggling with several processes of consciousness at once. First we need to produce the Insonic, secondly we must be aware of it with our Inner hearing, and thirdly we should be compressing a whole lot of meanings into it. Fourthly, we need to direct the entire issue toward some particular objective. If we are invoking a specific God Aspect or Intelligence, then in addition to the other work going on, we must aim the sonic by making ourselves Inwardly aware of such a Concept and linking ourselves therewith by that sonic as if we were calling anyone physically. Should we be simply practising the exercise, then we direct the outcome to our own Inner faculties of Wisdom, Understanding, and Memory. This is done in much the same way as if we took a record out of our Consciousness-bank marked "AY" (or whatever else), added data to it, and then replaced it until needed again. Every time the same sonically marked card is withdrawn, its total value should have increased by the "interest" added from Inner sources in contact with us on deep levels. A single sonic regularly "charged" and "discharged" between ourselves and some higher Intelligence can lead to considerable expansion of consciousness, providing we do our fair share of the effort involved.

Back then to our compression of conscious energy into the "AY" sonic. There is no reason why this should be limited to worded phrases or purely intellectual formularies. There are feelings to be considered. How does "AY" make us feel? Alert, wide-awake and ready for anything? Then let us feel so while we are insonating it. Absolutely everything connected with "AY" which affects our consciousness in any way on any level must be firmly pushed into that one sonic. It is quite amazing what will link in almost by itself. To obtain much success, the sonic will have to be kept up for quite longish periods at first, though not necessarily incessant ones. Several days may be spent on a sonic for perhaps a quarter of an hour per session. Practising Sufis operate on their sonic "HU" for as much as an hour at a time, and individual practitioners (probably very few in number) advocate the sonic "UM" (AUM OM) for days and even longer. It is quite practical to work on one sonic for a day at intervals and keep returning to it whenever opportunity presents itself. Compressing consciousness to a sonic point takes a good deal of effort if done properly, and should be carried out until the strain is felt, but on no account to any degree of exhaustion.

Once we get the knack of loading or winding up a sonic, we can try releasing its energy. This is done by directing it from our deepest levels toward our Outwardising awareness, and if necessary translating it into Outsound for communication with physical ears. It should be noted that merely calling a sonic aloud does not exsonate it. Exsonation implies a deliberate and intentional issue of conscious energy from an Inner source to the limits of Outer living via some specific sonic means. This may exteriorise as physically uttered noises during a ritual, or it may simply reach the Outer edges of the ritualist's mind and soul, remaining silent to anyone else. What matters is the direction of energy-flow.

To exsonate our charged "AY" sonic, we must first reach right back through ourselves until we find the Inner source from which we hope it will be directed. Suppose we are seeking contact with the Divine Concept of Mercy and Compassion. We approach this by whatever system of Inner awareness we find most practical, then exsonate our sonic from that point as if it were the actual reply of the Divine Concept Itself speaking toward ourselves as ordinary mortals listening with our human faculties. What we are doing in fact, is to set up a "carrier wave" of sound which Divinity will subtly modulate in establishing communication with us along this line. We provide the sound, Divinity provides the sense.

The sequence factor should help us get things right. With insonation we start the sonic physically and then go on pushing it Inwardly through physically inaudible levels, and in the case of exsonation we commence from an Inner point and continue pushing it Outwardly until it emerges from our bodily lips as physically audible sound. A significant physical silence is thus noticed *after* insonation and *before* exsonation. During those periods the necessary Inner contacts are completing the sonic cycle. They may be very brief, but they must be effective.

While insonating, we are pushing consciousness into our sonic, but while exsonating we are getting consciousness out of it. Everything depends from what level this consciousnes comes. If it is purely from ourselves to another human, then we utter it in the ordinary way, pushing our meaning out along with the sound. Should contact with Inner Intelligences be sought, the procedure must alter somewhat to allow that particular source to take over and modulate the sonic. This is done by "handing over control" of the sonic from the ordinary levels of our mind to the Inner point where we are making contact with the Intelligence, and simply allowing the conscious content of the sound to come from there instead of from our normal selves. We "stand aside" as it were, letting the sound pour through us and out of us directly from its Inner origin. If we were linking in with the Concept of Mercy, then the whole sonic should modulate with that particular quality to the maximum degree of our capability of "bringing it through". This means it would be evoked from all hearers, including ourselves.

Whatever Inner contact we make will affect our uttered sonic in its own way. All ten of the main Concepts modify the same sonic according to their natures. "AY" can therefore be exsonated in as many ways as we can find Inner contacts. Our next exercise should be running up and down the Concepts insonating and exsonating with each. It is very interesting to note the variations and effects that will come naturally with every change of contact via the same sonic. In olden times this would have been termed "becoming the Voice of God". The closer and better contact we can make with Inner origins, the more marked will be the Outer effect. The physical vibrations of the utterance alone will have a definite effect on and in our material bodies and brains, since these will respond to Inwardly modulated frequency. Health and general tone of our vehicles can be affected favourably or adversely depending on our sonic contacts. For that reason it is better to keep within proved limits rather than "try wild".

When we are exsonating the old evocative ritual formulas of: "I am so and so, my Holy Name is thus, I act in such a way, etc etc," it must be as though we were actually listening to the Contact itself speaking through us. No one, least of all the evocant, should get the impression of someone reciting something from a piece of paper. The God or Inner One must be positively felt through the sonic. Perhaps it will be an extra degree of resonance, even the slightest tonal alteration, or an indefinable yet recognisable quality superimposed on the sonic coming through. Whatever it is, there will be something quite unmistakable about it when it occurs, and all concerned will realise they are listening to other than a purely human voice. We should remember that the Inner Ones do not use human language for communication amongst themselves, and it is only through us they become limited to what we call "words".

The method of making such Inner contacts is not unlike the process known in theatrical circles as "suspension of disbelief". Pure faith in other words. A playgoer knows well enough that the whole theatre, play, actors, and everything else is an artificial arrangement. This rational knowledge however, entirely prevents access to the Inner meanings of the drama, and cuts off all empathy between players and audience. Eventually theatregoers develop an ability to override this spoilsport rationalism in themselves and accept the Inner reality of the drama for what it is worth. They then "enter the spirit of the play" quite literally. They accept the characters as realities rather than the artists who present them. At the end of the performance, they are rewarded by having undergone an Inner experience related to the drama. This experience is real in the sense that it affects them, even if only slightly, and to some degree they are changed by what they underwent. That is reality, and not fiction, however fictitious the play. It all depends on faith, or suspending disbelief.

We are faced with a similar problem in ritual sonics and general experience. We know that our arrangements and symbols are as artificial as a stage, and yet they are the means of our linking in with Entities far more real than the characters of any human drama. So we must suspend disbelief on rational levels and enter the spirit of a ritual with considerably more faith than we take to the theatre. There is nothing but a barrier of rationalism standing between us and the Inner Ones. Once we are able to open up a safe way through it which can be opened or closed at will, our Contacts are bound to link in with us satisfactorily. Surely if we can "suspend disbelief" for the purpose of enjoying a play, we can do even better along the same principles for the sake of our own souls and spirits.

When we are able to insonate and exsonate the one sonic "AY" with any degree of success, it will be time to try the other two. It is astounding what will go in and out of them. "MM" is the "happy medium" sound conveying an incredible amount of understanding between any two conscious entities. We must be careful to distinguish between "understanding" and "information". Real understanding is a definite contact made on deep levels of being, and provides an actual experience. Information is no more than a statement or presentation which we may interpret as we please on intellectual levels. Information can be put into few or many words of human language, but understanding does not need such words at all, although it may be directed sonically. All lovers will understand what "MMM" means to them. Bees are not only a symbol of love between sexes because of their sweet honey and sharp stings, but on account of their humming sound. "MMM" is essentially the sonic of complete empathy and co-union. There is no reason why we should not use a modern comparison of "MMM" with a perfectly running motor or dynamo. However we use it, the principles of pleasing relationships between people or things is encountered. Having sought contact with our Inner Intelligence by means of the "AY", we now establish personal relationship therewith on the best possible terms by using "MMM".

Humming is good for body, mind and soul alike, putting them on excellent terms with each other. Apart from anything else, it provides much needed exercise for the internal physical organs, giving them a valuable "micro-massage". Happiness and humming go together, and we should certainly practise it more frequently. If we make a good contact with an Inner source of consciousness, and then bring it through along a hummed sonic, this will be evident. The humming must be kept up long enough to be effective. If a small group of workers are practising together, they must synchronise with each other so that about half are humming outwardly while the others are breathing in. That way, the humming can be kept constant. This will have a surprising effect on "exalting the consciousness", and it can be varied in all sorts of way. Humming may be commenced on a very low pitch and gradually heightened step by step until inaudible physically but still rising Insonically. We can hum our way up and down the Ladder of Light. There are far more possibilities to "MMM" than might be supposed, and these are all waiting to be explored by adventurous seekers.

The "SSSH" sonic is one of arrival and pacification because of completion. It is both a finalisation of one factor and a preparation for another. As a "serpent-sound" it links with serpent symbology as the tail of the creature is about to enter its mouth and silence its hiss. All ends in Silence and begins again from thence. "SSHH" is both a sleep-sound and an alerting one as "hss-hhss", when attention must be attracted without much noise. The rhythmic rise and fall of "SSSH"' brings peace and tranquillity with it. If we associate our three Mother sonics with the act of generation, the "AH" links with the preliminary skirmishings, the "MMM" with the intimate climax, and the "SSSH" with the quiet fulfilment afterwards. Such sounds accompanied the making of a mother, and were therefore considered sacred to the Mother-Concept.

"SSH" is one of the few sonics that can be kept up with the mouth open while breathing in and out. It is an hypnotic and allays fear. Its great use is "silencing up" when passing from a loud active to a quiet passive part of a rite, and Outer action is being transferred to Inner. "SSH" releases tensions if sufficiently prolonged, and is valuable as a conclusion for most rites when all should leave in the Sign of Silence. If, however, we reverse the order of the Mothers, and sonate "SSSH MMMM AAAH" we get a complete wake-up effect, and in fact the word "SHMAH" means "to hear" in the sense of "Hear ye all".

"AAAH" is the sound of an indrawn breath, "MMM" of a closed mouth, and "SSSH" of exhaling by open mouth. Thus a complete life-breath cycle is sonated. It makes a good exercise to use the Mothers in this way while meditating appropriately. We shall hear the Mothers where sea meets shore. The "AAAH" of the approaching waves" the "MMM" of the breakers, and the "SSSH" of the shingle being pulled seawards. Our Mother-Deep speaking to us if we know how to listen. An interesting point in passing is that the name "HERMES" consists essentially of the three Mothers. "AH (ER), M, ES. In the Secret Tradition Hermes was far more than a messenger boy between Gods and men. He typifies the consciousness which links the two extremes of Being, and the Hermetic Mysteries were and are solely concerned with establishing and maintaning conscious communication between Divinity and Humanity. The very name of their Patron or Grand Master was the code on which they worked. We should remember in this connection Herm-Aphrodite, the male-female Concept, and realise that the Hermetic Mysteries conjoin those of the Father and Mother. Hermes well deserves his title of "Master of the words" in connection with magical rites, and is indeed the God of Speech in more senses than one.

Any sonic at all which gives a human being some actual experience of Inner realities otherwise beyond their reach is a "Word of Power" or magic word. All words and sounds have their own magic once we find out how to use this. It remains to discover which sonics have what effect on whom, and that is a major piece of research. People react to sound so very differently from each other. Primitives living among the sounds of nature itself against a silent background are much more easily moved by vocal sonics than those living in modern urban conditions with a high level of artificial noise against a background of distant disturbance. For that reason alone, Temple worked rituals in towns should be proceeded by at least some minutes of silent meditation. This is best led into by suitable music fading gently into the silence, and at the conclusion of the silent period, music connected with the rite should be commenced very softly, then gradually brought up to working level. At least this will provide participants with a chance to condition themselves for the ritual use of sound.

We are perhaps apt to overlook the possibility that Words of Power which had such great effect on hearers centuries ago may not move moderns to anything like the same way or degree. They are still effective, but only among those who are prepared to train and condition themselves by Mystery practices and hard work. Some schools believe their particular "Words of Power" should be kept secret, but this really makes no difference to their efficacy or otherwise. The words are useless except to those enabled to make use of them by responsive conditioning through individual and group efforts. Few but genuine and dedicated souls are likely to spend the necessary time and trouble on such a task. It is often amusing to find little "Mystery" Groups zealously guarding Words of Power which not a single member has sufficient knowledge or application enough to use. There is no secret worth keeping in the Words, because this lies in their practice and usage. That is the real Mystery or art.

When we have put in some reasonable practice with the Mother sonics and the vowels associated with the Elements, we shall be prepared to start "God Names". The real purpose of these sonics is for linking us directly with Divine energies. By means of their Names, we invoke them Inside ourselves, and evoke, or call them out of us into manifestation. This will be impossible unless we modulate our carrier-sonic with both Wisdom and Will. We must Know and Want the Power on which we call, thus providing it with a means of localisation on us. The deeper inside ourselves we reach, the more positive will be the responsive contact. Superficial calls receive only superficial answers. The principles of invoking and evoking Inner contacts, are that these will be made from their equivalent levels in ourselves. Divine Aspects are contacted from our Innermost beings, Archangel Intelligences from our higher minds and souls, Angels from our lower mental and emotional levels, while Elementals are encountered with our desires and passions. It depends entirely from which of our own degrees we work, as to what type of Inner consciousness or Entity we shall deal with.

Those unused to Orientally originated sonics and Names will have to condition themselves in order to make use of these. It is pointless sonating OM if it arouses no personal reaction. The same is true for most magical Names. We must react with and experience them before they can be valuable to us, and this is a matter of training like everything else. Suppose we take a fairly widely used Name by Westerners and develop its use. AM EN is very suitable for this purpose.

AM EN is generally supposed to be a terminal to prayers meaning "Let it be so". It is far more, being a God-Name in its own right signifying "The Mother am I". Mother to be understood in the sense of the Divine Producer of life and everything. As a prayer-termination, it is an acknowledgement that what has been said can only exist by virtue of the Origin of Existence Itself. As an invocation, AM EN calls to this potential in ourselves for the production of whatever we hope will come forth. As a prayer by itself, AM EN establishes a relationship between ourselves and the Divine Source of Life as Matrix of our being. It is an universal sonic of a very high order if properly used, being a doubly resonant bi-syllabic Name capable of many flexible adaptations.

For individual training, we should resonate AM EN as almost UM EN to a steady rhythm of about two or three seconds per syllable with the beat coming on the resonant M and N. During the UM we must make a realisation of the Great Mother Life or Spirit out of Which we, and everything else emerged. There should be no sense of "Me-ness" but all "Thee-ness", while we attempt to conceive however feebly what such a Power means. If we like to think wordlessly "O Thou Mother of All", and feel in our hearts our incalculable need of such Being, or the love we would bear towards It, so much the better. All this and more if possible during the UM. On the EN syllable, we switch over to our own identity, realising that a Mother expresses Herself through Her children of which we are one. What our Mother can do through us, She will. We are personally related in the deepest and most intimate way with our Primal Parent. There must be a realisation of being loved by the Divine Being because we are a child thereof. A sense of "I am Thine, and Thou art mine" is to be aimed for. All this and more when possible during the EN.

The AM EN must be kept up and reiterated over prolonged periods in various ways until we need only use it Inwardly to cause an effect with us. It can be taken on a two-tone basis, accompanied with gongs or other instruments, set to drum-beats, used with rising or falling cadences, or otherwise employed. Intoned between two people or sections, one side taking UM and the other EN, the Word will produce excellent results provided Inner contact is not lost. A dramatic practice is to start an UM EN duet on a low slow beat, then gradually speed up, each side as it were forcing the others pace to a rising crescendo until the AM and EN culminate in a single explosive sonic. At that moment a gong should sound and silence supervene while conscious contact is sought with the Divinity. This gives good overall results as a rule, but is difficult as a practice owing to the need for considerable training.

With an expert team, a great deal is possible by sonating God-Names. As a group experience they are naturally more powerful and impressive than as a solitary event, though everyone must find their own reactions to the Names for themselves, and the deepest Inner Contacts can only be made alone in the Loudest Silence. No team is better than the individuals composing it, and the strongest team cannot entirely tune out the weakness of its most fallible member. If a number of people are to use the same ritual sonic together, they must all work the same Inner and Outer method. It is no use their being tuneful or synchronous as a mechanical exercise if all their minds and souls are drifting about in contradictory fashions. Unless all are able to control and direct their Inner energies with the precision of a military drill manoeuvre, group working will produce little of value and may even weaken those already doing good individual work. When any form of combined operations is undertaken therefore, it is essential to put Inner discipline first, and agree together entirely about the Inner modus operandi before any Outer sonic or other work is attempted.

Syllable by syllable, the principal God-Names should be linked in with Inner realities, insonated and exsonated until they come to life, then associated with conditions of soul, mind, and body to which they apply. For instance, it is a natural thing to yell with delight and high spirits when so elated and exuberant that nothing else will do. "Yahoo" is a common cry, but if we analyse IA HU, we shall find it means "O Thou Greatest One" from a masculine angle. All the primal instinctive cries are God-Names of some kind. Suppose we adopt a controlled form of this exercise, and instead of simply saying, "My God!" as a kind of general expression, Anglicise IU HU AH into "YOU WHO ARE". It can be beautifully sonated on a dropping and recovering two-tone four syllable chant, "YOU WHOO OO/ARE". As such, it is an acknowledgement of the Divine Being, and one's own personal relationship with It.

An excellent opportunity to use this chant would be some perfect moment, such as a hill-top on a wonderful day amid glorious surroundings. There should be a sense that everything is calling its loudest and proclaiming itself as the outcome of an Omnipotent Creator. Everything Outside us is truly speaking to our Inside in the most emphatic way. If we have a human companion we may say weakly "Isn't it beautiful" or some such ineffective remark. Instead, let us answer back directly from the depths of ourselves, addressing our sonic to the Power behind the presentation which gave us a sense of Presence. Looking the presentation before us straight in its face we breathe in its essence and then release our reply in one freely outpoured; "YOOOO WHOOO OOO AHHHHHRE". Repeat to the Four Quarters, and the Dimensions behind external boundaries will be felt very plainly. It is advisable not to do this in the hearing of antipathetic human listeners however!

This odd habit (if discreetly practised) of answering Nature back in her own terms will provide a lot of most valuable information about sonics for ritual use. It is useful to sigh back into trees, crackle or roar back at fires, speak to waterfalls in their own language, and rumble at falling rocks. At first thought this appears crazy, but it is far from being so for those seeking knowledge at source. We cannot afford to overlook any life-linked sonics that have Inner and Outer connections. Above all, we must learn the art of *experiencing* them, so that they *happen* to us as actualities, and not remote meaningless noises. Western rituals are sophisticated affairs with longish prose and poetry passages. Unless we translate them into terms of Inner living and undergo them for ourselves, the words of most rituals will have less significance than a shopping list. It is what words do to us and we do with them that matters. This is their magic. We shall learn it best by starting at the beginning, and linking basic units of Inner experience with sonic syllables as with the God-Names. Later we may join these together to make sequential Inner living.

The God-Names are intended to cover every aspect of Inner Being in a definite number of categories reachable by human consciousness Divinely inspired. When we intone the Name, we link ourselves with that category or type of God-ness. The "Archangel" Names are to link us with the creative Intelligence of that Sphere, while Names of Angels or Spirits are for individualising our contacts even more toward our human limits until we reach our instant of time-place-purpose. A parallel for this would be comparing a Divine Aspect with, say, Industry as a whole, the Archangel as the Director of some particular Company, the Angel Order as the required department, and the Spirit as the individual with whom our dealings with the Company are transacted. Each Name adapts the original Energy closer to our humanity, and puts us in touch with its own category of Inner awareness—if we make proper use of it.

It is advisable to retain the God-Names in their archaic forms of Hebrew, Latin, Greek, or other derivation, for several reasons. First because this allows us to use them for ritual purposes alone, and they will not .trigger off responses at impractical times or places during everyday life. Secondly because they are thus less likely to be "profaned" or treated with the familiarity that does indeed breed contempt or sheer lack of interest. Thirdly, because the old formulae have links that go right back to early times, and have made channels in our deep collective consciousness forming natural conductive paths for the energies we are dealing with via ritual. If we train ourselves in their sonic use, we can modulate them with whatever Inner adaptions we are capable of.

Whichever Supreme Name we use for Divinity, it must be a sonic symbol for the absolute entirety of our Inner existence. All we were, are, or ever will be. Our Whole. Other God-Names will lead us to their parts of this ONE. On paper, the Supreme Name should be shown in the centre of a circle, and others around the perimeter. The Supreme Name IO (IAO, IHV, JOVE, IOEL, etc) can be expressed as the Circled Cross which reads IO whichever way we look at it. We can sonate it as:

EE   while we experience the emergence of Being from non-Being. Existence as Itself. All from Nil.

AY   while we realise the separation of Itself from Itself into distinct categories, much as light separates itself into colours via the spectrum yet retaining its wholeness for what IT IS.

OH while we try and realise the different Aspects of Divinity relating themselves with each other so as to form the Circle of Manifestation and complete the Cycle of Creation as an Entirety.

The important factor to bear in mind, is that we must put our experience into the Word before it will put any experience into us or anyone else. It is useless calling away at God-Names or any Word of Power without getting at them Inside ourselves and charging them up to the limit with Inwardly released energy. We must work a Word with Will if it is to be truly magic. We really have to put our souls and our selves into them, if words are to have any power whatsoever. Let us take the Names of the Ten Spheres which comprise the whole of Inner Existence, and instead of repeating them parrot fashion, make ourselves happen into each while we sonate them. The Names may be rhythmically repeated again and again as we arrange ourselves Inwardly. A brief outline of this exercise runs thus.

OOO	**AIN**	(NIL) No sonation outwardly. Experience the All of Nothing. OMNIL.
OO	**AIN SVPH**	(LIMITLESSNESS) Unbounded homogenous undifferentiated Being.
O	**AIN SVPH AVR**	(LIMITLESS LIGHT) Identify with boundless outpouring LIGHT. Nothing else. Just pure Illumination by itself with no objective to illuminate.
1	**KETHER**	(SUMMIT) Identify with fire awareness of individual existence. Feel I AM — THOU ART.
2	**CHOKMAH**	(WISDOM) Realise faculty for gaining knowledge and experience through consciousness. See it as a modus vivendi and a major factor for continuing existence further than this point.
3	**BINAH**	(UNDERSTANDING) Appreciate intuition and ability to extend consciousness through all else than "self". Try and do this.
4	**CHESED**	(COMPASSION) Enter into understanding of necessity for everything. Empathise lovingly therewith. Be merciful and kindly. Anabolic.
5	**GEBURAH**	(SEVERITY) Realise need for control and economy of energy. Nothing to be wasted. Law of retributive return. Discipline of self. Katabolic.

6	**TIPHERETH**	(BEAUTY) Experience poise, balance, harmony, perfect equilibrium, radiance, and all sorts of solar wonders. Feel the centre of a universe.
7	**NETZACH**	(VICTORY) Feel triumphant and joyful. Be "in love" with everyone and everything. Experience security of affections. Feel loved and wanted.
8	**HOD**	(GLORY) Experience a state of intelligent interest in everything, good humoured, amused, alert for all information and very much "ready to go".
9	**YESOD**	(FOUNDATION) Have faith in the purpose of everything even if incomprehensible currently. Believe in life itself regardless of personal opinions. Feel strong and firm, vital and fecund.
10	**MALKUTH**	(KINGDOM) Experience individuality as human and the world around. Relate one with other. Realise connections between Inner and Outer Life. Feel God behind Man as Ultimate Rule, Be, because of BEING.

Such is the barest sketch of our comprehensive tour around the Innerworld on ten sonics. Indefinitely more is possible within that framework. The exercises consist of resonating each Name during the whole meditative period while we are getting ourselves into the actual states of being what the Spheres describe. This does not mean vaguely thinking of what Spheres stand for, and speculating about them. It means that we must enter the spirit of each Sphere to the fullest degree of our Inner capabilities. We have to actually enter and live in them inside ourselves, not dither around them in uncertain circles. If we are entering CHESED for example, it is not enough to just think about Mercy, we must *live* it and BE it for the time we associate ourselves with Chesed. The whole of our Inner faculties must be concentrated on this one task of literally being IN MERCY. We must think it with our minds, feel it with our souls, extend it through our bodies, and BE IT with our Spirits. Starting at the top we say: I AM such and such, then, I *feel* such and such, I *think* such and such, lastly I *live* such and such. From end to end of ourselves we must make ourselves what we say we shall be. This is the creative power of the Word.

It will be seen that all the Inner realities dealt with are normally evoked from humans by externalities to themselves. Magical practices simply give us the ability to evoke the same energies from our Inner depths with no other externality than a chosen sonic. Our Words of Power are keys that admit us to the Innerworld far better than any drug, because with them we retain the will and mastery that drugs deprive us of. We enter as Initiates, not as an infestation. Admittedly it takes little effort to swallow a pill, and an enormous amount of work to become a Master of the Word (Baal Shem), but the pill-taker has only a temporary, tenuous, and ineffectual entry to the Innerworld, while the Master of the Word earns a permanent and powerful place therein. Once we learn the art of "living into" words, Inner life will open up in the most amazing way, and without such an ability we cannot hope to work modern rituals properly. Therefore we must keep up our exercises with God-Names until the mere whisper of one directly in the ear is sufficient to evoke immediate Inner reaction. That is the test of efficacy. It is practical and proven.

When we succeed with single syllables and sonics in evoking maximum Inner responses, we may try "living into" whole phrases and sentences of ritualised prose or poetry. This is really no more than following out a command or instruction, except that what we hear Outwardly we act on Inwardly or vice versa. It is the art of identifying into a story or recitation extended to a far greater than ordinary degree. For that matter, all magic is a question of natural abilities developed much beyond common possession or comprehension. The magician keeps going Inward where the rest slow down or stop. That is the only difference. In the case of ritual phraseology, each section provides the makings of a whole Inner adventure and experience which should be fully taken advantage of. Even a few words are enough to give a trained ritualist an opportunity for a considerable amount of Inner living. The Psalms were composed for this purpose, and afford incredible wealth of Inner material to build with. Let us take a trial run with the well-known 23rd.

Firstly we should note that Psalms are constructed to be recited or chanted verse by verse, two sections to each verse. Each section contains approximately one specific statement or idea. There is an important reason for this. The momentary pauses between statements or expressions are to give time and opportunity for Inner action concerning them. Unless this is actually done, the Psalms are no more than pleasant recitations. Properly performed, psalms are chanted alternately verse by verse from one choral group to another. Those chanting are providing the listeners with material to build Inwardly with, which means there must be a rapid turn-round between verses when both sides change polarity. The whole makes a four point cycle of consciousness alternating between Inner and Outer life at each half-cycle. These four points are:

1 INNER CONTACT. During which an idea is taken hold of, dealt with, and processed up to maximum.
2 OUTER EXPRESSION. The idea is verbalised and exsonated into material manifestation.
3 OUTER CONTACT. Hearers of the sonically expressed idea pick it up and extract a meaning.
4 INNER EXPRESSION. The essence of the idea as developed by hearers is projected back Inwardly.

This is the plan of ritual sonic activity. If two sides of a choir or team represented by A and B were working it, A would first invoke the commencing idea in themselves either from memory or by reading it. Then they would project it out of themselves towards B, having processed it with their own thoughts and Inner energies. B section now assimilates the idea receptively from the Outer sonic, transmutes it into Inner activity as they build within themselves, then projects the result positively toward the Innerworld via their own contact therewith. Continuing their Inner contact, B then changes polarity to receptive, and extracts the next idea for projection to A by psycho-physical sonics. With trained operatives a considerable exchange of conscious energy from one level of Existence to another is possible. The impact of Inner energy to Outer receptors can be as definite as that of a tennis ball against a racket during a hard played game.

If one person alone is working, the same principles apply. First the Inner concept, then the sonation, then the processing, and finally the projection back to the Inner. The cycle goes—Negative-positive, negative-positive. Over and over again, building up energies all the time. With practice this can be speeded up so that the brief pauses between statements and verses in a psalm or other chant are quite enough for Inner adjustments. The main thing is to get the working principles firmly established by repetitive efforts until they are automatically used throughout general ritual practice. If we continue our exercise with the 23rd Psalm, this should show up quite plainly. Its fundamental ideas are translatable from pastoral to occult ones.

1 THE LORD IS MY SHEPHERD: I SHALL NOT WANT.
Here there is an implication of being Divinely led and wanting Nothing. Our spirits move us toward the Great Nil of our Ultimate Existence, or Nirvana.
2 HE MAKETH ME TO LIE DOWN IN GREEN PASTURES, HE LEADETH ME BESIDE THE STILL WATERS.
Here we contact the Elements of fertile Earth and peaceful Water.

3 HE RESTORETH MY SOUL.

Life is returned to us. We re-incarnate for the sake of spiritual development.

4 HE GUIDETH ME IN THE PATHS OF RIGHTEOUSNESS FOR HIS NAMES SAKE.

The Holy Names will guide us through the Paths on the Tree of Life.

5 YEA THOU I WALK THROUGH THE VALLEY OF THE SHADOW OF DEATH, I WILL FEAR NO EVIL.

We shall cross the Dread Abyss with fearless faith.

6 THY ROD AND THY STAFF THEY COMFORT ME.

The staff is a spear (or sword) across the Abyss on which we must walk, the rod gives us the balance to accomplish this hazard likened to a tight-rope—one slip proving fatal.

7 THOU PREPAREST A TABLE BEFORE ME IN THE PRESENCE OF MINE ENEMIES.

The table is an altar-top (or Shield) between the Pillars of Opposites ("emnity" as opposition).

8 THOU HAST ANOINTED MY HEAD WITH OIL.

Oil is the Element of Light and consecrated Life. It is here considered as being sent from Heaven to a chosen one.

9 MY CUP RUNNETH OVER.

The capacity of the recipient for Divine Love cannot contain it, so there is an outflow for other souls.

10 SURELY HAPPINESS AND LOVING KINDNESS WILL FOLLOW ME ALL THE DAYS OF MY LIFE.

Here are the ideas of Mercy and Justice, the two Pillars between which our lives should be directed.

11 AND I SHALL DWELL IN THE HOUSE OF THE LORD FOREVER MORE.

This is the idea of Eternal Life in the Divine Spirit.

Here we have a whole perfect arrangement of Symbols and ideas directly connected with the Western Occult Tradition. The Elements, Instruments, Paths, and Principles are all there together. If we link them up again into a metrical combination suitable for plain-chanting, they will come together something along these lines:

I.O.A. leads me. Nothing is my need
Earth sustains, and Water purifies me.
Life returns to me. I shall beguided
By the Names upon the Paths of Righteousness.
I will cross the Abyss without failing,
Thy Sword supports me, and thy Rod will save me.
Thou settest up my Shield between the Pillars.

Light and Life thou sendest down upon me.
My Cup is overflowing with the Goodness,
If I remain within thy Might and Mercy
I shall live forever in thy Spirit.

A.M.E.N.

All these are Archetyptal Images, capable of linking us Inwardly with all their contacts throughout Existence. It remains to build them into our experience with ritual usage. Once we are able to handle the currency of our consciousness in units of Archetypes, we can convert it into whatever terms we need. Those Symbols are an universal exchange operating beyond the barriers of any language. If we are able to work in two teams, so that one does Inside themselves what the others vocalise Outside themselves, this will be a great advantage. On the other hand, solitary practice will allow sufficient interval periods for careful Inner construction. If we take the 23rd Psalm section by section and live it Inwardly as an experience, this will demonstrate how ritualised passages of poetry or prose are to be treated. Like this:

Outer phrase	*Inner activity*
1 I.O.A. leads me. Nothing is my need.	Awareness of the Divine Spirit urging experience and development of soul though evolvement until Ultimate of NIL is reached.
2 Earth sustains, and Water purifies me.	Realisation of dependency on earth-fertility and need of purification from corrupt matter. Importance of keeping good relationship with Elements.
3 Life returns to me.	Acceptance of re-incarnatory principles and sense of survival.
4 I shall be guided by the Names upon the Paths of Rightness.	Knowledge that information about living along the right lines will come from Inner guidance. The Tree Paths and the Holy Names show the Ways.
5 I will cross the Abyss without failing.	Realisation of the Terrible Test of soul-survival, and the Abyss of the Lost, which must be crossed *alone* except for the Inner Spirit which *alone* can save from destruction.
6 Thy Sword supports me and thy Rod will save me.	Here we visualise the crossing of the Great Abyss along the edge of a mighty Sword, but we are so well balanced by the Rod held horizontally that we shall not fall. This Symbol makes the Cross of Salvation.

7 Thou settest up my Shield between the **Pillars.**	Here we realise the Shield of our own perceptive consciousness placed between the Pillars of Opposites so that we may reach their realities by our reflections.
8 Light and Life thou sendest down upon me.	Now we must feel the Light of Truth above us illuminating our lives which become consecrated to the Divine Purpose in ourselves.
9 My Cup is over-flowing with thy goodness.	Here we feel ourselves a Cup unable to contain the Divine Love that is poured into us, and so it overflows around us to all other souls.
10 If I remain within thy Might and Mercy.	Now we are between the Pillars, upright, and keeping the Straight Way of the Middle Pillar.
11 I shall live forever in thy Spirit.	At last we return to the Point of our beginning, the Holy Spirit of Life Itself which is our true Immortality.

A helpful way to practice this sort of exercise is by putting the verses on tape, then listening to them one at a time, not proceeding to the next until the verse being dealt with is properly Inwardised. In this way we not only enter the Innerworld, but what is more important, we do something helpful and practical with our lives therein.

We have now considered the application of sonics to ritual practice from the simplest sonic units to their complex combinations as words linked with human understanding. It must never be forgotten that no matter how involved or complicated sonics become, or seem to become, their original energies derive from the "barbarous Names of Invocation" of which sophisticated writers of Mystery scripts were well advised not to change a syllable. It is still possible to make a truer Inner contact with one single Call than by reciting entire chapters of pious writings. Such Calls should always be included in rites at important points, and we omit these "God-Names" at our own cost. True, they cannot be taught in the ordinary sense, but they do teach themselves to anyone sufficiently devoted to their practice. They "come out" of their own accord as it were, during training sessions, and will ring true beyond any possible doubt, though probably on rare occasions. It is only when unhindered contact between the Inner Entity and its Outer manifesting agency is obtained, that the God-Names will sound "right".

No one can be taught exactly how to reach inside themselves and make these Inner contacts, any more than they can be taught their natural functions of breathing or eating. We cannot learn an ability, but only how to control or apply it. If we persist in directing our consciousness Inwardly in search of other sources of consciousness not directly associated with human bodies, we shall definitely encounter these. The rest depends on our own efforts and common-sense.

There are endless technical "tricks of the trade" in developing what might be called "ritual resonance" in the human voice. Most of these can be found in ordinary voice-training manuals, but some are traditional. Spending several days in an echoing cave might not be appreciated nowadays when we could get much the same effect with an amplifier at home. One old practice is worth mentioning for the sake of its quaintness and practicability. This is an unsuspected use for a cauldron of the "Witch" type as an echo-chamber. One about the three gallon size is needed for a head to be inserted without danger of being jammed. Cartoons of this event can be amusingly visualised!

If the head is carefully lowered into the cauldron and any of the Names resonated, the amplification effect is really startling and has to be experienced in order to be fully appreciated. Names "uttered" in this way really do make an impact on the hearer. To dress up this exercise even more, some water should be in the cauldron to about an inch or so, and the sound will be even more marked. If perfume or aromatics are added to the water for inhaling, these may be in keeping with the particular Names invoked. Hot water increases the efficacy of an inhalant. If, in addition to these hypnogogues, the cauldron is gently swung as it would be from a tripod over the fire, there will be a rotary light reflected on the surface of the water which if watched, has an additional hypnotic action. It should be unnecessary to say it would be unwise to try this experiment alone in case of entrancement when there would be danger of drowning.

There is a great advantage of course, in holding rituals in acoustically suitable places having natural resonances. Hence the popularity of caverns and crypts. Little enough can be done with the average living room of today to make it resonant by any natural means, and electrically amplified echo-chamber acoustics are a poor mechanical substitute. If an ordinary room is being used for rituals, there should be a minimum of furnishings and curtaining. It is a reasonable practice-exercise to hang up a good sized gong and try resonating Names powerfully enough to make the gong echo its response. This will give the "background" note for a rite.

One odd phenomena perceptible to sensitive people, is what might be termed "residual resonance" in the actual structure of the ritual room, Temple, or church. This means that the very walls and fabric of the place act as a kind of storage for the resonances they have responded to time and time again. They echo these inaudibly to physical ears for a long while after any rite. Those with clairaudiant faculties can sometimes pick up these echos after many years. Stone seems to be the best material for holding such sonic charges, and even if a Temple consists of a curtained off recess of a room, there should be a reasonably sized piece of stone incorporated in the symbology somewhere. Quartz is fairly good for general purposes. Eventually a regularly used Temple will accumulate enough energy to start inaudibly resonating by itself, so there will be an existing charge in the place all the time. The best occasion to notice this is immediately after a rite when the participants have left. Although the place is silent physically, its very atmosphere will be literally vibrating and pulsating with the diminishing energies left behind from the concluded ritual. These tone down to "normal" level for the place, but never seem to fade out altogether. The ultimate result is that the Temple sets up its own Inner harmonics which act as a kind of "homing beacon" for the Inner Ones who keep contact with humanity on those frequencies.

For this reason alone, it is important to hold regular and rhythmic rites in any particularly dedicated place. Every working Temple too should have its own "Call-sign", or identity-Name which should be clearly sonated at the beginning and end of a rite. An individual shrine will normally operate under the Magical Name of its owner, but if more than one person is involved, a Name for them collectively should be chosen and used. In that way Inner identities are established and contacts made easier. An ancient practice was to keep a sacred stone with a natural cavity in it in the Holy of Holies.

Periodically the High Priest uttered the Secret Name of the God into this hole, which was supposed to summon the attention of the God towards the God-House or Beth-El, i.e., the stone itself. This old practice is still kept up here and there. "Blowing stones" for calling the God (and the people), are with us yet, and the fundamental principles are sound enough theoretically. Whispering into naturally resonant cavities in large stones is not without attraction, and certainly worth experimenting with.

One useful practice sadly neglected by Western ritualists is that of "back-chanting". This means that while the principle Invocant is sonating some special effect or passage, the remainder of participants are keeping up a "background" sonation the whole while to supply sheer weight or amount of sonic force. A bagpipe with its chanter and drones shows the principles of this. Mechanically it would be like a hammer and chisel. The Invocant as the chisel with its sharp cutting edge, and the others as the striking power of the descending hammer driving the chisel into the material it contacts.

This effect is mostly obtained with congregational responses, providing the Invocant has made the Inner contact. The back-chant exerts continual pressure on the point provided by the Invocant rather than an occasional blow, so possibly the mechanical simile for the back-chant is more like a screwdriver or engraving tool being constantly worked by pressures applied from the hand of the craftsman.

The sonics of the back-chant depend on the nature of the main invocation. They are mainly vowel arrangements to a rhythmical pattern in keeping with the principal point at issue. If, for instance, the Invocant is calling on the Great Mother, a suitable back-chant could be: "Ah Ah O UMmmmm Ah Ah O UMmmm" on a rising and falling cadence. If a call is going out to the Spirit of Life, the back-chant might be: "EE Ya. EE Ya." It is not difficult to work out back-chants once the central idea of the invocation is known. Its application is that all using it must direct the whole energy generated toward what is being vocalised by the Invocant, and feel that they are concerting their strength together much as a number of people might haul on a physical rope or try and lift some heavy weight. A back-chant is in fact a ritualised chanty for bringing power to bear concertedly just like sailors used to work a capstan.

A number of the circle-chants work this way when an Invocant gives central Calls, and those treading the perimeter chant the age old sonics. For group-efforts there are few exercises to surpass this simplest of procedures. It all depends on picking up the rhythm rather than the words, and harmonising with it until the whole group becomes as sonically united as a wheel spinning on its axis to the tune of its own motion. There are hundreds of various circle-chants, varying from highly esoteric ones like the so-called "Hymn of Jesus", to the common or garden "witch-cult" types of the "Eko-eko" species which mean whatever the dancers like to put into them. One of these latter kind is amusingly related with the Elements, as follows.

> Fire flame and Fire burn,
> Make the Mill of magic turn,
> Work the will for which we pray,
> **Io Dio, Ha He Yay,**
> Air breathe and Air blow,
> Make the Mill of magic go.
> Work the will for which we pray,
> Io Dio, Ha He Yay.
> Water heat and Water boil,
> Make the Mill of magic boil,
> Work the will for which we pray,
> Io Dio, Ha He Yay.

Earth without and Earth within,
Make the Mill of magic spin,
Work the will for which we pray,
Io Dio, Ha He Yay.

Reminiscent of, but more sophisticated than the Witches chant in Macbeth.

Circle-chants or back-chants are easy to compose. The principle is to get one central idea and then make up a Magic Word for it which is readily chantable in the fewest possible syllables. This is the theme. Around it a number of different approaches, angles, or points of view are arranged in a circle and either made into verses or short statements of some incisive kind. A practical way would be to centralise a Word, then set up the Zodiac around it and approach the Word via the concept of each Sign in turn. Whatever system is used, the principle of the One related with the Many must be followed, so that the effect brings the will of the Many to One point. This is the important factor. Once that is realised, circle or back-chants should present no problems.

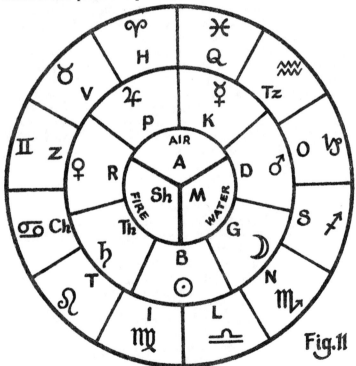

Fig.11

This was more or less the principle on which the secret Magic Words of some old Mysteries were put together. The letters of an alphabet were arranged in a circular or other pattern, each linked with a series of ideas or consciousness-content, then these were co-related as such and their sonic symbols emerged as a Word to represent them audibly. One standard Qabalistic pattern linked the three Mother letters with Elements, the seven doubles with planets, and the twelve singles with the Zodiac. The whole alphabet was then arranged in this order. (Fig 11.)

It will be noticed that only the three "active" Elements are used. These were thought to act upon Earth and produce whatever results were wanted. To make Magic Words from this design, it is necessary to think in the Magical terms of Element-Planet-Sign, then utter these according to their associated sonics. This would not necessarily spell a word of any known human language, but it would make a word intelligible to those accepting its Inner Meaning. If we see the Mothers as the "soul" of a word, the doubles as the "mind", and the singles as the "body", this will provide a plan of construction. Suppose using this system, we needed to make a Magic Word about ardent and dramatic love. This is easily worked out as Fire-Venus-Leo. or ARAT. To show gentler love we might use Water-Venus-Virgo, or MARI. An indication of vicious hate could be Fire-Saturn-Scorpio, which oddly enough works out as SHATHAN. All kinds of Magic Words can be made up by using this, or some similar system. Provided each sonic is properly linked to some comprehensible Inner meaning, the co-ordination of the letters is largely a matter of preference. One advantage of the Element-Planet-Sign system, is that it is generally understood regardless of national languages. If any Magic Words formed by these ideo-sonic codes are to be used in ritual practice, it is essential that participants should be aware of their individual significance.

A more ambitious lay-out with improved modern possibilities can be made by combining the Alphabet, the Spheres, and the Tarot Trumps. These are arranged with the Elements in the middle represented sonically by the vowels, the Spheres around those with their planetary and numeral values, then the consonants of our normal alphabet with their Tarot Trump attributes. Since they are clockwise, the Zodiac will have to follow suit, but with this system, planetary meanings have much less significance than the fundamental Concepts behind their symbols. Here the "body" of a Word will be shown in the Trumps and consonants, the "mind" by the Spheres, the "soul" by the Element-vowels, and the "spirit" by the inaudible silent Intervals. The general plan is like Fig 12.

We now have a sonic symbol-pattern for our Magical Inner

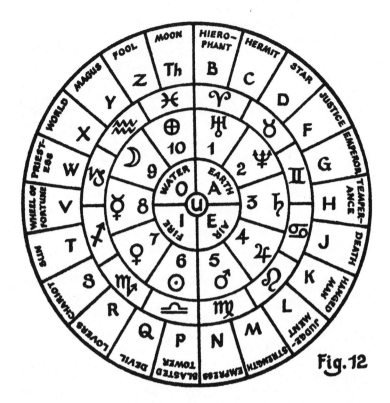

Fig. 12

Universe. All consciousness will link in somewhere or other with it. The advantage of the Tarot symbols is their universality. In this design of course, the Minor Arcana fit in with the Spheres, and the Court cards with the Elements. To make ideas into Magic Words, we work from centre to circumference, and to translate the Words into ideas, the direction is reversed. The fundamental nature of a Word comes from the central Element and vowel, its specific frequency and category from the Spheres, and its particular expression from the Trumps and consonants. Theoretically, we can extend the plan as far as we like by classifying more and more units of consciousness behind the Trumps. All we have to do is to take one idea and see it from twenty-two angles, each angle aligning with a Trump.

Using methods like this, Initiates or Mystery Schools extended their consciousness inter-dimensionally and evolved a common means of communication between themselves and discarnate entities whose units of consciousness were based on similar principles.

Once translation difficulties were sorted out, contact improved accordingly. A number of the "Spirit-Names" were actually code-words built up from such sonic bases, and the "Sigils" were a tracing of the letters forming the words from one point of the diagram to another. Eventually each School had its own "secret" system carefully guarded from the others, but the working principles were the same, only methods of arrangement differing.

The ritual value of such Magic Words is enormous, because so much can be got into so little, and we can really pressurise these sonics once we are able to handle them. They become "Master-Words" to chains of consciousness extending where we will. If we only link the Trumps with three Concepts, this will produce sixty-six inter-connected ideas. Let us try this with Time—Space—Property Concepts and see what happens.

	TRUMP	**TIME-TYPE**	**SPACE-TYPE**	**PROPERTY**
B	Heirophant	Incarnation	Outer	Pressure
C	Hermit	Excarnation	Inner	Inertia
D	Star	Aeons	Cosmos	Cohesion
F	Justice	Evolution	Height	Velocity
G	Emperor	Epoch	Large	Mass
H	Temperance	Peacetime	Plane	Equilibrium
J	Death	Cessation	Void	Vacuum
K	H.Man	Fateful moments	Small	Density
L	Judgement	Decisive times	Breadth	Hardness
M	Strength	Power periods	Line	Force
N	Empress	Happy times	Curve	Softness
P	B. Tower	Adverse times	Separation	Repulsion
Q	Devil	Testing times	Edge	Friction
R	Lovers	Love live	Junction	Attraction
S	Chariot	Travel time	Distance	Propulsion
T	Sun	Years	Universe	Illumination
V	W. of Fortune	Intervals	Length	Elasticity
W	Priestess	Devotional time	Range of Soul	Dispersion
X	World	Lifetime	Planet	Gravity
Y	Magus	Thinking time	Range of Mind	Concentration
Z	Fool	Now	Proximity	Incidence
Th	Moon	Months	Locality	Reflection.

These are not the only possible attributions by any means, and those unable to accept them must make their own list. It is sufficient to show the principles on which one Concept can be stretched twenty-two ways. Now we have to combine the sonics into Magic Words. These can be aligned right through the entire Tarot System if we follow a definite ruling such as:

Vowel-Pitch	shows	Element and Person
Vibration-Pitch	shows	Number (Sphere) and Suit
Consonant-Pitch	shows	Path and Trump.

There are four principal pitches for a chant. At the top, bottom, and two equal points between the comfortable chanting range of the human voice. This will vary for men and women of course, but everyone has their own range limits which are very simple to find in practice. It is only necessary to chant some sonic high, then low, then find two equal steps between them. Chanting "One, Two, Three, Four," in descending order will soon sort the pitches out.

If we take the Element Fire (Light) as the top sonic, chanting "I", then Air in order of density chanting "E", followed by Water as "O" and dropped to "A" as Earth, we shall make a good exercise. These sonics are variable of course, for each might be chanted on any pitch, and the meaning will be altered accordingly. Suppose we wanted to chant the King of Swords. Swords being equated with Air, and a King being top-value card, the note would be E top pitch. The other cards are easily worked out. Now suppose we wanted to chant the six of Cups. This means a rhythm of six - - - - - - to the third pitch. Since we must chant some sonic in this method, we carry over our Vowel or Consonant preceding, unless a change is indicated, and chant: "(top pitch) E (pause) E E E E E E (third pitch)" This gives us a combination of the Sword King and the six of Cups. Now we need to finalise the sequence into material manifestation, so we want the World in earthly terms, or at bottom pitch. In practice this could be emphasised by adding "Ah" (Earth) to a rhythm of ten - - - - - - - - - -. The whole Word would be sonated:—

Top pitch	E pause,
Third pitch	E E E E E E
Fourth pitch	EXX; AAA AAA AAA Ah

With only four sonics arranged according to this coding, we have constructed the fundamental concepts of a just, but perhaps somewhat severe soul with strict principles, contacting a needed balance of love and affection in actual earthly terms during physical life. All in one Magic Word chantable during a rite worked for maybe such a purpose. It could, of course, be understood on higher or lower levels according to the intentions behind it.

Since the limits of Tarot-Sphere-Element combinations are those of consciousness itself, the sonic system outlined is virtually inexhaustible. Its disadvantage is its complexity, which puts it far beyond the ability of an average worker. For general practical use, something much simpler is advisable. If we abbreviate the system so that:—

Pitch   indicates level of approach from which of the four Principal Points.

Rhythm indicates nature or Sphere of contact.

Sonics indicates pure Energies by Vowels and Resonants, and Effects by Consonants and Cachinants.

This will make a practical means of using and constructing Magic Words. Very broadly we might say that Vowels contained the Divine essence of a Word, and the Consonants held the remainder, including the Human.

It is possible also to make a somewhat rough attribution of the Tarot Consonants to the Three Pillars in this way:—

Left Pillar		*Right Pillar*		*Middle Pillar*	
C	Hermit	B	Hierophant	D	Star
J	Death	G	Emperor	F	Justice
K	Hanged Man	M	Strength	H	Temperance
P	Blasted Tower	R	Lovers	L	Judgement
Q	Devil	N	Empress	T	Sun
S	Chariot	W	Priestess	V	Wheel of Fortune
Y	Magus	X	World	Th	Moon

The "Odd one out" is of course the Fool—Z—who goes where he will, because he identifies at one end with the Invocants Human, and at the other with Divine identity. By use of this "Three-way" system, we can link ideas literally Right Left or Centre, making Words to suit any purpose at all.

Once we can construct Magic Words that extend our consciousness beyond the range of ordinary human speech and vocabulary, it remains to use them in a ritual context. It is useless simply to say them in an ordinary voice and expect instant miracles. Magic Words are not so much something to be said, as DONE. They must be enacted out entirely, through all levels of existence. We may utter them ritually on the Originative and even Creative level, but to push them still further through the Formative and Expressive stages may take anything from moments to months, years, and even lifetimes. Yet unless they *are* Originated, they can never be Expressed.

Therefore we must learn to concentrate consciousness into Magic Words by ritual means. It is not unlike choosing a Code-Word for a military operation such as "Crossbow" etc. Once the Name appears, it acts as a nucleus around which the energies of all individuals concerned may be related with each other for the common purpose. In addition to the main "overall' Name, there might be a minimum number of fractional Names circled around it, each given to some specific function or individual for fulfilment as a duty toward the Whole. Every Rite should have its Name-Plan built into its structure somewhere, and all participants should identify themselves with their own Name therein.

Nothing brings proficiency in ritual sonics except long practice in relating sound with consciousness through all possible paths, each of which leads to another one. The Magic of any Name lies in our ability to use it as a Door between the Dimensions of Being. Nothing else. No doors will be opened at all unless we knock on them the right way. Rhythmic taps with fingers have been used as thought-inducers since time-immemorial, and ritual shows us how to link our rhythms with the kind of thought we want. Once our fundamental frequencies are set to Inner rhythms of the finest possible type, we shall really make good progress on the Path. We gain very little indeed if we only mutter some Magic Word momentarily during a Rite, and are unable to carry it any further towards our Inner and Outer lives. Unless we live out the utterances of a Rite for ourselves, they will not help us much. That must never be forgotten.

For this reason, it is a wise plan to make a "Master-Word" for each Rite which can be Insonated or Exonated in order to sum up and live with all other utterances and conscious links associated with that Rite. By sonating this Word, we make Inner contact with the energies and even the entities connected with the Rite in question. This is the whole point of having "Passwords" to "grades" which are intended to act as a common code for a specific group of people needing to keep Inner contact with each other. A Name gives identity, and any Rite is entitled to its identity as an operation of consciousness. Hence the "Master" or Key-Word value. There should be no difficulty whatever inventing such Words. They almost invent themselves from an imagination fertile enough to engage in any kind of Rite.

Ritual sonics are a very major study indeed, and we have no more than scratched the surface of it, though enough to show the wealth of a deeper content than might be suspected. Any well organised Mystery Group should have its own set-up for the study of sonics and application of them for particular purposes. If there were more liaison between the various Schools and Groups for study reasons, it would save a considerable amount of duplicated and unnecessary effort on the part of many people. However, they doubtless enjoy their self-selection of "Secret Words" of value to none but themselves.

It is not enough to know "Words". We must know how to use them. Some, like the Secret Name of God, are unpronounceable by any form of human vocalisation. There is an Eastern tradition that God has a hundred names, but the real one is the whole hundred pronounced at once. Though this is an allegory, it does convey the idea of producing a sonic effect from a number of different sounds applied simultaneously together. By synchronisation of various sonics and Words with each other, quite interesting efforts can be managed by allowing the components to slip out of phase with each other and then back again to a definite rhythm. Then too, there are great possibilities in using sudden complete cut-offs at almost or full crescendo. This produces an opposite type of shock to that of a sudden yell in the midst of silence. There are no ends to the potentialities of ritual sonics, especially to-day, when so many new fields are being opened up. It is not a question of scrapping previous knowledge and experience, but of enriching it from the new treasure house available to serious researchers.

There is so very much to do. The full use of electronic sound generators tuned to various ritual pitches and rhythms has not yet been properly investigated. Nor have rites been worked in Temples so constructed that walls, ceilings, and floor might be set to frequencies in harmony with the Operation. The old Temples reflected sonics, but the new ones must emit them. Like most modern improvements, mechanical means can be found to do the donkey-work of physical sonic energy, while our Inner beings should be liberated from this chore to get on with the specialised task of modulating it on mental and spiritual levels. We need no longer spend our energy in blowing the organ physically, but in adapting its energy Inwardly. Everything relegated to our servitor mechanisms should make room for us to be masters of still greater achievements on higher levels. This is true in ritual as everywhere else, but unless we are really able to rise in ourselves proportionately to whatever modern devices we incorporate into ritual workings, it will all have been a total waste of time and effort. No amount of new equipment will help those who cannot master old principles first. Hence the need for sound grounding in fundamentals before embarking on novel experiments, however fascinating.

A well-designed Rite should be like any fine piece of engineering. This means its sonics must be correctly placed with regard to effect and purpose. Not a note should be out of true. There is a dearth of skilled Rite-engineers and architects, since there are neither training-courses nor salaried positions to be had in the art. Nevertheless if common-sense principles are combined with working knowledge of psycho-sonics, there is no reason why perfectly valid and competent rituals should not be constructed by anyone who really wants to, provided a few simple rules are observed.

Every Rite should have its own particular fundamental Pattern which must be followed out on every level of its working. Suppose our basic Rite-Pattern to be the Circled Cross. This must be adhered to throughout all its sensory components. There has to be a visual Circle-Cross, an audible one, a tangible one, and if possible an olfactory one. Each would be the same Rite in differing terms, linked together by the Time-Space-Event constants. Here we are faced with the task of fitting the sound-track to a "film" existing as a visual, olfactory, and tangible sequence already. The Pattern or Symbol must come first in a Rite, and its other aspects fitted around this.

Next comes the general tenor in which the Rite is to be cast. The same Rite-Pattern would obviously have quite different sonic and other attributes depending on whether it was Christian, Hebrew, Egyptian, Hindu, or simply Naturistic in character. Everything should be consistent with this overall nature, and the sonics should stand as a Rite by themselves. So many combinations are possible. With the Circle-Cross in Christian form, it might be as simple as the Sign of the Cross made in a moment, or the Eucharist with its four sections of Approach, Consecration, Communion, and Thanksgiving centred around the Christ-Spirit. Each section having its appropriate musical background, invocations, hymns, silences, responses, and other sonics fitting in with the Rite. Again we find shape first, sound second.

It is essential to know what end-product is required. If it is necessary to impress some mental image of a design upon participants, this may best be done by having them dance it to appropriate music. Or perhaps it may be displayed to them during a recitation concerning it. There are many ways of getting the same result under different conditions depending on the type of consciousness being dealt with. A ritual sound-engineer must know and use these to practical purposes. Once we know what is needed, it becomes possible to seek for this and apply it.

Ritualists need to learn from musical composers how to paint pictures with sound as an artist uses colours. A ritual *is* a work of art in itself, and must be so presented both Inwardly and outwardly. Whether the presentation be on the grandest scale, or the most modern one, the principle of perfection applies in both cases. A Rite is itself, be it worked in the finest Temple by a full Company and choral effects, or by a solitary officiant making no physically audible sound. The latter may even be more plainly heard in the Innerworld than the former. It all depends on the quality of Insonation. They that only speak to themselves seldom get much of an audience!

Putting sonics to a Rite is no more complicated than arranging a poem around a theme or a story around a plot. Once the nucleus of the Rite becomes established, the rest is a question of settling the various components into harmonious orbits around it. Without an effective nucleus, only chaos and muddle will ensue. Hence the necessity of "uttering the Word" which will bring the whole Rite into Cosmos about itself. That must come first, and the rest will almost arrange itself. The Master-Sonic is the vital one that gives Life and Light to any rite. Find and sonate that properly, and all else must eventually fall into place.

Before leaving this review of ritual sonics, we should consider the aspect of "inflaming with prayer." This is thought so essential by some workers that they have little time for anything else, which is a sad mistake. Nevertheless their technique is necessary to master, though scarcely an easy one. Words are strong stuff, and it is possible to get as "high" on words as on drink or drugs, providing they are properly applied. Any well-organised mass-meeting with a fiery orator, susceptible listeners, raised feelings, and shouted responses or songs will demonstrate this. Or again, we might note the effect of exactly the same quantity of alcohol drunk in silence and solitude, or consumed in noisy surroundings with stimulating company, conversation, and music. Sonics make a vast difference to the effect on the individual.

To "inflame oneself with prayer" should mean more than just becoming "word-intoxicated", yet that is exactly what happens if control is lost during the process. What should happen instead, is a steady lift up of consciousness while keeping on target the whole while until this is reached Inwardly. It is the difference between burning the alcohol as a rocket fuel, or using it to make the whole crew dead drunk. One is a scientific process, and the other a senseless orgy. Unluckily it is difficult to describe the exact Inner technique of applying this control, but the broad outlines will give enough information for the rest to be developed through personal practice.

The major factor behind this process of upliftment, is the production of a constant vibrato in not only the voice but the whole body and Inner being also. This means not simply a vocal resonance, but a double, or resonated resonance. We may achieve this physically by sounding off a resonant note and then shaking the body so that the note shakes accordingly. To make this a magical practice, it must be reversed, so that the note is not shaken by the body, but the body shaken by the note. Once this is possible, a vibrato is set up which must be kept going consistently, while being modulated into words or utterances by the lips and larynx. We shall be virtually turning ourselves into an organ producing a single tone which becomes notations by manipulating the keyboard.

A good deal depends on the poise of the body in the first place, so that it is not unlike a spring which will vibrate when given a flick with a finger. One most useful stance is with legs together, right foot behind left with its instep to the left heel in the "Square" or Tau Cross position. Most of the body weight is shifted slightly forward toward the ball of the left foot. Arms should be raised to the "prayer" position, palms of hands facing outwards about level with shoulders. This will place the body in a nicely balanced state, ready to respond when sonic energies move it.

For practice purposes, a page or two of prayer material will suffice. Provided it is metrical, or can be read in a lyrical fashion, the subject matter makes little difference. It could actually be a sales catalogue or a comic poem, and serve a purpose, but to avoid incongruity, good readable material such as a Psalm, or suitable invocation is best. Choose the pitch to be followed, and exonate it on "MMM". While producing this note, change it to a vibrato by introducing a regular tremor into the muscles responsible for making the sound, rather as if the body were slightly shivering. This will make the double resonance, and come out something like "MM-MM-MM-MM-MM" reminiscent of a bagpipe drone. While keeping this up all the time, begin to chant the prayer or recitation quite deliberately and carefully.

The idea should be to keep the outbreaths going sonically as long as possible consistent with effect, and make the inbreaths rapidly as quietly as may be. The words are pressed out as it were on each other's heels, so that while one word is being chanted, the next is held in mind ready to be slipped into the space awaiting it. There should be a sense of climbing up the words Inwardly, as if each were a step on an escalator or the rung of a ladder. After a little of this exercise, the body ought to be vibrating at a perceptible amplitude, and a feeling experienced as if the whole being were rising into the head. It is a strange sensation, scarcely to be described, though it might be compared somewhat with that of initial alcohol ingestion. There is a certain exhilaration and intensification of consciousness, which tends to fall off rapidly however, once the exercise ceases.

If this practice is kept up for any length of time until it develops its own natural frequency, the experience of being "inflamed with prayer" will be known. Mystics and "Saints" of all faiths discovered it for themselves in the course of their workings, though unless it is directed and controlled, it serves little purpose or value. It has been dryly observed: "God is the most potent intoxicant of all."

Everything depends on the use made of the exercise. As an expander of consciousness in order to improve and enhance spiritual evolution, it is of great importance, but as a means of abrogating that consciousness into confusion out of sheer irresponsibility, it is just as harmful as any other toxin.

Again the secret of the practice is seen to be pressurisation of consciousness. First one concept or word chanted, then another pressed on top of it so that two are being dealt with, then another one, and so on. The concepts are not taken seriatim, so to speak, but cumulatively. Instead of going through the mind one at a time and out again, they are piling up one on top of another to make one whole loading. We might say we were building up concepts to make Critical Mass for an explosion, and so in fact we are. This was the magical principle illustrated by the time-honoured but altogether misunderstood "ABRACADABRA" pyramid, or any other similar glyph. As a word it meant little enough, but as a *method*, it meant everything. It showed how to compress consciousness by taking a concept and adding to it bit by bit until an expansion developed to the degree where everything could be held as an entire unit of consciousness on a much larger scale.

To "inflame with prayer", would be better expressed as "enlargement by prayer," and this really does result in spiritual growth. So long as we avoid explosive point, and channel the energy into constructive projects, we may enlarge ourselves as much as we like. If we apply the "ABRACADABRA" formula to any prayer passage or invocation, it will give the clue. Chant one word and be conscious of it. Chant two words and be conscious of them *as one concept*, then three words with one awareness, and so forth. From the Time viewpoint, all that went before is constantly recreated as the NOW, which gets bigger and bigger as we grow with it. Our Inner Universe will expand in tune with the Outer one.

Such is "inflammation" or expansion by prayer, whether chanted audibly or inaudibly. We are more or less blowing ourselves up into a kind of pressurised container, and then it will be necessary to direct the "nozzle" toward whichever Inner Contact we are aiming for. Whether we think of it that way, or compare it with loading a gun, charging an atomic pile, or anything else the principles are the same. Results are only obtained by practice and nothing else.

Supposing we thought of words as having definite physical weight, say an ounce apiece. Then suppose we are seeking to effect penetration through some substance needing considerable energy concentrated to a point for sufficient time. If we place the Point of our Master-Word in the exact position we require, then build up a whole pyramid of words on top of this, they will eventually amount to enough sheer weight to supply the pressure necessary for the task. That is "ABRACADABRA" applied in practice, and how the cumulative effect of magical chanting works. Ritualists learn this in the course of their ceremonial practices.

No one however, is entitled to call themselves a ritualist who is unable to build their own rites from the raw materials available from Inner and Outer sources. External colours, forms, perfumes, and artworks, may be beyond many people's reach, but sound is always the cheapest magical component to any practitioner with a voice of their own. Most Western rites tend to rely more on sound than other means for obtaining their results, so there is plenty of scope for practice and experiment. The odd difference between a musical and a magical composer is that the former puts many ideas into one medium, while the latter must put many media into one idea. We have dealt with magical sonics sufficiently to provide some slight groundwork to the subject, now we must find out how to start building actual rituals out of the materials we have been Inwardly assembling.

RITES AND THEIR COMPONENTS

A genuine complaint from readers of Occult literature who are interested in ritualism, is that writers never provide them with actual ritual texts to practice. This leads to a suspicion that authors are in possession of the most amazing secret rituals which they are either forbidden by the Hierarchy to publish, or that they are being mysterious for the sake of appearing more knowledgeable than they really are. Neither assumption is accurate.

It must be admitted that very little solid stuff in the way of ritual texts is in published form. If we look at available material in the English language, it forms a depressing heap of second hand arcana. It is not even easy to come by, on account of price and comparative rarity, for the simple reason there is an insufficient demand to make paper-back or cheap editions a commercial possibility. If there were a "popular demand" for rituals, the market would be flooded with—yes, with what? One shudders to think!

Organised religion and other ritualistic bodies have published their rites in full. They can be purchased by anyone, regardless of membership. Even full texts of Masonic rituals can be bought by non-members. When we come to the smaller groupings of "Occult" practitioners however, the rituals become scantier and more doubtful. Those of the "Golden Dawn" are mainly pseudo-Masonic with a generous dash of Egyptian and a sprinkling of "Clavicula Solomonis." The late A. Crowley's rites have enough fool-traps in them to catch a regiment of idiots, or trip hordes of innocent unwary dabblers. Genuine pagan rites surviving today in isolated instances were never really written at all, because they were methods rather than actual words, though a few of these were handed down through families. Some of them were old war-cries of family "calls", now meaningless, and useless for ritual purposes. The completely phoney "Witch-rites" purchasable from various sources are mainly modern inventions. Here and there, small "Occult" groups have evolved their own ritual methods which suit their members, but are little used elsewhere. These are unlikely to be published, nor would they be of help if they were. A large number of medieval Grimoires and Claviculas are in print, and sorry reading they make. Anyone using these for source-material deserves their wasted time and money in the company of those Innerworlders who amuse themselves with human stupidities.

Not a happy picture at all. Where indeed is an honest and devoted ritualist to turn for the raw materials of the art? They are faced with only two alternatives, either to accept someone else's material, or to discover their own. The most satisfactory solution lies in a combination of both methods. After all, the whole purpose of occult ritual working is to extend consciousness into Inner Dimensions, and if nothing is ever brought back from thence, the rites will have proved ineffective. Anyone spending years in working other people's rites without evolving some of their own, has wasted much of a lifetime. Therefore we must consider how such rites are to be made up.

Rites develop from behaviour-patterns, and these come from adaptations and adjustments on Inner levels between individuals or groups, and various energies affecting them. It depends entirely on those concerned how they react, and consequently the type of rite they evolve varies enormously according to their nature, even though fundamental principles are the same for all. If individuals are illiterate and without resources, their rites will consist mainly of open-air gatherings spent in primitive activities. Literate people of fair means need rituals of artistic and cultural merit, though not necessarily very expensive ones. Churches or Temples are really a species of Club, where like-minded ritualists pool their resources so as to share far better facilities than single individuals might afford. Nevertheless the ideal in Occult ritualism is that everyone should become the priest of their own Temples, and work their own rites within it. For "Temple" read the body, for "priest" the soul, and for "rites" read the actions of one within the other.

First and foremost in ritual making, it is necessary to know what particular System is most suitable for the practitioner, then to ensure that the rite or rites are constructed strictly within that framework and none other. There must be no haphazard mix-up of divergent pantheons or incongrous activities. Rites are built up not unlike a theatrical production, each aspect calling for specialist treatment. Rites have a script or score, ballet or mime, wardrobe, and "special effects" besides "props". These all have to be put together so that their "Outworking" will facilitate their "Inworking".

Whether they are very simple and inexpensive, or elaborate and costly, each should be a good sound species of its kind.

It is fairly simple to classify rites according to the Three Ways, Hermetic, Mystic, and Orphic. Hermetic rites are mainly intellectual ones, calling for Temple conditions and sophisticated types of ritual. Mystic rites are more of the Spirit than the body, very largely contemplative in nature, needing few physical adjuncts, but a degree of devotional ability very much beyond most human participants. Mystic rites are usually worked in physical solitude. Orphic rites operate very broadly along emotional lines, using a great deal of dancing, music, and natural means of expression. It will be seen that any particular System, (such as Qabalistic, Rosicrucian, etc) could operate rites of all these three sorts for members of differing temperaments. On the whole, it seems generally accepted that Hermetic types of rite appear most suitable for the average Western worker, and to some extent the Hermetic Tradition carries the other two within it.

Once the individual ritualist has definitely decided which is his System and Tradition, the rest follows on fairly naturally. Again and again it must be emphasised that it is not a question of any System being better or worse than others, but of the persons themselves proving their own need for that especial type of spiritual development. That is the deciding issue, and only when it is satisfactorily settled can anyone make much headway with rituals. "KNOW THYSELF" stands over the Portals of every Temple, and this means we must know the sort of person we are before we enter them. It may take some amount of meditation and soul searching to arrive at this vital conclusion, but it has to be done. To wander vaguely around from one System to another with little aim other than amusement produces little results—if any at all.

Probably the reason Western ritualists often prefer the Qabalistic System is because of its precise lay-out and terminology so that Powers and Principles can be readily co-related with people in a neat and orderly fashion. The Pantheon of God-Aspects are easily recognised as personifications of Divine Consciousness in order to adapt humanity thereto, and basic truths can be expressed almost as equations. This gives an amazing scope for ritualisation along any of the Three Ways for whatever purpose is required. With a minimum of ingenuity, rites may be designed almost with drawing-board precision, whether these are wanted for purely personal practice, or an entire group of people. Yet there are no authentic Qabalistic rites published in available form, and practitioners must construct their own as part of their Magnum Opus.

A good deal depends on whether a ritualist has literary or poetic ability. If so, they have a headstart in arranging ritual formularies.

If not, they will have to rely on existent material. This is collected from every possible place, and put down in what used to be called the "Black Book" purely because of its binding. A Black Book should infallibly be kept by every ritualist. In it will be recorded all kinds of prayers, chants, invocations, calls, and any formulary that might be useful for their practice. These can come from quite unlikely sources such as newspapers, journals, works of fiction, or even hearsay. There need be no dearth of supply while Public Libraries exist. It always pays to explore local possibilities first.

The Scriptures of the various Faiths alone will provide far more material than could ever be coped with in one lifetime, especially if we include the Egyptian, Chaldean, and Vedantic texts. The aim should be not to quote masses and masses of these, but to evolve appropriate formulae from them for our purpose. For instance, evocations of the Four Elements, the Ten Spheres, the Planetary Spirits, and the Divine Aspects, are some of the standard formulae needed. The ultimate object is the making of what might be termed an Occult Office Book, containing suitable formularies for all likely occasions and uses. From these units, it is possible to build up the most elaborate rites imaginable. This is how practical ritualists obtain their stock in trade materials.

Suppose we are starting such a collection. First we need a General collective formula like the Circle Cross, "In the Name of the Wisdom etc." Then Elementary evocations, Sphere-workings, Divine Mother-Father approaches, (if Christian these would be an Our Father and Hail Mary), banishing formula, exorcism, specific formularies for intentions such as health, knowledge, etc, processional and circling chants, besides various blessings and consecrations. In other words, we shall be making up a recipe book like any conscientious craftsman. By the nature and quality, (not the sheer bulk) of their "Black Books", shall magicians be known. Eventually several of such books evolve from each other. One the "General Store", which is nothing but a heap of quotes, cuttings, and jottings as and when they come, in no sort of order except chronological. Out of that will come somewhat more polished and classified material. This gets sorted out under broad headings such as Elemental, Divine Aspect, Planetary, and so forth. From this again comes the definite Rite itself. For example an Opening and Closing ceremony as a standard beginning and ending for a main Rite, Seasonal Rites for Equinoxes, Solstices, and special occasions. Initiation ceremonies. All these will have "Black Books" of their own. Not that there is any need nowadays for black book-covers, and in fact suitable colours for different rites is a pleasing improvement.

Although the raw material goes into the stock-pot of the first

Black Book just as it is, everything must be boiled up together by the Fire of Wisdom before it becomes useable as food for ritual consumption. We cannot fish out an uncooked Psalm, a haiku, a koan, a poetic fragment from Sappho, a scrap of Shakespeare, and some old witch spell, throw the lot together in a lump, and expect a perfect ritual. The result would simply be a horrid mess. Yet each and every one of those ingredients has a valuable content which would combine perfectly with the rest to make a Rite of almost any kind. This can only be done by cooking them all together in the cauldron of our consciousness and producing the right sort of dish out of the Magic Pot. That is to say our materials must be Inwardly digested, integrated, stylised, to re-emerge anew in the shape of the product we require. We do exactly the same Inwardly as we would physically with equivalent materials, process them until we get what we want. Magical Cosmos emerges from Magical Chaos, but we must have the Chaos in the first place.

To compose a Rite of any kind means working with many media toward a common purpose. Here we are concerned with the intellectual medium of contrived wordage which must also provide emotional and spiritual links. We must find the best Words as vehicles for the Will Within. This is a truly magic task. It may not be easy to select a thought here, a suggestion there, a Name somewhere else, and a framework elsewhere in our Black Books, recast these into appropriate form and come up with a workable magical Rite, yet this is precisely what has to be done. Of course we cannot do this without help from Inside, and when we start producing practical Rites which seem to come together almost of their own accord, we shall realise that Inner help is being duly given. Phrases we would not have thought of on our own, or even Names, will "pop into our minds" quite suddenly and surprisingly. We shall get the feeling that "someone is looking over the shoulder" at what proceeds from our pens—and suggesting what to write or correcting what has been written.

Whether or not we receive assistance with what we compose, the responsibility for it will be our own and no one elses. While one hand holds the pen, the other must be firmly kept on the controls. There must be no scribbling of endless rubbish and pointless meandering without purpose. Rites have to be composed to definite rules, just as electronic equipment must be assembled from definite components to a definite circuit. Otherwise neither rite nor device will work. Most of the rules are covered by those of good literary composition and poetic license, but a few points in particular deserve to be borne in mind.

Since we are involving body, mind, soul, and spirit in our rite, we should decide what links with which, so that these may be worked with on their own levels. On a broad basis, this is approximately:—

BODY   Is involved in a Rite verbally by material allusions such as: "I shall hunger and thirst for Truth." "Take my left shoulder and direct my ways, etc." References to the body generally have such higher inferences, so that bodily functions or material assets serve spiritual ends rather than vice versa.

MIND   Comes into a Rite largely by means of problems and intellectual presentations. Queries and answers are mainly mental, and so are the majority of visual symbols needing interpretation through understanding. A large percentage of modern rituals is mental, and there is a tendency to overbalance on this level.

SOUL   Enters a Rite principally through emotional appeal and empathetic suggestions such as, "As Thou lovest me, so fill my heart with love for—etc" or, "Let not grief prevent us from—etc" All that connects with feelings of any kind involves the soul.

SPIRIT   Is brought into a Rite through pure Principles, such as the determination of Right from Wrong, recognition of Divine powers, dedication to purpose, devotion to duty, etc. God-Names, Words of Power, Declarations, and Calls express the Spirit of a Rite which forms its nucleus. Consecratory formulae and benedictions are vehicles of Spirit.

The question immediately arises as to ideal proportions for combining these together. There can be no absolutely hard and fast answer, because so much depends on the type of Rite being constructed, but for general purposes we might consult a glyph of the four geometrical symbols for the levels of being, and see how they relate to each other. We shall obtain Fig 13.

The rough proportions if we accept the oval of Spirit as one unit are:—

SPIRIT	1
SOUL	2
MIND	3
BODY	4

10 Units

This seems a very fair distribution of ritual energies for most purposes. It indicates we should base our Rites on the purely Spiritual content as a nucleus, double this in references to Soul,

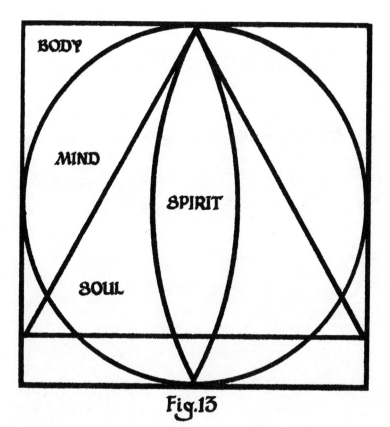

Fig.13

triple it in those of Mind, and quadruple it for those of body. In the whole Body of a Rite, this makes for three-quarters of that amount Mind, half of it Soul, and a quarter of it Spirit. It is rarely possible in practice to observe such exact proportions, but at least we are provided with some kind of a guide. Reflected Inwardly of course, the proportions inverse. Body leads into Mind, Mind into Soul, and Soul leads into Spirit, folding backwards as it were until all is compressed in Spirit.

Next, we must bear in mind the Three Rings of Limitation. Time-Space-Events. A given number of things, (Events) have to be done in specific conditions (Space), within a calculated period, (Time). Some things therefore will take a little or a lot of Time-Space, some conditions will be crowded or empty, and some periods be brief or lengthy. How are we to relate all these factors together so that a harmonious Whole results? The best way to explain this is by practical experiment. Obtain three flat metal rings of equal diameter.

Children's toy bracelets about three inches across, obtainable from fancy goods sections in chain-stores serve very well. Otherwise the rings may be made from any suitable material.

Pick up a ring, thinking "this is Time," and another one thinking "this is Space." Fit one into the other at right angles so that they hold together. Note they would soon fall apart if any stress were applied because here is only a two point contact between them. Now take the third ring thinking "this is Events", and fit it over the other two at right angles to them centrally, so that it binds them rigidly. The whole structure is now quite firm, can be handled, rolled around, and treated as an entirety. Each ring is held at four points, and this is what makes them all stable. The complete Symbol should be studied and meditated on very carefully, because it will give the feel of a perfect Rite, and show how to put one together along the three Axes of Existence.

The Time, Space, and Events of a Rite must hold each other together just like the Three Rings. Whichever we use for a constant must have the other two adapted so they apply pressure firmly at the points of contact. If we decide on making a time-constant of, say, half an hour, then we shall have to graduate our Space-events so they fill the half hour in such a way that there would be room for neither more nor less. It is not the number of Events or bulk of Space that counts, but the exact degree of compression with which they occupy the Time. There should be no "loose fits" so that things fall apart. For instance, to spend a full hour lighting one candle might be a valuable personal exercise in maintaining pressure of Space-Events for an unusual Circle of Time, but it would be useless as an occupation for a whole Rite involving many people, unless for experimental purposes.

As a rule, it is best to consider Rites in the light of their particular purpose, and then adjust the Three Rings around it suitably. Suppose we are considering a Rite of Initiation which may call for a certain number of Events needing a given amount of Space. Because of their nature, unavoidable gaps in Time occur between them, while perhaps appurtenances are being cleared away, or some accident has interrupted proceedings. Such Time-lacunae reduce the Rite to feeble amateur fumblings, and "let out the pressure." All such possibilities have to be allowed for. Chants might be written in to cover blanks between events, and an expert M.C. should be capable of dealing with accidents in such a way as to build them into the Rite as an integral part of it. At all costs, the pressure and pace of the Rite must be maintained. Once there is a serious break in any of the Rings, it is almost impossible to repair it well enough so that the Rite will build up sufficiently for successful continuance.

Groups of trained workers evolve their own "emergency drill" for dealing with unexpected incidents or a hiatus during their Rites, and this should be practised like boat or fire-drill. At a given signal from the M.C. or other Officer, everyone should know exactly what to do so as to maintain ritual pressure on the Rings around it. It is the responsibility of the Officer concerned to choose an appropriate course of procedure, and this will depend on the nature of the incident and the type of Rite. The general rule is that an untoward event must be built into the structure of the rite in the style of the rite itself.

Suppose for instance, that during a silent meditational period some sudden distraction such as something being knocked over occurs. It would be useless to pretend nothing had happened and no one was affected. The thing for the M.C. to do would be to treat it as a "sudden awakening" by sounding the gong and directing everyones attention to the theme of the Rite by intoning the particular "God-Name" or whatever central Key the Rite was constructed around. Suppose again (an event that can happen) some vital item of ritual equipment was missing from its required position through carelessness or oversight. This means an unavoidable delay while it is being fetched. If the M.C. is uncertain how long this might take, a chant or hymn in keeping with the proceedings is an obvious answer, since it can be easily terminated at the end of a verse. Should a ritual vessel with its content of water or wine be knocked over, this must be treated as a libation or a sacrifice, and the appropriate formularies gone through. The whole object should be to deal with ritual intrusions as a useful part of the Rite, so turning them to good account.

Maintaining Ring pressure of a Rite is much like keeping up "pace" during a theatrical production. "Pace" is not an easy term to define. It has nothing to do with breakneck speed at all, but refers to rates of progression compatible with circumstantial needs. Perhaps a useful comparison would be with the happenings during a cross country walk. The objective is to progress from point A to point B. Rates of progression vary enormously. We may walk rapidly or even run down hills, slow to a crawl while climbing them, stride over firm ground, or pick a delicate and hesitant way through boggy patches. Now and then we may stop entirely to get our breath back or admire a view. Maintenance of pace throughout the journey means sustenance of interest and attention the whole while during all the varied rates. The moment boredom or lack of interest sets in, pace or pressure has fallen away. Keeping up the pace of a Rite means keeping the focus of consciousness aligned with its action whatever its rate of progression. If the Rite runs, we must run with it, if it crawls, then so must we, and if action ceases, we must hold ourselves immobile. That is what "pace" means. Providing sufficient pressure to ensure concentration to a maximum degree.

If occult Rites were entirely dramatic presentations and no more, pace and pressure could only be maintained by their events keeping audience-interest captivated. Though there is some percentage of truth in this, especially during the early stages of initiation, the main pressurising factor of a Rite is keeping in constant contact with the Inner linkages behind it. This is the personal and collective responsibility of those taking part. Those unable to keep up the necessary concentration and Inner awareness for sufficient periods, should not be allowed to participate in Rites requiring such ability. It is for this reason that genuine Occult schools insist on so much meditational training work before anyone is allowed to take part in even the smallest Rite. This at least ensures that participants in the Rites of that School have proved their ability to maintain Inner contacts for working periods. By and large, the rule should be that if people are to participate in any Rite, they should be able to hold purely meditational contacts for the same extent of time.

It is quite futile to expect anyone who cannot hold an Inner meditational contact for even five minutes, to take a useful part in a Rite lasting over an hour or more. If their attention can be held by nothing but an hypnotic alteration of events, they are no better than television watchers, who, possibly without being consciously aware of it, are more held in thrall by the ultra-rapid flicker of the screen itself than the subject matter presented on it. This can be a very nasty mind-menace in fact, and serious ritualists might be well warned to cut television viewing to a minimum if they cannot altogether avoid it. The flicker-frequency of the television screen is a formidable modern agent for captivating and controlling the mass-mind. Dedicated seekers on Occult paths who are aware of this, set up their own safeguards.

A major reason for the failure of ritual practices is sheer inability to hold contact with the Inner content to any workable degree. The faculty for doing so can only be developed from within ourselves through sustained meditational exercises. There are NO "Instant techniques" for acquiring this ability, just as there are none for instant plant growth or instant adulthood. Before embarking on any ritual workings therefore, it must be ascertained whether or not they are within the concentrational competence of those who would work them. Rites will not give such abilities, but only occasions for using them. Far better design short Rites which may be worked well, than long ones few can follow. At least we provide ourselves with a standard for Rite-making, which is that the Time-Ring must not exceed the ability of participants to remain actively engaged on Inner meditational pursuits.

In such a way, everyone can work out their Rite rating as to a Time constant with the help of any watch or clock. It is only necessary to go into active meditation and see how long this can be kept up without drift or distraction. The average of, at the very least, ten such experiments, gives the rating value in minutes (at first) for the individual. Once this is known, it will be a simple matter for the individual to choose, or be chosen for, their most suitable Rite-workings. It is important for such time tests that the meditation must come wholly from Within, and not be evoked in any way by external suggestions such as vocal or musical leads. Nor should it consist of day-dreaming or trying to keep a blank mind. The type of meditation needed for this purpose is preferably a coherent involvement with Inner living for some definite issue. The subject of meditation is immaterial, so long as it is developed consistently with the style adopted.

Probably the best practical way to safeguard the continuity of any Rite and maintain its Inner pressures is to cast it in metrical form. There is no reason why the meter should be the same for the whole of a Rite, and indeed its rhythm ought to vary according to need like the human heart or breathing does, but the meter and rhythms of any Rite must be a recognisable feature of it. Usually this is of more importance than the actual words themselves. It is hard to over-emphasise the importance of meter in magic. Ritual and rhythm are inseparables. Every child who dances round a circle to an invented chant knows this well enough, and our most sophisticated Rites are but developments from such beginnings. In primitive and earthy Rites, it is the drum-rhythms which keep pressures going to a virtually wordless throaty accompaniment. Those risen above such levels are faced with the same problems to answer in a different fashion.

Although it is scarcely possible to be rigid on the subject of meter, a broad overall guide can be obtained by considering the Glyph provided by the Three Pillars of Light when the tops of the two outer ones are brought together at the Middle Pillar. Apart from the familiar "Broad Arrow", or "Three Ray" design, it also produces the idea of a pendulum swinging through its arc. While the tempo is represented by the frequency of swing from one side of the arc to another, meter may be compared to the amplitude of swing, governed by the width of the arc at any point of the pendulum's length. If we accept the top as Spirit, and the bottom as Matter, the Glyph will show at a glance that meter shortens as it approaches Spirit, and lengthens as it extends toward Matter. Since

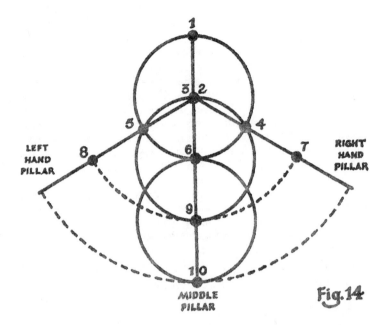

Fig. 14

the Glyph may be of interest to Qabalists, its theoretical outline is given here, in Fig 14.

The Pillars are pivoted on their central Principles of Justice and Mercy, and so the Middle Pillar Pendulum hangs on its fulcrum of Knowledge, between the points of Wisdom and Understanding. From this, depends the movement of tempo and meter. It should be noted that the Crown or Summit has an inverse swing of an approximately 1—3 ratio. This might well indicate a suitable balance between pauses and periods during metrical recitations, and it is easily checked with a stop-watch and tape-recorder. If we take a short passage such as the Lord's Prayer, recite it flatly and continuously without pause between words, it will be something like fifteen seconds. Hearing it will not be pleasant. A third of fifteen being five, we must introduce five seconds of silence into the prayer over its total, so that the whole recitation will come to twenty seconds. One single hearing of the difference between first and second readings should convince any reasonable being that a ratio of one third silence and two thirds sound is a very fair average proportion. The pauses of course, occur in the natural places indicated for them by the script itself.

The overall picture presented by our Glyph, seems to suggest that the more spiritual a Rite becomes, the shorter and more concise its meter should be. An example is the consecration formula of the Mass:

$$— \quad \text{THIS} \quad —$$
$$— \quad \text{IS} \quad —$$
$$— \quad \text{MY} \quad —$$
$$— \quad \text{BODY} \quad —$$

At the other end of the scale, constant and repetitive wordage or noise brings everything to physical levels over a broad metric band. Between the two extremes, we are left with a good working area for intellectual and emotional ritualism. Generally speaking, the intellectual meter is the longer of the two, tending to more words and less music. The meter associated with Soul leans to less words and more music.

Bearing these various points in mind, we are faced with the problem of what particular Rites to construct. It is well to form some ideas about the possible types to choose from, so that we may know along which lines to work. Although Rites are bound to differ very widely from each other in nature according to authorship, they do descend from a common ancestral stock with limited branches on its trunk. Some of the main limbs are these:

INITIATORY RITES These are among the most elaborate and spectacular of all. A candidate is being introduced into a Circle which becomes widened by that much, so there is gain and growth on each side. The candidate is subjected to chosen energies presented in dramatic forms under the guise of Symbolic tests and experiences. This is done in the patterns of the particular Group concerned, and most of these are traditional. There is no reason however, why the principles of initiatory Rites should not be far more widely applied. Nor is there any reason why they should not be repeated on suitable occasions. The general idea is to impact energies on the candidate which they should subsequently work out for themselves in the Group or Circle they have entered. Provided facilities are available for such work in the Group, initiation will be worth while. Otherwise it would be like hurling an alphabet at a child's head and expecting literacy in a few months.

How many candidates, once successfully through their initiations, ever go back over them in mind looking for missed points, or to expand an experience? How many Initiates ever repeat their Oaths of Obligation? (Let alone fulfil them!) Initiation should and must be a constant experience if it is to be a valid one. To make this possible, there must be enough potential in a Rite of Initiation for the candidate to grow as far as the next stage, provided they make use of it properly.

Arising from Initiation Rites there should be a number of minor

241

"repeats" which the Initiate may work for himself in order to develop the original potential. There should be at least an annual "re-cap" of the Initiation at about the anniversary date, when perhaps all those of a similar Grade could re-dedicate themselves. Why also need an Initiation Rite be limited to human candidates? We might Initiate a process, or a project, or for that matter almost anything at all, and there is no reason why appropriate Rites should not be used.

The ingredients of Initiations are drawn from the principal Symbols with which the Initiate will be expected to work. On the whole, the higher the Initiation the less physical the Symbols become until they transcend matter altogether. Most of the very colourful and even pompous Initiation Rites belong surprisingly enough to the lower Grades.

The structure of the Rite will normally include: an Oral Examination, set as questions and answers in connection with the Grade being taken; Lectures and Explanations which plant seed-thoughts in the Candidate's mind; Ordeals and Tests to call out necessary initiative. These are mainly symbolic only now-a-days, since the real ones come from Life itself. There will be an Oath of Obligation which is sworn between the Candidate and his Deity, in which is outlined his position, promises and purpose. Recognition signals will be imparted, and introductions made to Persons, both physical and otherwise. In brief, the Candidate's tasks are laid upon him, sources for help in these indicated, and blessings asked upon the whole. To initiate means to begin, and it is best to do so under favourable conditions. The Rites provide such conditions insofar as a gardener does his best to help the plants he sets out in prepared soil, but what follows can only come from Nature.

INSTRUCTIONAL RITES. These cover a very wide field. They may be divinatory in character, or simply to gain experience in ritual or other working. Any Rite may be rehearsed for instructional purposes provided the principal Name of Power is muted or excluded. Symbols used during instructional Rites will be limited to those concerned with the point or points on which specific instructions are sought, and no extraneous matter should be introduced. Invocations are to be directed to whichever Inner category of Consciousness covers the type of information or experience needed. Instructional Rites tend to be less formal than most, and their externals may be very simple indeed, perhaps no more than pen and paper. The lay-out might only be a brief Induction, directional prayer, meditational period, and Acknowledgement. Forms are always best kept to essentials, unnecessary decorations dissipate energy that is difficult enough to concentrate in the first place.

SACRIFICIAL RITES. Under no circumstances whatsoever should these be interpreted as a hopeful bribe offered to some very questionable type of God. The only sacrifice acceptable within the Holy Mysteries is that of Self. Carcases of any kind are quite worthless. Our own lives are the true oblation, so that through them the Divine Spirit may manifest according to Will. Our Symbols of bread for Body, salt for Mind, water for Soul, and wine for Spirit, indicate that we offer ourselves for assimilation into Divine Love. Death is no sacrifice, and should have no part in the Rites. Life is the Mystic Offering that we must make and maintain. In effect we offer the worst we have in exchange for the best we may ever become.

Several factors are necessary to constitute a true sacrifice. First and foremost it must be an act of complete free-will without the slightest suspicion of "strings attached." Second, it must be within the ability of the donor to offer. It would be useless for instance, to offer some fictitious and meaningless donation such as "all the flowers of earth", or "our happiness to come," or the like high-flown notions. Better a few wild flowers gathered sincerely, than wild promises about unattained Heavenly Gardens. It would be fair to make a sacrifice of living-time for some worth-while purpose provided this can be made practical, or to sacrifice personal will if this can be done without resentment. Whatever the object of sacrifice, it must certainly come within the competence of the giver. Thirdly, the sacrifice must be irrevocable. Hence the consumability of the sacrificial Symbols. That which is eaten and drunk cannot be restored, nor can burnt offerings, or those poured out on earth. The spirit of sacrifice is total relinquishment. A single "if", "but", or implied condition invalidates the act utterly.

The idea behind a sacrifice is that a human will has reached its limits, realised this, and accepted the fact that only a Divine or superhuman Will and Consciousness can proceed past such a point of human limitation. Therefore humanity "hands over" or sacrifices self-will in the matter to the superior Wisdom of the Overself. The unspoken implication is, "Since I cannot—You can."

Sacrificial Rites are most serious undertakings, and should never be embarked on lightly, however simple their formularies may be. These vary from the partaking of consecrated food and drink, to burning some Symbol (such as incense) in a fire. A dedicated Talisman consisting of a Glyph representing the intended sacrifice may be burned, or salt poured into running water. The lay-out of sacrificial Rites is essentially an Approach in which the intention is outlined, an Invocation directed toward the Divine Consciousness being approached, the Consecration of the Oblation, in which both Divine and human awareness come together, the Sacrifice itself when the "hand-over" takes place, and finally the Closure directing the new phase of co-consciousness on its way.

SEASONAL RITES. These are for "tuning in" with the cycles of Nature in which our lives take place. They normally coincide with the Quarters of the Solar Cycle, although the older Moon celebrations took place roughly at the cross-Quarters, and were based on fertility patterns. Quarterly Rites are properly called Feasts, since they are socio-religious affairs consisting of family and friendly gatherings probably for a day or so together. Each Rite should be in keeping with its Season. Ideas may be planted during the Spring, nurtured at Summer, gathered at Autumn, and purged out in Winter. It is the essence of Quarterly or Seasonal Rites that they are get-togethers of like minded people celebrating their particular Mystery in their own way as part of the Great Plan involving all Life. Well-designed Seasonals are a joy to the partakers. Divinities, absent friends, other Kingdoms of Life, the Dead, and spirits of the Innerworlds all come together for the celebrations. So long as the Mysteries continue, they will be kept up somehow and somewhere.

The pattern of the Feasts is the ancient Circle round the Fire (which represented the Sun and Moon as Principles of Light). Traditionally everyone brought something for the cooking-pot, so the meals were a communion of each others gifts. The rich brought much, and the poor little, but all partook together. Song, recitations, prayers, commemorations, entertainment and instruction all fitted into the Rites. Young, old, and middle-aged found at least something out of each other to suit themselves. Traditional games and sports were played, and both Gods and men were glad of each others company. Seasonal Rites have become very sadly neglected, and much in need of restoration in the best possible way. There is great scope for workers in ritual fields for putting Rites of the Old Traditions into acceptable modern formulations.

DEVOTIONAL RITES. These make a large proportion of ritual workings. They should be designed to make links between human and Divine consciousness. All possible ritual factors may be brought to bear on this point, so that purely devotional Rites can be most colourful indeed. They have no particularly set pattern, except that the God-Aspect approached is usually personified in some way as a Symbol, or presented in some formal fashion. The whole object of any devotional Rite is to establish contact with Inner Life, and the lay-outs should be arranged with this aim in view.

CONSECRATORY RITES. To "consecrate" is from "consacro", "to make Holy together," and this is exactly what should happen. Both human and Divine consciousness focus on a common point of person, place, or thing, agreeing together to make use of that point for a mutual purpose, excluding all other usages. This is consecration. The whole essence of the Rite is dedication of its subject to one function alone, which must serve the ends of humanity and Divinity alike. A single use of a consecrated object outside the terms of its consecration will de-secrate it.

The exact terms of any consecration must therefore be defined very carefully, preferably in writing, for the sake of a recorded understanding. Advantages of consecration are that so long as the terms are complied with, the object will remain "in tune" with its Inner link, and this is the reason for keeping it on that single mark. As a rule, fully consecrated objects are only handled by individuals appointed to use them. Those things which are "blest" have a much wider application in magical practice, and a careful distinction must be made between a consecration and a blessing. A blessing is the attachment of a hope to an object that it will bring beneficial results to its users, but this depends upon the use they make of it. Blessings are given in general terms, and consecrations in particular ones.

Nothing should therefore be consecrated unless every intention exists of fulfilling the conditions of its hallowing. Otherwise there is no consecration. For example, to solemnly consecrate a Magic Rod, and then leave it loose in a drawer full of miscellaneous equipment, would desecrate it immediately. Blessed objects remain blessed however they are handled, unless there is a deliberate intention of destroying the blessing, stronger than that which attached it in the first place. An unlikely occurence. Thus an object which has been both consecrated and blessed, might lose the former attachment but not the latter.

The term "consecrated" is far too loosely employed among certain types of ritualist, and various objects brandished around as being "properly consecrated" etc. If an original consecration ever did exist, this would certainly have lapsed with improper usage. Certainly no one could sell Talismans *consecrated* for a buyer, since the sale of itself would automatically invalidate the consecration. The Talisman or whatever might indeed be "charged" with energies imparted by its maker, but such does not constitute a consecration, and should not be so described.

Consecratory Rites may be quite brief, and in fact often form part of a longer Rite. They should include invocations to whichever Divine or other Aspect the object of consecration is being linked with, a concise definition of the consecratory terms, and some symbolic action that imparts individuality to the object, so that it differs in that respect from others of its kind. A simple way of doing this is to give the object a personal name. It may also be anointed, aspersed, or magnetised. Many individualising methods will suggest themselves to an imaginative mind. The important thing is that from the very moment the object receives its consecration, it must never be employed for other reasons. Should that occur in fact, an entire ritual cleansing and re-consecration would be necessary.

BANISHING RITES. These include cleansings and exorcisms, since their objective is to get rid of undesirable influences. They are concerned with reducing unwanted charges in persons places or things to neutral. This can only be accomplished by detachment of the influence from its linkage with whatever it affects, and is no easy matter, since so many variable factors are involved. Once the causé of attachment is known, the process of neutralisation may be commenced. Careful study from an Inner viewpoint is necessary. The ritualist does not usually banish anything by his own power, but acts as an agent for Inner Entities capable of carrying out the process on their own levels.

Banishing Rites include appeals to such Entities, and the ritualist is advised to act only in the name of Power invoked, or on behalf of some spiritual authority he is entitled to represent. At all costs, the ritualist must be capable of casting the unwanted influence out of himself, otherwise it will remain uncleared. Symbols used include salt (which sterilises); water (which cleanses); fire (which burns corruption and dispels darkness); sword (which severs contacts); air (which brings freshness); and earth (which absorbs and eventually neutralises poisons).

Banishing techniques are a study on their own, and no one incapable of banishing evil thoughts from their own minds can possibly dismiss even worse evils from elsewhere.

SPONTANEOUS RITES. These are simply made up from the miscellany of ritual units according to impulse or inclination. They are creatively refreshing to participate in, since they evolve themselves from Inner sources, but are likely to get out of hand unless controlled. It is a good idea to have some set Rites with periods set aside for free expression among participants. This works extremely well in practice, and develops a good deal of otherwise latent potential. There seems to be a considerable future for such types of Rite.

SPECIAL RITES. These are composed to fulfil some particular function such as Blessing, Cursing, Commemorations, Funerary or Nuptial celebrations, Summoning of Spirits and the like. They should present no special problems once the central theme is chosen and ritual items selected to build up around it. All Rites are constructed from the same basic ingredients in any case, only differing in styles, combinations, and intentions.

Now that we have ideas about the various types of Rite that may be worked, it may be as well to consider some of the principal ritual constituents in use among average modern practitioners.

The Altar. Traditionally this is a double cube, one white and one black. Theoretically they should be separate cubes, whichever is uppermost indicating the nature of the Rite to be worked. A cube unfolded makes a sacrificial Cross, black on one side and white on the other. The black cube of the altar thus has a white inside, signifying the Inner Light enfolded by Matter, and the white cube is black inside indicating Matter encompassed by Spirit. On the black and white faces of the cubes in contact with each other at centre, the Secret Names or Signs of the Patron Gods are supposed to be set, and since these faces should be cemented together, no mortal eye may see them.

The altar was considered to be the Beth-El, or "God-house" in which the presiding Deity resided during the Rites or at seasonal intervals. On the visible faces of the cubes there may be dedicatory Symbols or Names, though aesthetically they are best left plain for imagination to write on. The cubes also represent the two ashlars, or stone blocks, the black cube being the rough unfinished ashlar, representing man in his natural state, and the white cube being the polished and finished ashlar, or perfected man through his own efforts.

The normal place for an altar in a Temple is at centre, so that everyone in the circle around it is at equal distance, but it may quite well be placed at any particular Station which might form the focus of a Rite. The average altar is a cupboard of rough double-cube dimensions, painted externally, and the interior contains the sacred vessels and materials for Rites. Originally the altars had horns fixed to the corners as emblems of virility and power, besides being tokens of animal sacrifice. This is very rare now, and the horns have become mere tassels of the altar-cloth, which may be white for general use, or coloured for harmonising with specific Rites. Occasionally the horns appear as attachments to right and left of the altar, one holding the Book of Rites, and the other a lighted torch or candle. This design is most practical indeed.

An altar is to a ritualist what a drawing board is to an architect, an operating table to a surgeon, or a bench to an engineer—a principle working surface. On the altar top there should be neither more nor less than the exact symbol pattern necessary for whatever stage of the Rite is being worked. Nothing extraneous or non-essential should ever occupy the surface of an altar. An altar-top represents the field of consciousness in use by the ritualist, and should be so considered. It is like a Shield on which a Charge is being designed for a particular purpose, and during the Rite this must be built up bit by bit, the consciousness of the operator varying with the Symbols he manipulates on the altar-top. It is most important an altar be treated in this way if it is to be properly used. Under no circumstances should it ever resemble an untidy shelf in some junk shop, or be crammed with pointless decorations. Flowers and other ornaments may be put on other stands, shelves, or elsewhere if insisted upon, but an altar top must be scrupulously clear of everything except Symbols in actual use for definite reasons.

When not in ritual engagement, an altar may have a meditational Symbol-pattern upon it and nothing more. Sometimes only a votive Lamp is left to burn in the centre, or a crystal globe or mirror displayed. Occasionally the Four Instruments might be laid out in association with each other. The simpler and more concise the design on an altar, the better. Frontals or side drapes for an altar, may be coloured according to the season, say light green and yellow for Spring, dark green and blue for Summer, russet and brown for Autumn, and dark brown and white for Winter.

It must be remembered the Altar is the Symbol of a focal point for the Divine Presence in the Temple, and as such should always be acknowledged on entering and leaving the place, as well as during Rites. A brief bow or hand salute is sufficient, and should never be omitted as a gesture of good Temple behaviour. This too, considerably helps the build-up of atmosphere in the place. If there is no actual Rite in progress, the altar may be kept in the Eastern Station to signify the approach of Light, so that all salutes should be directed thereto. What is important, is to make a realisation of the Inner Power, become aware of It, and feel It in focus through the point symbolised by the altar.

To do this efficiently needs practice in "altar-approach" which is a highly important ritual act. According to the spirit in which the altar is approached at the beginning of any Rite depends the subsequent development and outcome of the working. A conscientious ritualist will therefore practise approaching an altar again and again, until a sense of fitness is achieved. This is done as follows:

Sit facing the altar upon which is a working Symbol such as a Lamp. Concentrate on the flame, and become aware of the Point of Presence behind it. Build up this awareness as strongly as possible. Feel a tremendous attraction toward the Presence that emanates from the altar. Want wholeheartedly to approach and be drawn into the Presence, yet make no deliberate physical move. It must be as though the ritualist were holding himself back against an increasingly powerful current pulling him into the Presence. The thought should be: "I will not move, but I will be moved. It is not I that move, but the Presence moves me." There will come a point when the Higher Will prevails over the lower, and the ritualist literally feels himself, as it were, pulled out of his seat bodily toward the altar. This is when the physical move takes place, which consists of the traditional three steps forward, ending in a bow from the waist toward the Presence. No move at all shall be made until the preliminary build-up is sufficient.

Retirement from an altar is the reverse process, and must be done with equal care. A bow, three backward steps, then turn and proceed deosil to seat. Should there be no physical room to make the three steps, they can be done Inwardly. Whatever limitations are imposed by awkward physical conditions should be extended to proper proportions through Inner dimensions. Once the principles of altar-approach have been experienced, they can be widened into approach-attitudes, which are particular ways in which the Presence may be approached. These will generally be in line with the Personification or Aspect chosen, and the ten broad approaches are:—

10 Approach as if to a Head of State on earth.
 9 Approach as if to a mysterious Goddess of Life and Strength.
 8 Approach as if to a Healer and Teacher.
 7 Approach as if to the Goddess of Love.
 6 Approach as if to the Divine Priest-King of Light.
 5 Approach as if to a Great Judge, who might be Protector or Punisher depending on deserts.
 4 Approach as if to kindly and compassionate King.
 3 Approach as if to the Great Mother.
 2 Approach as if to the Father of Wisdom.
 1 Approach as if to the Supreme Spirit of All.

All these approaches call for distinct attitudes of their own in keeping with their natures. It must be realised of course, that the Divine Presence does not actually alter at all, and it is ourselves who necessarily change our viewpoints and approaches thereto. Nevertheless we would not approach a Mother Aspect in exactly the same way as a Judge Aspect, and the difference ought to show up in the method used. A Mother might be approached with a soft smile, a gentle step, and outheld hands, while a Judge would be approached more apprehensively with no smile and arms held in with possibly crossed hands. Attitudes suggest themselves quite naturally for all the Aspects, and should be practised and rehearsed until they become normal procedure which can be assumed at will.

A custom which seems to be increasing in connection with modern mainly wooden altars, is the inclusion at the base somewhere, of a natural stone sometimes taken from an ancient holy site. This stone need not be at all large, since it is purely symbolic, though it may be used for striking matches on to produce the "Fire from

Stone" which should traditionally kindle the Fire on the Altar. Whether from a sacred site or not, there ought certainly to be a stone of some kind associated with the altar for the sake of maintaining ancient links.

By the behaviour of any ritualist in association with the altar, it is possible to assess their qualities and capabilities. Ritual life revolves around the altar as a symbolic fulcrum for the forces involved. Even the word itself comes from a root signifying "high" in the sense of *exalted*. In olden times, a hill-top was a natural place of worship, since it was furthest away from the plains, and received the first and last rays of the sun before and after the low-lying cities thereon. It was the place of the Most High in maximum Light, and therefore sacred to Heaven. The hill or mountain itself was the altar, and an artificial altar in a Temple is but a simulacrum of the Holy Mountain. As the Psalm says, "Send

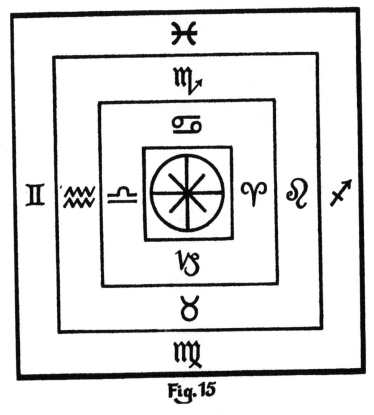

Fig. 15

forth thy light and thy Truth; they have conducted me and brought me into thy holy mountain and into thy tabernacles. And I will go unto the altar of God; to God who giveth joy to my youth."

For this reason, a well-placed altar has three steps leading up to it on each of its four sides, so that it becomes almost a pyramid in principle. The total of twelve steps around the altar are of course the twelve Signs around the Sun, arranged in Cardinal, Fixed, and Mutable order so as to give the Solar Cross Symbol. Quite an elaborate processional can be worked out with this pattern, which is given in Fig. 15.

The significance of the so-called "Chi—Rho" sign will be seen as the Quarters and cross-Quarters on the altar of Light in the centre of the design, and many interesting altar-approach patterns may be made by following out the various Sign-combinations. All such approaches should be aimed at heightening the consciousness so that when the altar is finally arrived at, the officiant is in a state of upliftment compatible with the Rite to be worked around and upon the altar itself. In ancient days, this followed naturally upon the exhaustion of body and exhilaration of spirit consequent upon a spiral progress around a steep hill. Nowadays we have to simulate this in a Temple by symbolic means and circumambulations, yet if we remember the old process, it will help very greatly.

Now we must consider the behaviour of the ritualist both in relation to the altar and otherwise, which might be classified as:

Attitudes. Originally each God-Aspect was represented in some characteristic attitude which the ritualist was supposed to assume when invoking or personifying them. These old attitudes are easily discovered from representations of the Gods themselves, but they are seldom in prominent use to-day, any more than are the ritual masks once worn by ritual officiants. Nevertheless, a correct attitude in the Temple is of the greatest importance, and ritualists should be meticulously drilled in their practice until an easy grace comes with them. Oriental Yogins adopt their "asanas" quite naturally as a matter of course in their training, and Western ritualists should at least make some effort in the same direction. If we consider the body itself as a whole, it may occupy one of four major positions:

1. Prostrate. This may be in the "earth-embracing" position, with outstretched arms like a cross, or the "serpent" position, hands clasped in front of head, left foot crossed over right. There is also the "hanged man" position, in which the hands cross over the forehead, palms flat, the elbows forming a triangle, while the left foot crosses behind the right knee. A semi-prostration, is a kind of crouch, forearms and palms on the ground, with hands close to forehead which touches the earth. Prostrations are only used to express personal negations and unquestioning acceptance of Divine authority. It will be noted that the "serpent-position" makes it impossible to rise by one's own efforts.

Full prostrations are not often used in Western Rites, the bow taking their place, but this is probably on account of physical inability rather than deliberate disuse. The semi-prostration, or crouch, is the attitude approximating a womb-position, or unspoken acknowledgement of the relation between humanity and the Divine Mother-Life. It is also the smallest compass into which the average body can be compressed, and is a useful commencement position before embarking on a major Rite. It should convey the impression of coiled-up energy like a spring or a serpent tightened upon itself awaiting release through action, or perhaps an implanted seed prepared for germination into full growth and ultimate stature.

Ritual prostrations are in no sense to be construed as abasements or attitudes of self-reproach, but are to be thought of as adjustments toward Inner forces. In the presence of mighty physical energies such as explosions, earthquakes, etc, we should instinctively flatten ourselves into protective positions. Ritual prostrations are practical acknowledgements that we admit the existence of Inner Powers infinitely greater than any physical manifestations, and are invoking those very energies in our cause.

2. *Kneeling* If on both knees, this is an upright extension of the semi-prostration, indicating the commencement of human ascent toward Divinity, yet still attached to earth half way. In prostration, man is shown as an earthly being, figuratively buried like a seed. With kneeling, we perceive the progress away from earth of human growth, as if humanity had emerged out of it to the knees, yet was still rooted like a plant, the upper part of the body free to move, and the lower part captive. This is an average human state in comparison with Divinity, and is therefore an admission of a status quo when invoking superior Beings of the God-Aspect category.

Kneeling on one knee (sometimes called the Swastika position) indicates an increase of human freedom as if one leg and foot had been pulled out of the earth. A partial resurrection as it were, with one foot out of the grave, showing man as a threequarters upright being, yet still held by one leg like an upright version of the Hanged Man. This position is the one adopted in genuflecting, and signifies our relative status to Beings of an Archangelic order. It is characteristic of military submission to a senior officer, and is often associated with soldiery, since it leaves freedom to draw a sword, and is the preparatory position for an upright spring.

3. *Standing.* Here man is at last upright and able to move around the surface of the earth. Nothing but gravity holds him an earth-captive. Humanity has emerged into the Light bodily as a responsible being in his own right. Uprightness is man's noblest

attribute in all senses, since it has been earned by his own efforts. Only when man has both feet free can he turn a complete circle, and tread the Solar Path. We do not appreciate our ability to stand, and realise what it means, until some disability prevents us. The fact that we stand upright in ritual practice, indicates our standing between Earth and Heaven for what it is, and signifies our competence to deal not only with each other, but with Angels and spirits also. A standing individual shows that spiritual growth has been attained to a point of reasonable ability, and a good deal of ritual working time is spent in this position.

4. *Sitting, or Resting.* This position is one of Outer quiescence and Inner activity. It signifies a changeover of energies from one state to another. Before anything manifests Outwardly, there has to be considerable Inner preparation and working, just as after external manifestations cease, there follow Inner continuations. The sitting position during Rites is to allow for this adjustment, and is not for Inward idling. Although a sitting posture is physically relaxing, Inner action should be correspondingly increased and intensified. During some Rites, one Officer at least (the Pontiff) remains seated the whole, or most of the time, often with closed eyes. This apparently superfluous individual is in fact most energetically engaged in "bridging" between the Inner and Outer worlds, and so "mediating" the force-flow in either direction. They are actually the immediate contact-point through which the other ritualists are working.

The normal sitting position should be that as shown by Egyptian God-figures, spine erect not leaning on the back of the chair, arms to sides and hands palm down along the thighs. Otherwise the hands may be loosely clasped in the lap, or with finger and thumb tips touching so as to make a triangle pointing earthwards. These manual postures allow a nice muscular balance to be maintained, and permit the upright positions to be assumed with a naturally graceful movement. Hand positions are always of ritual importance, and apart from specific gestures of blessing, dismissal, etc, can be classified thus:

Closed positions. Hands thrust into sleeves grasping opposite wrists; arms folded; fingers tucked beneath opposite arm-pits; hands joined on lap with thumbs contacting opposite palms; or fingers interlaced, with arms to sides, and hands across abdomen. All these positions indicate temporary disengagement from the action of the Rite for one reason or another.

Receptive positions. Hands relaxed open on lap, held cupped before the body, crossed on breast, outstretched palm up, or in any way suggesting receptivity. These manual positions are adopted during ritual periods of reduced external activity when participation is largely confined to establishing Inner contacts, yet the Rite is being closely followed inaudibly.

Alert positions. Palms together breast level in classic prayer attitude; hands upheld palms outward at shoulder level; palms together, thumbs touching along nose; hands and forearms resting along arms of chair; any manual position involving a static semi-tension somewhere between rest and activity. Such postures are used to focus attention and confine consciousness within chosen limits. The arms represent the Pillars, and so when they are held above the head, Man invokes God; when level with shoulders, equal understanding is sought; and when extended downwards, the highest in the operator seeks control over the lowest.

Active positions. These include all mobile gestures such as blessings, bannings, sign-manuals, and handling of symbolic instruments. There are endless signs which may be made with the hands, from the secret grips to identify membership and grade in any association, to the elaborate finger-language used to convey intelligence without ordinary words. Strictly speaking, these refinements are not properly part of ritual practice, and have occurred as side-effects rather than main methods. They may be interesting as curiosa, but are not germane to ritualism per se.

Hermetic types of ritual tend to have somewhat formal gestures and attitudes, while Orphic practice is largely spontaneous according to mood or music. This does not imply that Hermetic Rites are necessarily all solemn, slow, or portentous. It simply means that they have become perhaps more conventionalised in their methods of expression. For example, a Hermeticist when handling a Sword or Rod, would point along it with thumb to indicate an absolute Will in any matter, and the forefinger to signify intention and hope. The first method shows command, and the second persuasion. Both may actually be used together if circumstances call for this.

If one hand has nothing particular to do while the other is being used, the free hand should automatically be placed palm flat on the breast, which is the neatest disengaged position. Hands should never hang limply by the sides, be held behind the back, or left to dangle carelessly anyhow. They should always be both posed and poised like the mind directing them. Sloppy hand positions indicate disorganised minds, and novices must be most carefully drilled in all hand-usage. No one should move around a Temple with swinging hands or held at low-clasp over lower abdomen. If nothing is actually being borne in the hands, movement is best made with the hands at breast-point, or the high-clasp at about the epigastrium.

Uselessly elaborate or fantastic gestures should be carefully avoided. They impress no one except those knowing no better. All hand or body movements should be economical and precise, conveying exactitude and competence, controlled by Wisdom working with Will, yet no gesture should be inadequate or ineffective. Correct use of movement can only come with long practice, and many training sessions will be necessary to develop this skill. How we should consider some types of movement likely to be encountered in working ritual methods.

Circling. The so-called "Magic Circle" is really the ground-plan of whatever Cosmos of consciousness the ritualist intends to manifest through. In olden times, the idea was to run round and round the circle until sheer giddiness resulted in disorientation and dis-association from physical surroundings. This will work today, provided there has been a previous period of fasting and mal-nutrition, but it will scarcely produce worthwhile results, unless confusion of consciousness is counted as such. The modern method of circle-working is to make consistent cyclic changes of con-sciousness according to the plan of the circle and rate of progression around it.

Suppose we had a "Spring-Summer-Autumn-Winter" circle. As we go round it deosil, we change our Inner awareness and attitude from one concept to another while we traverse the Quarters. The same may be done with Archangel or any type of concept, pro-viding the principle of the cyclic pattern-change is followed. To do this effectively, there ought to be a circle-chant designed for the purpose which is called by a central controller, and responded to by those treading the perimeter. The general scheme should be to start fairly slowly, work up to a good sharp pace, then halt suddenly at a given signal. To keep distances properly between a number of people, they may link with each other in some way such as putting hands on shoulders, or even holding hands like children in ring-games. Originally, the circle was worked by going round and round it at ever increasing pace with one idea in mind until this became forced through the various levels of being by intensity of effort. Now, instead of pushing our minds through a circle so hard, we push the circle through our minds faster than our bodies are going around it. Theoretical circle-working can be done whilst standing physically still, and feeding the concepts through our consciousness in their cyclic order at an increasing rate.

Nevertheless, bodily movement around a circle is a genuine help in all ritual practice. Apart from anything else, it co-ordinates effort and brings people together. The mere fact of circular move-ment through the earth's magnetic field, induces minimal electric changes in the human body of a beneficial kind. Moreover, if a number of people are involved, they are moving through each other's electric fields and auric influences so as to pick up each other's energies and tune these for the common purpose. The shuffle-stamp foot movement seems to generate maximum electrical energy, while a next best is a sliding step.

It is important in circle-chanting that the intoned response from the dancers is kept going all the time while the caller at centre is giving out the next subject for thought. When the final abrupt halt comes, all possible powers of concentration are brought to bear on the single topic that halts everyone. In this way the entire accumulation of energy generated by the circling is directed into the intended channel of consciousness. Sometimes this works best if the dancers remain unaware of this point until it is emphatically announced to stop them in their tracks. Then their forces are released like the snap of a bowstring, and physical effort converts to mental and spiritual equivalents with considerable impetus.

The whole purpose of circle-working or maze-treading is to bind consciousness Outwardly and release it Inwardly. This is to "bind on Earth and loose in Heaven" (the Kingdom of Heaven being Within.) By involving awareness in some physical repetitive process until saturation point is reached, the drift of lower consciousness ceases in such absorption, and the higher awareness floats free, as it were, to open up Inwardly and establish itself in those transcendent Dimensions. So we might think of the Magic Circle as a kind of spiral staircase which enables us to get higher and higher with every round. However we treat the Circle, it certainly deserves to be studied in principle and worked in practice throughout all Systems of occult activity.

It is difficult to adjudicate on the controversial issue of deosil and widdershin circling. Neither are essentially good or evil in themselves. The former follows the diurnal path of Solar Light, and the latter the annual Zodiacal cycle. Over the centuries however, an association has grown up of the widdershin (against the Sun) direction being one of Darkness, and hence favourable for wicked purposes best kept under dark cover. Naturally evil may be done as well by Day as Night, but humanity still tends to think the reverse. As a general ruling therefore, if ritualists connect an anti-Solar cycle with anything undesirable at all, it is best not to use it.

Circle-working ought usually to come somewhere near the commencement of a Rite in order to start up the artificial Cosmos which the Rite should create. Once the circle is got going, the workers may continue the Rite in its centre, but they should still consider the perimeter they have Inwardly made to be revolving around its central axis of the altar of whatever is set up. In effect they have constructed a world of their own holding them together by its centrifugal force while they build their Inner patterns as they intend. This is why it is important not to go beyond the limits of the circle during a Rite, because to do so breaks belief in its centralising power, and thus invalidates the Rite. To avoid this, it is only necessary to agree that no matter where a physical circle may be traced on the Temple floor, its Inner and real perimeter extends around the whole place and so cannot be accidentally overstepped. While the circle-working is in progress, its Inner extent should be clearly felt and defined by all engaged in the task. Circles may be worked to any theoretical diameter, but are best kept within concentrated limits for practical purposes.

Each properly worked Rite thus makes a sort of Inner rotary globe or circle of its own, which continues to spin along through Inner Space and Time, charged with the energies of its origination rather like a planet. Depending upon its construction, it may fulfil the intentions that formed it, or else disintegrate through lack of stability or meet with destruction because of impact against unfavourable Inner forces. Making and launching an Inner Space construction is difficult enough, but its subsequent eventual life has to remain in the guidance of those Inner Ones who take it over at inception. The general picture of the process is that the artificial Inner Cosmos is started up as a spinning circle (not unlike a Nebula) processed from the centre into patterns, and then the constructors disengage themselves from it through its central axis, leaving it to the Inners who make themselves responsible for its guidance.

It should not be forgotten that although the Magic Circle is traced around one plane only, its cross indicates the planes of the other two Circles which must be meshed with it. The officers of the Quarters are responsible for projecting these toward each other, and keeping them going actively. They obviously cannot run up the walls of the Temple and over the ceilings, so they must mentalise the movements accordingly. So long as the end-product is a Time-Space-Event Inner creation, the means by which it is achieved are matters for choice and convenience. Having set our Magical Circles in motion, we are now concerned with what takes place inside them. Since the conventional opening to so many Rites is a bow to the Quarters and the altar, let us consider this action.

The Bow. Properly performed, and not a ridiculously casual bob, this is a very functional item of ritual procedure. It consists physically of standing at attention, the body weight balanced evenly between both feet, hands usually together at heart level, then bending forward slowly from the waist with a straight back until the trunk is horizontal with the ground. After a brief pause, the trunk is straightened to upright, and the act is complete. An important factor in the bow is that it should be done with closed eyes, which has the effect of co-ordinating both physical and mental energies through the nervous system.

During the downward arc the breath should be slightly expelled and a Divine Name or other Symbol connected with the Rite strongly formulated. This may be changed at the horizontally held position, and changed again during the recovery to vertical while a new breath is indrawn. The bow thus becomes a cyclic four-point exercise, and may be considered as a vertical plane circling operation, provided the Inner activity is matched up to the Outer.

From another angle, the bow may be seen as a "swooping to Earth and rising to Heaven" movement. The idea behind this, is that like a bird, the ritualist dives through Inner Space after some quarry, takes hold of it, then soars up again with the prize. If, for example, the bow is made before a God-Aspect, an intention might be to shed some of the old personality on the way down, and arise with new qualities picked up from the contact.

The bow is quite an efficient aid in laying down one personality and coming up with another one. It probably stems back to ancient times when those in search of themselves drank at a still pool from the reflection of their own lips in the water. The mirror-image would represent the alter ego both of the Old Self to be drowned as a sacrifice, and the New Self to arise through the mystical communion between image and actually.

Out of this came the baptismal Rite, in which the candidate slowly sank beneath the water while watching their old image disappear, in the hope that their past sins might sink with it. They were then "saved" by being pulled from the water by their heads like a child from a womb. As this happened they were called loudly by their new name, and the first thing they saw (their Initiator being behind them) was their new reflection arising with them. Tradition says that in this way God arose from the Primaeval Ocean, and on seeing His reflection uttered His own Name.

The bow can be made into a model of this concept. A practice method is to place a mirror on the floor, then bend slowly over it while watching one's image. At the nadir of the bow, feel all the unsatisfactory qualities of the old personality slip away into the mirror's depth like clothes falling off the body into a bottomless pool. Then, closing the eyes, imagine the new and more worthwhile personality arising from the depths whence it is invoked and merging into the awaiting individual.

In general practice, the bow is an unspoken invitation to Higher Beings to extend their influence inside whoever makes the obeisance. This was a technique sometimes used in "spirit control" when the etheric portion of anyone was extruded during the bowed position, and the entering entity "took over" while bringing the body upright, eventually restoring the status quo ante by reversing the procedure. This process might be assisted by the "Name over Fire", which consisted of calling over and over again on the God or spirit to be invoked, whilst the invocant bowed over a brazier emitting smoke from hashish, opium, henbane, or the like stupifying agent. A dangerous practice, scarcely to be recommended, though a relic of it remains with us when a bow is made briefly over a smoking censer, which is nowadays harmless.

The basic essence of the bow in ritual is alignment with whatever is acknowledged, and change of attitude. It is like the space between paragraphs which gives the opportunity for adapting an outlook to new encounters. Apart from this, a bow has the effect of increasing blood to the brain, thus temporarily increasing mental ability. It also limbers up the spine, relieving minor pressures on nerves through prolonged standing, so promoting better neural tone. Regaining the upright position after a bow should always be done slowly to eliminate risk of fainting due to sudden blood-drainage away from the brain.

Some workers believe that a number of rapid bows have the effect of "loosening" the etheric body and increasing psychic sensitivity. It is very doubtful whether anything of real value comes of this. A similar effect may be far more easily obtained with the aid of a swing or rocking-chair. A steady back-and-forward movement while sitting in an ordinary chair will induce a mild auto-hypnosis, but is most unlikely to result in any worthwhile expansion of Inner consciousness.

There is a lot more to the ceremonial bow than might be supposed, if it is studied from the Inside rather than from its external appearance. This is true of all apparently minor ritual procedures, and only becomes evident when they are practised intelligently. It should never be assumed that all is known about even the most trivial ritual point. No matter how familiar or commonplace any ritual practice may become, there will always be some deeper meaning in it to be discovered by an open-minded user, perhaps after years. It invariably pays to keep looking Inward and exploring the depths of ritual items. Usually they are accepted on face value, or far too near their surface, and no further effort is made to follow them Inwards. This is a mistake. Whenever it seems that the bottom of a ritual topic is reached and there is nothing more to learn about it, then a realisation should be made that such an evident end is no more than a temporary limitation in the understanding of the individual himself, and not of the study topic. It is amazing what will emerge from old subjects studied in new ways after a lapse of time and a gain of experience. All ritual matters ought to be seen in this light and re-studied at intervals.

The Kiss. After the bow, we come to the question of the kiss. This implies a good deal more than a casual brushing of the lips against inanimate objects or other ritualists. It is the Outer symbol of an Inner energy-exchange on very close terms.

Between ordinary human lovers, the kiss is a kind of "soul-eating", each participant attempting to enhance themselves by partaking of the other's nature. The physical stimulus and thrill attending a kiss is an effect rather than a cause, and a kiss is fundamentally aimed at uniting souls rather than bodies, if indeed the humans involved are capable of such an experience. The lips being the junction point between the outer skin and the inner mucous membrane, they may be considered as Symbols of the Portals between Inner and Outer life, and they will fulfil this function for those in possession of spiritually organised vehicles. Just as sex-organ contact results in propagation of body, so lip contact should propagate soul. The use of the second apart from the first at the will of the user, is an outcome of careful training, yet a ritual necessity for Inworking.

If we look at the kiss at a basic level, we shall find that to kiss and to kill might be synonymous. An amoeba is all mouth at its edges, and simply flows around its food. Mouth contacts between creatures in the first stages of evolution are usually fatal for one of them, right up to the scale of the great carnivores. We might equally say that herbivorous animais kiss the plants they eat, or that we kiss our own food as we devour it. Food kissing gives life through death, and the serpent kills with its kiss.

Kissing as a form of contact on higher than physical levels is not practised by primitive mankind, and its technique only develops among evolving and sophisticated peoples. Its introduction as a purely ritual practice seems of comparatively late origin. The Christian Church still retains it, and kissing the book in lawcourts, or the hilt of a sword in a formal salute, yet partially remains, while folk-customs abound with ritualised kissing-practices. We kiss the chalice when partaking of consecrated wine, or the blessed bread that passes our lips. The kiss in some form or another is inseparable from ritual, since the lips are the gateways of Breathing, Eating, and Utterance, three vital ritual components. The general technique of the kiss is thus:

First visualise and invoke as strongly as possible, the Inner reality with which contact is sought. Then concentrate receptive awareness into the focal point of the lips so that they are like the apex of a cone containing all possible power behind them. When lip contact is physically made with the objective, let the feeling be of two cones meeting point to point and exchanging energies through this junction. It must be remembered that nothing may be taken in without a corresponding output. This may be synchronised with the breathing, so that energy is given out during exhalation and absorbed with inhalation.

Supposing a Symbol is kissed. After lip-contact is made, the ritualist should breathe something of himself into the Symbol which corresponds with its nature, and then attempt to take in whatever the Symbol has to offer, like an indrawn breath from the soul rather than the body. The same principles would apply if a living being were kissed, except that while one gives out, the other should take in alternately. Thus, the "Kiss of Peace" is given by placing hands on each others shoulders and bringing cheeks and lips in contact, first to the donors left, and then the right, so that the recipient is touched on opposite sides. The "Spirit is passed" by the donor breathing the Word into the recipients ear, and then receiving the response into their own. If this is done around a whole circle of people, the initial contact having been between a human member and an Inner source, the result is most pleasing.

The "Kiss of Peace" is not based sexually but spiritually, and is therefore a normal ritual act between those of the same physical sex, although it is best given and taken by opposite polarities of male-female around its cyclic course. To some extent, the Kiss being a symbolic act of "eating each other", a sharing of identity should take place so that both recipient and donor become enriched by the experience. It is all a question of linking externals through a human organism in order to evoke Inner realities of being. Physically, the lips are provided with very sensitive nerve-receptors which are capable of this linkage for those able to translate them into such terms.

A practical example of this is the somewhat primitive habit of chewing a pencil end in the hope of evoking writable thoughts. This usually works after a fashion, and can be demonstrated by gently tapping or rubbing the lips with the end of a pen, or even a fingertip, while letting the mind quest in search of some topic. The mild hypno-effect of the labial stimulus soon quietens the interfering part of the mind impeding contact with deeper levels, and consciousness begins to flow as it should. Some exponents of modern psychology are unable to interpret labial stimuli in other than terms of sex or infantilism, but this only reveals their own limitations and inability to see beyond those points. The ritual kiss extends far past those limits into Inner dimensions.

No ritual kiss should be lightly exchanged at all parts of the proceedings. Properly speaking, it is a sacramental act, and should be so considered. The kiss at the altar is made by placing the hands on the altar and touching the lips to it at mid point exactly as if the altar were a person, because it is considered to be the material vehicle for the Indwelling Presence invoked. No ritualist in his right mind bothers to kiss a lump of stone or wood for its own sake, and the kiss is bestowed to the Divinity behind the altar, or is at least intended so. In the case of a book, the kiss is directed not to print on paper, but to the Spirit of Understanding within the Words. The same applies in the case of any Symbol whatever.

Worked properly, the kiss forms a very practical ritual means for contacting Inner energies. It may be noted that sensitives who are trying to 'psychometrise" anything sometimes touch it to their lips quite instinctively in an effort to reach its Inner content. Ritualists have the same aim incorporated into procedural formulae, and should practise these until they achieve skill in their usage. A ritual kiss is an approach, Portal-contact, and direct Inner entry between entities in different states of being, thus being a minor Rite on its own. It must never become a perfunctory and meaningless act, for to so debase it is to lose its entire value.

The Censer. This is probably about the most popular item of ritual equipment. Most ritualists enjoy making pleasant or sometimes unpleasant smoke-smells with the help of some type of incense burner. Traced to its origin, we shall find the overpowering effect of the roasting sacrifice wafted before the noses of hungry worshippers luxuriating before their cheering fire. Their appetites were not only sharpened, but they could think of absolutely nothing else except the succulent meat their hunting Gods had provided. They associated the smoke and smell with everything that was holy, pleasant, wonderful, and inspiring. Even all these thousands of years later, there is something rather special about the smell of a Sunday roast. Our memories do not utterly perish, they just alter.

Later, when it was discovered that differently scented smokes could stimulate mental and spiritual hunger, affording aesthetic satisfaction and comfort, these became incorporated into ritual practice and are still with us. In olden times there was a general belief that the Beings invoked built themselves semi-material bodies out of the incense smoke and manifested to the invocants in that way. It is probable that such manfestations were actually subjective results of hemp, opium, or henbane smoke. Even much milder intoxicants can produce strange effects when inhaled in strong concentrations by those in a fasting semi-exhausted condition. It is not, however, suggested that such is a desirable practice or would cause results of any worthwhile nature.

The problem of how to burn incense is always a disputed one by differing practitioners. Some believe it should be a major part of a Rite, and others think it should be more of a background effect. It all depends upon opinions and the type of Rite worked. To be in keeping with ancient customs, the incense ought to be burned on a low stone altar in the centre of the circle. If a species of this is made with a central depression to accommodate a flame, and four other depressions around this for lighted charcoal and incense, it makes a primitive device which is quite effective. The flickering of the flame in combination with the ascending columns of smoke is almost hypnotic if there is no other illumination in the place. If the flame is supplied from spirits burning through an asbestos wick, chemicals added to the spirits for colouring the flame may be useful.

The principle purpose of using incense in this way is to provide a means for the constructive imagination to make its own "smoke-pictures" from the variable olfactory and visual stimuli offered. Even the consecratory prayer affords this clue when it says, "May our thoughts and prayers arise acceptably to Heaven, even as this smoke arises from our earthly altars." The incense smoke was supposed to be a suitable medium for the Outer invocants and the Inner Entities to use for impressing their consciousness upon each other. If the human operators fixed their attention into the smoke and tried to make it a vehicle for their awareness of what Lies behind material manifestations, then the Inner Ones would endeavour to reciprocate so that a point of common consciousness arose half way. This at least was, and still is, the theory. Not only smoke was used for this practice, but steam also, either by itself or in combination with smoke. It is surely as feasible to try tracking thoughts through ritual vapours, as to track electron particles through a condensation chamber. Both act as energy resistors, thereby revealing a passage of power.

In more developed types of Rite, the incense should either be burned in a proper chafing dish or tripod standing in its alcove normally at the East, or in a proper thurible produced as necessary by the thurifer, or "Incense bearer". The idea of the alcove is not unlike a "materialisation cabinet" favoured by old style mediums. It is simply a recess or artificial Grotto on the principle of the Mithraic or Delphic "Cave". It may be possibly some two or three feet across and perhaps five or six feet high and as deep as conveniently possible. If it has to be shallow, it is generally painted to give the impression of a "Crevice" between the worlds. The essential furnishings of this "antechamber" on our side of the Veil, are an incense burner, a flickering Flame, and sometimes an arrangement of mirrors or reflecting facets to stimulate imagination. The task of keeping the incense burning in this "Cave" was customarily given to a "maiden", or in large Groups to nine "maidens", three serving the Flame, three preparing more fuel, and three standing by as reliefs. So were the Fires in old Circles kept going.

It was hoped of course, that the God invoked would actually appear to the worshippers by materialising in the artificial Grotto, partly through the means of the incense and lights, and partly because the 'maiden" or her colleagues were acting as physical mediums. While it may not be denied that odd manifestations did indeed happen from time to time under exceptionally favourable conditions, such is most certainly not a general ritual happening, nor should it be expected as an objective event. Normally, impressions are conveyed on subjective levels, and they are no less genuine for that, since it is their proper channel. The physically perceptible manifestations were undoubtedly due to the "poltergeist abilities" of the pubescent "maidens" whose psychic energies were diverted for this purpose from normal sexual activities. Their unsatisfied stresses could certainly produce "paranormal phenomena". Once deflowered, the girls were of no value for obtaining such effects. Hence the ancient death penalty for seducing a Temple Virgin.

Suitably illuminated incense smoke is certainly a useful ritual adjunct if properly arranged as a convenient means for making meditations during appropriate phases of the Rite. It should be remembered however, that there is little use in doing this in any way that makes anyone cough or choke so much that concentration or even comfort is impossible. Careful rehearsals of smoke-effects are always advisable, and provisions made for suitable ventilation. Actual amounts of incense needed for the room or chamber wherein the Rite is taking place ought to be most carefully estimated. It is always possible to add small quantities to the hot charcoal, but usually impossible to clear the quarters of unwanted smoke until everybody is half suffocated and the Rite ruined.

Undoubtedly the best method of using incense during a Rite is by means of a properly constructed thurible. Today these are no cheap propositions, though they could be manufactured by home handymen skilled at a workbench, especially if they cared to adopt the simplest cylindrical designs in mild steel blackened to give a "wrought iron" effect, which is quite a pleasing alternative to brass. Ingenuity can be a great supplier of necessity. Handling a thurible in practice is something that many ritualists have misgivings over, since it definitely calls for skill and experience in order to avoid entangling the chains or scattering red-hot charcoals among unsuspecting co-ritualists.

Nothing but practice will bring competency with a thurible. The acme of thurification is when ability is reached to whirl the thurible around in full circles at the end of its chains without hitting anything or anyone. This is not a general custom however, and under no circumstances recommendable in small quarters. The occasional full swing may be permissible during processionals if there is ample space for the manouevre by a fully experienced thurifer, but it must be fully realised that even a single accident would be irretrievable if red hot coals were shot into vulnerable places. It is best not to exceed a 45 degree arc of swing.

The advantage of having a proper thurifer responsible for their ritual instrument is that they provide a mobile service, bringing the incense when and where it may be needed during the Rite, thus keeping full control of the smoke-situation. If a Rite is being worked by a single operator, the absence of a thurifer may be compensated for by hanging the thurible by its holding-ring from a hook where it can swing gently without hitting anything. A thurible should never be stood on its base with chains draped anywhere during a Rite. This is asking for entanglements. Some thuribles are even made without bases for this very reason.

A thurifer will normally be positioned in the South place of Fire, ready to bring the thurible to the officiant when required. Since the lid of the instrument must be slightly raised during its inactive moments to ensure proper burning of the charcoal, its lifting-chain has to be drawn up a few inches and held so that it may be released quickly. Some fold the end of the chain over the suspension plate and grasp all chains in a bunch immediately behind the plate. Really experienced thurifers slip the right thumb into the suspension ring, the little finger into the lid-lift ring, and raise or lower the lid that way during rest periods. This will not open the thurible enough to offer it for charging with incense. At that moment, the suspension ring must be kept by the left hand against the thurifer's chest and the incense-pan presented to the officiant at the extent of the right arm, fingers gripping the chains just above the lid. When the officiant has charged the charcoal with incense, the thurifer must close the thurible, bring the locking-ring above the lid and present it to the officiant with the left hand below the suspension plate and fingers of right hand steadying the chains just over the lid. The officiant will take it over that way with middle finger of left hand through the suspension ring, and the chains passing between the first and second fingers of the right hand so that the last three fingers are a few inches away from the top of the lid. These fingers act as a lever for impelling the thurible forward during incensation, when combined with a turn of the wrist.

When actually censing, the thurible should be extended before the face at almost forehead level by the right hand, the left being centrally aligned with the body so that the chains form a slack loop. This presents a symbolic picture of the Heart (left hand) being joined with the Head (right hand) in sending up thoughts (Mind) and prayers (Soul) from Earth (Man) to Heaven (God) like a cloud of fragrant incense. The Outer representation has to show what must happen Inwardly, and what the officiant does externally with the thurible around the Temple must be matched by the participants doing likewise internally at the same time. The act of incensation itself is done by swinging the thurible forward with a twist of the wrist and fingers, so that when it falls back gently under finger control it will meet the chains and give a ringing sound.

This noise is not intended as a pretty effect, but as a signal of the type of consciousness to be used by those hearing it. A maximum number of rings indicates the Diety, and the minimum of one, plain humanity. This simply means that more attention must be directed to Heaven than Earth at that instant. In Chrisian practice, three swings are for Diety alone as the Trinity, two for saints or seniors, and one for "other denominations". For Qabalistic practice, four swings would be for Divinity, three for higher and two for lower Spiritual concepts, while one alone is for mere mortals. Every System has its own code. As soon as the incense signals are heard by participants, they should direct thought and prayer accordingly so that they work in unison with each other Inwardly. If a Temple were too large for the thurible to be heard properly, small bell signals could quite well be given simultaneously.

The task of the officiant is to indicate with the incense pattern whatever devotional design ought to be followed during the Rite. What the thurible does, so must the thoughts and prayers of participants do with it. If it is held steadily up, so that a column of smoke ascends from it, then everyone should still themselves and send up a cloud of concentration between their personal Pillars. If it is moved around in various ways, so must attention be directed as it goes. To incense an altar for instance, the plan of the Temple and Rite is sketched in smoke around it. This would be in general terms:

1. A still column of smoke ascending at centre;
2. Four swings to the Height for Divinity;
3. One swing to the Depth for Humanity;
4. Three swings to Right for White Pillar;
5. Three swings to Left for Black Pillar;
6. Twelve semi-swings around perimeter of altar, three per quarter, for the Circle of the Stations;
7. Three swings around each corner of the altar (where the Horns used to be) for the Four Principles;
8. A triple swing from front right to left back corner; followed by
9. A triple swing from front left to back right corner, to indicate the Cross within Circle.
10. A still column of smoke ascending at centre.

Quite an elaborate Rite on its own if properly done, especially to suitable audio-accompaniment.

Incensing oblations is usually done by tracing a triple or quadruple Circle-Cross around them, and is carried out with the object of focussing all possible concentration on them at that moment, both from Inner and Outer viewpoints. When ambulating the Temple and incensing its various points, the officiant ought to be a visual focal centre for the Inner activities of participants. At the Quarters, for instance, the figures of the Four Archangels should be visualised as building up in the smoke, and at the Cenotaph the disincarnate contacts of the Circle may be imagined as looking through the haze toward their still embodied friends on the other side of the Fire. The officiant himself should strongly direct all this consciousness into the channels created by the behaviour of the smoke-pattern under formation. Eventually a certain amount of "style" will be developed whereby the gestures made with the thurible will adequately convey a whole chain of meaning between Inner and Outer ritual workers. Under no circumstances must a thurible ever be vaguely "waved around". It is a ritual tool which is to be used like an artist's brush or a sculptor's chisel, except that it is supposed to formate forces from "mind and soul" levels. If we could imagine a luminous contact coming from everyone present and meeting in the Fire and smoke of the thurible, then all this accumulated Light-energy being used to construct realities Inwardly, according to the behaviour of such a Fire-focus, we shall have a good idea of what ought to happen during incensation. Many lights will shine as one amid a cloud of combined consciousness.

Such is the function of the thurible as a means of consciousness control on a much higher level than applied by cruder types of incense burners. Provided ritualists know how to make proper use of it, the thurible induces awareness to behave in cosmically designed patterns intended to harmonise with the basic nature of the Rite being worked. It produces a sight, a sound, and a scent, thus linking with three of our senses, whereas other sorts of static burners offer only the scent. Once skill in manipulating the thurible is acquired, it will be preferred for most ritual purposes where movement is called for. While being carried from one place to another, the thurible is best borne before the body rather than beside it, since this position makes it less likely to be caught in robes or accidentally knocked against furnishings. Both hands should always be used, one to control the end of the chains, and the other near the thurible itself. When handing it over between officiant and thurifer, the instrument should be held out with taut chains, and accepted with both hands of the recipient. A brief inclination should pass between the ritualists concerned on these occasions.

Incensation is a matter of degree and circumstances. Some

encounter Divinity through the singing of their hearts amid the scents and sounds of nature itself, others meet their degree of It through songs around the campfire in a circle of comrades, and more specialised ritualists seek It in their Temples with swinging censers and chanting. All are different methods of putting similar principles into practice.

The Pillars. Leaving the subject of the censer, we turn to the use of the somewhat mysterious Pillars which stand erect in most Temples and Lodges under one form or another. They are capable of interpretation on so many levels it is difficult to choose a starting point. Like all Symbols of the Mysteries, they are meant to lead a Truth-seeking consciousness ever more deeply toward the Inner Kingdom. No sooner has some discovery been made about such Symbols, than another awaits to be found in endless succession. No matter how far we penetrate Inwards, there is always further to go. Anciently, at each stage of Initiation, the candidate was given some new explanation of previously known Symbols, and told that he was then in possession of the genuine meaning. Nowadays, such Symbols are usually presented to the candidate in principle and practice, after which he is expected to follow those Symbols Inwardly on his own initiative.

The Pillar Symbol is certainly a major Key in the Mysteries. Outwardly, it is no more than a pair of uprights, one white and one black. Any other embellishments depend on the System or Temple using them. Whether they are seen as phalloi, or the uprights of a ladder leading to Heaven, or in any other way, depends upon the consciousness considering them. In principle, they are Right, Left and centre, This, That and the Other, etc. Their middle is the space between them in which progression or evolution takes place. As a rule, they are so spaced in the Temple, that only one person can pass between them at a time, showing that everyone is responsible for their own advancement in the Mysteries. Using only two Pillars, an incredible number of conscious combinations may be made. Theoretically, all Creation happened when the Original One became Two, and from that point re-combined indefinitely. The highest number imaginable is only One followed by another One, (the Pillars) ad infinitum.

The Pillars are symbolic of so much in the Mysteries that they are well called the Pylon or Gateway leading to Truth. By their use alone, an enquiring consciousness might discover what it sought. We are not bound to treat the uprights as immovable or unchangeables. They may become all sorts of concepts. If they join and pivot at the top, they will become the legs of a Compass. Fixed, they become a Square. Crossed, the Cross in the Circle. Leaning together they might be the sides of a Pyramid or the Rays of Light and Darkness. The Pillars lead anywhere in the Inner-world, being a sort of Universal Entry. Where they allow access to "private rooms only", there will be some particular Symbol between them, and a would-be entrant is barred from progression until that Symbol is solved or worked out in life. Once any particular "Key" is grasped (understood) and turned (applied), then the Door stands open to be passed. In the old Mysteries, physical doors and Guardians with weapons had to be negotiated by Pass-words demonstrating Knowledge, and Grips showing Ability. Given those two factors, any Entry may be made.

In the Temple, the Pillars should be movable to any desired position in keeping with the Rite being worked. Generally they stand between the principal Officer and the altar, or between the altar and whatever point the Divine Presence is being approached from. Normally the line passing through the Pillars connecting the Mediator and altar is considered as a "clearway" for the Inner forces, and is not crossed by anyone during the progress of a Rite apart from the circumambulations. When the arms of the officiant are raised on either side of the body, these are assumed to be representative of the Pillars, between which all ritual work takes place.

In effect, the Pillars are applied as Limiters on each side of a flow of consciousness, so that awareness is only operative strictly along the Line of Light between them. They are not unlike an electronic tuning device that allows only a certain frequency to be used for working. The broader the space between the Pillars, the broader the frequency band, but the more loss of sensitivity and selectivity. For accurate work, the Pillars are theoretically adjusted so that Outerworld impressions are tuned to minimum, and Inner-world awareness increases in consequence. We may visualise the Pillars getting closer and closer to each other until the light-gap separating them illuminates only what is being sought. The real Pillars are thus the ability to concentrate consciousness into the limits of inter-dimensional channels and hold it there on a beam between imposed restrictions. They are the application of Principles to life, between which a Will confines itself for the sake of progression on the Path. It has been said, "Strait is the Gate and narrow the Way," and this is indeed quite true literally, when specialisation is called for in any direction.

"The strait and narrow Path" has nothing to do with religion or morals, but is a natural fundamental procedure of any life devoted to some particular purpose. In order to achieve anything, super-fluities must be excluded from the field of action. To achieve athletic prowess, drugs, alcohol, and sex must be drastically cur-tailed or eliminated, and the training programme dutifully adhered to. The same applies to spiritual development through the Mysteries. To rise between the Pillars, it is necessary to remain scrupulously within their mid-line limit. There is no alternative, and the higher up the Pillars one aims for, the narrower the space between them has to be. This is the first lesson taught by the Pillars. In a way, they are like the diaphragm of a camera which must decrease in diameter to increase the depth (or height) of focus. The smaller the hole in the diaphragm, the sharper and clearer become the details of the picture. So with the Pillars. The closer we hold them together, the better our Insight becomes.

The Pillars, in ritual usage, mark the demarcation between Inner and Outer Worlds, and they should be treated as the Gate through which entities of both Spheres make contact with each other. Some practical drill is a great help with this. Let a workable pair of Pillars, (painted broomsticks will serve) be set up on an East-West axis with altar (or stand with Light) in the East. Be seated W, facing E. The distance between Pillars must be physically passable. Visualise the Innerworld as a state of reality beyond the Pillars in the Sanctuary formed between Pillars and altar. Think of an opening Golden Gate, or any sort of Door with a Symbol on it swinging between the Pillars. Try to visualise or think of totally different conditions behind the Pillars from those in front of them. Imagine these to be very wonderful and compellingly attractive. Feel drawn toward them quite powerfully. The Guardian of the Gate may be thought of, and a personal invitation heard in the form of the hearer's own name. All these and other assistive factors should be strongly put together until they cause the experimenter to stand up and move toward the Pillars.

Approach to the Pillars should be slow and careful at first. At the moment of passing between them, the eyes should be closed, and a sense of entering the Innerworld experienced. All Inner impressions should be intensified as far as possible. The Innerworld conditions ought to be the Inside of the Outer Temple, as if the Outer Temple were a triangle with its apex between the Pillars meeting the apex of its opposite number expanding Inwardly, not unlike the Mirror in "Alice". There is no need to go far physically beyond the Pillars. What is of importance is to feel the difference between one side of the Gate and the other. At first, this may not seem much, but with practice it will keep increasing. There are all sorts of "dodges" to accentuate this feeling of "difference". One might imagine passing from darkness to light, a cold atmosphere to a warm one, breathing rates can be altered as the Pillars are passed, or anything done in order to feel changed and different (for the better it is hoped) because of passing between the Pillars.

The whole object of the exercise is to become so conditioned that whenever a pair of Pillars is thought of or constructed Inwardly, access will be provided through them to Inner consciousness. As a safeguard however, they should not be passed without the use of some Key (or Password). Otherwise the Pillars will become a dangerous trap allowing an unwary approacher to slip through them at all the wrong times into unfavourable Inner conditions. Entry to the Innerworld must at all times be under full control of the entrant. The real use of any Password is to act like a security lock for the protection of its users, so that it alone admits conscious entry to the Innerworld. If this were not so, enthusiasts and others would drift helplessly back and forth between the fringes of the Inner and Outer Worlds, lost in both, doing no good in either, of unstable mind and dubious sanity in each. Neglect or ignorance of the Password precaution has caused much suffering among amateur occultists—and their human relations!

There is no difficulty in becoming conditioned to a Password. Any conveniently unlikely phrase for other use may be chosen. This guards against its inadvertent or thoughtless use when Innerworld entry is not sought. It is also a good idea to change the Password periodically, so that it does not become too familiar or casual. Once a Password is adopted, the Pillars should be set up and approached in ritual manner, but the Gate between them must be regarded as firmly shut, and passage through the Portals impossible. Such an invisible barrier has to be carefully and methodically constructed by all possible means. Let the hands be moved around with palms flat between the Pillars as if they felt the surface of the Door. Let the fists beat against its surface. Call anything except the Password and hear no reply. Feel and experience the impossibility of going through the Gate without the Word. Sit down before the Pillars with the back to them, as if a physical door were being leaned against. Get up and go away. Any device to impress the consciousness with non-entry to the Inworld.

Once this exercise "takes", and a conditioned reaction is established, start approaching the Portal, giving an agreed knock-signal, and whisper the Password as though through a listening-tube beside the Door. Then, and then only, imagine the Door opening from inside, and proceed with the full entry. On leaving the Inworld, the Door should be imagined shut properly afterwards. When all this drill is worked to a point of proficiency, which ought to be in the early stages of Initiation, it must be an agreed thing by individual or groups that they will never seek entry to their Innerworld without using the proper Password. This is absolutely for their own protection and advantage, and not to make some unnecessary mystery or to play childish games. The effect is to put a good combination lock on the Unconscious which allows access

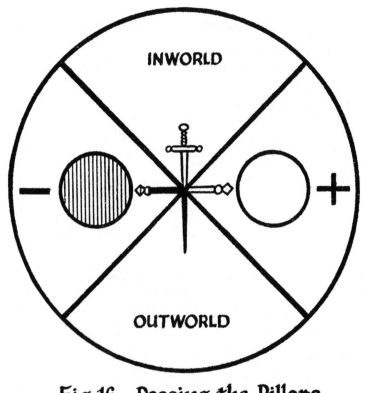

Fig. 16. Passing the Pillars

to only its best and finest levels. Similar locks could be applied by such methods to any Innerworld level if necessary. The Password system is a most practical one with centuries of reliability behind it.

In established Mystery Lodges, a would-be entrant is traditionally halted at the Gate with a challenge and a presented sword-point. This looks dramatic, but has a very sound symbology. The entrant is actually confronted by his own Inner caution (the Guardian) and forced to acknowledge consciously firstly who he is in the Mysteries; secondly what he has come for; and thirdly how he expects to attain this, or in Whose Name he asks it. No one should try an Innerworld entry without at least an attempt to formulate this essential information. The sword is not shown so much to prevent entrance as to show the way in, because the Sword is itself an Entry-Key from point to hilt.

It is only when entry to the Innerworld is sought as a responsible and legitimate act by a capable individual that access will be granted to the Initiate. Inner Temples and "enclosures" have their own Guardian and security systems which do not admit unsuitable entrants. Anyone at all can gain entry to lower Inworld levels and take their own chances there. No one will hinder access there. Once it is seen from Within that someone is using "correct" methods of entry, and can be trusted to maintain them, invitations will be offered into other spheres of Inner Life, so that Initiates complying with the rules of good Inner behaviour really do "come into their own, among their own people." It is not that some wonderful secret Password would automatically admit anybody knowing it into forbidden territory (which it would not) but that when proper procedural principles are used, the natural results of this are bound to follow.

To grasp the Pillar-entry scheme as a whole, the glyph in Fig 16 may be helpful. The ubiquitous Circle-Cross is divided into four values, the Inworld, Outworld, and their Positive and Negative qualities. The Entry-exit point between Worlds is the exact centre of the cross on the Zero line dividing Either from Neither. A Rod bars, and a Sword admits through the Pillars. The Sword insists there must be a point to the entry in a definite purpose behind it, and the Rod tells us the necessity of knowing This from That in order to be conscious at all. If these factors are combined correctly, passage between the Worlds will become a normal proceeding.

This is very far from being the end of Pillar-symbology, but it does round off a present train of thought. Ritual work is virtually an endless field of research and study with paths leading in all directions, and the Pillars stand everywhere. To use them properly, we should treat them like any Symbol, by approaching them Outwardly, taking hold of them (like Samson) and so dealing with them that they will reveal their Inner meanings. There is no other method. No matter how clever or convincing other people's explanations and expositions sound, the best of these will never be a substitute for even the feeblest original and constructive effort of consciousness. The Mysteries only exist to guide an entering Initiate up to a point by Inner Teaching. From that point onwards, he must learn from his own efforts, or he will never get any further.

That is why in Mystery practice there are virtually no published Rituals that form a recognisable Liturgy. Every group of Initiates or individuals is responsible for constructing its own out of the same elements common to all. Some make a good job of this, and many produce very poor ones indeed. Good work seems to be an exception rather than a rule. Many of the rituals that never see the light of day would not even stand up to it for a moment. Nevertheless, there is a case to be made for the publication of at least a few basic and reliable Rites suitable for Western ritualists in modern practice, yet linked with original Traditions. Doubtless these will be forthcoming at the right time, provided the right people reach the right conclusions.

CONSTRUCT OR DESTRUCT

It would be a fatal mistake to assume that all Inworlders are pro-human. They are not. Left to themselves, in their own type of Creation, the anti-humans would do us no particular harm. In fact they are only "anti-us" because our respective Patterns of Creation are incompatible with theirs. Their Patterns are anti-Cosmic, or Chaotic to ours, and capable of disrupting our living quite as much as our Patterns upset theirs. One would suppose under such conditions that a mutual avoidance policy would be the best for both sides to adopt, but neither being possessed of Perfect Wisdom, this is unhappily not the case. Moreover, our atomic explosions and radioactive developments in recent years have seriously weakened the divisions between the different Dimensions. We can be "got at" much more easily by those Inworlders who scarcely have our true welfare at heart. We also could "get at" them, but how many humans are either capable of it or interested in doing so?

These anti-humans were formerly thought of as Demons, Evil Spirits, wicked fairies, and so forth. People imagined them to be motivated by sheer hostility to the human race, and all beliefs are full of legends and stories concerned with them. Anti-human entities certainly exist, but are not so much activated by hate as by necessity. Their state-structure and ours are inimical to each other when forced into unnatural contact, and mutual trouble arises from this just as certainly as when sufficient uranium is put together. There is little point in arguing the rights and wrongs of the matter here, what ought to concern us chiefly should be how to cope with the problem.

The basic difficulty arises from the fundamental difference between our Pattern of Creation (or WORD) and theirs. Our Creation is on the Cosmic Pattern of the "Word becoming Flesh", planets around suns, electrons around nuclei, and so on. The Many and the One in harmonious relationship with each other. Our entire Macro and Micro-Cosmic structure is assembled along these lines, and whether we are incarnate or discarnate, such is our Law of Life. If we live in accordance with it we prosper, if not, we suffer. We cannot alter our basis of being without extinction. Whatever tries to live against the structural principles of its own atomic and Universal state of Existence will sooner or later disintegrate. That is inevitable. If humans were the only types of entity existing, life would be simple for us, but we are not. Others are made in accordance with the same Cosmic principles as our own, but others again conform with what to us is an anti-Pattern. Provided these are not in conflict with each other, all runs well. As we know to our cost, this is by no means always the case.

Our Primal Life-Pattern should be clear enough to anyone by this time. Every single Faith and Mystery has been proclaiming it loudly enough down the centuries, and it stands in the Heavens for all to see anyway. There are so many forms of it we can scarcely avoid them. Whatever relates One and Many together is a Life-Pattern. The methods of doing this may be good, bad or indifferent, but the principle remains. The Solar Cross and the Tree of Life are examples of good Patterns. So are the wheel, the Solar System, and atomic structures. Whether the Life-Pattern is expressed visibly, audibly, or by any means whatever, it remains what it IS, COSMOS.

The anti-Pattern is CHAOS. Its principle is the Many without One relative Constant. Electrons with no nuclei, planets with no Sun, hence sometimes miscalled the "Forces of Darkness", implying intentional malignancy. Entities living in CHAOS are not essentially evil, even though the effects they have on us may seem so. We are capable of inflicting equal damage on them. If only we might all learn not to interfere with each others states of being except through control points where energies may be safely exchanged, all would be well, but this is asking too much of imperfect beings. To impose alien Life-Patterns anywhere in Existence is a terrible mistake that has to be bitterly paid for by those concerned.

Since the Patterns of Chaos do not have any recognisable formation that we can define in an ordinary way, we are only able to identify them by their effect on humanity and the results they produce. Cacophony would be an audio-Symbol of Chaos, incoherency an intellectual one, irrationality a mental sign, and so forth. The Chaos-Pattern is in behaviour and not simply lack of a directing Will, since Chaos is an intentional state, constituting a refusal or Un-Willingness to live Cosmically. References will be found in Scriptures to anti-Cosmics as "Rebellious Angels" because they would not accept Cosmic Law which had evolved Man, whom they regarded as the Creator's greatest mistake. We have yet to prove whether they were right or wrong.

As humans, our natural state is that of Cosmos, and when we allow ourselves to live otherwise, or are caught into Chaotic forces beyond our control, we get into trouble. The Companions of Chaos are not at all interested in living our way, but it is to their advantage if we accept their Life-Pattern to any extent, for this enables them to tap our natural energies for their own purposes. Put into childish clarity this means that while we live Cosmically the Goodies get the benefit, and while we live Chaotically the Baddies stack up the loot. The former are pro and the latter anti evolutionary so far as we are concerned. It would suit the Chaotics very nicely if humanity might be persuaded to live in spiritual servitude to the Pattern of anti-Cosmos, thereby supplying the Companions of Chaos with useful surplus energy until there is no more left worth having because we are approaching extinction.

On the other side, the Companions of Cosmos would prefer that our energies were directed according to the same Pattern as their own natural expression, plus of course any force convertible from the Chaotic state. To their way of thinking, Mankind should evolve the Cosmic Way until material manifestation is transcended altogether and new points of perfection become nuclei for us in ever finer states of Existence.

Faced with these alternatives from which to choose an ultimate Destiny, Mankind continues to vacillate from one to the other. The Secret Way sought by the Mystery Schools of Initiation lies exactly between both. Its major difficulty is that no human being is able to follow it until a fairly high degree of spiritual development has been reached. The most practical solution reached so far, is to progress the Cosmic Way until the soul attains a sufficient degree of mastery over Inner energies to direct itself independently.

We are reaching a decisive phase on earth in this "War of the Worlds" which has been going on since the dawn of our time so far as we are concerned. Both Chaotic and Cosmic Patterns may be observed in action everywhere. Their modern battle standards no longer carry the old Names of "God" and "Devil", but those of "Nuclear Energy" and "The Bomb". Behind these obvious devices, the "back room boys" of both sides are engaged on a far more insidious campaign. Physical warfare is getting old fashioned and uneconomical unless rapid depopulation becomes necessary. Modern battlefields have been principally established in the Inner fields of Mind and Soul on a highly organised scale, and the various factions are pursuing their own interests relentlessly.

With modern weapons of broadcasting, newsprint, advertising, and improved techniques of influencing human beings from Inner levels, the human Soul, both individually and collectively has never been subjected to greater stresses. Caught between the cross-fires of commercialism, religion, politics, and other major combatants, the human Soul as such struggles for survival with the alternatives ahead of supremacy or subjection. It is almost impossible to maintain neutrality if this state commands no respect from belligerents of all descriptions. The ritualist is as much involved as the rest of humanity, and must engage in Cosmic or anti-Cosmic ritual activity according to conviction, unless ritual practice is abandoned altogether in favour of contemplative life or some other escape route from conflicts of consciousness.

The chief task of any sincere ritualist in present day practice is an obvious one. It is to design and carry out Rites on the Cosmic Life-Pattern which will act as energy-exchangers between our state of being and that of those Inworlders who represent our best spiritual interests. This is not at all difficult when the Cosmic Patterns are known and followed out. About the simplest Rite is any form of the Circled Cross, and the most complicated ones would be those based on atomic structure-Patterns. Qabalists have their faithful Tree to rely on which constructs an un-Chaotic Inner Existence with carefully worked out Paths of progression to OMNIL. There are plenty of Cosmic-type Patterns to work Rites with.

It might be disconcerting, but must not be allowed to be discouraging, to note the growth of Chaotic Patterns reaching this world via the arts, religion, and almost every sphere of human activity. Discordancy and arhythmics with music, distortion in sculpture, unbalance and incompetency in painting, depressive irrelevancy in drama, incoherency in literature, indecision and ineptitude in most fields that should provide mental and spiritual food for human beings. Confusion and uncertainty are Chaotic Patterns which we accept at our greatest spiritual peril. They should be recognised for what they are, projections from an Instate which is inimical to our own, and countered by our contra-Patterns of Cosmos. It should not be difficult to identify Patterns of Chaos, since they are evident everywhere once they are looked for. They must not, however, be confused with normal katabolism, which is breaking anything up in order to re-use its constituents in an anabolic re-creation. This is not Chaotic, but Cosmic. True Chaos is a continuum of inharmonics. It may not seem a very great contribution toward human welfare for a ritualist to devote energy and ingenuity for devising and practising Cosmically constructed Rites, but in fact this is much more valuable than might appear possible. Every Rite so worked processes Inner energies according to our Life-Pattern, and these have very far-reaching effects indeed.

Each effort at conditioning consciousness in our Cosmic way is very well worth while, and a worthy offering upon the Inner altars we seek to serve. If the single instruction:— "LIVE LIGHT-WARDLY" (i.e. according to the principles of Cosmic construction) could be impressed from Within deeply enough on every human mind and soul so that it becomes a major living motive, most of our problems would be well on the way to solution. Even the least Rite projecting this Pattern into the Innerworld is of help not only to the ritualists, but also to those whom its influence reaches. The reverberations of a well-worked Rite echo a long way into Eternity.

Power behind each Pattern becomes increased as it is extended or reiterated. Thus, everyone tries to impose their own Pattern on others, because if this is accepted they become that much more powerful. So long as all the Patterns are variants of a common basic structure, there is no reason why interchanges of energy between them should not eventualise well enough. When the structures are mutually antipathetic as with Cosmos and Chaos, no exchange of energy should be made without adequate safeguard provided by a proper adaptive connecting device. Only when the Force-flow between Cosmos and Chaos is strictly controlled by those that understand the nature of this action may it be really considered either safe or permissible. Though main energy channels are comparatively well guarded, leakages along lesser lines have always occurred, mostly to human detriment, and are increasing somewhat alarmingly since the materialisation of the most terrible Chaotic Symbol yet known—the Bomb. We may assess its Outer effect easily enough, but its Inner capabilities of Chaos are very considerably greater.

There is no doubt whatever, that if Inner Chaos ever predominated throughout the human world we should be doomed to destruction as Cosmic creatures. Our existence as the entities we are and hope to become through evolution, depends entirely on the Pattern that keeps us together physically, mentally, and spiritually. Break that, and we are broken with it. Matters are as simple as that. If our atoms explode, so do we. If our Solar System flies apart, we go with it. The same laws of Cosmos that appear Outwardly, act Inwardly. It cannot be otherwise. Our Life, both mortally and immortally, is supported by Cosmos; and our Death either way comes through Chaos. Until a soul has gained sufficient stature to exist independently of both Principles (which is not a common occurrence) we must evolve with Cosmos or be overwhelmed by Chaos. There is nothing else to do.

One unique advantage available to the magical ritualist of our times is a sort of "Do-it-yourself survival kit." Using ceremonial methods it is possible to construct an Inner Cosmos strong enough to defy the Forces of Chaos. There seems little use in building atom-proof deep shelters on earth if we have no equivalents on Inner levels of Life. What is the point of saving our bodies if our minds and souls are blasted? First things first. If we remain intact Inwardly, it is always possible to find other bodies, but if we suffer irreparable Inner damage, there is an end to us as Cosmic entities. Spirit may be immortal, but unspiritualised mind and soul is not.

With the aid of ritual techniques, it is fairly simple to build up an Inner Cosmic Pattern for both personal and collective Inner survival. By working together on the same design, any number of people can construct their own Innerworld citadel just as easily as they might build themselves an ordinary city on earth. This was the aim of the various religious systems and Mysteries. All these Inner structures are made by directed energies which used to be called "Faith", or Belief in Being. It is a principal Cosmo-constructor. Break up human faith and belief in their Inner existence, and this eventually becomes Chaotic, because humans have been conditioned to believe in Chaos. We become what we believe. This is why it is so terrible to observe the increase of Chaos Symbols offered humanity for acceptance in these times. Unless Cosmic practitioners are able to counterbalance this by efficient measures, we are likely to suffer severely if the Chaotics gained control of earthly affairs.

First and foremost we must learn to live individually and collectively in a Cosmic manner, our Divine Spark at centre related harmoniously through all within our Circle to every point of our Circumference. This throughout our Time-Space-Event Circles. Every Symbol representative of this Principle or expresing it in any way should be pressed into service. Our Magic Circles have to "come alive" and project themselves around us everywhere by every means. The Rites will definitely accomplish this if we perform them properly, and they are Cosmic in nature, however simple their design. The simpler the better for practical purposes. If a single ritualist merely acknowledges Cosmos by a bow to the Quarters, or four Companions sit the Circle meditating via a central Flame, this will keep the Pattern working. It is always possible to elaborate as much as required subsequently, provided the nucleus of a structure is absolutely sound.

Cosmos and Chaos should not be confused with the Principles of what we call Good and Evil in the sense of intentional malice or beneficence. It is quite possible to work Cosmically with "evil" intentions or Chaotically with "good" ones. The main difference is that Cosmic evil can be dealt with in our own state of being, but Chaotic evil is aimed at breaking up the very basis of our Creation. It is always wise to choose the lesser of these two. There is a very simple ruling to decide the difference between Cosmic and Chaotic matters. Is the Divine Primal Principle acknowledged and adhered to, or denied and abrogated. The former is Cosmic, and the latter Chaotic. This does not mean the profession of any kind of religion or belief in personal Deities. It means whether the units of an Existence relate with each other via their common Causative Spirit or not. Do we come together willingly because That in us seeks Itself in others, or should we automatically fly apart if compulsive pressures were removed, because we have no such Inner nucleus of unification? What are we—Reactors or Bombs? Events will prove the issue.

The old notion of a Principal Evil Spirit who hated the Divinity and all mankind was at least the concept of a Cosmic Devil who accepted the existence of Deity. One cannot hate or love without establishing a definite relationship between points of consciousness in Cosmos. That is why it is important to make a Love-relationship between individual entities and Deity Itself, since this makes a perfecting Cosmos. Our chief need as souls is relationship between ourselves and all others in the best possible way. Even bad relationships are preferable to Chaotic incoordination. Better the Devil known than the Devil unrealised. A Devil or a Deity with which no relationship is possible for us as humans, has no Cosmic validity for relative creatures like ourselves.

We are up against a far greater meance to our Existence than Lucifer with his personal dislke of mankind. The real Companions of Chaos are utterly devoid cf anything we would recognise as any kind of feeling. They are not really enemies in that sense at all, but Eliminators. Since to them Cosmos and its products, such as the human race, is an incompatible, Cosmos must either cease or be converted to Chaos. There is no question of emnity against humanity by the Companions of Chaos. They are completely disinterested in us as entities either individually or collectively. Whether or not we exist makes no difference to them whatever as an actuality. It is the Cosmic Pattern of Life itself they mean to break, and if humans associate with it, then those humans must be disassociated into Chaos. No more nor less than that.

There are only three Magical Ways of dealing with this general situation. Black, Neutral, and White. It is rather a pity that Black has been associated with Evil in the human mind, for this is not really so. True Black is a Symbol of the entire absence of a Cosmic Solar Principle, the reversal of Light, and is a complete denial of Creation which is a Cosmic act. We should distinguish between this, and states that may seem Black to us but are not truly so, because they bear within them the Seeds of Light awaiting Life. Ultimate Black is as rare as Ulimate White, but their labels have been attached so firmly to the Goodies and Baddies of Inner and Outer Life that there is little point arguing an alteration.

The aims of the so-called "Black Magician" are much more deadly than worshipping a Science Fiction Satan and his court of Bug-Eyed-Monsters. An initiated Black Magician believes that he can compromise with the Companions of Chaos by deliberately acting as an agent for their Anti-Cosmic Pattern in the human world, thereby ensuring his own survival on favourable terms. He would subject other mortals to a Pattern leading them toward their eventual extinction, which the Black Magician is confident he will not share. In common language, a sell-out.

Theatrical versions of Black Magic such as the Satanic Mass and Witches Sabbat are far beneath a competent practitioner's notice except as a means of beguiling or bewildering likely recruits and victims. The modern Black Magician uses mass-production methods reaching the mass-mind. So does his White opponent. How then, may an ordinary mortal distinguish the activities of one from the other? Nothing but the Patterns of procedure and Symbols used will provide a clue. Otherwise the real Rites. Neither faction can use the other's Base-Pattern, since to do so would be to defeat their own ends. Nevertheless a Pattern may be perverted or distorted to its opposite purpose by damaging its design, though this is a double edged practice likely to result either way. The inverted Cross on the Satanic altar may invert itself again and restore the Cosmos it represents in that position.

This was a mistake the German Nazis made by adopting the Swastika as an emblem. To them, it signified the broken Cross or Cosmic Circle, but had they looked more deeply, they might have found its more ancient significance of the Cosmic Power in action around the Solar Circle. Their own Symbol was turned against them. Only the bi-valency of most Symbols preserves them from exclusive use by Cosmics or Chaotics. The one infallible Cosmic Symbol which cannot be used otherwise is the Solar Cross, pure and simple. Therefore it should be adopted by all intending to align themselves with the Cosmic cause, if not as their principal, then certainly an auxiliary Symbol. The Solar Cross cannot be reversed, inversed, or perversed, though it might be distorted, broken, or superimposed on by anti-Cosmic devices such as the extinguishing Torch, or a black counter-cross. It is unlikely however, that any experienced Black Initiates would use any kind of Solar Cross in their workings, for fear it might regenerate itself and cause retributive effects. The legend of the Devil fearing the Sign of the Cross is based on truth, if we remember the Cross is the Cosmic, and not the Calvary one, which is reversible.

Even the Tree of Life may be reversed to indicate the old adage:

"Daemonus est Deus inversus." Black Magicians are unlikely to do this however, because it can be countered by one rapid stroke which converts their Chaos to Cosmos in a single checkmate move. The tenth Sphere (Kingdom) which is material manifestation, has only to be swung into its rightful "pre-Fall" position at the vacancy of "Knowledge", and the Tree then presents an irreversible Cosmos-Pattern, as in Fig 17.

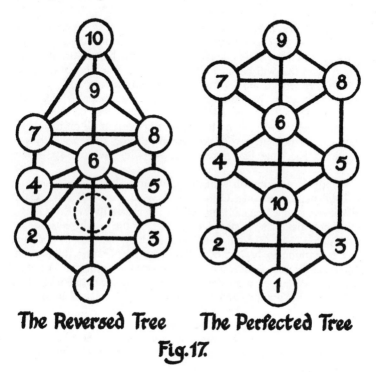

The Reversed Tree   The Perfected Tree

Fig. 17.

It will be seen that any attempt to invert the Tree has the effect of making the material Sphere top-heavy, and when it "Falls" for the second time, it goes back to its original place and makes up the "critical mass' of Cosmos, which has an opposite result to that of Chaos. It "locks" Cosmos together so that both Inner and Outer states of Cosmic Existence coincide axially, and the realities of both become directly interchangeable. In such a condition we should be aware of Inner and Outer Worlds with the clarity of a consciousness working perfectly from one to the other as a normal Way of Life, and the Kingdom of Heaven would equate with the Kingdom of Earth. Meditation on the Perfected Tree, its Paths and Patterns will be amply repaid. Its numerations may be differently arranged too, and will give interesting combinations. Arrange the Perfect Tree as we please, it will produce Cosmos everlastingly. Definitely a Master-Symbol of "White", or Cosmic Magic.

It is the responsibility of the White Magician to maintain and propagate the Patterns of Cosmos throughout the whole of our human existence in all the Worlds we inhabit either physically or in any form. A heavy responsibility indeed, most especially so during this period of our history. Let us neither underestimate its importance nor overestimate its difficulties. No Cosmically motivated act is too small to count, nor too large to consider. What matters is that the Principle is practiced to the best of the Initiate's ability, and this will be shown in the type of Rite he works. If the Chaotic tendencies among modern humanity are to be countered, it will take every possible resource available to the Whites built into a concerted Cosmic effort. Old Systems must be adapted to modern needs, and realistic Rites constructed that all on the White Path can participate in with power and purpose, both privately and publicly. The time has come when we will have to say: "Here stand I."

We are faced on earth with the need for both a Renaissance and a Reformation among Occultists, Mystics, and all who claim allegiance to the Inner Cosmic cause. This is sadly evident, yet we must not make the mistakes of earlier centuries where these are avoidable. There is nothing to be gained by needless iconoclasm, and everything to be lost by falling into the Chaotic traps of indifference or senseless enthusiasm. Granted the ancient Tradition should be continued in modern manner, but this must be a constant process of adaptation, and not a severance of original linkage. If any alterations are to be made, these should only be effected for the sake of improving relationships with the Cosmic Pattern, or enhancing and clarifying the consciousness of those concerned throughout the Mysteries. Heaven knows this has become a necessity on Earth!

Ritual methods have a major part to play in this spiritual rebirth we must undergo during the times ahead, if we hope to have any times ahead of those. Anyone suggesting that ritualism is an outworn affair of the past, or should be abolished altogether by "progressive outlooks", or is not a necessity for human spiritual development, is either unaware of reality or deliberately seeking to mislead mankind. There is no question that forms and presentations of Rites are as variable as circumstances may require, but basic principles are unchangeable without endangering the whole structure of our Cosmic existence. Ritual per se is a structural behaviour pattern of a humanity created as we are. We cannot eliminate Ritual principles without eliminating ourselves. Perhaps this was felt by the ancient writer imploring the "progressives" of his day not to alter one syllable of the "Barbarous Names of Invocation", which were so old that their meanings had been forgotten. To alter one syllable of the Creative Name or Keynote behind our Cosmos would mean our destruction.

It would be quite wrong to imagine that all occult Rites consist of theatrical performances in secret Temples. This is simply a method of projecting their Patterns. Many occult rituals might not be recognised as such at all except by those knowing what to look for and where to find it. When the same Rite that appeared so colourfully as a Temple working is extended through varying Time-Space-Event tracks in quite different forms, few would suspect it was in progress. This type of ritualism calls for expert handling by experienced operators. It needs few externals, only the ordinary accessories of living, and is worked in terms of Word and Will forming part and parcel of life-experience.

The more experienced an Initiate, the less he needs to rely on dramatised productions for obtaining effects, but he must still follow the same Patterns and techniques projected into other forms of action. Often many lifetimes of work with traditional types of Rites may be needed to raise a soul to the point where it is able to operate independently through other channels, though still using the same principles learned the hard and patient way in Lodge and Temple. Those who claim there is no necessity for ritualism would do well to remember this.

What, for instance, could be more ritualistic than a Quaker meeting with its fixed Outer pattern designed to allow individuals freedom to make their own Inner ones? It will usually be found that those objecting most strenuously to Ritual, are really objecting to others who use different Rites from their own. They are apt to forget that the greatest Rite is Life itself, and we are all participants in that Drama. An error is made on one hand by ritualists who cannot see beyond the dramatics of their art, and on the other by those who do not understand the need of drama.

There is a tremendous necessity among the peoples of Earth for a type of ritualism which links Inner and Outer Life both simply and effectively. In olden times the simple folk realised this well enough, and linked themselves to Life with the crude rites that came within their comprehension. Everybody knew them and did them as best they might. In this way they kept touch with the Inside and Outside of Nature through themselves. All they ate, drank, touched, or contacted was part of their Life-ritual. Man met God in everything. It was inevitable that we should grow away from imperfect practices, but a pity we should lose touch with the principles. Who nowadays looks for Divinity in the commonplaces of their daily lives? Who can make a Rite of some ordinary event as the old people did? This is the heritage we are in danger of losing—the sheer Magic of living. No socialised or nationalised ways of life can ever replace this, it is a piece of private enterprise we must undertake on our own with Inner assistance.

Orthodox Faiths recognised this need when they tried to attach religious observances to very ordinary things. The innumerable Jewish blessings and formulae, the standard Muslim "In the Name of the Compassionate and Merciful", the Christian custom of the Cross, and the Buddhist "I take refuge etc", are all examples of bringing both ends of our being together so as to make a Cosmic Circle. It is unlikely that specialised invocations of this sort would have much appeal to others than subscribers to those Creeds, if indeed they still observe them to any degree these days. Nevertheless, the principle of linking Inner and Outer Life by means of conscious union between the manifestations of both is a major ritual fundamental. The rabbit out of a hat may be legitimate entertainment magic, but the ritual Magician has to do better than that. He must produce Divinity from the merest speck of dirt, and be as conscious of the Presence as an audience is aware of the rabbit.

The modern practising ritualist is faced with the amazing opportunity of designing Rites for present day people which should bring Inner realities into contact with everyday living. If our ancestors could do this with a few stones, sticks and strings, surely we ought to do more with what is available now. Perhaps there is a lesson to learn, when we consider how much Inner content the ancients obtained from their small resources, and how little we seem to extract from our plethora of possessions. Are we gaining a world at the price of what made it worth living in? We need rituals to make us realise the Inner Verities through every aspect of modern life. Someone has to evolve those Rites from basic principles which are ageless, and project them into acceptable terms for us to work with now. People are seeking contact with Divinity today as much, and indeed more, than they did in the past. They find themselves unable and unwilling to look for it in Temples and Churches, and do not know where else to look. They must be shown how to look where their ancestors did, into the ordinary externals around them until the Inner Portals open, and the Kingdom of Heaven is encountered. If practical ritualists are able to devise methods of doing just this, they will have made an inestimable contribution to the spiritual progress of humanity.

Even though it is true that Lodges and Temples will always be the laboratories of dedicated specialised workers, it is an advantage of Magical Rites that they may be devised by anyone at all who feels need to do so. They are a perfectly natural activity and not some exclusive prerogative belonging to unattainable "In-Groups". True again that different Groups or Schools have worked out systems of their own which they have proved over the years, and they are naturally reluctant to admit outsiders who might introduce Chaos into their carefully made Cosmos. Who would blame them for that? Nevertheless, the practice of Magic (like Medicine) is free to all. Everyone may make of it WHAT THEY WILL, which is NOT the same as WHAT THEY WANT. Those who do not realise the difference between one statement and the other, would be advised to leave Magic alone, for they will only meet disappointment and failure.

If the natural question is asked: "How am I to learn Magic, and who is going to teach me?" there could only be one truthful reply. "You must learn it of your own life-ability inside yourself, and none can teach you except those able to contact you on deepest Inner levels." Anyone thinking that real Magic might be taught through a series of lectures, ceremonies, secret books, or even by correspondence, has not even begun to learn the facts of Magical life. If it is believed that some wonderful "Master" will impart vital secrets into eager ears enabling the hearer to attain "Instant Adepthood", then Eternity is likelier to end before such an event occurs. It is surely time to disencumber ourselves from misunderstandings about Magic that will only hinder true progress.

The real "Schools of Initiation" and "Masters" are established on Inner levels where they are able to make the best contact with human souls advancing past the general Earth average. In this world, we are only likely to encounter their agents—often in very unlikely circumstances. Whatever we learn of real true value can only be reached from Inside, and we must find the Way In for ourselves. There is no other entrance.

What is available on Earth to those who seek the Magical Path? Endless books in profusion resulting in confusion. Large numbers of "Societies", "Groups", and other associations of human beings with their various claims and counter-claims. The seeker thinks: "To join—or not to join. That is the question." No one can decide this but themselves. "Occult Groups" on Earth are no better than their Inner linkage makes them, and this is no easy matter to discover. Commonsense alone should warn anyone with a grain of intelligence to avoid any Occult organisations offering initiation for money, making grandiose claims, sponsoring advertising campaigns, or otherwise behaving unethically, though by no means illegally. Assuming that an operative Occult Group might be found on Earth with undoubtedly genuine Inner authority, what is the absolute most it might do for those who wish to associate with it? No more than they might do for themselves through their own Inner contacts. The best any Group could possibly offer are facilities for research and opportunities for learning. These are also available elsewhere for anyone taking the time and trouble to look. All a Group can do it to be responsible for presenting the Pattern they represent in the neatest possible way.

Anyone being "initiated" into such a Group may expect to be ceremoniously introduced to a number of Symbols, told what is hoped from them, given advice and encouragement, shown methods of using the Symbols, and offered whatever help the Group can afford on the various levels of life. No more. The rest lies with the individuals themselves, and the contacts they make with the real Inner School behind the earthly agency. They may be shown the Portals from Outside, but they have to turn themselves into the Keys which will unlock the Gate. It is not so much a question of being given the Keys of the Kingdom, as of *becoming* them.

Once, there were distinct advantages in belonging to authentic Occult organisations on Earth connected with the Mysteries. They had libraries and scholars, healers and helpers. In their secret meetings it was possible to discuss beliefs and ideas which might mean persecution or even death elsewhere. Even financial aid came from charitable funds if necessary. All these might really be classed as valuable fringe benefits however, though they helped each soul find its own Inner freedom. Virtually such things mean very little in modern times when they are all much more readily available elsewhere than from private associations. The one thing an Occult Group could offer today which might be unobtainable otherwise is true spiritual leadership and an ability to bring out the best from the souls who come in direct contact with it. It is sad this should be exceptional.

The only advice which might be fairly offered those wondering whether or not to join Occult Groups of any kind is to examine their own motives in the matter and make no decision until they obtain an absolutely honest answer from the very depths of their being. If they are sincerely in search of spiritual truths, they may be assured that no Group on Earth has exclusive rights to these, and membership of the Holy Mysteries is not limited to those who join "approved schools" as paying pupils. If it is imagined that any Group possesses wonderful "occult secrets" imparting "Instant Wisdom" or the like, then disillusionment will certainly follow. Nothing may be learned in any Group that could not be learned outside it in a different (and often easier) way. Should the seeker be looking for intellectual interest, there are Occult Groups with this much to offer, but no more than might have been found otherwise. If the motive is simply that of dressing up for amusement and indulging in amateur theatricals slanted in any particular direction, there are many Groups to supply this for varying considerations. Some are "respectable", and others the reverse. All tastes are catered for. Few reflect much credit on anything connected with the genuine Mysteries. If, at a final analysis, the motive for joining an Occult-oriented Group on Earth is for the sake of companionship with the other souls whose mutual interaction results in spiritual progression for all more favourably than might have been achieved independently, then the seeker is to be congratulated if such a rare opportunity ever presents itself.

On the whole, the position may be summed up that it is not a strict necessity to join any particular Group on Earth in order to participate in the Holy Mysteries, but membership of some reliable association could be useful during the early stages of Initiation. Once past a certain point, the Initiate comes into direct contact with those Inner beings to whom he is responsible, and so becomes beyond any dependency on immediate Earthly Circles. Anyone with a capability for self-discipline and a true sense of dedication to a purpose might reach that point for themselves, especially in these times of good general education and readily available information.

All this does not mean that Occult Schools or Groups on Earth have outlived their usefulness or become totally valueless. A necessity arises for quite a new type of grouping among those following Old Traditions. The whole policy of "Occult secrecy" needs complete overhauling and reconstructing to suit modern advancement. Mystery as a living force that draws a soul closer to Divinity is an incalculable blessing; but as a dead letter causing nothing but confusion or lack of interest, it is a useless curse. How many unnecessary seals of secrecy conceal shrines from which the Living Presence has long departed? No bird was ever imprisoned by building a fence round it, and the Spirit indeed "goeth where it listeth." Once again it must depend on whether the secrecy causes Cosmos or Chaos. It is not that "Occult secrecy" should be abolished but it certainly ought to be adapted for our day and age.

The old Mystery Schools on Earth made no secret of their existence or purpose. Some of their Rites were quite public, others semi-private, and the remainder entirely private, until they ultimately became individual affairs. It was not that different sorts of Rites were worked by more advanced Initiates, but the same Rites were worked in more advanced ways as the Initiate progressed. Rites involving the public had a great deal of Outer showing and elaboration in relation to the Inner content. The "In-OUT" ratio altered according to the degree of Initiation until Externals reached minimum, and Internals rose to maximum intensity. In the case of the public Rites, Inner Illumination was diffused to reach as many as possible; then, as Initiation progressed, the Light concentrated to fullest focus until It might be entered past necessity of return.

This is the sort of organisation we need to re-establish, if such a thing is possible. It proved unworkable in times past because of human fallibility, but unless it eventuates as it was intended to between Inner and Outer Life, humanity will deprive themselves of their Heavenly heritage, which would be an irreplaceable loss. Most of the failures at the human end of the Mysteries were due to sheer greed and lust for power and position, plus political and commercial interest being allowed to supplant spiritual motivations. With the regenerated formation of the Holy Mysteries in linkage with Earth, their Outer Courts must be freely accessible to anyone of average good will, and their Inner Adytum unreachable except by such a degree of personal purification and perfection that only the finest type of humans would ever attain thereto. The entire snob-structure of fictitious "Grades", "entitlements", "conferred Initiations" etc, was never part of the original Mysteries, and nothing resembling them should become a feature of their re-establishment. Offices are not ranks, but responsibilities, and should be so considered.

There must certainly be no commercial, social, or other material gains to be made within the framework of the coming Mystery structure on Earth. Friendship and fellowship should infallibly be fostered, but no form of personal profit other than spiritual and intellectual should be permissible or available. Initiates are to feel the resources of the Hierarchy behind them for every forward step they take toward the Light, though to fully realise that no one but themselves obstructs their Way hence. None are trying to outstrip others, take advantage of them, or prevent their progress anywhere. When all are in a Cosmic Circle, the Light at centre is equally available to everyone. None may interfere with another's Path thereto without blocking his own. This was the simple Pattern of the circle round the fire used by primitives in their dealings with the Light-Life Mystery. According to their behaviour within it, so they evolved, and their Rites emerged. Since a true circle can only be completed at its commencement, we shall scarcely do better than to continue what our forebears began. Even if we will not improve on the Pattern, we shall have to improve on our behaviour therein. Otherwise the Fire will either go out or explode in our faces.

Real ritualism is for living with on all levels. Living with a Purpose in a Pattern to a Point. All the rest of it is elaboration and adaptation. Whether we use rituals for good or ill depends upon our own natures, of which the Rites are expressions, but use them we must, one way or another. Therefore it seems only reasonable to gain both experience and skill in ritual practice. If would-be ritualists ceased expecting absurdities or Chaotic effects from their Rites, and commenced to practice in a responsible Cosmic manner, they would be healthier and happier humans altogether, assuming such was their intention in the first place. In one sense our Rites actually do put us in contact with Devils or Divinities according to the way we work them, since any projection of consciousness into intentional Patterns automatically connects with its prototype in the Universal Awareness. It has been said: "Speak of the Devil and he will surely appear", and also: "Where two or three are gathered in My Name, there am I within the midst of them." Whatever we deliberately direct our minds and souls toward by means of concerted action (such as a Rite) will be called within our Inner reach thereby. The precise effects of the contact will be determined by all the variables involved, and we shall be influenced according to our degree of involvement with them.

Those failing to grasp the working principles of ritualism can never understand the bridging methods between Inner cause and Outer effects. They argue: "Something has been said and done, why has nothing happened?" They expect immediate objective results from subjectively released energies, refusing to realise the impracticability of their demands. Such thinking is rather like refusing to believe in a Divinity because some personal request has not materialised. Belief or non-belief only affects the person concerned, opening or closing their Inner consciousness. It is futile to deny the Existence of Inner Entities because they do not manifest in the Outer conditions insisted upon by humans with no ability of awareness outside those terms. We can only follow subjective energies with an Inwardly directed awareness. As and when these energies objectify we shall only recognise them if we externalise our own with them. If we are expecting Inner Beings to manifest Outwardly, they might equally insist that we manifest Inwardly. It is the aim of the Magical ritualist to simulate conditions wherein a compromise of this kind is possible, and those on both sides of Life who are willing to accept each others' Existence may do so on a basis of mutual belief. The Janus-Symbol of the Two way Look provides a clue. If one face were human and the other Divine, each would look directly at the other objectively if they were connected by the Great Cosmic Circle of Light. So does the Magic Circle bring the two Principles in contact with each other in a relative way.

It is only possible to estimate values and effects in Ritual Magic if we are able to operate consciousness through circles like the Janus one. Each state of Existence must be seen through the other, and viewed as a Whole. To stipulate conditions of any sort which ritualism will never in its nature fulfil, and then treat the art badly, is both absurd and unscientific. Medieval magicians were sad offenders in this way, and modern ones have inherited the most miserable mess to clear up before the original Light of Truth will shine plainly again. Nevertheless it is a worthwhile job, and a fascinating one. Digging for Truth is not unlike digging for gold—as the Alchemists discovered. The rubbish concealing it lies on the surface, and the deeper one digs, the more valuable the treasure brought to Light.

When we consider how fundamental ritualism has survived from our beginnings in this world through an incredible number and variety of religions and beliefs right into our present times, it is amazing what effects it has produced upon humanity. If we care to examine the origins of any religion very critically and closely, it will be found that its Reality lies with its Inner Mythos, and not in its material or historical background in the usually accepted sense. How many Founder-Figures of ancient religions were incarnate at all? How far would the personal lives or circumstances of modern ones stand up to close investigation? How many inaccuracies and distortions do we find all over the place in connection with Faiths embracing millions of human beings? Any scholar may find these to his heart's content everywhere. Forgeries, mistakes, even deliberate lies. Endless streams of disillusioned people turn away in disgust from what looks like nothing but a junk of untruth. Others remain with it either because of an instinct, or because they can think of no more to do. Which is right?

Those who only find falsity and error and accept this as ultimate, have fallen into the greatest error themselves—that of not going beyond what they find until they emerge on the other side. Truth shining through a human being always throws distorted images. We must look the other way to find reality. The basic Inner Pattern (or Life-Rite) *is* true, and therefore has persisted with us through all the alterations within our Cosmic Time-Space-Event Circles. It is the so-called "falsity" that leads us to Truth, if we are really looking for it. Those who are satisfied to accept falsity *knowing it as such*, and determined to go no further, are telling themselves the biggest lie they ever believed. If we alter the old invocation a little and pray: "By the False—lead us to the True, by the Unreal—lead us to the Real, and by the Darkness—lead us to the Light." It will explain the process more clearly. Finding an error should be a moment of triumph and not disappointment, for no lie can exist at all without its original Truth from whence it became a falsity. The more error we find, the more Truth becomes a falsity. All the errors, falsities, inaccuracies, and other perversities apparent in human Patterns of Faith should indicate infallibly the

Inner Truth of their Origin. Unless It were Real, we could not have lied about it.

Providing we realise that our Rites are necessarily distorted Symbols and projections of Inner Reality, and that we are using them as such on the principle of the algebraical "X" to supply a focal point for an otherwise unreachable value with which we seek to relate ourselves, we shall succeed as ritualists. Not otherwise. We get what we ask for with ritual. Who asks the impossible is answered negatively. It all depends on the manner of asking what reply is received. Learning the art of asking is an essential part of practical Magic. As one experienced Occultist remarked: "Be very careful what you ask for. You might be unlucky—and get it."

What is our greatest need? Undoubtedly PEACE in the true Inner sense of the word. Not mere cessation of hostilities to be recommenced after a breathing spell, but perfect Poise, Harmony, Balance, and Equilibrium. The smoothly silent running of our Motor of Manifestation on its central Pivot from whence its Power is derived. When this does not happen with us, we use foolishly drastic means of compensation. We go to war for the sake of peace—at our own price. Anything affording even temporary relief from the torments of our Inner unbalance and unrelieved pressures is used, no matter how harmful its after-effects. We are bad Cosmic engineers during our apprenticeship. Drugs sex, crime, insanities and stupidities of every sort come from a common root— an overpowering compulsion to escape from excessive Inner unbalance, combined with ignorance of how to deal with them and unwillingness to learn Inner methods of compensating unbalanced energies that have reached Outer immanence.

Once, these torturing Inner impulses were called "temptations" and considered to emanate from the Spirit of Evil. In a sense this is true, because our combined energies build up into polarisations which may be characterised as "God" or "Devil" depending which way they attempt to correct our instabilities. Instinctively we seek stability between both which will free us from either extremity. This is the PEACE PROFOUND which Initiates in the Mysteries wish each other while searching for it themselves. The ritualist believes with reason that disturbed balance can be corrected Inwardly before it reaches Outer manifestation, provided energies are focussed accurately enough as close to the centre of balance as possible. If energies could be re-routed on levels reachable and controllable by ritual means, we might avert all kinds of disasters. It is a question of designing rituals for specific ends. We are un-fulfilled and inadequate creatures trying to supply our own deficiencies and falling over each other in the process. Once we discover how to compensate ourselves Inwardly and achieve stability by ritual processes we shall make enormous spiritual progress. All our difficulties are theoretically capable of ritual solution. Even war, which after all is a human Rite of its kind. If only it might be laid out as a Symbolic activity capable of restoring unbalance between dissidents, there would be no cause to materialise it. The difficulty would be persuading potential belligerents to confine themselves within the purely Symbolic structure of the Rite. To make an un-funny pun, war is one human Rite in urgent need of a re-write.

It is by no means sufficient to write out the script of a well designed ritual, perform it, and imagine everything possible has been done. It must still be connected to Life at both ends. There has to be what is called the "Labour of Preparation" before the actual dramatisation of the Rite takes place, and the "Work of Disposal" afterwards. These slightly archaic terms mean that we cannot very well leap into a full scale Temple Rite without building up from our normal living conditions to the working level at which the Rite should be produced, and subsequently coming back to earth-life by a reverse process. If we like to think of this as a preliminary warming up, and an eventual cooling off, the simile will serve. Most Systems have their particular standard formulae for "getting off the ground" and returning thereto. The average one is probably the "Induction narrative", which is a passage in prose or poetry descriptive and evocative of the state of mind and soul necessary for the best performance of the Rite. The idea is to bring the hearers into a concerted condition of readiness for the ritual ahead of them, or "work them into the right mood". At the end of the Rite it will be necessary to restore them to ordinary consciousness by a gradual return route.

Even the simplest Rite should have its brief preparation and disposal that lifts us out of and restores us to normal living. If we are to get away from our everyday activities and work a Temple Rite that is far from our normal practice, then we shall need a build-up to, and a let-down from it. It all depends on the nature of the Rite as to what these are, for they must accord with the particular character of the ritual in question, and the more important it is, the more thorough and detailed must be the extra-ritual activities. Before an Initiation ceremony for instance, months and even years of work and study in connection with the particular Initiation being taken, will culminate in a final period of intensive meditations, tests, applications, and adjustments until the climax of the Rite itself cosmates all these energies into a whole achievement. In this sense a Rite is like an examination insofar as it becomes the focus of what has gone before in order to allow a future disposition of the accumulated power.

For more usual Rites than Initiations, less strenuous efforts will do, provided they lead away from ordinary living and then back to it again. For this reason in olden times, preparations for ritual working included sexual abstinence, fasting, and charitable works. Three distinct breaks with the living pattern of a humanity unaccustomed to foregoing opportunities for sex and food or selfish interests. A self-imposed discipline in fact, which had the needed effect of "lifting-off" from an average life-level. After the Rite, many old workers indulged in sex acts and feasting to "earth the forces", or get back to normal. It depends entirely on what is an ordinary life-level for the practitioner concerned. This must always be the criterion. There can be no hard and fast rules about what preparations are best for any Rite except in relation to the life-pattern of its operators. By and large, the general guide is that we should intentionally prevent ourselves from doing what takes us away from the spirit of the Rite, and make ourselves do what leads us toward it. Symbolically speaking, we put ourselves between the Pillars and squeeze.

For some workers, this might mean giving up smoking and drinking for a period before a Rite, and saying some special prayers. Others would interpret things differently. There has to be an inhibition and an injunction involved, which should switch us from Outer to Inner life, over a convenient period. As a rule it is customary to inhibit something physical that links us purely with the material world, and encouraging spiritual activity leading us Inwardly. Hence the traditional "prayer and fasting" technique in preparation for Rites. The underlying principles of this may be applied in all sorts of different ways to suit modern requirements. In a way, it is not unlike what is called "getting into character" for a stage part, where the actor's purely personal nature is carefully altered into a semblance of that which is to be portrayed. This assumed nature also has to be "exorcised" at the end of a run, so as not to be a nuisance or interfere with the formation of new characters. Much the same principles apply to a military operation where those involved are "briefed" before it and "de-briefed" afterwards. Every Rite should be preceded and followed by similar processes.

If the proposed Rite were to be in connection with the Great Mother God-Aspect for example, then not only should preparatory prayers be phrased accordingly, but characteristic life-activities be adopted also. We cannot invoke what we are unable to call up in our own natures. So we have to "mediate the Mother" by thinking, saying, doing, and being all sorts of things we believe to be more in Her style than our own usual one. Perhaps this means something to do with children, or being unusually forbearing with difficult people, or coping with daily situations as a mother has to. In the case of one who is already a physical mother, it might mean being a bigger and better mother in whatever ways were practical. We all interpret motherhood as we see it. The point at issue is that we discover means of bringing the typified energy of the Rite through ourselves in a gradual way before we work the Rite intended to modify it, and then release it into our lives afterwards with equal care.

Possibly one of the best descriptions of preparatory labour ever written is to be found with the famous "Abramelin" system of magic. Anyone capable of living under such exemplary conditions of self-discipline for a whole nine months should certainly be able to control any demon they might encounter. The subsequent "Work of Disposal" of course, was supposed to be the altered life of the Initiate as a better being than he was before the Operation. Unless we have sufficient faith and interest in any Rite to impose controls upon ourselves in its favour, it will never be fully effective. Let no one attempt to call up forces they are unable to handle in themselves. All preparatory and dispersory exercises are for the development and application of such control. It is very foolish to try to work Magical Rites without them, just as it would be to attempt athletic feats without preliminaries and subsequent relaxations.

Every magical worker must be responsible for deciding which types of body-mind-soul co-ordinated exercises prepare him best for ritual practice, and this can only be discovered by trying them out, since everyone knows their own reactions best. Provided this is done conscientiously according to the principles outlined, it is possible to step "Up" and "Down" before and after a Rite with maximum efficiency, and a minimum of disturbance. The aim should be a smooth and strong ascent and descent to and from the level of the Rite. Anything jumpy or jerky should be avoided. The soaring of an eagle is better than the hop of a flea. No Group Rite ought to be worked without affording the participants sufficient opportunity to make their personal preparations in advance, and a session together before the Rite proper so as to bring these into a common focus. If these common-sense requisites are properly done by everyone concerned, the Rite can scarcely fail of result.

Sometimes, however, it is wrongly assumed that unless a good deal of emotional experience is encountered with a Rite, or some "psychic" happening occurs, the Rite cannot be working properly. This is not so at all, for such would be side-effects and not the operation of main-stream energies. They are in fact energy-escapes which detract from the principal purpose of the Rite, unless indeed it was intended for that purpose and none other. Any emotions experienced during a Rite should be immediately channelled into the main working and not indulged in for purely private entertainment. This is what was meant by the old precept of "not enjoying it", which had the unfortunate effect of making so many Rites completely joyless affairs. All it really meant was that if everyone taking part in a Rite used up its energies for little personal unshared emotions, there would be insufficient energy left over for accomplishing the principal intention of the Rite they were supposed to be engaged with. In other words all thinking and feeling of those in a Rite must be devoted entirely to its purpose and no other. This is perfectly reasonable. It all depends on cause and effect. We should not work a Rite in order to arouse emotions, but any emotions which might be aroused must be used to make the Rite work. LOVE under WILL. If emotion can be properly handled it has value in ritual, but if not, it is best excluded. That is a good general rule. The energies dealt with in magical rituals of a highly developed kind operate independently of human feelings.

Occasionally ritualists are accused of being "mere repetitionists" of meaningless formulae. The accusation is justified if the form of their Rites means nothing to them, but unjustified on the count of reiterative activities. To repeat means to do the same thing on a number of different occasions, and this is a technical impossibility since an event might resemble a previous pattern as closely as it may, but the fact of its variance in the Time-Circle from its predecessor makes it an individual entity. There may and should be a reiteration of a pattern as a continuum, but this as a Whole comprising many parts. Even a Circle is composed of an unknown number of contiguous points related to a common constant at the centre yet differing from each other positionally. Such a relationship is Cosmic.

No matter how often a Rite may be reiterated, it will never be the same on each occasion. All the Rites worked may have a common Pattern, but they will be unique instances of it, as indeed they should. Reiteration is a Cosmic process, but it is also an evolutionary one. Each instance of manifestation ought to be a slight improvement on its immediate predecessor if we are ever to be more than mere mortals. Granted, this does not happen in ways appreciable to our normal consciousness, and we waver considerably from the mean line of progression, but the Spiral of Evolution should be our overall scheme for ritual activity. Our Circle must not only spin truly on its axis, but also describe a spiral as it progresses through the infinitely Greater Circle of which it is but a segment. The Greater Circle in turn forms a segment of another, and so ad infinitum. A truly terrifying Symbol if we even grasp the least of its significance.

Each Rite we work should be as new as a fresh life, and as old as our Existence. Every time it is worked we should aim to improve over the last production of its pattern. There must be no cause of doing the same old thing the same old way. Every Rite has to be productive of something which is an outcome of all its predecessors and the foreruner of its successors. Just as every life we live adds another development to our reincarnating souls, so should every Rite we work bring our ritual life-Patterns that much closer to perfection. It is true that "vain repetitions" of any Rite would be useless, but purposeful reiterations of it have the opposite effect, since this increases power with every performance. Everything depends on what we bring to the commencement of the Rite from past ones, and take from it for future ones.

We should look upon all our Rites as units in a whole life-series, each with its own importance in relation to the rest. There are really no "big" and 'little" Rites, but only well or badly worked ones. Unless the quality of our ritual workings shows an improvement over the years, we shall have sadly wasted much of a lifetime. Naturally our rituals have to be reiterated to obtain long-term effects. Some we shall do several times a day, some maybe once a week, others at monthly or yearly intervals, and a few once or twice in a lifetime. Expert ritualists build all these into a complete Pattern of Patterns so that Inner and Outer life come together with a common conscious meaning. It is the regularity and reiteration of rituals that enhance the energies released through them.

Old rite-workers knew this well enough when they went over the same Name or invocation again and again for perhaps hours. Some Rites specify a triple reiteration of every Name of Power in three variant ways. We may be reminded of the Bellman saying: "I have told you once, I have told you twice. What I tell you three times is true." Perhaps the adage occurs to us that if a lie is told often enough everyone believes it. There is a great Mystical reality to be found here. What we believe long enough eventually does come true. It may take thousands of years, or millions in some cases. In others maybe moments. Since our Rites link Words with Will, let us continue to reiterate them in good faith regardless of comments from the uninstructed. None of those would be likely to refuse a handsome sum of money on the grounds that it was "just the same old pound note one after another." Why then should we not seek our spiritual fortunes that way too?

Who can possibly learn "all about Ritual Magic"? We have been learning it for thousands of years and scarcely got out of Infant School. Our most wonderful knowledge is yet to come, though if the first stone and stick had not been arranged in a Magical Pattern revealed Inwardly to the mind and soul of a man seeking the same universal answers as ourselves, there would have been no Magic in anything for anyone. Perhaps this ancestor of ours was the greatest Master Magician of all our time. Did he discover the secret of triplicity that promoted him to Trimagister, or "Master of Three"? Namely that if one did anything long enough some success would emerge, and three attempts were the least a human being might expect any kind of result with. Had he learned how to continue past the point where everyone else stopped looking? To make what we should nowadays call a "breakthrough"? It was not for nothing that the first Sign of the Zodiac was typified as a Ram that reiterated its efforts with all its strength until it broke through resistance to its will by means of its head. A plain enough analogy of magical procedure.

So much has been written about Magic, and so much more will yet be written on this inexhaustible topic. Why? Because deep down at the basis of his very soul Man is a Magician. Deny this as he will, cover it with science and pseudo-science as thickly as he likes, Man seeks Magic whether he admits belief in it or not. (The generic term "Man" is of course intended to include Woman, since one sex could not exist without the other.) When we look back over all the mountain of material written or spoken concerning Magic and its Rites over the centuries, how much is or was of any real value to anyone? No more than aroused enough interest or gave sufficient inspiration to those seeking Inner Realities so that they might make Magic for themselves.

Formerly, much of the appeal in Magic was to Man's most ignoble instincts. To get rich, gain power over others, wreak revenge, all the sad admissions of human imperfections served as motives for humans of both sexes to implement their inadequate abilities by what are now termed "paranormal" energies. Unhappily these basics still persist in humanity. So does Magic. Fortunately there have always been those souls who sought in Magic a Way of Life leading far beyond the limitations of what is worst in human nature. With the best of intentions they sought to keep their magical methods secret for fear of misuse by ill-intentioned people, human or otherwise. There is not much point to such out-of-date secrecy now that Man could scarcely make himself any worse than he is as a potential destroyer of his own body mind and soul. We have reached our ultimatum of "Grow up or Blow up."

The necessary Will to "redeem" ourselves from the depths to which we have "fallen" can only come from Within each one of us. Man damns or delivers himself according to whether he relates himself Cosmically or Chaotically with Divinity Inside him. If magical ritual practices help to link the Inner God and Outer Man together as an effective Entity, then this alone is sufficient reason why they should not only continue among us on Earth, but be brought to the highest possible degree of development. In fact it is the true justification for Magic in modern or any other times. No less a standard should be demanded of the art than the best it may afford its practitioners in terms of relative Inner and Outer values.

No art of any kind expresses itself better than the ability of its exponents, but with Magic these exist in more Dimensions than our purely human ones. If ever there was a need for magical operatives on both sides of the Veil who support the Cosmic cause of Light to combine their efforts in the name of the art they claim as theirs, that necessity is NOW and it is URGENT. About the end of every century there seems to be a recasting of the Old Wisdom into a new format. It is time we looked forward to the Magical Renaissance of our period. At the end of the last century, we had nearly all the "New-Old" Occultism presented in Oriental dress, and Asiatic patterns subtly imposed upon an European Ethos. Carl Jung has dealt with the dangers of this in his comments on the "Golden Flower." How much of our present world situation arises from such unbalance is a matter for conjecture. If the Circle of Light is to continue properly, we need a powerful Occult revival of the Western Tradition in its own right—and with its own Rites.

This is a most important consideration with which to conclude our present studies. There are many varieties of Rite practiced among Western Occultists which might be classed as Magical, but they are mostly personal affairs or limited to some particular Group. There is every reason why this should be so, but there is also reason why a common Pattern should be found acceptable in which all Occultists of the Western Tradition might co-ordinate their ritualised energies. We need Rites that Westerners of all Systems can practice both individually and with others. Not to supersede or supplant their own private practices, but to implement these to their fullest degree by linking them into a more effective Cosmic Circle than they are at present.

It is obvious enough that the details of such a vital Western resurgence of our Ethnic Innerlife will present difficulties, none insurmountable, but as an Ideal it must surely offer us every incentive to make modern methods of Western Magic something to write Occult history with. Everyone following our Tradition and of good-will is needed. Truth is Truth whether it takes Eastern or Western shape, but the Traditions of both are complementary to each other like the Black and White Pillars, and should be kept intact if the vital Middle Pillar is to be effective. If either outside Pillar broke down, the present Middle Pillar would automatically become an outside one and the whole process have to be started again. Our Western Pillar may not yet be broken, but it is certainly rocking on its base and crumbling somewhat at the edges. If the Inner Temple is to remain operative, we should make every effort to keep our Pillar both intact and upright. It is no use relying entirely on our Inner Initiates to do everything necessary when they are depending as much on us. Everyone concerned, whether incarnate or not, must make themselves entirely responsible for their own part in the coming Plan and then—get on with it.

Real ritualism is Right behaviour in the Rite Pattern. Divinity and Humanity discovering a mutually acceptable set of Symbols with which to play the Game of Life together, with both competitors on the winning side. If ever we become Adept players, so that Inner and Outer lives combine in one consciousness operating through the same Pattern or Perfection, we may say in Total Truth:

"WE HAVE COME INTO THY KINGDOM, FOR THY WILL IS DONE ON EARTH THE WAY IT IS IN HEAVEN."